THE OTHER SIDE OF SILENCE

The Other Side of Silence

A Guide to Christian Meditation

Morton T. Kelsey

PAULIST PRESS
New York   Paramus, N.J.   Toronto

Cover Design: Nigel Rollings

Library of Congress
Catalog Card Number: 76-9365

ISBN: 0-8091-1956-0 (Paper)
ISBN: 0-8091-0208-0 (Cloth)

Published by Paulist Press
Editorial Office: 1865 Broadway, N.Y., N.Y. 10023
Business Office: 400 Sette Drive, Paramus, N.J. 07652

Printed and bound in the
United States of America.

Acknowledgments

Roberto Assagioli, M.D., PSYCHOSYNTHESIS: A MANUAL OF PRINCIPLES
AND TECHNIQUES. New York, The Viking Press, 1971. Used with the permission of
The Psychosynthesis Research Foundation, New York, New York.

T. S. Eliot, "Burnt Norton" in FOUR QUARTETS. Copyright 1943 by T. S. Eliot;
copyright 1971 by Esme Valerie Eliot. Reprinted by permission of Harcourt, Brace, Jo-
vanovich, New York.

Louis Evely, THAT MAN IS YOU. Westminster, Maryland, The Newman Press, 1965.
Used with permission.

Edward Fischer, "The Journal as Worship," from WORSHIP, vol. 47, no. 8. Used with
permission of Edward Fischer.

Baron Friedrich von Heugel, THE MYSTICAL ELEMENT OF RELIGION AS
STUDIED IN SAINT CATHERINE OF GENOA AND HER FRIENDS, Vol. II.
London, J. M. Dent and Sons, Ltd., 1927. Used with permission.

William Johnston, THE STILL POINT: REFLECTIONS ON ZEN AND CHRIS-
TIAN MYSTICISM. New York, Harper & Row, Publishers, 1970. Used with permission.

To Paisley Brown Roach,
faithful co-worker and friend.

Contents

Part Five

Adventures on the Other Side of Silence

Introduction

Many people seem to feel that meditation is not for everyone, particularly Christian meditation. In fact more and more people, seeking a way of getting down to cases spiritually, have turned to Eastern ways of meditating in the hope of finding some discipline that the ordinary individual can follow. Much has been written about these Eastern disciplines. But neither the Western novices in Zen or Yoga or Transcendental Meditation nor the more experienced writers about them seem to realize that there is a powerful and unique Christian method of meditation available to any ordinary person who wishes to use it. This Christian way of meditating can bring many people a whole new vision of reality and new effectiveness in their living.

As a matter of fact, Jesus of Nazareth was the most democratic and down-to-earth of all the religious leaders the world has known. He offered a way for common people to encounter and experience God. His way is not just for the intellectuals or the full-time professionals or the particularly adept. It is for everyone, particularly people like the publican who do not think they have a chance and those whom life has beaten down. Simple people and beginners can have a genuine encounter with God. It is a matter of learning to respond to the presence and love of God which He already offers us. It is very much like Dante's conception of heaven, in which each person has a particular place, while everyone who enters at all also has some basic experience of the whole of the heavenly spheres.

This is quite a different idea from that found in most Eastern meditation. On the one hand, the idea is to respond to the loving concern of God so well expressed in Jesus of Nazareth. Most people can learn this response, and the broken, downtrodden and oppressed of this earth have the easiest access to this response. The poor in spirit, the hungry and the seeking have a special advantage. Our part is mostly to accept the hand already stretched out to us.

Eastern religions, on the other hand, usually stress the painstaking discipline by which one detaches oneself from the world, losing personhood or individuality and merging with the Cosmic Mind to become one with pure consciousness. The basic difference between the two is whether one sees ultimate reality as a Lover to whom one responds, or as a pool of cosmic consciousness in which one seeks to lose identity. It takes an extraordinary amount of living and experience to decide between these deeply different views of life. A snap decision could be made only on the basis of prejudice or naïveté. In this book I am trying to present some of the evidence for the Western point of view of ultimate reality as Lover. This most basic idea of Christianity is not given much consideration today in either religious or secular circles.

We in the West live in an age which has doubts about people's ability to reach out of the physical and material world and touch anything at all. The first-rate scientists have passed beyond these doubts. But it is popular science, usually fifty years behind the times, that influences the average individual, and popular science is still caught in the kind of materialism that confines us to a space-time box. If the modern world sees any way to get out of the box at all, it would probably say that this could be done only by religious professionals who give their total attention and effort to a break-out experience. And the tragedy is that most Western Christian professionals have forgotten how to meditate and they are caught within a view of the universe no longer accepted by modern science. And so people, hungering for a spiritual dimension in life, turn to the East, to TM, to Yoga and to Zen.

Since the aim in most varieties of Eastern meditation is to lose one's personhood in the experience, there is no personal way to describe what is sought or experienced. With the exception of Transcendental Meditation, which has developed easier techniques and some quite specific goals, these are very difficult ways which only the adept can follow, open only to a select few and which Westerners must generally enter blindly. Those on the outside are not drawn in; they are simply to live on in reflected glory until they come to a more favorable karma.

There is no doubt that the experience described by the advocates of Eastern meditation is a real and valid one, and we can learn much by studying those from both East and West who have experienced it. But there are other ways of experiencing the same reality, and they are just as real. Simple peasants sometimes have equally important experiences in the Eucharist or praying the rosary or repeating the Jesus prayer. Still others find it by turning inward through imagination—which is one way of experiencing reality—and meeting the divine Lover who then draws them on to deeper religious experiences. Many people, religiously untutored, have used this imaginative method unconsciously as they conversed with God in a natural way about even the trivialities of daily living. The windows of ancient Gothic cathedrals and the icons of Eastern Orthodoxy have also been launching pads for numerous individuals to enter this imaginative venture.

Thomas Merton was one writer about the life of prayer who came to realize that imagination has creative and constructive uses in the contemplative life. In conferences he held not long before his fatal journey to the East, Merton spoke at some length of the need to liberate imagination and allow it to be used for the purpose of discovering relationships between things, creating symbols, and finding special or new meanings. He noted that imagination can discover real meanings, not just produce distractions and delusions, and he stressed reading the Bible imaginatively, both as a way of exercising imagination and also to find the full meaning contained in the Bible.

These discussions, taped at his conferences, were published in his posthumous book, *Contemplation in a World of Action.* Merton knew both the life of the cloister and secular life. He knew heights and depths of the interior life, and also the prejudices in our culture against using imagination. If he had lived longer, he would undoubtedly have had much more to say about this subject. His discussions suggest in various ways the importance of my own reasons for writing about imagination and trying to show its place in our prayer life. His ideas open the way to discover how imagination can be developed to lead one into a deep and fulfilling relationship with God.

In the pages to follow we shall consider one simple way in which such an encounter can be found. This approach is particularly helpful for those who have doubts about the possibility, or the value, of meditation for whatever reason. It requires no great gifts. Most people who are capable of listening to their dreams can use this method. It is not the only way, and it may not touch individuals of certain psychological types. However, many people with whom I have shared it have found it most helpful. Some of these people were members of the parish church of which I was rector; others heard about it in my conferences, held here and abroad, or in my classes at the University of Notre Dame. I hope it falls into the hands of still others who find it useful.

The encounter with God and the Risen Christ is a present possibility. This is verified by those who turn toward Him, find new meaning and hope and love, and are then transformed by this experience. What I am trying to offer is an understanding of one neglected method of meditation in general use in the days when Christianity was most alive and creative. This is not a manual intellectually demonstrating the possibility of the encounter. I have written such a book: *Encounter with God.* This is a practical manual for those who would like to try out this method of finding the encounter, learning what it is like and practicing it.

I am deeply grateful, first of all, to the band of people who met with me for nineteen years in the Thursday morning prayer group at St. Luke's Church, and to the Reverend Stuart Fitch who assisted so ably with this group, in which so many of the ideas suggested here were tried. I am also much indebted to those who have attended my conferences on meditation and have offered so many suggestions. I am particularly grateful to the students at the University of Notre Dame—graduates, undergraduates, seminarians, priests and ministers, nuns, directors of religious education in various denominations—who have worked with me in courses on religious experience and who have given me so much honest feedback and so many helpful suggestions.

I am grateful to those followers of C. G. Jung, Max Zeller and Hilde and

James Kirsch, who showed me the reality of the spiritual world and how one could reach it, and so opened me to an understanding of what the early Church Fathers were talking about in their discussions and meditative writings. I am also thankful beyond words for the friendship of John Sanford who has shared with me, listening and discussing nearly every aspect of the spiritual world, and to Leo Froke, a wise friend, psychiatrist and student of literature, who has shown me so clearly that meditation and religious experience can lead to maturity, rather than away from it; and to Richard Payne who suggested that I write down these thoughts.

This book would have been harder to write and to read without the careful and clarifying editorial attention of Paisley Roach. My wife and I have spent hours talking over the subject of the book, and she has also spent many hours reading each draft and helping to put it within the range of nontechnical readers.

I am deeply appreciative to the University of Notre Dame du Lac for providing an atmosphere in which such works are stimulated and encouraged. I owe much to discussions with my friends David Burrell, C.S.C., Maurice Amen, C.S.C. and David Verhalen, C.S.C. who have listened and responded to many of the ideas and practices that are presented.

I am also grateful to Carmela Rulli, Shirley Schneck, Beth Gadberry and the faculty stenographic pool who have worked hard putting the manuscrpt in final form.

PART ONE
A Basic Perspective

1

Encountering God

Can people's lives be touched by God? Can we actually find our everyday activity given new vitality by the reality of God's presence and wisdom? If this is possible, than what can we do to open ourselves to such experience? What preparation is needed, and how do we go about finding such an encounter?

These are the kinds of questions that come up when people meet together to consider and talk about ways of deepening their religious lives. There is always concern about whether God can be reached at all. Over many years I have wrestled with this problem and I have come to the conclusion that there is no good reason to assume that one is limited only to experiences of measurable, physical things. Nor is there any reason to doubt the validity of one's religious experiences. These experiences deserve consideration, and there are grounds for believing that they point toward God Himself.

Starting with this premise, the best way of discovering whether this religious belief rests on reality or not is to open oneself as best one can to a relationship with God. Our purpose in these pages is to explore ways in which we can become open to experiences of God and know that relationship with Him is possible. This is the aim of meditation and of meditative prayer.

It is not my purpose to give a history of the devotional masters and their methods, although I have learned a tremendous amount from them over the last thirty years. I have found inspiration and guidance in these great leaders, from Origen and Gregory of Nyssa to St. Teresa, St. John of the Cross, Francis de Sales, Fénelon, John Woolman and Douglas Steere. But it was only when I was introduced to certain findings of depth psychology that I began to make the fullest use of their methods for my own religious development and to help others who came to me. Through one branch of depth psychology I found an understanding of the human soul that made the need for religious meditation very clear. I was then able to pass the knowledge of these masters of the devotional life through the cauldron of my own experience. Only by trying them out in actual practice can one learn which of the various ways of praying are most real and healing today for each individual.

What I hope to provide are simple and direct suggestions that can help ordinary people to open themselves through meditation and be touched by the reality of God. My purpose is essentially practical. I shall discuss the prayers of others very little in a theoretical way. Instead we shall be considering ways in which modern Christians can tap the resources that have enlivened the Church and its people in its most vital periods, and these will be mainly practical suggestions. It is not that history and theory are *un*important, but rather that reflecting upon them is mostly a waste of time until one has the raw material of an active prayer life with which to test the experiences and the ideas of those who have gone before us.

What Is Meditation?

The first years of my ministry showed me one thing more and more clearly. If I wanted to go on speaking as a pastor—or even simply as a Christian—about the reality of the Christian life, I needed to have some experience of what I spoke; otherwise I could not live with myself. And, incidentally, I discovered that when I did speak from even the slightest encounter with God, others showed an interest that seemed to carry over into action. But most of the time I found that none of us—even those who really should have been stimulated by my words—was trying very hard to get closer to that reality.

I found that I could read the Scriptures and say my prayers and offices with little sense of contact, almost no experience. Most of this activity came from my conscious mind. I was reading the Bible like a student, voicing the prayers mostly as thought forms, and more and more the feeling grew of something lacking, of facing a dead end. At this point I began to see that some kind of religious experience was important. Experiences of God were needed, not just at conversion or as some specially consecrated breakthrough, but available to people's ordinary lives, my own in particular. I needed relationship with Him as a regular and sustained part of my life. And it was then that I found the real meaning of meditation.

It is easy enough to say that God is seeking us, and even to stress how central this understanding is to Christianity. But it is harder to realize that we have to prepare so that God can break through to us. *Meditation* is simply the way we prepare, setting up the conditions that can help to make this possible. It includes various practices, even quite diverse ones, all aimed at making experiences of God as available as possible. But obviously this does not mean summoning God like a cosmic bellhop. What meditation does mean is a way for us to unlock the door and come out from the places where most of us have been hiding. It is the process of opening ourselves to the realm of nonphysical reality in which God can touch us far more directly than in the physical world. It is that kind of prayer in which we seek relationship with God, and in this sense meditation is the preparation and foundation for prayer.

perhaps asceticism is nec for beginning meditation but does in continued meditation drive us to asceticism? there is a relationship of prayer to fasting

So often prayer carries with it the idea of asking for favors. Of course most of us are well aware that prayer is broader than this, and that any act of turning toward God and relating to Him must be included. But in actual practice most people, both lay and religious, make prayer either a matter of formal repetition or of asking for changes in the world around them.

In meditation, on the other hand, there is a fresh emphasis on prayer as one way of meeting and relating to the One to whom one prays. Meeting God and learning what God wants of us become far more important than what we want of God. Yet the amazing thing is that when we pray in this way, we often receive better than we would have dared to ask on our own. This is also the way Jesus taught His followers to pray. In the Lord's Prayer we are told to begin by speaking directly to the Father and hallowing His name, putting the first emphasis on meeting God and expressing appreciation for what we have found. We then direct our attention to His kingdom and His will, showing our readiness to relate to His ways and wishes. Only then do we go on to ask for ourselves. Later on I shall say more about this prayer and its use in meditative practice.

Most people seem to feel that meditation is an esoteric practice that can be attempted only by the most holy. It is my experience, however, that encounters with God are much more available than we have been led to believe. These encounters occur most often as men open themselves to an inner realm. It is true that for a long time it was thought that only ministers or those in religious Orders could have any real contact with God through inner or spiritual experience. They did it for us. They were the spiritual masters, the mediators, the mystics who had gone the route of complete and utter commitment to God. Until quite recently there seemed to be no reason to question that this was the only way of finding a viable and valuable experience of God; the first and most essential requirement was asceticism and a total renunciation of one's worldly goods and interests.

One of the real discoveries in depth psychology has been the finding by one of the foremost groups in this field that we all have access to an inner realm. It is not just the saints. Ordinary people can turn inward and be touched by an experience of God and be transformed and renewed. If the essence of mystical experience is contact with a level of experience other than that of sense experience and reason, then all of us have this contact whether we know it or not. Most people are aware of dreams, intuitions, visions, hunches and other experiences that give a glimpse of something in addition to the physical world. But where does one, with only the ordinary problems of doing the best one can in the outer world, turn for instruction about these experiences of another realm? Unless we are forced to look for psychological help, most of us are left with no real approach to this realm where God and His direction could be found. There are very few spiritual directors in the modern Church, Catholic or Protestant. This is one reason so many people today are turning to the wisdom of the East.

Of course, if mystical experience is understood only as an imageless and blissful union of the soul with God, then the mystical encounter with God is less available to ordinary people. Probably that experience is not meant for all people. That kind of prayer was stressed by leaders like St. John of the Cross and St. Teresa who lived in an age that was already occupied too much with the nonphysical world and the supernatural. Their followers were trying to leave all concern with the material world behind, and it was a wise suggestion that they should not get too caught up in visions and fantasies.* But our world today faces the problems of quite a different outlook on life.

Today most of us are so caught up in the outer, material world that we forget that there is a nonmaterial inner or spiritual realm of existence. Our task is to come to know that realm again, and to realize that in it one can find sustaining and fulfilling experiences of God that give direction to the whole of life. Unless there is some such reality that can be reached, how can prayer itself make much sense? Why pray, if one is only calling out blindly into the void? Yet through meditation and the images that are evoked, one can touch and come to know the reality of the Other who is actually there.

The Inner Experience

What I wish to share about meditation are things I have discovered in thirty years of struggle. For me they have been fruitful years in which I encountered an Other with whom I could share every experience of confusion and anxiety, hope and thanksgiving, of sorrow, joy, discouragement and renewal. The Other of whom I speak has sometimes been a vague presence and sometimes a burning reality that brought relief from tension and misery, or again at times a wisdom offering specific directions and guidance that rescued me from intolerable situations. And at rarer moments this Other gave a joy and fulfillment that made the whole business of life worthwhile. I have also come to realize, through years of studying modern thought, that there is no good reason to discount these experiences of the Other or to attribute them to self-deception or wishful thinking. What I have come to know through my relationship with this divine reality stands on its own two feet.** Those who experience this reality do not have to defend it.

---

*In their own experience, however, St. Teresa and St. John of the Cross dealt very adequately with visions and fantasies. In their writings their experiences are set down in detail.

**For the reader who is interested, the thinking which supports this kind of experience is presented in some detail in the first part of my book *Encounter with God* (Minneapolis: Bethany Fellowship, Inc., 1972).

Even so, it takes courage to write about these things, and there are two reasons for my doing so. In pastoral counseling I discovered that it was often helpful to share things from my own meditations and methods of praying. I found that this was not only a sharing of myself, but of something more. I was also sharing the strength that was given me in relating to the Other. As some of these people tried the same kind of practice, they found the same presence and reality of the Other that I found. Activity like this was one of the very factors that enabled them to find their own strength and to begin dealing with the full gamut of life.

At the same time I discovered that there was—and still is—precious little published today to which I can refer the people who want to learn how to open themselves to an experience of the divine or the Other. I found next to nothing written about prayer and meditation that takes into account the discoveries about the human soul made by depth psychology in its seventy-five years of activity. Freud, Adler, Jung, Maslow, Carl Rogers and Rollo May might as well not have existed for all the importance they seem to have for writers on prayer.

Yet the masters of the devotional life and the depth psychologists need each other. They have each discovered something of the reality of the human soul, and each discipline has something important to say to the other. There is a burning need for us to see meditation in this new light. So many modern Christians have trouble with praying because they do not see how it can make sense in this complex modern world. Some psychological thought has made the complexity more understandable for us. The work of C. G. Jung and his followers has led farther than that. Their thinking and practice have helped many people to become aware of a need for prayer today. When the discussion of prayer leaves their discoveries out, it cuts off much of the sophisticated reading public and these people have as much right to prayer as anyone.

There is need, of course, on both sides. One of the great weaknesses among even the most religious depth psychologists is simply that their findings have not been tempered with the experience of those men and women who have plunged deepest into their relationship with God. These psychologists have not grasped the range and depth and richness of that experience, and so they can offer guidance only part of the way toward it. They often do not realize how common these experiences are to the ordinary "normal" person. Then there are psychologists who mistrust the entire experience of prayer and religious meditation, and these psychologists leave a great gap just where most of us need some direction and assurances that the road ahead leads somewhere worthwhile.

On the other hand, devotional writings, even down to the present day, have often left much to be desired. Some manuals insist upon the idea that we cannot grow in relationship with God without developing contempt for our emotional lives, our bodies and the physical world in general. Many of the classical Western writers have neglected the immanence or ever-present quality of

rejection of "contempt" could be facile

God and the ways of finding Him within this world as well as beyond it. The result has often been practices so ascetic, one-sided and rejective of the world that they even caused emotional disturbance in some followers. It is difficult for the average reader, lay or clerical, to sift the wheat from the chaff in this writing, even though popular devotional works of the last fifty years have sometimes suggested practices quite foreign to the total message of Jesus of Nazareth. Through the best of psychological understanding, however, we can find balance in our devotional lives and a return to His wisdom and practical directions.

No one has yet shown more clearly than Dorothy Phillips and her friends did thirty years ago what a close relation there is between the great devotional masters and many depth psychologists. In their anthology, *The Choice Is Always Ours*, the writings of these devotional masters and depth psychologists are set side by side. By listening deeply and sometimes translating the language, one begins to realize that the master of prayer and the depth psychologist are often speaking of the same reality. Each is expressing the same truths. Their own words show that there is an undeniable agreement or affinity between these two ways of understanding human beings. Both of them are deeply concerned with our need to stop and to pray, to question and to contemplate. Yet again and again I am tempted to ask: who or what am I speaking to and who is listening?

Quite recently I was told by the editor of a large denominational publishing house that he knows of no modern book on meditation which shows how valuable the insights of depth psychology are in Christian devotional life. In fact I had already been told by a major Catholic publisher that they had reviewed their titles and found they had brought out no modern work on the practice or practical methods of meditation. The books on prayer either repeat the same old formulas in their antiquated garb, or else they suggest that the traditional ways of prayer and meditation are no longer possible.

In my travels, lecturing to both Protestant and Catholic groups, I have learned over and over again how many religious professionals are abandoning any active practice of daily prayer and meditation. This is almost universally true among both religious communities and puritanical religious groups in which the members have been alienated by the strict and world-denying practices that have been so common.

There are good reasons for this failure to integrate psychological wisdom with religious practice. Among Catholics, Vatican II has given a freedom to examine and to abandon many religious practices that were never before questioned. At the same time many religious people have been frightened away from psychology because of the negative attitude toward religion on the part of much of the psychological community. But this attitude, although it does persist, is certainly no longer the total view. In addition, as Karl Rahner has noted, there is the great theological gulf fixed between the mystical or ascetic position and the more rational theological tradition.

Thus the practice of prayer and meditation has been doubted on psychological grounds (and some of the practices advocated by leading medieval writers *were* extreme), and it has failed almost entirely to gain the support of rational theology, much of which casts doubts on the contact of ordinary people with God. For a long time only authority kept the practice of meditation intact throughout the Church, and when that faltered so did the practice. At Notre Dame, which is unquestionably one of the world's great Catholic universities, we have awakened to the fact that only one course is offered in the practice of religious experience, and this by a non-Catholic. When the question was discussed, there were even a few who remarked that such a subject had no place in a university curriculum because it was not an academic subject.

Those who are informed about young people and the counter-culture know what an emphasis there is on meditation and prayer in these subcultures. Their use of hallucinogenic drugs is not just a reaction against a square adult society; it is often an attempt to break through the ordinary boundaries of human experience and make meditation easier and its results more real. Among college men and women (and older people as well) many are turning to Eastern forms of prayer, from Hare Krishna chanting and Zen meditation to Transcendental Meditation, in an effort to find some reality or experience beyond the immediate one. These are reactions to the materialistic and rational attitudes of the grey-flannel-suit culture, and they may even be healthy and encouraging signs.

These individuals are trying to fill the gap in their lives that was left when Christian forms of meditation were either forgotten or relegated to the dustbin. It is no wonder that both young and old turn to some place outside the Church to find a way that can bring them into contact with a deeper dimension of life. Where does one learn about the art of real prayer and meditation in a language that makes sense to us in these last years of the twentieth century? *And people are incurably religious.* There is no doubt that there is need.[1]

Even so I find that I am hesitant in writing about this. Although I know that there is need, and even though I have had to wrestle with bringing my own life into relationship with the Other over many years, I would still rather be silent than write the pages that are to follow. There was good reason for Jesus's instruction about praying in secret. And indeed, it is possible for me to write about these experiences only because I was asked to do so for a real purpose. There is nothing unique in these experiences of my response and interactions with the Other. I was driven by personal necessity to relate to God and have found this relationship necessary not only for my own life, but in the lives of others as well.

I write these pages on meditation and prayer as a beginner, even and *especially* after thirty years of practice. As Archbishop Anthony Bloom has written in his excellent manual, *Beginning to Pray*, we are all beginners in relating to God. Indeed, in every real relationship with human beings every encounter is new and a beginning. Our human relationships have a tendency to go sour the moment we assume that we know the depth and direction of another life. The same is certainly true of the unfathomable Other, or God; every turning to Him is a beginning, and in our turning we are all beginners.

One of the things that I have learned in talking with people over thirty years is how open one must be to communicate with any other person in depth. I have also learned that the truths enabling me to relate to people are usually even more significant in my relation to God in my meditation. The more deeply one knows humankind the more open one is to know God. One comes to understand what it means that we are made in His image. Every opening of myself to God in meditation opens a new door with new potential and possibilities.

As I share some of these personal and intimate experiences, my hope is that this will encourage others to turn inward in some similar ways, and then will lead them into examining their experiences and seeing how these compare with the ones I describe. We can also read some of the devotional classics and discover that the present generation is not so different from generations of earlier centuries as we sometimes think. There are also the works of those psychologists who believe that there is a place and a need in our lives for religious experience. By exploring in these ways we can find that there is a reality beyond ourselves with which we can communicate and which can transform our lives. Any practice that leads one into deeper relationship with this reality is part of the practice of meditation.

The Material

This attempt to share something of the experience of meditation will be divided into several quite different parts. In reality these are inseparable elements of a living process, but in order to understand either the process or its elements they will be taken one part at a time. The human mind can hardly take in such a whole process except in an intuitive flash, which can almost never be communicated except by the greatest of artists, and art is certainly not my forte.

We shall look first of all at the problem of the intimacy that is involved in meditation, since in speaking of this aspect of life one reveals one's depth. Then we shall discuss the relation of psychological types to the inner life, and, finally, in this section we shall consider how art is related to meditation. From this basis we shall go on in Part II to lay out one by one the elements of the atmosphere or environment in which it is possible for Christian meditation to grow and develop.

In Part III we shall consider several ways in which the individual can prepare to get into the practice of meditation. We shall discuss setting aside the time for meditation, the purposes of becoming silent, and various ways of encouraging silence, including keeping a record or journal.

In Part IV we shall go on with the preparations for meditation, considering first the importance of understanding the experiences that are sought and knowing our point of view in seeking them. This will bring us to the gateway of the inner world. We shall look at the nature and use of images, particularly as found in dreams, and then at other ways of awakening imagination. We shall then review briefly our need for historical tradition and ritual, the purposes of keeping a religious journal, the need for a group with whom one can share the experiences of meditation, and finally the need for spiritual direction.

We shall then consider how to go about "doing" meditation, using Biblical stories, dream images, and images from other sources. I shall try to show how negative moods can be changed into images and then brought before the Risen Christ so that one can be delivered from these moods, and how this practice can help one in depression, anxiety, or anger. This will help us to see how meditation can transform and stabilize one's emotional life and, with that, one's total outlook, especially actions toward others and toward society. We shall go on to discuss the practice of meditation in healing prayer for both ourselves and others, and from there we shall see how this fits naturally into intercessory prayer in general.

In the final section I shall offer examples of meditations that have risen spontaneously over the years, concluding with a description of the way in which we can pray the Lord's Prayer. These, it is hoped, will offer some signs along the road to the universal language of prayer.

2
Intimacy, Art and Meditation

One reason that we so often discuss prayer only superficially and intellectually is because this, in some ways, is the most personal and intimate aspect of one's life. Speaking about it is like laying oneself open for public examination. Our meditations reveal what matters most to us, and it is not easy to stand naked before others in our weakness and fear and exaltation. Perhaps it seems strange that contact with the Holy should be such a difficult experience to share. Yet this is like telling of the intimate aspects of one's love life.

In reality meditation is the record of one's love life with God. Sharing it with another person is like taking someone into the bedroom scene where one learns that all love has its ups and downs. I have discovered in listening to people that it is only after I am really trusted that they will tell me of their deepest religious feelings, their hopes and experiences and commitments.

This reluctance to speak about religious experience stood out, almost like the walls of a building, among students at Notre Dame. When they first came in to talk, it would be about some book or idea. If I passed muster in that situation, then in another hour of listening and talking I might hear about problems with parents or a brother, or in the dormitory; their sense of loneliness and isolation and problems of identity. And after that test I might then be admitted to a room full of sexual fears and tales of sexual peccadillos, some not so minor. But there was still another level of sharing which I found only when they were quite convinced that I would not doubt or ridicule or pressure. It was then that I was admitted to their religious experience, their sense of the presence of God, their feeling of closeness and desire to serve and know Him better.

It takes courage to share in this way with a friend and counselor. Allowing another person into this deepest level of our human experience makes any of us ultimately vulnerable, for it allows the other person to discover where our deepest values are and where we can be touched. We are exposing to another human being the center from which we move or wish to move. This demands real courage. And it requires even more of us to open ourselves in depth to the Other who is at the heart and center of reality. Most of us are afraid to try because we have not been able to take the Christian revelation really seriously.

We have heard so much about justice and judgment and the wrath of God that it is hard to believe anything else in our nerves and cells. Even when we try, in our heads, to accept what Jesus Christ reveals to us about the ultimate reality in the universe, we are not truly convinced. It is so easy to find anger and retribution among people, to learn about criticism and lack of acceptance even among our closest friends and family, that we keep on projecting upon God what we have known from people. There seems to be little reason to expect anything else. And so it requires real courage to turn to the center of things, to face that reality and find out what is there.

We are not really sure that Jesus knew what He was talking about in the story of the prodigal son, when He described God as that father who stands peering into the desert waiting for a wayward child to come home so that He can pour out upon the child the incredible richness of His love and concern. This is too good to be true. At the same time it threatens our whole way of life. If we should turn to the center of reality and actually find that kind of concern and love, then our lives, many of our motives and reasons for being, would be turned upside down. No wonder it takes a genuine act of will, first to believe that God could be like this, and then to act on that belief.

Then, too, we have to turn away from the idea of popular sentimentality about God being loving. Freud was certainly right in criticizing that kind of religion, which he described as a longing to return to the womb. It expresses a superficial desire to be taken care of by an indulgent parent without conscious consideration of what life is about. But this does not come out of a genuine confrontation with God, with "Love." Even parents, when they love in the deepest and wisest way, try not to indulge their children and make them dependent. As long as dependency is needed, they offer it, but their real desire is to encourage the child to step out toward maturity. How can we expect any less of God? Those who have the courage to face the reality and be confronted by that Love are refined and transformed by the experience. They do not fall back into childishness very easily.

Being confronted by love means responding, giving back freely to the Other. And what can we possibly give to God—that is ours to give—in return for His love? St. Catherine of Siena was once asked this, and she wrote back that the only thing we can offer God of value to Him is to give our love to people as unworthy of it as we are of His love. Really meeting the God who is love means stepping willingly into the refining fire to be slowly remade and changed into the kind of love that one has confronted. Some even turn away from human love to escape this demand upon them. They realize how powerful that experience can be, and they resist being opened up to forces outside themselves which might loosen their ego control of life and change them. Love is indeed a powerful experience; one can be caught by it and forced to change, which is painful for most human beings. And the touch of a loving God is no less powerful and dangerous than that of a human love affair.

The Ways of Relationship

Sometimes we conceal our relation with God in prayer because we are afraid that others are closer than we are, that someone may be further ahead. But once we have turned and are actually seeking to confront the Other, then we will almost certainly find a need for someone to talk with. Real confrontation with love demands sharing of this experience. And in sharing we realize that all of us, even the best, are babes in the woods.

So much growth and transformation are possible in one's relationship with God that those who are trying are like the laborers in the vineyard.[1] There is little difference between the one who has labored all day and the one who has been at work for only an hour. The first and the last are not far apart. And each of us, the best and the least alike, needs other human beings with whom we can share our deepest experiences and safeguard against deceiving ourselves. We each need some person with whom we can talk about any of these things, any level of experience, and we also need a group—which of course can be only two people—with whom we can pray. Although a real confrontation with the God revealed in Jesus Christ often comes alone and apart, in the desert or on the solitary mountain top, it draws us toward other human beings. This is a natural and integral part of the experience of meeting God. When it fails to happen, something is wrong.

The practice of prayer and meditation is as complex and varied as human life itself. As we confront the reality of the Other, we bring every part of our being, our ideas and thoughts, our plans for the day, for the week, for our entire life to the Other. We disclose our fears, our hopes, our human love, our thirst for more than human love, our anger and vengeance, our depression, sorrow and lostness, the values that are important to us, our adoration and joy and thanksgiving. Leaving out any part of the spectrum of human life makes prayer and meditation incomplete, and that is like meeting a person whom one hopes to know better, only to find that the relationship cannot grow because the other person dares to share only a small part of himself/herself.

What is true of human relationships at their deepest and best is even more true of the relationship with God. It is not very hard to know when we are at our best in relating. At those times we want to know all about the other person, including the darkness and shadow, so that we can love or care for that individual better. If one loves, one can bear everything. And the incredible mystery of Christianity is that God wants to know *us* in that way, in total depth and reality, the darkness as well as the light, the anger as well as the love. Indeed our human desire to know and love some other person in depth springs out of the very nature and reality of God Himself. This is perhaps the most essential way in which we are made in the image and likeness of God, this way of needing to love and to be loved.

I have had one particularly good friend who taught me much about this. He once shared the very depths of his broken life with me, a life indeed broken by alcoholism and sexual fear, failure in school, failure in life. Gradually my friend came together. He began to be able to deal with life. He got a job. He kept it. Jointly through the support of AA and through a vow renewed each week at the altar rail, he stopped his drinking. He got married and then went to work in another city. He lived there, creatively and independently, for three years. But when he came back and we talked, it was apparent that something had happened between us. We did not really seem to communicate. Then a time came when we discussed this. And it came out that my friend had felt that he did not want to bother me with any more of his shadowy darkness, any of the weakness that of course did not just evaporate. We both realized that he was keeping a part of himself from me and that this actually prevented the relationship from being real. Once it was clear that we were both losers, that we each needed to know a whole person and not just a mask or portion, then we were friends again.

Almost the same story could be told over and over of our relationship with God. As long as we feel that there is some part of ourselves that we cannot lay out and share with God, then we cheat Him fully as much as ourselves. For some inscrutable reason, something hidden deep in His nature, He wants to meet the totality of us, good, bad and indifferent, in the greatest depth. And only then can His love touch every part of us and transform or change the whole.

For this reason the meditative process is a many-faceted jewel. There are as many different sides of meditation and prayer, of meeting and confronting the Other, as there are sides of human life. If there are parts of us that we do not bring to the Other, it is like letting part of the gem go uncut. So many people like to emphasize certain forms of prayer or meditation such as prayer of thanksgiving or adoration. But these are completed only when one's prayer life involves all the other aspects of his life, from one's anguish and despair to volcanic and explosive anger. There are prayer forms appropriate to each of these sides of life. If we want the transformation that can come, we need to bring all parts of ourselves before the Presence. Sometimes the very things of which we are most ashamed can become the most brilliant part of our being when they are touched by that Presence and changed. This was the change that the alchemists were talking about when they hoped that the base metal might be transformed into gold; they were speaking more of the base metal of their human nature than of the metal in the furnace.

Some years ago Louis Evely set down these thoughts about sharing and love:

Love must express and communicate itself.
    That's its nature.
    When people begin to love one another,
        they start telling everything that's happened to them,
            every detail of their daily life;
        they "reveal" themselves to each other,
            unbosom themselves and exchange confidences.

God hasn't ceased being Revelation
    any more than He's ceased being Love.
He enjoys expressing Himself.
    Since He's Love,
        He must give Himself,
            share His secrets,
            communicate with us
            and reveal Himself to anyone
                who wants to listen.[2]

These words speak a very profound truth. Love can begin only as we begin to allow others to really know us. We can begin to love and be loved only as we bring all of ourselves to the other person, all of our disappointments, our joys, our angers and hopes. This is the nature of love and communication. It applies as much between God and a person as it does between person and person, and perhaps even more. For this reason we shall say quite a bit about prayer in fear and anguish, in anger and sorrow, since modern piety mostly seems to assume that we cannot find God through these experiences. Yet, any good parent expects to love and comfort children, to help them pick up the pieces when things seem to go wrong. God is certainly not less than a human parent.

Communication is a growing process. As one comes to trust more and more, one reveals more and more. Sometimes these will be things which looked so black that we buried them deep in the unconscious. We could not bear to keep remembering them. As trust and concern and love begin to grow, even these things can be brought out of the darkness. And until then few of us can ever become free of the nagging fear, hidden in the heart of nearly every person, that no one could really stand us if we actually let them see the totality of our being. I recall one young man with whom I worked for over two years before he was able to reveal the things he disliked most about himself. When he finally did, the change in him was miraculous.

It is not easy for us to realize that the One who is love does care for us. We have to bring the more secret parts of ourselves up slowly and let the reality of the One who is love be tested. This takes courage, patience, time. In fact one of the reasons why I believe in a life after death is the way communication with the Other develops. Even in the best of lives this reality is just beginning to grow at the end of that life. Even when we have known this experience of communication with the Other early in life, and realize all along that this Other is trying to communicate with us, our lives are just not long enough to bring all the parts of them and all of our actions into accord with the Other. There is no good reason to believe that the One who begins this process, and offers us all the care we are able to take, then will end the process just as we are beginning to experience it. On the contrary, every now and then an experience comes to one or another of us which strongly suggests that this process goes on after our physical death.

Human Types and Meditation

If this is true, then quite possibly there is meaning in the fact that we have suggested that meditation can be as varied as life itself. Since each person is unique, each one will have an individual way of relating the totality of his or her being to God. Other people's ideas may be helpful, but only one's own way which is uniquely individual and personal, will offer a relationship with the Other that is real and meaningful.

We have become so accustomed to thinking of human beings as sociological abstracts that we forget that no two of them are identical, any more than any two leaves are identical. When even our fingers and toes and voices leave a distinguishing imprint, it is no wonder that our personalities also differ in many unique ways. There have been several attempts to find some order in this variation, some rule of thumb that would make it easier for different types of people to understand each other better. One of these theories is the understanding of personality types developed by Dr. C. G. Jung. This theory, which is one of his most important contributions to psychological thought, has been tested experimentally by Isabel Briggs Myers. The test she developed is very helpful and not difficult to use.[3]

Jung's theory suggests that there are sixteen basically different types of individuals, and that each type has its own characteristic ways of taking in information and organizing it. Many of our fundamental divisions over prayer and ritual may well be understood as different ways in which different types of individuals prefer to relate to religious realities. When we love another person we try to understand and relate to that person just as he/she is, and we do not expect him/her to be a carbon copy of ourselves. My experience of God is that He is far more understanding than we are at our best. After all, He is the creator who has made us and given us different ways of responding and relating to this world. Apparently He wants each of us to seek Him in whatever way is the best for us individually, and He honors each personality and does not try to force us into any particular pattern or mold in order to relate to Him.

Our task is for each of us to find the way that is best for oneself as an individual, by first learning how one functions best, and then developing one's own relationships to the Other in that way. There are certain universal principles, of course, which must be followed. Beyond that, in order to find the deepest kind of relationship with the Divine, one needs to know oneself and the strengths one has been given so that they can be used in seeking and responding to God. Later on there is a time to try other approaches and methods. But until one has tested one's own way, it is not wise to adopt another person's meditational practice without knowing whether it will lead as far as one might go by following one's own way.

It is so easy for a religious leader to assume that the way which is meaningful for him or her must be equally meaningful for everyone else. This has presented a real problem in many denominations, and also in religious Orders in which the actual devotional practice of one leader could be made the rule for all. For about sixty years many Catholic Orders followed a meditational practice based almost exclusively on the approach of Adolphe Tanquerey, who adopted the ideas of St. Teresa of Avila and St. John of the Cross. This method holds that the use of images is an inferior way of meditating and seeks to place the whole emphasis on mental communion in an imageless void. It has value, particularly for certain individuals, but certainly not as an exclusive practice. The needs of various types of individuals could be met if other approaches, like the very different practice of St. Ignatius of Loyola, were available.

Still, there are two sides to this matter of the individual's personality type and his/her way of relating to God. God expects those of us who seek Him to keep on growing, learning to use our personalities more fully so that we will be able to know and relate to Him more and more completely. This goal makes it even more important to know one's own strengths and weaknesses so that each of us is prepared both to share with others and also to learn from them. At this point, trying out and sharing someone else's way of meditating is important, both for the leader and for the follower. This is one way that each of us can find hidden parts of ourselves and bring them to the meeting with God. With this in mind, let us take a look at our differences in personality structure and how they relate to devotional practice.

There is first of all the very basic difference between the extravert and the introvert, between one whose interest lies in the outer world of people, affairs and tangible things, and one who is comfortable being alone and turning inward. Since extraverts find meaning among people and in doing things, their prayer life will probably be geared to service with and to others. They are likely to find God more often present in the outer physical world than through inner experiences of quiet. Yet extraverts also need time for quiet and reflection; otherwise they have no chance to integrate what they have experienced among others and find its significance for their own growth and their deeper relationship with God.

Introverts, on the other hand, already find the inner world fascinating and easy to deal with. They are very likely to have no trouble finding an inner experience of God's presence, and then look down on those persons who find their meaning largely in the outer world. Since they enjoy quiet, it is relatively easy for them to find time to meditate and seek a personal relationship with the Other. Their need, then, is to be called back to the outer world in service to other humans and to society, which is difficult but necessary for them. Unless they will get out and deal with the realities of the outer world, both beautiful and sordid, their devotional life tends to become unrealistic and detached. Certainly it would seem that the introvert and extravert need each other if each is to find the deepest and most fulfilling devotional life.

Instead, this difference between two types of personality has probably been one real cause of discord and schism in the Church. In his tremendously important book *Psychological Types*, Jung has suggested that type structure may have been a basic factor in the great theological split of the Middle Ages when reason and revelation, the natural and the supernatural began to part company. In this clash between nominalism and realism, the nominalists were basically interested in the outer world. The realists were caught up by the inner world and its structure. This seemed to them to be the ultimate reality. For them the image or idea that came to the mind was more real than the outer physical thing which was mediated by sense experience. Because of this personality difference, neither side could see the possibility of getting along with the other, and so the conflict was brought to a head.

Besides such differing attitudes toward the outer world as a whole, most of us develop at least one of four functions that we use in dealing with the realities we encounter. Two of these are functions of perception, which involve taking in information about the world, usually about parts of it in which one is interested. The other two relate to judging, deciding about how to organize and use this information.

A mature individual generally develops one of these functions highly, another to a lesser degree, and then leaves at least one buried in the unconscious and seldom consciously used. We can sometimes learn to work with this fourth function, but this is usually not wise until we have developed the ones that are easy for us to use. By experimenting in the weakest area before working consciously to find the strengths that can be used, one usually ends up undeveloped in all areas. After we have learned to function well in our favorite area and can use an auxiliary or secondary one, and after finding a nodding acquaintance with our third function, we can then investigate what our inferior function can do for us.*

The first pair of functions, by which one receives information, are the perceptive ones that are called the *sensing* and the *intuitive* functions. Those persons who prefer to use their senses, the sensing type, are interested in individual details. Generally they like repeatable situations and are more comfortable in a well-known environment. They live in the "now" timewise and are usually "get-it-done" persons, doers. Action is their response to prayer and also to the rest of life. They often find religious pictures, crucifixes, icons helpful. Their prayer life will tend toward structured and familiar prayers, some often-used meditation. They are likely to be conservative in their meditational practices. They have real need to go out from their meditation into social action and correct what needs correcting.

In contrast, the intuitive persons are more often interested in unconscious data, in perceptions that are received in some way other than by sense experience. The unconscious is their ballpark, and they enjoy it, either observing its influence in the outer world or directly in the inner one. They are likely to be innovative religious leaders, interested in renewal in the Church. Their time sense is in the future and they are "thinker-uppers." They seldom can handle the details of what they think up, however. The inner life is very meaningful to them, and since they use images and understand their meaning, they will probably be bold in trying new ways of meditating. They find themselves at home in imaginative praying.

In religion it is important that the conservative, stick-by-the-rule leader does not quench the enthusiasm of the intuitive person, and also that the intuitive does not expect the impossible of sensing individuals, but allows their prayer to lead them into *doing something* about what they perceive. At the same time, each has a great deal to learn from the other. The intuitive must learn that there are bounds beyond which one cannot step without danger, and that one's own value has its roots in tradition, while the sensing person needs to realize something of the vast openness and freedom of the imaginative, intuitive world and its possibilities.

I recall one clear-cut example of this. I was working with a woman who came to me in real depression, whose personality seemed to be limited only to the sensing function. When I suggested looking within and finding an image

---

*The undeveloped function, being in the depth of oneself, can often give a person access to the depth of one's being, and using the inferior function is sometimes a way of allowing the powers of God to reach one most dramatically. Marie-Louise von Franz and James Hillman have written wisely on the importance of the inferior function.[4] The great mystic Jakob Boehme demonstrated its importance by developing his understanding for years around the experience of a ray of light striking a shiny pan. His inferior sensing function opened the way to him and he worked for years to integrate it.

that would help her express her feelings of difficulty, she protested that she simply could not use creative imagination. There was nothing there; no images would come. Yet, when a change finally began to take place in her, it happened when she realized that she had felt bound and that this had made her depressed. Suddenly she imagined that the bonds were dropping away from her body, and there was an experience of release which had a remarkable effect on her whole life.

The other pair of functions have to do with two essentially opposite ways of organizing the data that one receives. These are the rational or judging functions that determine how we deal with the experiences that come to us, and they are known as *thinking* and *feeling*. The person of thinking type likes to classify and arrange things according to logical or intellectual values, while the feeling individual prefers to base decisions and actions upon human values.

The first term is easy for us to understand. The thinking person is essentially interested in logical relationships and how the world fits together into a total scheme of meaning. Time for these individuals runs in a straight line from past to present to future, so that they see things in historical perspective. Their concern is with ideas and relationships between them, and they just aren't much concerned about how other people are affected or whether others are upset by their understanding of things.

The description of a "feeling type," however, is harder for most people to understand. This term has nothing to do with feeling in the ordinary sense of either emotion or physical sensation. Instead, it means making evaluations on the basis of how things affect people. What is important to the "feeling type" individual is the personal value or the value for others of the act or thing or person or idea. People are important to "feeling type" individuals, and they organize their actions and thoughts around human values. Their sense of time is rotary, moving from present to past to present. They arrive at their values by matching experiences that are meaningful to them in the present with those that have been meaningful in the past, and they organize their lives according to these values. They are generally quick to grasp and understand the values of others and the meaning of what is happening to them, while ideas and logical connections are seldom important to them.

The thinking types usually build their meditational life through connections with ideas and theology. They find philosophy important and value the effort to understand God within a framework of ideas and in the historical process. To them God can be apprehended by the mind as well as through experience. Their devotional life might seem cold and detached to the feeling person, and they need the correction and support of human values and close personal relationships.

Feeling individuals, on the other hand, find the greatest religious value and meaning in personal service and intimacy. The intimate Eucharist, where there are horizontal relations between people, is often very important to them and probably more significant for them than a majestic liturgy or a finely constructed sermon. Much of their meditational life is expressed in loving action toward others. But at the same time, they also need help to awaken their thinking function, first simply to evaluate the results of their actions, and then to see their place in a more total framework so that they will be able to communicate to others the meaning they find.

In *The Kingdom Within*, John Sanford has suggested that Jesus expressed the ultimate of what human beings ought to be by combining these various types of personality in perfect balance. He was able to turn inward and relate to the inner world. He was also able to deal with the outer world as no other human being. He cared about people, and yet He could defeat the scribes and Pharisees in intellectual battles. He had the most comprehensive intellectual framework. He perceived the beauty and meaning of the outer world and at the same time was uniquely open to the intuitive depth of humankind. Since we human beings are nowhere nearly as balanced as He, we can use only two, or at the most three, of these capacities. But as we do learn to use them, we can put them to meditational use for our own growth. And a part of this is learning to be tolerant and accepting of those who have other ways of responding to the divine.

It is important to realize that each type of person has to take his/her own avenue to find and explore his/her relationship with God. God is found in many different ways. The important thing for me as an individual is to find a way that will get me there, into that relationship, so that I can begin to grow. For teachers of the religious way the important thing is to learn how to encourage different ways of responding, to discover how they differ from their own, and how others can develop their own relationship. They also need to study the language and the expressions of others. Most of the devotional manuals were probably written by introverted intuitives (as they would usually be the only ones who would care about writing them) and so they must be translated to be understood by other types.

Whether we are directing our own lives or others' it is wise to realize that our type structures can change as life changes within and around us. Thus, practices which may be very meaningful at one time will not be as important at another period of our lives. Real life is fluid and ever changing, and so are real people, particularly in their relationship with the center and core of reality. When we are "stuck in cement" and cannot change our meditational lives, they suffer just like our relationships with other human beings. Creative human beings keep changing and adjusting to the complexities and varieties of life, to new experiences and new people, and also to God.

Meditation and Art

As we write about our relationship with the Other, we cannot avoid getting close to poetry or art, for we are expressing the deepest and most powerful emotions that we can have. Some people scorn art because they confuse it with entertainment. A friend wrote to me: "By making us aware of alternatives, art allows us to participate more fully in life. Most of what is called art is for the most part not art but entertainment. Its purpose is rather to make us less aware, to dull our senses, to confuse us, to give a false feeling of security and success. These forms of entertainment are drugs for the mind and soul, drugs to ease our pain rather than tools to use in curing the illness or at least letting us live with it creatively." There is a place for relaxation and entertainment, but this is seldom a major part of our relation with God.

If there is indeed an Other who seeks us and who wishes to love us, and we are not aware of Him and do not relate to Him, we are certainly not dealing with the totality of life. Perhaps the greatest expressions of art are those meditations and flights of imagination which express our relations with God and which enable other people to see the possible alternative ways of finding the reality of One who really cares for them and will direct them in their total being. Sometimes art, which merely shows us the futility of life without the Other, can drive us on to the alternative, but the great expressions of art and religion are those which show us the futility and meaninglessness and then the way out. It is here that Dante, Goethe and Shakespeare are masters indeed, but the greatest masterpiece of art is the Bible and in particular the gospel narratives.

Each of us becomes the artist as we allow ourselves to be open to the reality of the Other and give expression to that encounter either in words or paint or stone or in the fabric of our lives. Each of us who has come to know and relate to the Other and expresses this in any way is an artist in spite of himself/herself. The reason for the tragedy and futility of so much of modern life is that it has lost this dimension. The art which reflects only the barrenness of life shares in the meaninglessness and absurdity. In the deepest sense religion, in which the individual has not been touched by the center of which we speak, is cold and unfeeling. It does not know the fire and expression of art. Art, which has not touched the same center, either is bravado in the darkness, despair, or debases itself into entertainment. In the final analysis meditation is the art of living life in its fullest and deepest. Genuine religion and art are two names for the same incredible meeting with reality and give expression to that experience in some manner. The experience of this reality demands expression. This is part of the experience. Those who have been badly hurt or disappointed by churches can perhaps recover something of the reality by seeing the process of meditation and prayer as the final and sublime art form and the most creative way of living out a life.

It is only dangerous to view meditation as art when we do not take art seriously and so refuse to see that real art is working one's salvation out with fear and trembling. When art is seen merely as one's attempt to reach aesthetic perfection, then it loses its seriousness and becomes a plaything and not a reality. But this is only possible in a world which does not know the reality of the spiritual world and so sees art merely as a human product and not a revelation of more than human harmony and meaning.

Jung warns against viewing one's record of inner experiences as art, either written descriptions of fantasies or paintings of the inner moods. One must be careful not to view these as "art" because then they lose their seriousness and their power to bring us into touch with another realm of reality and to produce a transformation within us. One of the ways of cutting us off from the spiritual world is simply to view this as mere art or mere aesthetics. Henry Miller speaks with power of the reality of art with a capital "A" in his *Open Letter to the Surrealist* written in 1938. This kind of Art is very close to meditation.

One critic who saw the opening performance of T. S. Eliot's *The Cocktail Party* on Broadway remarked that he felt like leaving the theatre on his knees beating his breast. The same critic would probably not have been touched by the ordinary religious service. Yet he caught the utter seriousness about salvation and the reality of the spiritual world which is found in so many places in Eliot's poetry, in the children's stories of C. S. Lewis, particularly *The Lion, the Witch, and the Wardrobe,* and in the novels of Charles Williams. We find the same quality in even greater measure in Dante's *Divine Comedy*, Goethe's *Faust*, and in a more hidden way in some of Shakespeare's plays like *Measure for Measure, The Tempest, Lear, Hamlet* and *Macbeth*. Only a cheap, disillusioned or frivolous art is antagonistic to religious experience and meditation.

Where the Church fails in its task, God uses whatever channels are open, whether they happen to be artists or psychiatrists. One psychiatrist friend once said, "Morton, there is a place for religion in the Church as well as in the psychiatrist's office."

Humankind stands as a bridge between two worlds. Our greatest moments are when we have met, nakedly and face to face, the reality that saves and transforms, and then express this as part of our assimilating the experience. Our records of such experiences give us a further step on the road. They also give others light to find the path they must follow. Everyone's encounter and record brings more light and consciousness into this world and allows the forces of darkness to be beaten back.

PART TWO

The Basic Climate
for
Meditation

3
The Climate of Meditation

Living things need an appropriate climate in order to grow and bear fruit. If they are to develop to completion, they require an environment that allows their potential to be realized. The seed will not grow unless there is soil that can feed it, light to draw it forth, warmth to nurture and moisture that unlocks its vitality. Time is also required for its growth to unfold.

Those who have lived near the desert know the miracle of a rainy year when suddenly a whole mountainside turns orange under a blanket of poppies, or a valley becomes a fairyland of color. The seeds have been there. The soil and the sun and the warmth have been there. Only one thing was lacking, and when that last climatic need was fulfilled, life was profuse beyond imagination.

Meditation is the attempt to provide the soul with a proper environment in which to grow and become. In the lives of people like St. Francis or St. Catherine of Genoa one gets a glimpse of what the soul is able to become. Often this is seen as the result of heroic action lying beyond the possibility of ordinary people. The flowering of the human soul, however, is more a matter of the proper psychological and spiritual environment than of particular gifts or disposition or heroism. How seldom we wonder at the growth of the great redwood from a tiny seed dropped at random on the littered floor of a forest. From one seed is grown enough wood to frame several hundred houses. The human soul has seed potential like this if it has the right environment. Remember that only in a few mountain valleys were the conditions right for the *Sequoia gigantea*, the mighty redwood, to grow.

How, then, do we provide the right environment? What are the conditions for the soul which are equivalent to the sun and rain, the soil and warmth for the seed? First of all, the soul requires a spiritual environment with which it can react and in which it can grow and mature. This is the reality of contact with a spiritual world. Then it must be prodded from within by human need, the moisture that makes the seed swell and burst its own limits and so start upon the growth process. Until we realize that we need something beyond our own humanness, neither prayer nor meditation become a reality.

And then there is the reality of love which seeks out and desires to touch us and bring us to itself. This unique Christian understanding of God is the light of the sun which draws us forth. Christians have been entrusted with the knowl-

31

edge that God is like the loving, caring Jesus of Nazareth who cared enough to die for any individual, even if that person had been the only one. This understanding gives us the assurance that there is nothing to fear in the ultimate confrontation. Instead, it means allowing oneself to be open to this almost incredible love. But this still requires one more condition for the reality of continued meditation.

It is this final step of allowing our lives to be expressions of that love in outer action that provides the warmth needed to encourage the seed to grow. The expression can take innumerable forms. One person may express that love by attempting to change a rotten social structure that warps and deforms human souls, another by making love more real to those one already loves, letting more of one's concern become apparent. It can be expressed by visiting a crotchety old neighbor with a cup of warm soup, or on a battlefield by lifting some water to the lips of a dying man. And these things are not only the highest good in themselves; they also keep our feet on the ground, guarding us from the danger of becoming so involved in spiritual things that we lose our humanness and our touch with outer reality.

For both the seed and the soul, these things all take time. In both cases there is need for patience. Most of us know enough not to poke at the seed to see if it is sprouting, or try to hurry it along with too much water or fertilizer or cultivation. The same respect must be shown for the soul as its growth starts to take place. Growth can seldom be forced in nature. Whether it is producing a tree or a human personality, nature unfolds its growth slowly, silently.

It is so difficult for human beings to understand that more than one condition may be needed to realize some possibility. We seem to have an insatiable desire to make things simple, to reduce every complexity to one cause. It is difficult for us to adjust to the world around us as it is. While there is no harm in trying to simplify things enough to understand them, too often we try to force reality to fit some rigid pattern of our own ideas. Where meditation is concerned, we need to realize two things. Meditation is simple and natural, like a seed growing and becoming a tree. At the same time it requires the right conditions, conditions not provided by the secular world today. If meditation is to touch reality, we must seek out the right climate.

4
The Spiritual World
as the Soul's Soil

Most religions believe that humanity is in touch with a nonphysical or quasi-physical realm of reality. We are in touch with a physical world of rocks and trees and enemy tribespeople. We are also in touch with a spiritual world inhabited by the spirits of the dead, by demonic and angelic powers. Religious ritual, prayer and meditation were once ways that people used to deal with this spiritual reality, and being able to deal with that realm made a lot of difference about how life went with them.

The early Christians believed that they were in touch with such a world, and that Jesus by rising again gained victory over the powers of evil in it. A decisive victory had been won, and the Christian with the Eucharist and meditation shared the victory of Christ and gained control over evil forces. Since evil afflicted them morally in sin, psychologically in mental illness, and physically in disease, they gained power over these things. There was nothing more important for the early Christians than keeping in close touch with the source of that victory, and ritual and prayer were what kept them in touch with it. The importance of ritual and prayer in this framework can hardly be overemphasized. They enabled Christians to face a hostile world with love, and even to face death with joy.

Some comprehension of the reality of the spiritual world, as separate from, but related to, the physical world, is crucial to this view of meditation. If there is no such realm, meditation at best is only talking to oneself, and at worst it verges on stupidity and illusion or outright madness. It is very difficult to open materialistic Western people's eyes to the reality of the spiritual world. There is no way to find this reality except by trying something which they have been taught leads nowhere. This is one of the reasons why it so often requires desperation to get secular persons to try opening themselves to this reality which is new to them.

It was easy in medieval times to believe in the spiritual world. It appeared to people in that age like an extension of the physical world. Hell was straight below them in the earth, and heaven started just beyond the top of the highest peak. It stretched away in ten ascending layers represented by the planets and stars, up to the highest level where God reigned in the perfect wholeness of the Celestial White Rose. They did not lack pictures of the soul's place and significance. A person *was* the center of the universe, immersed in the world to which the soul belonged as well as in the bodily one, himself/herself the main concern of the creator God. The person's spirit was the only thing that really mattered. For this reason the great mystics and spiritual writers of the late Middle Ages could indulge in ascetic practices that today seem almost abnormal. Neither St. Teresa, St. John of the Cross, nor St. Catherine of Genoa speak much about dealing with the spiritual world. It was almost too much around them, too much in their imaginations. They hardly took the physical body, its values and its needs seriously.

Then began the study of the patterns of physical matter. Beginning with the movement of the stars and planets, step by step to the laws that govern the tiniest atom, they showed that humankind was far from being at the center of the universe. The human being was pinned down to a bit of matter revolving around a lesser star at the edge of unimaginable reaches of space. The philosophers of the Enlightenment came to doubt that humans could reach anything beyond themselves, or that anything more than human ever touched them. And finally, with Darwin's impersonal principle of human evolution, the modern world began to doubt whether a human being has any soul at all. A human being might well be just a set of conditioned responses, or one more material thing in a material universe that can be studied and picked apart and which will be discarded in the end.

It is next to impossible to maintain a meaningful practice of religious meditation within a belief pattern like that. Only the most resolute or the most unconscious are likely to keep on reaching out to something beyond themselves if this is what they really believe about the universe in which they live. They may see meditation as a kind of inner dialogue that sometimes produces interesting results, but will this draw many people to pursue it faithfully? Perhaps a few aesthetes and a few strange cults will keep at it seriously, but for many of us it has become difficult to see what there is of universal and urgent value in the practice.

 Frankly, with the breakdown of scholastic thinking in the Catholic Church and the rise of liberal and existential thinking in most Protestant Churches, few people see any place for the soul as an independent, irreducible reality with a probability of persisting. By the same token neither is there a place for an environment, a soil, with which the soul can interact. Yet our very real souls are just what we are trying to work with in meditative practice, and the soul needs its activity in the nonphysical environment in addition to its very real involvement in the material world.

Please note that I am not suggesting that the soul can act and react only in the spiritual environment, only with the reality that is of the same stuff as itself.

What I am saying is that there are two realms of reality. And the soul, which is quite an amazing reality—like the redwood seed, far more amazing than we usually realize—can move in two different worlds, and must move in both of them if it is to realize its potential. Like the tree, it has its roots in the earth and its branches in the air and must have both to survive.

In several other books,[1] particularly in *Encounter with God*, I have tried to show that there is no good reason to doubt the reality of the spiritual or psychoid* world with which the soul has much in common and with which it can interact directly. As for "knowing" that there is no spiritual world nor any spiritual substantiality to the soul, it rests upon the doubter to prove this. This is a negative proposition, which is the most difficult kind to prove. To demonstrate that *no* spiritual reality exists, one must show that either one knows *everything* about the world, or else knows the very essence of things. And both of these assert a kind of knowledge that few thoughtful people of today would claim to have. Especially in this case it would be hard to sound convincing, when so many in all ages have maintained that, when conditions were right, they touched a reality which made anything within this physical world seem pale by comparison.

There can be little question about the way Jesus of Nazareth believed. He expressed quite clearly His understanding that we are in contact with two different worlds. This is seen in one after another of the parables where He often used some description of the physical world to illustrate what He was revealing about another realm of reality. It is seen in His various references to the angelic realm and in His teachings about the evil one, as well as in His understanding and healing of the one possessed by the demon, and also in His own experience on the Mount of Transfiguration. While Jesus certainly showed a thorough appreciation of the outer material world in all that He said and did, He also wanted men to know their relation to the world of spirit. This is assumed in all His teachings about prayer, which make sense only within such a framework. It is strange how seriously we take Jesus's moral ideas and then ignore His worldview. Yet, if Jesus really was the incarnation of God, He probably has something to tell us about philosophy as well as morals.[2]

The world-view of Jesus has more in common with the ideas of late Judaic and Greek thought than with early Hebrew thought. It may well be that God waited until the climate was right to bring His son into the world. This happened when humanity was ready to experience the reality of God's love, when it could awaken to the realization that this reality can be touched whenever the conditions are right. It is not that God has to wait for us to *make* the conditions,

---

*Resembling the psyche or soul. This is the world which we know through the unconscious and it has been called the collective unconscious or the objective psyche by Jung.

but rather that He has to give us time to adjust, to recognize our need and be open to His love which is always ready to come in.

At the time that Christ came it was not extraordinary for people to deal with this realm through which God could be experienced directly. This, anyone could do. It was their natural birthright and did not require extreme asceticism or esoteric knowledge. Instead the kingdom of heaven was right at hand, ready to be entered.

The most vivid experience of the early Church was that of the Risen Christ. For these earliest Christians the experience was so real that when it came to setting down the record about Jesus Himself, they sometimes confused the teachings received by the Church from the Risen Christ with those that Jesus had given to the original disciples. The reality was so close to them that they did not even realize they were creating a problem.

Yet it has taken generations of historical criticism of the New Testament to come to a real picture of the historical Jesus.⁵ We have begun only recently to realize that He was known in both ways, first by the New Testament writers in the historical record, and then for centuries by the apologists and Doctors of the Church as a spiritual reality. This was possible because they were still aware of how close the spiritual world is to humankind and how they interact. Indeed the Greek Orthodox Church has not varied from this basic view of the world. Only in the West, when the thinking of Aristotle and scholasticism came to dominate Western theology, did it become difficult for people to realize that spiritual realities can touch their lives in the here and now.

The great Fathers and Doctors of the Church who gave us our Trinitarian Christianity continued to express their knowledge of humankind as a bridge linking two worlds. They saw humanity with one side joined to the physical world of matter, and the other immersed in the nonmaterial but even more real world-of-spirit, and the human soul or psyche as the instrument of communication between the two. What they were expressing might be pictured in a diagram. (*See* facing page.)

The space on each side of the central line represents the two realms in which the human soul or psyche (represented by the ellipse) exists. We do not need diagrams to realize the many forces which affect humanity in the physical world (the area on the right), and so we detail only the lesser known realities that touch humanity from the nonmaterial world on the left. Consciousness and rationality are represented by the portion of the psyche extending over the dividing line into the area of space and time. The larger portion of it extends deep into the world of spiritual realities. As is shown, two of these realities can sometimes be encountered in the world of matter, but the human psyche provides their most effective meeting ground.

What this sketch suggests is that we have greater depth than conscious rationality reveals, that in this depth there is a reservoir of memories and unin-

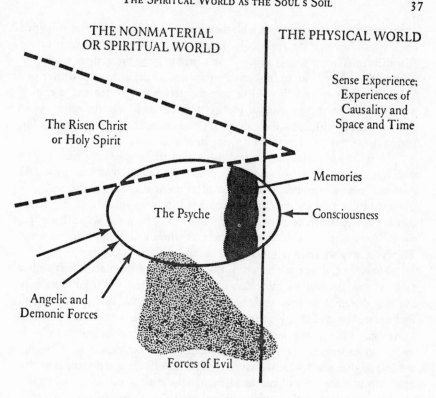

THE NONMATERIAL
OR SPIRITUAL WORLD

THE PHYSICAL WORLD

Sense Experience;
Experiences of
Causality and
Space and Time

The Risen Christ
or Holy Spirit

Memories

The Psyche

Consciousness

Angelic and
Demonic Forces

Forces of Evil

tegrated instincts and fears, and also a deeper level through which we find contact with the separate realities of the spiritual world. A person needs to be in touch with this depth to have a "single eye," to be whole.[4] We need to become as aware of it as we can so that we are not moved willy-nilly by either a fragmented part of ourselves or some unknown element of the spiritual world.

This is usually a difficult task, to know whether one is moved by something within one's ego or possessed by an element from beyond it. But there is a compelling reason for trying to find out, trying to become as conscious as possible of this depth. One's being can be touched and even penetrated by the powers of evil, as well as by the creative force that is often called the Holy Spirit. Most people who turn inward find a war going on within them between the powers of destructiveness and the force of light which the early Church knew as the Risen Christ.[5] This is a struggle which one cannot win by one's own power, but only by being open to the reality of the Risen Christ and allowing Him to win the victory.

Meditation is the practice, the art of letting down the barrier that separates one's rational consciousness from the depth of one's soul. In Christian meditation

It's inner work

one is trying to come into touch with the spiritual world in a way that will open one's whole being to the reality of this creative and integrating center, or the Risen Christ. The purpose is to allow the Christ to bring the split-off, conflicting parts of one's being into fruitful relationship, and at the same time deliver one from destructive evil which seeks to keep the person fragmented and operating unconsciously. In this way one is brought together and given the single eye— that new center of being which allows a person to operate at more nearly full potential, creatively and freed from giving in to destructive impulses.

In reality, Christian prayer and meditation make sense only within some such framework. Unless we find a power like this beyond ourselves, we would do better to stay as conscious and rational as possible and try not to fool ourselves. But if prayer and meditation are what I have suggested, then few things that we can do are more important for our lives. Only in this way are we able to reach out to the reality that can make us whole and bring us to maturity. This is the way we grant full reality to our sonship through Christ.

How, then, does one find out if this is true, or if there actually _is_ such a realm of spiritual reality? How does one find out if there is a realm essentially like that described by Jesus and the early Church? I know of only one way to find an answer, and that is to try the same method the scientists have used to learn what is true about the physical world. This is the way of repeated experiment and experience. We can expose ourselves to experiences of this other world, and then ask if what we have found tallies with the descriptions of others. Have we, as many others have stated, found something more lasting and significant than is found in the purely physical realm? Only experience can decide whether this is true or not.

In this sense meditation is the laboratory of the soul. Like the physicist studying the atom, or a biologist working with the cell, or the psychologist trying to understand a complex, the person who turns inward learns about the realities that are found there, their patterns and how to relate to them. While this comes by experience, still one does not start from scratch, any more than a scientist would blithely forget everything in textbooks and try to reconstruct it all every time an experiment is performed. The scientist and the explorer in the spiritual world both need the accumulated wisdom of the past, even when it has to be questioned and sometimes brought up to date.

But one great difficulty in learning about the spiritual world today is that we have forgotten how to use much of the wisdom that is available to us. It often seems that the only place to go for guidance is to the Eastern religions which, it is true, can tell us much about our inner world. But when it comes to the practical effect of meditation on the things that are important in Western life, Eastern thought leaves a real gap. We are then faced with an undesirable choice. We can accept the Eastern idea that the outer reality of life is transitory or illusory and of no great value, or we can turn back to the standard values of our own world and go on leaving spiritual realities out of our calculations about the world that matters to us right now. What we in the West generally fail to realize is that we have another choice, although a difficult one, and that our task is to learn what our own tradition says about this question and then go ahead and try it out.

There are a few things, however, that all of us probably need to realize at the outset. First of all, a strong ego, a strong consciousness is indispensable if a person is to find relation to the spiritual world through meditation. Having an ego is not bad. It refers to having a strong and stable center of one's personality. To go upon this way one has to give up the ego or self, and one cannot very well give up something that one does not have. The person who has never become established in the outer world is in no position to turn resolutely to the Risen Christ and allow Him to take direction. Our first obligation is to sink roots and find our point of view so that we are able to stay on course and take this kind of direction.

Much nonsense has been written about the spiritual world by people who were trying to open themselves to this realm before they were ready for it, without realizing that they were courting disaster. The most extreme example of this is the psychotic who encounters the spiritual realm. Psychosis is a kind of mental illness that can result from failure to develop an ego. The psychotic lacks any barrier to hold back the tides from the depths of the soul and veers with every current, good or evil. The psychotic has just as great religious experiences as anyone else, just as valid ones, but the problem is that he/she is not able to do anything about them except talk, having no life of his/her own into which such experiences could be integrated.

One reason that many people are leery of taking the inner world seriously is that they see it merely as a world of illusion and psychosis. In fact where there is no understanding of the reality of the spiritual world, the tendency is for most people sooner or later to view all religious experience as some kind of illusion. Yet this thinking does not fit the facts, as the philosopher Henri Bergson has shown so well in *The Two Sources of Morality and Religion*. For one thing, our world simply does not produce any finer or more effective people than the men and women who are dealing maturely with this inner reality.[6]

In taking this inner way of meditation, however, even the person with the strongest ego needs to realize that there are dangers, that one faces a vast world of contrasting and often conflicting realities. One might say that the mountains are higher, the oceans deeper, the colors even more vivid than in the physical world. Certainly the forces of light and darkness stand out far more clearly than we are accustomed to. And in the spiritual world we find not only greater beauty and creativity than in the physical one, but also the reality of destructiveness and ugliness, of evil itself.

One of the saddest misconceptions of the modern world is the notion that something which is spiritual must necessarily be good. In reality something can be truly evil through and through only when it *is* spiritual. It is usually in the spiritual world that such evil takes shape, when a subordinate or partial good takes over, pretends to be the central or the essential good, and becomes unmitigated evil. And there such evil is encountered, naked and direct, as the author of Ephesians described clearly when he wrote about putting "on all the armour which God provides, so that you may be able to stand firm against the devices of the devil. For our fight is not against human foes, but against cosmic powers, against the authorities and potentates of this dark world, against the superhuman forces of evil in the heavens" (New English Bible, 6:11f.).

The inner way, the way of meditation is dangerous. Any practice which brings us into contact with forces from the spiritual world in this way puts us into the middle of a mighty struggle. To enter this arena for curiosity or diversion can be disastrous. Indeed there is only one thing more dangerous than entering upon this way, and that is *not* entering it (assuming you have a developed ego), for you then allow the destructive forces free play. If you do not get into the battle yourself and try to stay in touch with the forces of light, you become a blind target. You allow the forces of destructiveness to enter and eat away at your own soul, or else you project them upon other colors or classes of persons, other races or other nations. Whomever the darkness seizes in this way becomes an instrument of destruction and cruelty, sometimes even sucking a whole nation into cruel and bloody acts.

I know of no way that this danger can be met and overcome except by the way of meditation, and this is not child's play. But then neither is life itself. Most people are beset by difficulty and danger both from without and within. Most times when we do not see the grim reality in the lives of others, it is because we have closed our eyes to it. But the message of Christianity is that if we will first try the inner way—dangerous as it is—and seek the kingdom of God, we will find help on the road ahead. The way of Christianity, as we shall see, provides solutions, hope, and victory, and the Good News is for both the outer world and the one we can find within.

And how does one come to believe in such a world of spirit? Is it by faith? Heavens, no. The spiritual world can be discovered and experienced by anyone who really wants to find it. One acquires this knowledge by making the same hypothesis that others have made, and then experimenting with life. Faith, on the other hand, is given; it is a gift of trust that one does not stand alone against the forces of darkness in that world, but will find them already in flight from the powers of the Risen Christ. Faith is what gives one the confidence to go ahead and learn about the reality of that world, to use the practice of prayer and meditation to open oneself to it. This is the way one tests any hypothesis—by action, not by saying what he thinks or believes about it. Discovering and coming to know spiritual reality requires the action of meditation. In fact, the time one spends in quiet and openness, in imagination and introversion, is far better evidence of one's actual belief about this world than any theological declaration. It reveals just how much one believes and wants to know.

This is like the story, told me recently by one friend who is a priest, about a man who came to the edge of an abyss which he could not cross. As the man stood wondering what to do next, he was amazed to discover a tightrope stretched across the abyss. And slowly, surely, across the rope came an acrobat pushing before him a wheelbarrow with another performer in it. When they finally reached the safety of solid ground, the acrobat smiled at the man's amazement. "Don't you think I can do it again?" he asked. And the man replied, "Why, yes. I certainly believe you can." The performer put his question again, and when the answer was the same, he pointed to the wheelbarrow and said, "Good! Then get in and I will take you across."

What did the traveler do? This is just the question we have to ask ourselves about the spiritual world. Do we state our belief in it in no uncertain terms, even in finely articulated creeds, and then refuse to get into the wheelbarrow? What we do about it is a better indication of our belief than what we think we think. Are we willing to take the time and effort to test the hypothesis that there really is a spiritual world available to us? The practice of meditation will not be very meaningful unless we do, and no amount of thinking or reasoning can take the place of experience.

5
Cracking the Husk:
Man's Need for God

It is hard for self-reliant modern men and women to ask for help from beyond themselves. All through modern history there have been voices telling them to rely on themselves, that they need nothing else, and in recent times the volume has stepped up among Western thinkers until it almost drowns out any other idea. Most people have become convinced that human life is essentially a do-it-yourself proposition. We reach our goals by carefully planned social conditioning and by working hand-in-glove with matter and the process of development that is seen to occur inevitably in matter. Few people stop to ask whether they can achieve their full potential, their full growth, without first finding God.

Is it possible for men and women to run their lives adequately without turning to God and becoming open to the realm where God is found most directly? In many ways we human beings *are* like seeds that wait for moisture to break open their husks so that they can sink roots and begin to grow and develop, and this raises a real question. If we are like seeds in the way we have suggested, do we need to have the husks of our souls cracked open so that we can sink roots in the spiritual world and find direct contact with God? In fact, should our souls be exposed to this realm? At the outset it must be admitted that the answer is not a simple and easy one.

Most of us would rather stay put than seek such an experience of growth. This process of allowing new life to open up is like death and resurrection for human beings. One gives up life to find a new way, like the seed that gives itself to nourish a living, growing plant. While the seed seems to have no choice, the person must choose to experience dying in order to live, and this is painful. Few of us will knowingly expose ourselves to such an experience unless we are convinced that it leads to growth too valuable to avoid.

If one believes, on the other hand, that all growth is a natural result of developing and experiencing in the physical world, then it is foolish to test the soul in this way. As the story at the end of the last chapter suggests, there is a dangerous abyss between the experience of these two realities, and we should not attempt to cross it unless we sense an actual need for the direct experience. As long as we are quite sure that we can stay on this side and find all the fulfillment that life offers, we probably have tasks enough for one lifetime. Sooner or later, however, the prospect of death sometimes forces some of the most confident persons to turn toward this other reality whether they are ready or not. We are almost certainly ahead of the game if we have already seen this ultimate need and allowed ourselves to be opened up to God and the world of spirit before the ultimate need catches up with us.

Let us now turn to the questions this raises about a person's outer life. We shall then consider the kind of cracks that open the souls of some people to this reality, often without their understanding or even recognizing it, and how other people are opened to the need to search for it. Finally, we shall examine the dangers involved in trying to open another person's life, and the question of whether there is need for everyone to go the inner way. First of all let us ask about the claim that humanity has come of age, which is Bonhoeffer's view, and that we no longer need direction from beyond our immediate world.

Man Come-of-Age

If our human problems could be neatly packaged and sent to the low bidder for solution, we would learn at least one thing. The biggest bundle would certainly be the one labeled "Problems of Self-reliance and Maturity." To become mature, adult men and women have to learn to stand on their own feet, tackle their own needs and work with whatever powers they are given. It takes us human beings most of a lifetime to try to become mature and independent. This is known as developing a strong ego which is essential if one is ever to go the inner way. And even then, most of us never quite get over the wish to be babied and taken care of by other people. It is no wonder we often confuse human maturity with becoming independent of God.

Religion itself can be used as a crutch. The worst abuses of power have probably occurred because people wanted to rely on God as a defense for their action or inaction. Religious people have often looked for reward and fulfillment in a future life instead of doing the best they could to bring justice and renewal and fullness of living in this present one. At times they have even concealed their desire to keep the *status quo* by convincing themselves that something like slavery was meant to be and that men and women are foolish to think they can change what is considered the "divine order" of things.

On the other hand, what do we have to show for the abrupt swing in the modern world in the opposite direction? In the past century we have had a taste of "coming of age" and trying to make it on our own. Yet with all our technical "know-how" and skill in reasoning and diplomacy our world seems to race toward overpopulation and pollution and self-destructive conflict. Millions die of hunger and over half the world's children go to bed hungry most nights. Preparation for war absorbs an enormous share of our energy, and over the last one hundred years we have fought the bloodiest and most damaging wars of all history. It seems ironic that the phrase "man come of age" was brought into popular usage by a man who was about to be hanged in a Nazi concentration camp.[1]

In spite of the tremendous increase in medical knowledge, physicians often find that they are baffled by the mental and psychological difficulties of their patients. Almost everything that we moderns write or produce imaginatively tells of our problems and despair in living at the present moment. We come face to face with the ultimate prospect of a meaningless void without hope of a life after death.

Fifty years of Marxist experiments all over the world have apparently left many people in those countries with the same feeling of despair. Marxism is simply more honest than our present Christian culture. It makes no pretense that we can create our own world or solve our dilemma by conscious will. Of course there is no God to turn to, but the ultimate reality is replaced by the almost religious belief in the materialistic process working in history. According to this belief a people must give themselves to the working out of this rational (dialectical) process. Marxism recognizes that we need something beyond ourselves, but this is seen only as an impersonal principle that grinds on without possibility of changing. Trying to reach dialectical materialism by meditation would be like trying to pray to a drill press. In Marxism, a person's need to be self-reliant is not recognized nor is there any possibility of meaning beyond the individuals and their involvement in the historical process.

We need to use our own ability and to muster all our intelligence and power to put our own house and world in as good order as we can. But once we have done our level best (which we often seem unable to do), we still need something more. Both efforts are needed. It is not a matter of choosing between human ability and divine power and direction. We need to give our best effort to this present-day world and *still* ask humbly for help and guidance. Many modern thinkers, however, reject this understanding completely.

In *Walden II*, B. F. Skinner, for instance, describes a utopian communal life in which there is no need for religion or God. People's wants are filled in perfect balance by proper conditioning or training. There is no anger or hostility; everyone is creative, and no one seems to worry about life after death. Dietrich Bonhoeffer also denied our need for God in a different but even more idealistic way. He believed that we were ready to come of age so that we no longer needed God and would worship Him only because we want companionship and fellowship. This is a beautiful idea but one that I have not found true to life in the lives of people I have known.

Apparently both Bonhoeffer and Skinner had doubts they did not express. Skinner speaks of feeling a certain aimless boredom in life, which makes one wonder if he is convinced by his own utopia. A close friend of Bonhoeffer's has written of how he carried bottles of sleeping pills and tranquilizers to give people in times of stress. He evidently thought people needed something but didn't expect religion to give it. Indeed, the suffering that was ultimately inflicted on Bonhoeffer by the Nazis suggests that people are not quite ready to take over and run things without God; nor in my opinion are pills a very good substitute for God.

People still find a need for something beyond themselves after they do the best they can and then look honestly into the depth of their lives. Trying to ignore this with a stiff upper lip does not help them become mature. They become truly mature as they first develop all the capacities they have, recognizing both failures and weaknesses, and then turn to God for further wisdom and understanding and power. There is no basis for the idea that our human struggle is opposed to our need to rely on God. People who plug for total self-reliance are usually making up for some lack in themselves, while those who insist on total reliance and dependence on God are generally trying to keep people dependent on a repressive religious institution. God, I believe, wants us to use all of our human abilities which are, after all, given by God in the first place and when that is not enough, God Himself gives something more.

In over thirty years of parish life ministering to all kinds of people, I have found no one whose life was totally secure and without need. This was true in a comfortable parish in suburban Los Angeles, and I have found it true in the academic community, as well as in lecturing from one end of the country to the other and in Europe. Insecurity seems to be the common lot of all human beings. Among every group, young or old, wealthy or poor, people whose lives seemed rich and full and powerful, as well as those that were empty or oppressed, there has been a deep need felt which the individuals normally found difficult to express to others.

Most of the time people are able to keep up a good front and appear and often feel confident and satisfied with life. Our society seems to demand and reward this kind of self-sufficiency. But behind the human mask are often pain and hurt which make it possible to experience real confidence and satisfaction in life only by KNOWING that a loving God is there. I have found some people who reach this reality through the Church and the rituals that express it in action, and others who have come to it through the practice of meditation. Neither of these ways, however, is easily available to many individuals today, who have lost the reality of the belief system. The experience of recovering it is not one I would wish for any of us, but in all my reading and personal experience I have found no alternative for those who come face to face with a meaningless universe. You can then keep your guard up and perhaps risk going to pieces, or else you must allow yourself to become like the seed and be opened up to new life.

Neurosis: MORBUS SACER—*the Holy Sickness*

Many people, in fact, have already had the husk of their souls cracked open, although they ordinarily will not admit it to a world that considers self-sufficiency a prime virtue. They are suffering, mostly in silence, because they do not see any place to turn. My encounter with the pain and need that fill almost every crack in our social facade was in the parish of which I was rector for twenty years. I had been forced to admit that I, too, needed help, and once I was willing to speak to a few people of my own need, it was like a dam bursting. People came to the church with their problems—children and husbands and wives in trouble, parents who had been rejected. One by one their stories came out, from sexual fears and rigidity to affairs on the side, alcoholism and sometimes even the threat of jail; from meaninglessness and inner hurt to depression, neurosis, and physical illness.

At times it was almost like ministering to a parade. In the twenty years I was there more than sixteen hundred families came to the church, most of them because they needed help, and many stayed to become members for longer or shorter periods. I came to know most of them, sometimes in depth, and I could scarcely put my finger on one whose life was complete and satisfying, with no need for God. As a rule the most important help we offered these individuals was in finding a way of relationship with a God who cares. They kept coming, because in other places they found mostly the idea that Christians are to be perfect and that ministers must be a symbol of that perfection, not a gateway to let the problems of the human soul tumble out and make an opening for God to get in.

People are not much different in other places. Recently I gave a healing mission at Trinity Church on Wall Street in New York City. For three nights the church was filled with people seeking healing, and the most common need they expressed was to find meaning, some meaning that would help them bear the inner pain they suffer. Too often, however, all they find is advice about how to stay busy and get their problems solved, or else they are advised to forget them and keep up a brave show like other people. The trouble with well-intended advice like this is that it leaves the pain and agony locked up inside the soul where most often nothing can touch it.

In fact, the deepest dread and pain, which existential writers reveal so well, seldom comes to the surface until people are relieved of the struggle for existence which keeps them busy all of the time. So long as they are completely absorbed by the problems of getting enough food and fuel just to stay alive, they seldom have to face the despair of meaninglessness. Working with people at all levels of our society has brought home to me how often the greatest misery and pain occur along with great wealth. These people have no outer problems important enough to keep their attention diverted from the emptiness of their own being. With no outer problems, they are exposed to the reality of the inner or spiritual world. They feel as though they are naked and alone and are usually guided only by fear of what might be found if they looked within for meaning. This is one reason for making almost a fetish of bridge clubs and bingo parties. If one is busy enough it isn't necessary to look within.

Anyone who is stripped in this way and forced to look inward usually faces fear and agony. Like solitary confinement, this exposes us to the depth of our own blackness. We often find whatever meaning we have known disintegrating; there is fear of finding only a void, fear of death and dissolution (particularly in this time when so few people see any place for an after life), and the threat of condemnation. These are elements of the confrontation that are described over and over by writers from Paul Tillich to Jean-Paul Sartre. Although Tillich in *The Courage To Be* writes of finding the God beyond god, other people see man caught forever in a blind nothingness that most people try to escape. They are afraid of finding only the pointlessness of Beckett's *Waiting for Godot* or Sartre's *Nausea*.

This terror of looking directly into the blackness and finding only experiences that seem meaningless and devouring is worse than any sickness. Yet the blackness is there; the need is not to escape it, but to go through the inner darkness and find meaning on the other side. There is still no better description of the darkness than the words of St. John of the Cross in *Dark Night of the Soul*. The idea sometimes heard today that darkness can be avoided and we should find God only in joy and celebration, in peace and comfort, is a grave delusion that perhaps reveals our present lack of experience. We are apt either to begin this way in some darkness and depression or else be caught up by it somewhere along the way. Celebration is fine and comes after deliverance. Beforehand, celebration is often hollow and false and naïve.

Often the opening from the outer conscious realm to the inner is made for us, and we are then thrown into this inner world. When this happens our husks of ego defenses are shattered in one way or another. Perhaps one has known an experience of love, or the breakthrough of a searing religious experience—sometimes about as pleasant as Paul's encounter on the Damascus road—or perhaps one is struck by neurosis: all three of these common human experiences can often open us, through our own need, to another dimension of reality. Of course love can be dismissed as merely the gonads at work, and religious experience can be seen as illusion, but one cannot ignore the pain of neurosis. It often forces comfortable modern men and women to unmask and seek help.

The new profession of psychiatry, which is dedicated to relieving the increasing anxiety and agony of people today, has begun to awaken to these persons' need for religion. As Jung originally noted, behind every neurosis lies one's separation from that reality of which all living religion speaks. There is a growing awareness of the importance of this understanding and of the point Jung made that he had never seen a neurosis healed until contact with more than human reality had been reestablished. My own experience has borne this out in more than one way.

breakthrough: love/ ecstasy/ neurosis

In working with college students, particularly over the past six years, I have found that their neurotic problems spring far more often from a refusal to deal with religious reality than from ordinary pathology. For them neurosis is often the "sacred illness" that forces them to seek meaning. Few of them have suffered any other trauma than comfortableness. Their pain and suffering result from being cut off, for one reason or another, from their religious roots. Many of them are aware of their need for meaning, and they are usually perceptive enough to realize that they will not find it until they encounter a new level of inner reality. Some of them are willing to take the time and effort for the inner way, rather than merely shopping around for an easier behavioral answer to their problem.

Depression is another experience of which I have some first-hand knowledge. This is such a common expression of need today that it is often called the common cold of modern psychiatry. One should have real sympathy for the medical profession in their effort to do something for depression besides prescribing a mood elevator—which is about as effective as aspirin is in getting at the cause of a cold.

I have no reservations about the need of people who are sick in this way, because my own introduction to the realities that are the substance of religion did not come through seminary or the Church, but as a result of being plunged into the black depths of myself in depression and anxiety. At the time I was in real need; the need affected me physically as well as psychically so that living itself became an intolerable burden. I could find no priest who seemed to know much about the depths of the human soul and was willing to enter those depths with me. Although the problem was a religious one of healing the human soul —one I have met in dozens of people since then—the Church had forgotten how to deal with it. There were no Christian shamans* or medicine men!

In an agony of trying to offer others a meaning that I did not have myself, I had to have help or be destroyed. At that point Dorothy Phillips realized my need and shared her own discoveries with me. One reason I turned to her was because I knew of her work on the profound anthology, *The Choice is Always Ours*. Through her I found help—from a man who had escaped from a Nazi concentration camp, and who believed that there is a reality that can touch and save. This was Max Zeller, a Jewish follower of Jung who not only started me toward healing but taught me to read the gospels again. In the light of what I was learning through him I read and reread the New Testament.

Here in these pages I began to find the reality of the loving, saving God whom the early Church knew so well. I woke up to the fact that this was not mythology that could be discarded, but a reality. The Church, I found, had gone

---

*I have suggested ways of providing this help in a booklet, *Finding Meaning: Guidelines for Counselors* (Pecos, N. Mex., Dove Publications, 1974).

right on touching people at this deep level as long as it still believed in the victory of Jesus Christ over the powers of evil. There was nothing inconsistent here with what I had learned through my psychologist friends. Instead, they had opened vistas of reality to me that were not only religious but specifically Christian. For the next eighteen years we tried to make our parish a place where these insights could be shared. With the help of the thought and practice of Dr. Jung, we tried to make it a place where people could bring their needs, become open to them, and learn to use the most basic Christian ways of dealing with them.

Physical Illness

For many of the people who found their way to my church, the first need was to get over some kind of physical illness, very often psychosomatic in nature. Even when things seemed to point only to psychological distress, we always made sure that the person had a thorough checkup by a good physician before counseling could begin. Specifically physical problems can be masked (as well as aggravated or even triggered) by psychological distress. Sickness of any kind, from neurosis to purely physical ailments—including organic diseases, infections and psychosomatic disorders—can be an expression of a person's unconscious need.

Indeed, sickness in all forms is one of the most common ways unconscious need shows up in our society today. With all the improvements in medical treatment, a larger percentage of people require care for illness than ever before.[2] Repressed fear and anxiety can interfere with our resistance to bacteria or to cancer cells and can literally destroy our bodies in dozens of ways. Medicine has come to recognize the deadly potential of this kind of stress.

There is no more effective way for Christians to realize their own needs and to help deal with the needs of others than by sharing in the work of healing. They can do this, first by knowing their own fears and anxieties and helping others to become aware that they have these emotions, and then by helping to reveal and share the base of real meaning which gives people the security and courage to deal with fear rather than letting it build up in unconscious tensions. In the process, some healing miracles do happen, and sometimes this process also gives an individual gradual healing. As people face and handle their problems, they often find complete health of body, mind and soul. By using prayer and meditation much as the early Church did to bring hope and healing to people, we open both ourselves and others to the healing reality of the loving God. I shall be ever grateful to Agnes Sanford for opening me to this ministry by her books, her down-to-earth lectures, and her personal friendship. Our need for healing can start the soul's growth toward health and wholeness.

In addition, the medical profession is suffering today from more than a century of separating physical healing from its spiritual and emotional base. As a profession, doctors themselves show more problems with drugs and alcohol, neurosis and divorce, as well as a higher suicide rate, than any other profession. I worked for four years with groups of senior premedical students at the University of Notre Dame who originally asked for a course in which they could examine the problems of suffering, dying and death.[3] They asked for this course because they had discovered these statistics about the profession they were entering, and they were alarmed. They all came to much the same conclusion: The detached medical attitude does not work very well when a doctor must deal constantly with human misery and suffering and fear of death. The patient is not satisfied and the doctor develops unconscious guilt. On the other hand, the physicians who relate to patients with empathy and understanding need some belief in a pervading meaning to it all—some experience of the Other who gives meaning when nothing else does—if they are to deal with these things day after day and not go under themselves.

If our need for meaning is to open us up to the reality that can give this meaning, however, first of all it has to be recognized. Whether one is a doctor or a theologian, lawyer or politician, or simply a layperson who depends on these other human beings for an approach to the realities of life, the first step is simply to acknowledge that one has tried to depend just on human resources and that this leaves a great deal to be desired.

Reflecting on the Needs of the World—the Reality of Evil

It is all too easy for most of us, immersed in the comforts of Western civilization, to forget what basic needs exist outside of our charmed circle. As long as one stays put, making the regular rounds of business and friends and gossip, one can stay shielded from the difficulties of people even in the next block. For example, the people in Palm Beach seldom stop to think about the conditions of the migratory workers hardly ten miles away. Yet anyone who takes the trouble to look at the surrounding world will find more than enough need to question the why, what and how of it and search for some ultimate meaning.

Some people, of course, are insensitive to anything beyond their immediate concerns. They bury their heads in the sands of comfort with no interest in finding the Christ by going out to the hungry and thirsty, the prisoners and the sick. Others are sensitive in the extreme, so sensitive that they dread being hurt. They are afraid of life as it is, and often they try to escape through alcohol or drugs. Gertrude Behanna, who told her story in her book, *The Late Liz*, once remarked that wealth was what made it possible for her to go the alcoholic route; it kept her wrapped in cotton batting so that she did not have to face either herself or the world.

But most of us are in between. We live in relative comfort psychologically as well as physically, and this makes it difficult for us to imagine what it means to struggle just for a little to eat and a place to lay one's head. We can hardly picture our own children crying with hunger each night, perhaps with not even enough clothing to keep out the chill wind, nor do we really comprehend how helpless most of the world is in the face of natural disasters like famine and flood and pestilence, or for that matter when faced by injustice and cruelty from higher up.

Certainly there has been enough war and violence and organized destruction in this century. In every part of the globe we can find the victims of humanity's senseless cruelty, aggression and ability to hate. The casualties do not occur just on battlefields or in devastated cities and concentration camps. They occur wherever there are tensions between people—between racial groups and in families, on the streets of every city where human wants fester until those affected become violent. The same forces are usually found in our system of justice, wherever one person or group has taken responsibility for enforcing the law and inflicting punishment on others.

If people were more aware of their kinship, they would be deeply sensitive to the suffering that is caused in such basic ways wherever it exists, whether in Vietnam or in a European concentration camp, in Bangladesh or Chad or in our own country. Their hearts and souls would be so flooded by the sense of human need that there would be little problem about turning to God. Every effort to alleviate that need would make them more open to the presence and action of the Other in their lives. Few of us, however, are this open to human needs, even our own. We often respond magnificently to a crisis, but then the awareness peters out, and whatever we found from beyond ourselves is absorbed into the concerns of our own personal "normal" living.

Often it is easy to see that the person on the receiving end, the one who suffers deeply, is forced to seek help beyond what people can give on their own. We easily admit that there are no atheists in foxholes, and even the experience of the concentration camp has forced some to search for God. In the pages of the book, *Night*, Elie Wiesel lays bare his own experience of despair, of watching every hope die in the hell of the concentration camps, Auschwitz and Buchenwald. Then in other works he goes on to show how the loss of everything of value brought him, first, to give up hope of finding any ultimate meaning, and then to search within himself until an ultimate meaning was revealed to him from beyond himself. This is one kind of need that Christians in particular should understand, for at the center of the Christian experience stands man's inhumanity to man, the God-man on a cross.

The teachings of Jesus suggest, however, that we should not wait until we know all about suffering to find our need. We need to be delivered from the source of our inhumanity, Jesus taught, and He told us first of all to pray, "Deliver us from the evil one." Then in various ways He showed that the task is to look within and to know what is causing the trouble and whether we are nursing anger or harmful desires in our hearts. Our job is not just to wait for evil to happen in the outer world and then try to do something about the pain and agony it causes. Instead, Christians are to recognize the source of evil within

cosmic evil

abuse of
a very
technical
vocabulary

themselves so that they can seek help in order to stand outwardly against it.

One way is certainly to reflect on the need and suffering in the world. If one looks honestly at the things that happened, for instance, in the Communist and Nazi concentration camps and in Laos and Vietnam, there appears to be a superhuman force in the universe dragging us down from the goals we express. As Jung suggested, only someone with a warped sense of humor could honestly claim that the death ovens of Dachau represented only an "accidental lack of perfection" or an absence of good. In our own time we have seen a cruelty overtake otherwise normal and civilized persons which one might call bestial, except that this maligns the instincts of the animal world.

It is often easy to identify this force within oneself. This force is like a death wish which attacks a person in depression and anxiety, fear and rage, as many people find when they turn inward. No matter how much one struggles against it, this force is still there ready to tear the person apart and drag him/her down into icy isolation. None of us escapes its destructive drag entirely. Some people simply give way to outbursts easily, while others bottle up the lousy feelings it arouses and suffer the effects of tension. Either way the effect is uncreative and hostile to love and growth. The novels of both C. S. Lewis and Charles Williams portray the primal force of evil in all its ugliness. I have also written at some length about it in other places.[4]

The idea that we have outgrown our need to turn to God for help in dealing with evil, or the idea, in fact, that there is no such thing as cosmic evil, would be funny if it did not show such a tragic lack of understanding. This force has to be faced and dealt with or it will keep on turning our homes and our world into a battlefield. We sometimes find it hard to understand why Jesus said that the poor in spirit, the meek and sorrowing are blessed, but perhaps it was because they are the ones who know they can't manage their lives by themselves. Once a person realizes that there is a spiritual or psychoid world as well as a physical one, that person learns that there are forces of evil more destructive than the simply human ones, and that these spiritual forces of evil are those that the individual cannot deal with on one's own. They are more powerful realities, like the force of gravity or some other force of the universe, than many of the more recent ways of thinking about Satan or the evil one would suggest.

We can be so protected by life that we fail to see the depth and power of evil, and we wonder why all the to-do about something that should require only some real intelligence and reason. This failure to comprehend evil as an autonomous force with a power to affect human life is a kind of unconsciousness that can lead to disaster. As Berdyaev remarked, the powers of evil certainly appear to be at least as intelligent as the powers of light. He made these remarks as he was looking back over his life with the communist revolution and the two world wars, all of which he had survived.

I remember a conversation I once had with a brilliant and creative theologian who was denying the reality of evil as an autonomous force. We reflected a little together and realized that he knew little outside of the college community, which was a protected one indeed. He had never known real tragedy or violence or inner agony personally, and in dealing only with rational concepts, he had no need to postulate the reality of evil and look for a power that could save him from it. He had about as much idea of the danger of evil as most of us had of the danger of radioactivity before Hiroshima.

When we do awaken and realize our own helplessness, then the second door is opened to the inward way. The realization of our spiritual poverty and our need for help from beyond ourselves is the moisture that breaks open the seed. This breaking of the husk fulfills the second condition for the practice of prayer and meditation. It takes great courage, however, to enter this door or to seek for this moisture unless life has already done it for us. Once the depth of your soul has been penetrated, you have little choice; either you follow the religious way like a search for rare treasure, or else you must turn back to the ordinary world with resolute detachment and probably despair. At times one wishes one could back up and start over, but consciousness was apparently designed without a reverse gear.

Is the Need Universal?

Today, however, we find a rash of methods for cracking people open without counting the cost or looking at the way ahead. In encounter and marathon groups a person is broken down by fatigue and group pressure. Many people have found them renewing and restoring, but these groups have also had a high percentage of casualties. They offer little protection for the person who is not ready or capable of facing the full depth of inner darkness, and this person may then go to pieces. Even the modified form of encounter group used by the Episcopal Church for training religious educators did not work as expected and those "T-groups" were finally abandoned. The person in such a group often was opened up whether ready for it or not, and then that same person was left without a continuing support group like a seed with no soil in which to sink its roots and with no help provided to find this soil.

Drugs are used indiscriminately by people who have no business trying to enter another world with no one to guide them and not even the preparation of getting along adequately in their natural world. Andrew Weil has written wisely about the dangers of using drugs apart from religious ritual* in his perceptive

---

* My own view is that it is best to leave drugs alone entirely. There are better ways to open up the soul. Many people try the drug route only because the Church has failed to offer the safer ways to open up one's life to experience and growth. People need more than the physical world offers, and they will turn to drugs as long as no other way is available to them. Passing laws and trying to enforce them will not eliminate the use of drugs. But there is a good chance that offering the inward way of meditation to those attracted to the drug culture could bring about that result.

book, *The Natural Mind*. Methods like séances or using a ouija board open up some individuals to real trouble because they do not realize the dynamics of the inner world they are dealing with. It is like Pandora's box; once it is opened, it is impossible to close it. We shall say more about these dangers of the inner way later on.

Eastern religions try to make the same opening and then give the person a specific way to follow without considering the fact that one cannot lay one's own culture aside and discard it. You may accept the Eastern approach, but you are forced to leave a part of yourself behind. The religion of fear does much the same thing. It cracks the individual open and then submits one to inner and social pressure to go a certain route. If one deviates, one will either be ostracized or condemned to hell. The effects of this kind of training are so destructive that one wonders how a religion supposedly concerned with love could have turned to this method. It defeats love entirely by walling off parts of every personality so that one cannot even know the whole person, let alone love that person. Many people have been scarred for life by the use of this method. They are so damaged by this kind of religion that they never learn the meaning of love or its healing effect on the personality. While a certain amount of fear may be healthy for some individuals, it is almost always destructive to apply any such religious idea wholesale, without considering individual differences.

There are also individuals in some groups who decide that everyone needs to be cracked open and proceed to put pressure on everyone around them. Often they have enough power to keep the heat on until people submit, and this is much like the police tactic of brainwashing, which has been developed to a fine art in some communist countries. As both Jerome Frank in his book *Persuasion and Healing* and William Sargant in his *Battle for the Mind* show, the forces at work in this type of religion and in communist brainwashing are the same. In one case they are applied consciously and deliberately; in the other it is like the preparation for a primitive initiation rite in a tribe. Either one of these methods can be thoroughly demonic. We are simply more aware of how detestable the conscious and deliberate practices are than the unconscious religious ones.

At one time the survival of Christianity depended upon a fellowship who knew what it was all about. As long as the early Church faced the threat of being wiped out by a hostile empire, every Christian was given three years basic training before being baptized and received into full fellowship. The inner husk of old attitudes and old images was broken down and penetrated by a new reality so that every Christian knew both the need for God and the need for community. All Christians had to have a faith that prepared them to meet death, if necessary. Today, however, the pressures seem to be of a different type.

For one thing, there is a collective Christian attitude that still works very well for many people. They accept and use the rituals, dogmas and daily practices that express Christianity in the fullest possible way for them, and the person who is embedded in this attitude may need nothing more. Religion then acts as a buffer between religious realities and the individual. It is like an electrical reducer that brings the 1,000 volts of direct contact down to the 110-volt current that any of us can use. As Jung commented more than once, within the Roman Catholic Church, in the full catholic doctrine and practice, there is a deep psychological wisdom that can keep men's lives in order. When a person's life is contained within that religious framework and the Church symbols are alive and meaningful to the individual, the inward journey is simply not necessary and may even lead to disaster.

A great many people, however, find that ordinary religious practice has lost its meaning for them, and they are threatened by pressures from within. They look for meaning and try to find some source of power or of the energy to put their lives in order. In the Church these people often feel only more pressure to act or to be something different from what they are. There is good reason for them to try the inner way of meditation. They have less to fear from being opened up further to the darkness within as they are already seeking something beyond it.

Then there is a group who have little tolerance for any kind of religious way, inner or outer. These people often project their darkness onto others, arousing the hatred and anger that lead to war and other violence. They have no approach to reality except through the outer world, and they slip easily into the delusions of psychosis. A psychiatrist friend recently told me the story of one such patient who had suddenly stopped seeing him. After several months the man came in to thank my friend for curing him. The doctor was curious, and asked what had happened that led to being cured. "Don't you remember?" the patient asked. "You told me to find a cause and get busy on ecology or keeping the streets clean or fighting communism. I went to work on the communists, and I've been fine ever since." In those few months he had started a hate group and brought nearly five thousand citizens of the area into it. For these people the inner way of meditation may be less dangerous for others than the things they attempt to do in the outer world.

In addition, there is one group who, without exception, require this experience of direct contact with spiritual reality, both destructive and creative. These are the religious professionals, who undertake to mediate the realities of religion to others, often to people who have lost faith in what the religious institution stands for. Unless there are leaders who know the experiences for themselves, it becomes like the blind leading the blind.*

---

*While many religious Orders use some practice to bring novices into contact with spiritual reality and give them a way of dealing with what they find, these practices break down when no one believes that there is any spiritual reality with which to deal. I know of at least one attempt, however, to rebuild a novitiate program by using the understanding of C. G. Jung. It is described by Fr. John Welch, O. Carm., in his unpublished doctoral dissertation on the "Implications of Jungian Theory for the Education of Candidates for the Catholic Priesthood."

The pressures on people today seem to be directed more and more toward greater consciousness. If the constant drive toward growth and consciousness does express our greatest need and wholeness, then certainly not everyone should be exposed to this experience whether needful of it or not. Many people are getting along with their task of growth quite well as they are, and the place to start growth is by examining their own lives and what their desires and expectations are. After this is decided there comes the need to find a fertile soil, to seek direction, fellowship and encouragement from those who have already gone this way, and, above all, to be sure one is following a serious goal and has some map of the inner world that one is entering. The inner meditative journey is not a weekend excursion to a land of sun and happiness. It is a way of life for people who actually feel a need for it and who have become conscious of their need. In the final analysis this is a way for people who have been unable to find meaning by other methods. It is important to break open the ego to deeper reality but it is nearly impossible to legislate one way for all people and one can only do it on an individual basis and with the greatest care.

6

To Whom Do We Pray?

The way that you pray, the form and direction your meditations take, depends largely upon the way you view the world in which you find yourself. If you think that you are part of a purely physical universe, you may understand meditation as a method of controlling the brain waves in order to improve your physiological and emotional condition. If you then turn to Transcendental Meditation, you will say your mantra faithfully for twenty minutes twice a day, and probably you will find what you expect.

Or, if you really envision all life ultimately merging into the effortless, suspended bliss of Nirvana, then you will try to make your meditation another step toward release from the illusion and burdens and pains of this life. You will consider it a way of entering a state of imageless enlightenment in order to experience the bliss of mature relationship with the universe. This is the way of meditation found in Zen and other disciplines derived from Buddhism.

Christian meditation in its most developed form is quite different from either of these. It is based on a view of the world that finds each individual important, both in the material realm and in the nonmaterial or spiritual realm. In this practice of meditation one expects to meet someone, and the encounter is usually experienced as a relationship with a person. Even to talk about it one must generally resort to images. Sometimes the encounter itself is experienced in vivid inner images. This is something we shall take up in detail later on since many Christian groups in recent years have frowned upon allowing images to enter into meditation and prayer. Yet one of the most helpful methods that historical Christianity has offered to reach this encounter is by using images.

Outer aids and actions may also help to bring one to the encounter, and of course there is no reason why Christians should not use the techniques of Zen or TM or Yoga. These are valuable so long as one is aware that there is another element in Christian meditation, an addition that makes it quite another practice. Christian meditation is not a way of escaping from one's condition. Rather it is something we undertake in order to bring the totality of our being into relationship with a person, an Other to whom we can relate. Before anything else this means stepping out in trust, experimenting to see if one does find such a reality of the loving Father or the Risen Christ.

real love ≠ projection

It is not likely that any of us will find out whether there is a loving and forgiving Father waiting to be met until we do try to turn to Him. So long as one will not even consider the idea that such a reality might exist, one's chances of finding out are slim indeed. It is like finding a vein of gold; not many people strike it rich until they believe that there is gold to be found deep in the mountains and that it is valuable. The same thing is true of finding God. Through meditating we explore in order to know more and more of God. But before He is discovered, a person only *believes*; through experiencing a relationship one comes to *know*. Believing is a stage on the way to knowing. Consequently one of the main conditions for effective meditation is to gain some idea of the reality we are seeking. This is found in the Christian story. It is the Good News of Christianity; it asserts that God is like Jesus, that at the heart and core of reality is the same loving, forgiving concern expressed in the life and teachings of Jesus and in His story of the prodigal.

I can almost hear an audible protest: Isn't this wishful thinking or merely projecting humankind's fondest hope into the heavens, refusing to admit what God is actually like? If we stop to reflect, however, it is harder to say that this is the kind of God men and women really wish for. The reality of love revealed by Jesus demands real relationship and, as I have tried to suggest, this is difficult for us. Most of us are quite willing to be cared for, to be coddled and protected, but it takes great courage for men and women to relate, even to each other. Real relationship is not often found among human beings.

Much of the time what passes for love is merely projection, which can actually keep individuals from knowing other persons. We project a part of ourselves upon the other person and actually do not see that person. When real love does occur one finds that an individual is accepted by the other person no matter what is revealed about that individual, and this kind of love is not easy. How often in counseling, people turn away from me temporarily or get angry with me because I try to be accepting. This situation allows individuals to look at parts of themselves which seem totally unacceptable. It is a very painful thing to be genuinely accepted. Then there is no reason not to look at oneself. All of one's excuses are swept away. One cannot say, "I can't talk about this because you won't understand."

Whenever real love and relationship develop between human beings, they face the demanding task of coming to terms with the less pleasant elements of themselves. God offers us a far more accepting love than any human relationship, and we actually shy away from it because of the deepening honesty and growth it requires, both of which involve shedding one's skin time after time. This is difficult and demanding.

Yet Jesus of Nazareth tells us to approach God by addressing Him as "Abba." This is one of His unique contributions to religious thought and practice. Christians are told to turn to the very force that moves the sun and other stars and speak like small children who need their father and call out "Daddy!" knowing that they will be answered. In other religions, and even among many "Christians," there is a very different idea of God.

Most of the world pictures the ruler of the universe like an Oriental potentate who must be approached almost crawling on one's belly. His justice is not questioned. He is feared, because He is infinitely distant, infinitely just, and He administers the justice with a heavy hand. Often He appears very much like an almighty steamroller whose majestic will and wrath and judgment must be accepted with resignation, without hope. There are even people to whom God appears to be an unreasonable tyrant who strikes out angrily one moment and comforts and heals the next. No wonder people have little desire to relate to such a God and prefer to leave prayer to the professionals. Those who hold such ideas of God deep within themselves cannot help but pray very differently from Christians who find the love of a father for a child at the heart of their most central experiences.

The Prodigal Father

According to Jesus of Nazareth, God is a prodigal, spendthrift love. He spelled it out in His great story of the father and son, which should probably be called the parable of the prodigal father. Not only does the father receive his son back without a word of criticism—knowing that the son is judging himself too much already—but he brings out the best that he has. Instead of ordinary clothes he brings the best robes, instead of a meagre meal they kill the fatted calf, and instead of recrimination he places rings on his fingers. Even toward the self-righteous elder brother, he is open and caring. Instead of chiding him for being interested only in justice, the father practices reconciliation and begs him to come to the party and join in their rejoicing. This, as Jesus Himself revealed, is the kind of God men find when they turn to Him for relationship, for a re-connection to the life that they need.

Such a God is not made in the human image. This kind of caring is simply not found among men and women naturally. It results only when they catch a picture of this infinitely loving God and are raised above the human condition. Although in rare instances we do dream of such a world and such relationships, usually we are afraid to believe that either we or God could be this way. We do not dare to reach out toward God courageously, risking the hope that He may be like that. Until we are willing to take that risk and venture on this path, we actually limit the fullness of relationship that God wishes to give. It is difficult for a human father to relate with affection and warmth when he is mistrusted, rejected or held at arm's length. He cannot give all he longs to give. It is no different with the heavenly Father who is far more sensitive to our actual inner response to Him. If one sees God as a vicious tyrant or Oriental potentate one robs Him of the opportunity to give us love.

Taking such a step is radical action. Few of us are able to contemplate acting in this way until another person has demonstrated such action toward us and reassures us that it is safe. Even then it takes a lot of meditating before one can break out of the human pattern of revenge and anger, retribution and destructiveness, and consider taking this risk oneself. One reason that many Christians find this so difficult is simply that they are afraid of God. It has never occurred to them that He might be exactly as Jesus described Him in words and life and so they keep their defenses up at all times.

The main point of the doctrine of the Trinity is simply that God is essentially the same as Jesus of Nazareth. They are not only alike but the same in being. How many battles the theologians had on this issue. It is an important one. In the same way that people turned to Jesus of Nazareth twenty centuries ago in Palestine, we can turn to Him as the Risen Christ and find the same creative energy which made this universe and still pulsates through it. And if we really believe in the Trinity, we will let it show in our lives. This does not depend upon our ability to explain the intricacies of this mystery or how well we know the history of its being understood. Real belief in the Trinity is determined by how we act toward God, how we meditate, how we pray, and especially how we treat our fellow human beings. As I have said before, and probably will say again, our actions tell more about what we really believe than all our intellectual formulations of doctrine.

If one turns to God then, with some expectation of finding the reality expressed by the Trinity, what will one look for God to be like? Certainly if God does unite the qualities of Jesus of Nazareth and the prodigal father, He is better than any human father. First of all, He understands the human plight, the tensions and agonies of human life and how prone we are to being swept away either by selfishness or by evil. He knew what it was like to be a human being in Jesus of Nazareth, and He cares about us no matter what we have been or done. He is like Aslan in C. S. Lewis's *The Lion, the Witch and the Wardrobe*. He gives free forgiveness and receives us back the moment we pick ourselves up and start back toward Him. Incidentally, Christianity is the only major religion of humankind that makes such a far-fetched offer. God asks only that we treat other people the same way as we are treated.

He also gives us freedom. There is nothing that can really prevent us from turning away from Him or mocking Him. He has confidence that in the end nothing else but relationship with Him will satisfy us, and so He waits. He knows that only love given in freedom and only relationships founded on freedom are real. His desire for us is not to pin us down but to see us grow and develop just as far as our potential and our opportunities will permit. In order to help us achieve our greatest potential, He offers us healing and transformation.

One of the great joys of childhood is sharing in some creative action with a parent. In a similar way God wants us to join with Him in expressing His creativity and love. Each of us has a place within His plan, a destiny which is not like a straitjacket but is rather a potential in which our greatest effectiveness and joy are realized. Finally, when we turn to Him and ask, we can expect guidance and help, and we can expect it even more than from a human father, for He has the knowledge and the vision of what we are able to become.

The early Church believed in such a Father and they experienced the reality of the Risen Christ in their midst. They knew Him as one who gave relationship, love, concern, wisdom, power, healing and transformation. I doubt if they could have had this experience without the revelation of God which Jesus presented. This conviction shaped their meditation, their sacraments, and opened them to a new level of experience of God. In order to reach the deepest levels of relationship to God one has to put imagination to work and start upon the daring venture of seeking a God who is loving beyond any experience we have and fulfilling in a way that few of us have even dreamed of.

Of course, all of the universe is not one garden of joy and love. We wonder where evil comes from. How can a just and loving God permit the agony and hell we so often encounter? If we do not follow Jesus of Nazareth and the early Church Fathers and see the reality of a powerful force of evil abroad in the world, we are likely to see God as its source and recoil in horror. Here human attempts to find a reason and to avoid any dualism often turn us away from the loving Father who stands ready to receive us. How is it possible? I do not know. I only know that those in the Christian tradition who have known Him best agree that meeting Him is meeting unbounded, overwhelming love.

This takes some doing, because it makes demands upon our capacity to respond and to love. Through meditation we can locate this precious vein buried deep within us and begin to open passageways of belief in this kind of God and the experiences He makes possible. Meditation is one way that brings us to this power and helps us stay open to it so that we can become what we are capable of being. Finding this kind of God enables us to grow into what we were meant to be. It is a wild gamble to look for a God like this, but what do we have to lose?

7
The Creative Power of Love

Often the elements we have been discussing are all present, and yet we find no life, no vitality in meditation simply because we separate it from morality. We see no connection between our prayer life and our actions. The two, however, cannot be separated for they are of the same fabric. What we do with our lives outwardly, how well we care for others, is as much a part of meditation as what we do in the quietness and turning inward. In fact, Christian meditation that does not make a difference in the quality of one's outer life is short-circuited. It may flare for a while, but unless it results in finding richer and more loving relationships with other human beings or in changing conditions in the world that cause human suffering, the chances are that an individual's prayer activity will fizzle out.

Loving actions provide yet another condition that is needed for the soul to develop through meaningful meditation. They provide the necessary warmth so that sprout of new life can break through the surface and continue to grow. One of the great contributions of the Hebrew prophets was their understanding of the direct interplay between people's everyday living and their approach to God through ritual and prayer. They believed that the only sure basis for relating to the just God was to show justice in one's own actions.

While the revelation of Jesus of Nazareth goes a long step beyond justice, He, too, showed the absolute necessity of revealing to others the qualities of God which are revealed to us. Giving some of the same love is a prime condition if we want our prayer and meditation to be worthwhile. In our own time, Martin Luther King exemplified the connection between prayer and loving action as few have done in any age. His prophetic words are written in his book, *Strength to Love*.

Meditation and the inner way are like a spiral staircase. The first steps bring us to a realization of the nature of the God to whom we are opening ourselves. Then if we are serious about going on and not just pretending or hypocritical, this realization requires putting what we have learned into action, coming to a new level of caring for others or of action in the world. Once we are trying to act upon the meaning we have found, we are ready again for a new level of meditation; and again with new insights into the reality of the Risen Christ, we are given new understanding of what our actions ought to be and a new basis for directing them. At one level we may become open to the joy of many different relationships, or at another to the sorrow and suffering that make for sympathy with untold numbers of people and their condition in life. As each level of experience is actualized in our relationships with other people, we find again and again new levels of community with God. This seems to be an unlimited process. In this way real social action grows from an experience of God.

In Friedrich von Hügel's study of the life of St. Catherine of Genoa one can follow this process at work in a life that is certainly one of the most attractive examples of medieval piety.[1] St. Catherine is easier to identify with than many of the cloistered saints, and step-by-step the effect of her search was reflected in action. Her initial illumination arose out of discouragement with a meaningless life. The experience made it possible for her to continue in her marriage, living with her wealth until much of it was lost and giving the best of her love to her husband. After his death she protected his mistress and illegitimate daughter. She moved to a hospital to care for the sick and destitute there so long as her physical health remained. In each act of giving she left a record of how the richness of her communion with Love (as she called God) grew and developed. In her will she continued to show her humanness, leaving her precious objects to favorite relatives.

How does one go about shaping one's life so that it will manifest this love, giving of oneself even when one's own needs cry out to be met? Certainly this is not a simple matter, and elsewhere I have tried to approach it in some detail.[2] Here it is necessary to sketch these ideas only briefly to remind us that looking inward and staying in touch with the reality that is found there requires keeping the door open both ways. It is so easy for us to forget that accepting from God nearly always means passing it on by doing something active for others, even if that activity is only listening and sharing oneself with others.

First of all, such love is not created by one's own effort. It happens when a person allows the love discovered inwardly, through meditation and ritual, to pour out through life in action. Since this is not our first and foremost human reaction, it does take effort to cooperate with this creative reality when one finds it. Allowing love to work through us takes some doing, but it is far more certain than relying on our own efforts. Unless we first find the reality of the Other who gives love, our attempts to imitate it are often self-seeking, shallow and egocentric. The trouble comes not so much from our intentions, but from the fact that so many well-intentioned people force love. They go out in caring for others and make valiant efforts to love without first discovering the difference between the reality they are trying to express and unrecognized self-seeking. Because they try to go ahead without seeking experience of God, they often spoil what should be a transforming contact with the reality of love, at best reducing it simply to a human level.

Probably the best way to describe what I mean is by another diagram, this

* of Ignatius: love that comes from above

one representing two individuals facing each other. The ellipse on the left desig-
nates one who is trying to be open to love through the religious way and then let
it flow out to another person. Each is surrounded by the physical realm and the

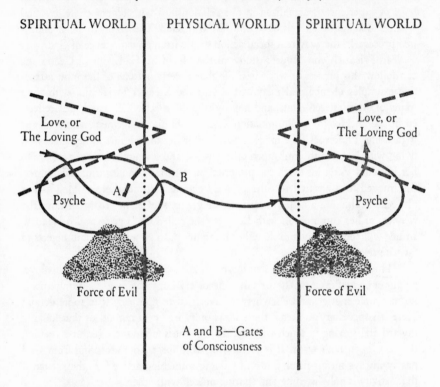

SPIRITUAL WORLD | PHYSICAL WORLD | SPIRITUAL WORLD

Love, or
The Loving God

Love, or
The Loving God

Psyche

A

B

Psyche

Force of Evil

Force of Evil

A and B—Gates
of Consciousness

spiritual realm, as suggested in the diagram on page 37. The dotted lines A and
B suggest how one's conscious psyche is usually contained; they are like gates
that can be opened. As the first individual turns inward, gate A is pushed back
so that the individual is open to experiences of the spiritual world and can seek
contact with the creative reality of the loving God. For a time that person is
largely absorbed by this experience, but as this reality is found, it becomes clear
that it cannot be kept just for the self. The person allows gate B to swing outward so that it no longer remains fast shut. Then something of the love which
has touched the one goes out to the other person. It breaks through similar gates
around that person's consciousness and seeks to find contact with the same reality within another.

There is really no way that we can help other people become open to relationship with their fellow humans and with God except through an expression
of love. Otherwise they remain fortresses that may be conquered and brought to
subjection, but not to open relationship. What we have to learn, to begin with, is

how to open the first gate so that the reality of love can work in us and then flow toward others. As this love reaches another individual, then that individual is opened to the loving Father who waits patiently at the doorway of every soul. Indeed, where there is genuine love for another person, it is as if God communes with God through two human beings.

One of the main purposes of meditation is to expose us to the reality of the Father in such a way that we can become the kind of people who are able to love. His life radiating through us cleanses, heals and transforms us. Then we can truly love in the way that Jesus asked of us. He did not tell us that we are His followers when we are great at meditating and religious activities, but only when we love one another as He loved us. This is the ultimate criterion of our lives, which can be fully realized only as we turn inward and open ourselves to God.

Love in this sense is characterized by its lack of self-seeking. It gives with no strings attached, expecting nothing in return. I remember one student telling me that it was quite easy to give this kind of love. We talked about visiting a friend in the hospital day after day during weeks of illness. But then I asked how she would react if she were to get sick, and the same friend made no effort to look in on her. And *that* was a different story. How subtly and unconsciously we lay our expectations upon others. The beginning of Christian love is when we give them up, insidious and clinging as they are. St. Francis put this truth at the heart of his famous prayer when he wrote: "O Divine Master, grant that I may not so much seek to be consoled as to console, to be understood as to understand, to be loved as to love."

The person who gets this idea begins to find the meaning of the life of Jesus of Nazareth. We can no longer be emotional children once we are trying to allow this kind of love to flow through our lives. We have already touched the meaning of dying and rising again, and we know the reality of the spiritual world. Even so, it is not easy to open the second gate outwardly, even part of the time, and every one of us needs a check list of practical suggestions. Let us outline very briefly some of the ways of reaching out toward different people and also how meditation is involved in the giving of love.

The Ways of Loving

The most basic premise for giving love is knowing the person one loves. Before there can be any real love, one must find out what the other person is like. One has to become aware, conscious of that person's true being, in order to love that very person and not some image of one's own that one projects upon the other. It is altogeher too easy to believe that I really love someone when all I am doing is enjoying my own ideal of what I would like that person to be. And probably the surest way of finding out the difference is by listening to the other person, allowing oneself to be open and sensitive to that person's real reactions.

Listening to others is an art that can be learned. Learning to listen to God helps, but it also works both ways. We listen better to God and the beings of the spiritual world when we allow ourselves to be open to human beings and their deeper reactions. At the depth of every human being is a shy, timid spirit like a beautiful bird. As long as one judges or throws out personal opinions, that inner depth, that spirit remains hidden and afraid. To discover what is there, one must learn to be quiet and wait with openness, expecting a response. This is the first step in Christian living with one another. Christian fellowship and community do not begin until we have learned to listen to other people just as they are. Only then can most of us begin to discover this essence of our souls.

If a church or religion really wants to create community, it will provide experiences to help people learn to listen to one another. Most people have the best of intentions, but they are not secure enough to express love to others by listening in depth when the others express some idea or intention that they believe is wrong. It takes real security within oneself to be open to the totality of another human being. In this listening we give neither approval nor disapproval. We accept the other's ground of being and the other's system of values just as they are.

Listening with this kind of openness means allowing one's whole being to become involved without worrying about whether it is accepted or not. One reason most people are unable to do this is that they are unable to love themselves. In listening to people, one finds that below the surface very few of them can really abide themselves. It is because of this that solitary confinement is so painful; when one is shut off from the outside world, one comes face to face with oneself. Yet how can we pass love on to others, as Jesus asked of us, unless we can accept that love and understanding for ourselves?

For my own part, I have found no other way of accepting myself than to open the door to the Risen Christ through meditation; about this I shall say a lot more later on. Allowing Him to come in, I find that He cares for me just as I am, that He would have died for me if I had been the only one. This realization makes it possible for me to accept others and allow them to be what they are without expectations. In this way I find the power to face the destructive force that sometimes creeps up from within or sometimes strikes from without, instead of projecting it upon others and rejecting them. What I have learned about personality types is also helpful. Knowing how many different types of people there are makes it easier for me to listen to them without trying to force them into one mold, the mold that suits my own personality type.

For thirty years one of my main tasks has been listening to people. Among all of them, children and young people, husbands and wives, alienated friends, lonely people, there have been few who felt that they had been really listened to and cared for, even by those closest to them. Yet this is one of the most creative ways of allowing love to flow through us. As St. Ambrose once suggested, there is probably no better way of starting to make love grow than to begin expressing the love we already have toward those around us, toward our families and close friends. These are the very people we often feel do not need to be told that they are loved, and so they carry away from daily living the impression that we do not really care for them enough to express it.

If one can realize that there is need for love close at home, growth can begin right there, with the healthiest kind of groundwork to build on. We do not have to worry too much about our own feelings at the time; what matters is doing something that makes the other person feel loved. The test is not just whether we feel loving; it is more whether or not the other person feels loved by us. Christian love is not complete until the other person feels loved through contact with us.

As we turn toward a wider circle, however, a different kind of action is obviously required of us. Is there a way of expressing real love to a neighbor or acquaintance, to one's employer or employee, to a friendly clerk in a store, or a shy member of one's club or church? Certainly it is easier to know if one can put an arm around the person and sense a reaction. But there is definitely another way, as a friend of mine discovered when he was faced with difficulties in administering an industrial plant for which he was responsible.

This man was not afraid of prayer, and so he asked what to do. The answer that he was given offers an unparalleled description of the way of love. Out of the blue he heard the words: "Create those conditions whereby each individual may develop to the maximum of their potential within the opportunities at hand." When he tried to follow that instruction explicitly, the reaction among his employees was like the lifting of a cloud. Love is not only feeling; it is action.

Any of us can develop this means of expressing love if we will take the trouble to think about the needs of others and to commune deeply with the source of love. In all kinds of less intimate situations—at work, or at play, and particularly in the classroom—one can bring love to the people one encounters by giving them room or space in which to live and grow. Or at times we may find that love requires us to support another person when events are forcing growth or change on that person. Some individuals need stability in order to grow, and sometimes they simply need the confidence to stay put when change does not mean growth.

Even those whose influence seems limited can start by watching and caring how their actions and words play into the environment around them, and making the effort to put love into action. In the process they cannot help but come to know the source of love more deeply and truly. Again, it is like a spiral staircase.

In similar ways one can reach out to strangers once one realizes that the need is there. The first problem is really to recognize the stranger, and then to ask oneself, "How does it feel to be alone in a strange land?" There are few experiences more devastating. We humans are social beings who hardly live at all when we are cut off from others. Only those who have a deep and genuine relationship with God can stand being ostracized for any length of time. While our society rarely banishes people purposefully today, the same results are found in the rooming house districts of our great cities, where the suicide rate is the highest in our land. Another of the loneliest places in today's world is any of the huge college campuses where there are few opportunities for deep and honest encounter between individuals. There are even strangers in our Christian churches, people who, tragically enough, come and then leave with no one reaching out a hand to them.

One problem is simply to notice that they are there. Before we can even try to offer them love (extraverted-sensation-type persons will be best at this), we must first forget ourselves and the clique and look around. Most places we go there will be someone who looks lonely, someone withdrawn at the edge of a group, even with a look of pain. Once we have noticed them, it still takes courage to step out and speak, to make contact. This is particularly difficult for introverts, very nearly as difficult, in fact, as it is for extraverts to turn inward and wait in silence. One may even be rejected and have to try again. It is certainly a good thing that we can see our capacity to love grow as we reach out to strangers. So often there is a grateful response which lets us know that an act of reaching out has brought results.

There is one difficulty we usually escape when it comes to loving our enemies. Generally we have no trouble noticing either the people who cannot stand us or the unpleasant ones we cannot stand, particularly if we have never tried to forgive them or relate to them. If we avoid those who seem to be enemies, however, and do not try to accept them into our lives, we become stunted both in personal growth and in finding reality in our devotional lives. Love implies forgiveness. It is hard for us to realize, but actually the only requirement the loving Father places on us, once we come to know Him in meditation, is that we forgive as we have been forgiven.

Our first task is not so much to make contact with these people, but simply to stop our unkind actions toward them. Most often this means simply stopping our chatter about them, laying aside our almost unconscious backbiting reaction to them. In the beginning it was hard for me to realize that there was no point in discussing the flaws of other people, that all it really accomplished was to lessen my ability to love anyone. We all take a certain perverse pleasure in hearing a spicy story, or being the first to know a spiteful tidbit, and the key that will open up more room for love to work is simply the determination to struggle with this petty egotism that makes us vengeful.

Then, when we are making a real effort not to hurt people no matter how much we dislike them, we can begin to pray honestly for them, and we can expect some surprising results, especially in ourselves. Starr Daily was the one who first made this clear to me. Quite a few years ago he explained to me that he believed it was not his friends who made him grow, but his enemies, because he had to grow to take them in. By looking for the creative or positive in another person, and seeking other elements in that individual to which I can reach out, new capacities to love and to respond are born in both of us.

The warmth that is provided by our capacity to love is as necessary for the soul's growth as any other part of the meditational way. It radiates from our efforts to express love to those both at home and farther away. It comes from our acceptance of others as they are, from learning to listen to them and becoming sensitive to their needs. It increases as we look out for the strangers and welcome them, and particularly as we work at trying to transform our enemies into friends. Steadily the warmth that is given by this kind of action draws the soul toward the reality of the loving God. Step by step the soul's reach grows, so that it becomes easier to find the One who is love through meditation and to carry more of His love out actively to others.

8

A Word of Warning and Encouragement

Meditation is not something one should do simply because others are doing it. It cannot be undertaken like an aesthetic exercise or merely for diversion. Whether we expect it or not, in meditation we are opening the door to another aspect of reality, potentially just as rewarding and sometimes even more dangerous than the physical world. Not many of us would turn a child loose in the physical world without teaching that child, as best we can, how to get around safely in it.

We take pains to teach our children not to touch the stove when it is hot, to protect them from deep water until they have learned to swim, and from other natural dangers. We try to help them learn about the perils of this modern world, to be careful crossing streets and not to play with machines and electricity, or with drugs and alcohol. Yet we are often like children ourselves when it comes to getting around in the inner world.

The problem is that most of us have been brainwashed by experts. We would like to believe that something real could be reached in meditation, but the materialists are at the helm and they see only a world of illusion within. No matter how sincere we are in believing that there is a place to find God, we cannot go along with today's materialism and take the inner world very seriously. If we are forced to conclude that these experiences are only the creation of our own minds, then we are not likely to worry much about preparing to deal with them creatively. More likely we will try to free ourselves from the inner world as quickly as possible, figuring that it is important only to understand how these illusions interfere with our reactions to the outer, physical world. One finds the same attitude on the part of many teachers of meditation, East and West. This world of images is only illusion and should be systematically dealt with and then repressed and ignored.

Certainly there is a danger of illusions coming from the inner world, and learning to deal with them is one part of the preparation I am talking about. On the other hand, simply acquiring knowledge about this world is far more difficult than ordinary study of physical things. Just as in the physical world, there seem to be many spiritual things that are destructive when handled in one way, but open up new life when we approach them differently. In addition, there is a reality of radical evil found in the inner world that is bent on seizing power and destroying the individual. If we must realize that we face this reality, as Jesus and the early Church did and as Jung seems to understand, then the task is even more difficult. One is then much like a soldier at night trying to avoid a stalking enemy.

Knowing this, why would anyone willingly choose to venture into a realm so difficult and dangerous? The answer, at least, is not very difficult. The experiences of the inner world are the prime realities that give us our approach to life, the basis for our widely varying emotions and feelings and values. If we don't deal with them directly, at the point of entry, these realities can operate autonomously within us. We can become puppets of the inner world, sometimes pulled happily by forces of light (which unfortunately have a way of shifting), or perhaps more often sucked into aggressiveness and destruction. Those closest to us may suffer from our moods and actions, from the attacks of depression and anxiety, from the almost impossible egocentricity that results. Or our bodies may become the target, afflicted by psychosomatic illness in one of the many ways I have described in *Healing and Christianity*.

If we are free of such problems, if we are healthy in body, mind and personal relationships, we can probably avoid looking inward, unless we become tormented by the collective ills of society in which we all share. So far, however, I have run into very few people whose lives were going this well at every level. When we really look at our actions and reactions to others we may realize how often they are unconscious and unsatisfactory, and this can be the first step toward an inward venture. Others, of course, start from necessity when depression or anxiety or some other psychic discomfort pushes them without their having to become aware of their need so intellectually. Physical illness, again, may require an entirely different approach. Sickness can force a reconsidering of the whole of one's life, and sacramental healing of one thing or another can be the opening to another realm of reality.

Most of the people I have known needed this relationship with the inner world more than they realized. When their masks were down, it was clear that they did not need judgment. They were already dissatisfied with themselves, already judging themselves too much. I have found in counseling that my task is often to encourage people to be more gentle with themselves. Many of us really need to discover what is good about us and to develop these qualities rather than to concentrate endlessly on all that is wrong. Often people who are the most vocal about their religion are lacking in balance for just this reason. They are practically unconscious of their best qualities, and they try to make religion compensate for what they feel is the muck in themselves.

These and the many overzealous souls who actually are psychotic probably account for the belief that the religious experience of turning inward can lead to mental illness. This understanding is quite prevalent among the general public as well as among many psychologists. It is true that one kind of mental illness consists in becoming lost in the inner world, in the unconscious. In psychosis the individual becomes so occupied with the inner world of psychic realities—both personal and impersonal—that he or she fails to relate to the outer world. The psychotic's actions are irrational in relation to the world of other people and things because he or she responds only to experiences of the inner world. It is the only thing that is real for that person. People who are psychotic are definitely sick, and they can damage themselves and others, particularly if they come into contact with destructive elements in the inner world and become possessed by them.

There always seem to be people who try to reduce religion simply to the act of turning inward and reveling in what is found there. But this is a very immature idea of religion. Similarly, when meditation is reduced to going inward and luxuriating in either images or simply feelings, it does not touch the real meaning of religion. In genuine religion, looking inward to discover what is there is only the first step. The real task begins as one learns to deal with the images and feelings that arise, and then goes on to relate them to one's practical, outer life at the office, helping or playing with one's children, or going on a vacation with friends.

Many of the medieval writers on the life of the spirit warn against too much concern with the images of this inner world. The men and women emerging from the barbarian Dark Ages were too close to the unconscious and needed their enthusiasm curbed. St. John of the Cross and St. Teresa are classical examples of this emphasis. Our world, however, faces a different problem. It fails to realize that most of humankind's great religions are essentially ways of showing people their way in the inner world and then relating this to the world of outer reality.

Our trouble in dealing with the inner world begins at the point where we see ourselves in the driver's seat, responsible for our own actions, with no need to go back and discover a step at a time how our rationale is born out of interaction with spiritual realities. It is when men and women begin to feel that they have a rational knowledge of all there is to know about religious ways of dealing with these realities that they go off the deep end, with destructive results. Real maturity starts with realizing that we must go back again and again to the source and keep seeking practical religious wisdom and methods of handling what we find. We all remain beginners at this level.

Playing around with either the spiritual world or the physical one without this guidance makes us vulnerable to all kinds of forces we cannot control. We in the West have learned a great deal about matter and how to release its energy, but we are babes in the woods when it comes to understanding how spiritual forces influence what we do with our science. Eastern peoples, who are basically more introverted, have learned a great deal about accommodating themselves to the spiritual world, but they have not worried much about understanding matter.

Since none of us is likely to suggest with a straight face that we in the West might wake up one morning without our drive to acquire scientific knowledge, it is up to us to discover the ways of becoming mature in using our science. Our first task is to admit that our responsibility does not end with learning all we can about the physical world. We have a lot to learn about the inner, spiritual realities and whether science is being used for good and in accord with our religious values, or whether we are playing a dangerous and destructive game.

The dangers of playing around with the unconscious, with spiritual reality, may be harder to grasp than the tangible dangers of playing with an automobile, or with war or atomic energy, but they are just as real. Whether one uses the ouija board for thoughtless fun, or picks up the *I Ching* or tarot cards just to relieve the boredom of a rainy afternoon, these ways of reaching unconscious or psychoid experience are capable of opening a person to levels of spiritual reality that are more than can be handled; or if dream interpretation or a séance is treated like a parlor game, the results can be devastating. They are often not very different from the effects of opening oneself to this level of reality by using drugs indiscriminately.

Recently a group of high school youngsters in the Midwest, all of Catholic background, learned this lesson quite unexpectedly. They were together one evening and, just for fun, decided to hold a séance around a picture of Bobby Kennedy and invoke his spirit. They turned off the lights and stared at the picture on the table lighted by one candle, chanting, "Come, Bobby, come." Suddenly there was a change. The face seemed to come to life, and they felt there was a presence in the room. They were frightened. Then from downstairs, where no one was aware of all this, they heard a commotion that halted things quickly. Another young person downstairs had gotten up from a chair and keeled over unconscious.

In another instance a young woman I know has suffered real agony because she made the mistake of treating an ouija board like a plaything. One rainy afternoon she and her sister began to play with a board quite innocently. After a question or two she found herself thinking of the spoiled child of a friend she expected to see the next day. Suddenly she found herself asking if the boy could be disciplined. Almost electrically the pointer board moved under their fingers to spell out "yes." The next day at a meeting where she had expected to see the friend, she learned instead that the mother and boy had been badly injured in an accident the evening before. Their recovery took months, and during that time this young woman learned to live with guilt and anxiety.

Experiments of this kind are like children playing with matches, innocent souls looking for excitement with no wish to harm themselves or anyone else.

Being truly devoted to evil, in fact, probably takes as much effort as being dedicated to God. Most people are incapable of working up the energy to design a Manson family, or to engineer a kidnapping like that of Patricia Hearst. They would not go near a black mass, and probably do not even believe the lasting effect that is reported by those who have. They simply fail to see the absurdity of allowing oneself to be open to these realities without knowing the dangers.

As long as one believes that there is no evil and that spiritual reality is relatively benign, there is no particular reason for caution. This is why our belief systems are so important. People who would take no chances around high explosives or a racing car will often expose themselves blithely to dangers just as great simply because they cannot see that they are there. Yet, strangely enough, this is a realm that requires an approach in a spirit of openness, detachment and respect. The fire of creativity that is found here can burn the house down as well as serve to heat and light it, and there are elements in this realm that can possess and constrict life or sometimes destroy it outright.

Some of the clearest reminders of these dangers come from writers who were the most aware of the imaginative way they made contact with creative energy. The novels of Charles Williams and the hobbit myths of J. R. R. Tolkien deal deeply with the problems of demonic and destructive realities. Mary Shelley's *Frankenstein* opens up the life-size problems of a modern world creating its own psychic image, and the more recent best-seller by William Peter Blatty, *The Exorcist*, presents a thorough and convincing case for the reality of demonic possession.*

Williams and Tolkien were central to the group at Oxford who shared a lifelong pursuit of imagination. *Frankenstein* was created when P. B. Shelley and his friends decided to play at writing ghoststories and wagered on who could turn out the best. Shelley's wife, who was still in her teens, won hands down with the little book that turned out to be one of the great horror stories of all time. Among this group there was no realization of the seriousness of what they were doing. William Blatty's way of using the ouija board today is well known, and there are other creative writers who show at least some awareness of the dangers of experiencing the psychoid or spiritual world.

As Dr. Jung points out, however, simply understanding the danger is no protection. Creative individuals who try to use their contact with the depths *only* for artistic or aesthetic reasons seldom differentiate between the destructive and creative aspects of this reality and may lose their ability to find the full creativity that is possible. When people lose sight of the central reason for being in touch

---

*Movie audiences obviously do not all share Blatty's conviction about the reality of evil. Some of the untoward physical reactions to *The Exorcist*, which occurred wherever the movie was shown, were undoubtedly suffered by people who expected just entertainment and had no outlook to help them handle this depiction of spiritual evil.

with this realm, they generally put themselves at the beck and call of whatever realities emerge, with no power to choose between those that may be good, bad or indifferent.

One of Jung's important contributions to psychiatry and philosophy was to show that people in the West need to learn how to deal with the inner world as well as the outer one. He also made his own confrontation with the unconscious. In his description of it in the sixth chapter of *Memories, Dreams, Reflections*, he reveals how terrifyingly real these inner experiences are. He exposed himself to them because he felt that the only way he could offer his patients the direction and help they needed was to know the experiences that came to them out of the unconscious and to discover for himself how these elements of the spiritual world could be dealt with. He wrote of this period:

> An incessant stream of fantasies had been released, and I did my best not to lose my head but to find some way to understand these strange things. I stood helpless before an alien world; everything in it seemed difficult and incomprehensible. I was living in a constant state of tension; often I felt as if gigantic blocks of stone were tumbling down upon me. One thunderstorm followed another. My enduring these storms was a question of brute strength. Others have been shattered by them—Nietzsche, and Hölderlin, and many others. But ... from the beginning there was no doubt in my mind that I must find the meaning of what I was experiencing in these fantasies.[1]

St. John of the Cross describes the same kind of inner agony and dark night of the soul during his inner journey, but he gave few concrete suggestions for dealing with them, except to block them out and hang on for dear life until the love of God breaks through. He actually discouraged his followers from using any images, and suggested that it is better to remain in the darkness simply waiting for dawn to break.

Jung, on the other hand, carefully recorded his fantasies. He found that this and, even more, his ordinary business and home life kept him stable enough to work with them to gain understanding. "It was most essential for me," he noted, "to have a normal life in the real world as a counterpoise to that strange inner world. My family and my profession remained the base to which I could always return, assuring me that I was an actually existing, ordinary person."[2] Three things seemed to make the confrontation possible for Jung. He knew that he was undertaking it for very good human and professional reasons; he had an unswerving conviction that he was obeying a higher will; and he realized the importance of his caring relationships with his patients, friends and family. The net result of his search for understanding is to offer a real promise to those who face the necessity of seeking similar experience.

The Promise of Experience

What I am suggesting is that—although entering the spiritual realm is dangerous—if the three main conditions for going inward are met, then the perils can be lessened and largely avoided, and one can begin to think about some of the real rewards. These conditions, which we have discussed as making up the climate for meditation, are: (1) to be conscious of personal human need, particularly in starting on this way; (2) to realize that there is a spiritually creative center, a higher, loving will that has already conquered evil; (3) to keep working to form real human relationships. They are all so vitally necessary that without them the process dead-ends or worse.

If one enters the inner spiritual territory because of human need—either one's own or another's—one will be on the lookout for the dangers that are encountered. In Jung's case the need was certainly there. He knew that he had to make the experiment, but Jung did not have the wisdom of the Church. For centuries no one had tried to describe the relation of the Christian story and its images to a person's own spiritual venture, and he did not know the magnitude of the task or the difficulties he would encounter. It was only sheer strength, along with an unconscious Christian conviction that there is a meaningful reality at the root of things, which kept him going on without breaking at one point or another.

Following where others have gone before gives us a real advantage. We are not only aware that this is a dangerous way, but we recognize at least some of the dangers to expect. It helps in the outer world to know if there is quicksand in a certain area, or if a certain stream is polluted or a field has been mined. Potential disaster in the inner world can be avoided if one reads the warning signs.

One of the main purposes of religion, Christian or otherwise, is to provide such warnings on the inner way and other road signs to guide and direct the individual. It helps just to know that others have gone this way before, since each of us, however close we are to others, steps alone into the inner world. If we do so recognizing the seriousness and danger of the task and going inward only if it is our call to enter, then the chances of getting lost are greatly reduced. There are some who should not try the inner journey. If there is any question about it, we should seek a guide or companion and give up the journey if it seems too dangerous.

Going ahead takes courage and perseverance. Once there is recognition of real danger, there are only two attitudes one can take—courage or cowardice, going forward or retreating. This is characteristic of the inner journey. One of the seeming tragedies is that once one has become aware of this inner world, there is no way to become *un*aware of it, to become *un*conscious again. For my own part, I am well aware that it is not virtue or trying to be "good" that keeps me on the inner way half as much as knowing that abandoning it would be more painful and destructive than keeping on. Turning back can result in deathlike rigidity or in losing one's bearings even to the point of mental dissolution.

For me as an individual, the inner world demands that if I am to gain my life, I must be willing also to lose it. This is an individual path; it is the way of the hero and heroine who offer their lives without knowing whether they will be selected for the quest or where the way will take them. For some the heroism consists in turning toward the outer world and learning to use the insights of others in it. There are some whose way leads to becoming mediators of the inner experience, while for others the task is to find and work with a mediator. The way is different for different people. And even the mediator becomes this only by the grace of God.

In *The Courage to Be* Paul Tillich points out how necessary it is to pass through meaninglessness and guilt and death if one is to find the reality on the other side. Perhaps the truest sign of adulthood, of our maturity, is the willingness to endure an immediate pain in order to find an ultimate good. The neurosis that infects our present-day society may well be the opposite symptom of immaturity. Today's neurosis often looks like a psychic tantrum thrown by a person unwilling to move out into the battle, even though this would mean finding the One who cares and would bring that person through. The trouble is that few of us are really sold on this possibility.

As difficult as it may be, it is important for us to admit the belief, no matter how tentative, that there is such a loving reality at the heart of this world of ours. Perhaps we do see ourselves in a world that is indifferent or even hostile to humankind. In such a world only the strongest really dare to turn inward and find what the reality actually is. But this is just where historic Christianity has something to say.

The Christianity of the New Testament and the early Church tells us that the battle against evil and danger has essentially been won. Humanity has been ransomed and freed from the powers of destructiveness and annihilation. Because of the victory given through the cross and resurrection, we have no reason to fear the ultimate conclusion. The ultimate nature of reality is revealed in Jesus Christ, in self-sacrificing love and concern for ordinary people like you and me. We don't have to be heroes and heroines or world-denying ascetics to pass through the realm of spirit. Even so, it is a difficult task. Following the Christ is no light or airy undertaking. It is dying and rising again; it is losing one's life to find it. But there is confidence in the final outcome. The victory has been won. It is a paradoxical way, very difficult and yet quite simple.

No one can be convinced of this; but any person can step out in hope, keeping an eye peeled for experiences that reveal the victory and the guidance in this other realm. This is not a matter of faith. Faith is a gift that comes, the gift of assurance that the powers of light have conquered and will keep on defeating the darkness. Hope, on the other hand, is our own attitude of looking steadfastly toward that victory and trying to order our lives toward it. Hope is a far easier attitude to live with than despair and disillusionment.

I remember one of the first occasions when I began to learn this. A person for whom I cared very much was terribly sick. I woke up one morning realizing that it would not do any good to brood over impending disaster, and so I deliberately chose to hope. This brought me through. I was able to go on ministering to the dying person and to face the eventual death. I learned that I could hope in spite of everything, and that it was far more creative than gloomy foreboding.

It was hope like this that made Christianity possible. The early Christians knew that they were risking everything and still went to Eucharists which led into the arena. They were ordinary men and women like most of us, fired with a hope that resulted in firm faith. It is just as possible for us to face the inner struggle with meaning as it was for them to stand up against torture and death.

But this is not a practical possibility unless one has the hope that a reality that gives meaning is there. The importance of admitting some such tentative belief can hardly be overestimated. The hope of the Good News lifts ordinary people to the hero and heroine stature and protects them on the inner journey. Because one dares to hope one is able to turn inward without just wandering around in a wilderness. Through hope the inward way has direction and a goal, and Christian meditation becomes a process of discovering the reality of the loving Father revealed by Jesus Christ. Those who consciously follow this way are rescued in almost incredible ways, both inwardly and outwardly.

There is also protection in trying to live one's outer life in the way of concern and love. Nothing gives a person better roots in the outer world than loving someone in it and offering the best of oneself first to that individual, and then to others, whoever they are. Without this base every other connection to the outer world leaves a gap for resentment and hatred to creep in; one is then rooted for sure in this world with little protection from the destructive elements of the inner one. As Jung described so dramatically, the best insurance for a safe journey inward, one that does not turn sour and lead to difficulty, is to find fellowship in the outer world and warm, intimate relationships that are growing and developing in love.

One reason that members of the early Church emphasized community and fellowship so much was that they knew the dangers of going this way alone. In fellowship with another person who is also on the inner journey there is additional protection from the dangers experienced by Jung and others who had to go it alone. It is best, of course, to find a spiritual director with whom to talk, but even another neophyte upon the journey is better than no one at all. There are also prayer groups in which one can listen and share and test one's experiences, and each of these relationships can provide deeper understanding and a new base for love to grow.

We have sketched the general conditions that make it possible for meditation to be real and fulfilling and also as healthful and free of danger as possible. As we turn now to the specifics, it is from this base that we shall consider the actual practice that can lead us to know something of God and His direction in our lives. Everything else that I have to say in the pages that follow is written with these conditions of the spiritual climate in mind. We shall now look at the human preparations that are necessary to realize this way of inward exploration and discovery.

PART THREE

Preparations
for the
Inward Journey

9
Time

Unless one takes the time to turn inward and be silent, meditation and the spiritual quest will not get very far. We seldom find God in a hurry, or in bits and pieces of reflection on a day of busy activity. I am told that Dr. Jung once remarked, "Hurry is not *of* the Devil; it *is* the Devil." There is simply no better way to keep ourselves out of relationship with God than by simply having no time for Him, having no time to look within in meditation.

An efficiently busy life, which keeps us occupied without being harried and keeps our attention entirely on interesting outer things, is probably more potentially destructive of spiritual growth than debauchery or alcohol or hard drugs. These obvious indulgences usually at least lead to emptiness, and sometimes to despair, and in such times one is dangerously vulnerable to being found by God. On the other hand, a quiet, efficient and busy life spent continuously in good works can shield an individual most effectively from any plunge into the depth where God dwells. Time for silence is a prime requisite for finding that inner depth through meditation. Obviously there is a connection between one's capacity to be still and the uses of one's time, but for the moment let us take one thing at a time and then try to see the relation between them.

Human beings are indeed wondrously made. They have the capacity to stay busy no matter how much or how little they have to do. As *Parkinson's Law* puts it, "Work expands so as to fill the time available for its completion."[1] People have a way of keeping their time filled with the job at hand, whether it consists of writing one letter, or buying a loaf of bread and picking out a birthday card, or in doing the work of two or three people, say, by teaching a class schedule, running a counseling practice and caring for a family. Time is more elastic than we ordinarily think. Although there are limits to its elasticity and one must be careful in a full life that important parts of it are not shortchanged, time does expand and contract according to what we do with it.

The reason that most of us fill up our time and stay busy is that we are afraid to be alone. We do not want to deal with everything we find in ourselves. One thing I have learned from practically thirty years of listening to people is that nearly all of us have our own inner monsters. It seems that if we will just keep busy enough, we won't have to deal with them. But that is an illusion. If they are there and we do not deal with them, then the monsters usually seize upon and raise hob with our families and children and friends, the very ones who least deserve their "dirty tricks." In fact, if we stay busy enough, we do not even notice the mischief our inner demons are doing to others.

The best story of this is one I have told before, but it is so much to the point that it bears repeating. It is told about a clergyman who came to see Dr. Jung on the ragged edge of breaking down. He had been working a fourteen-hour schedule, and his nerves were played out; his hands even trembled. Jung began by asking if he wanted to get well, and the minister said indignantly that of course he did. Jung gave him a simple and inexpensive prescription. He was to work just eight hours a day and sleep eight. The remaining hours he was to spend all alone in his study, in quiet. This seemed easy enough and he agreed to try it and was quite hopeful that the tension would be relieved.

That day the clergyman worked only eight hours. At supper he explained to his wife what he was going to do, and went into his study and closed the door. And there he stayed for several hours. He played a few Chopin Études and finished a Hermann Hesse novel. The next day he followed the same routine, except that in the evening he read Thomas Mann's *Magic Mountain* and played a Mozart Sonata. The following morning he went back to see Dr. Jung, complaining that he was just as bad off; and obviously he was.

Jung carefully inquired about how he had followed instructions and heard what he had done. "But you didn't understand!" Dr. Jung told him. "I didn't want you with Hermann Hesse or Thomas Mann, or even Mozart or Chopin. I wanted you to be all alone with yourself." At this the minister looked terrified and gasped, "Oh, but I can't think of any worse company!" To this Dr. Jung made the reply that has been repeated so often: "And yet this is the self you inflict on other people fourteen hours a day." Isn't this uncomfortably close to sadism, to inflict on others the company one cannot abide oneself?

This, in broad srokes, is the story of so many of us who cannot enjoy being alone. When we take no satisfaction in our time alone, and make no provision for it, we are running away from ourselves. Either we fear that there is a devouring void within us, or else we glimpse something disturbing and demonic enough to try to escape from it. In either case it is not very gracious to try to share that self with other people all the time. One reason why suffering and disaster, defeat and agony are openings to another realm is that they bring us to such a complete halt that we cannot avoid looking within. It is the only thing left to do. How much more sensible it is to stop and look for that dimension before life catches up with us.

Often we think that we really do not have time to stop. Time often seems to have an inexorable power over us which keeps us from stepping out of it. We get so caught up in clock time, in the rushing moments, that we forget that time has another dimension. Each moment has a meaning, an eternal one.

While most of us Christians are caught in time, our Eastern brothers and sisters have been deeply wise about the meaning of each moment, and in the *I Ching* they have spoken about this wisdom. In this we can learn from them. But just as we Westerners often fail to understand the eternal dimension of time, so they often fail to see the urgency of the plight of humanity caught in the flowing temporal process. It is not a matter of either one or the other. Both of these aspects of time are real, and both are important.

Stopping Time

Bringing time to a halt, one friend has suggested to me, is very much like stopping a car when one sees the "STOP-LOOK-LISTEN" sign at a railroad crossing. Perhaps a few drivers are going slowly and can simply coast to a stop, and there are always some who have to come to a screeching, protesting halt. But most of us are somewhere between the two; we have to put the brakes on, but in time because we have learned that the signal shows us there might be a train coming. It is not that God is like a freight train bearing down on us—although that is the way some people do see God. It is rather that we have come to believe, or even to know, that He is there, and we have found that our need will overtake us if we do not stop.

For my own part, I find that my life can get painfully out of kilter, and the only way it can be kept in any sort of balance and harmony is to have stopping times. Even when things look good, I have to realize that I am not very interested in having the meaninglessness that the existential writers describe catch up with me again. I had better agree with St. Augustine that my heart is restless and finds rest no other place but in Him. If I want to find the satisfaction that all the ideas and comforts and gadgets of this world fail to provide, I find that I have to stop time in order to look for another dimension. I have to stop dead in my tracks in several different ways.

The first of them is a daily time of anywhere from fifteen minutes to an hour, and this is the most basic way and the one that requires the most discussion. I first learned about this in the seminary. Coming out of an agnostic background I took the seminary very seriously. I went to all the morning chapel services, and one morning when I came a few minutes early, I found a handful of people already there. I began coming earlier myself, and realized that six or seven were there each morning in quiet before the service. They were alone, but together. In these times of openness I first began to sense a presence seeking me out. Then, almost suddenly, I was responsible for a parish and out of touch with the fellowship of a daily chapel service. I did not realize until much later what a severe loss it was not to have this time of quiet inner reflection.

The services and outer activity of the Church are designed to feed the individual search for God. For me, as timeless and indispensable as the sacraments are, much of their meaning is swallowed up and lost unless I take some time apart and in quiet to stop the headlong rush of time and let the Risen Christ speak afresh. The sacrament itself is set in a framework of silence in many churches. As I learned the hard way, we must take some of our prime time, whatever is the best part of the day for us, to stop for reflection and openness to the Other if we are to realize the depth of meaning that is found in Christianity.

It was a psychologist who first made me really aware of this. As I have mentioned, my deepest problem was trying to minister with a gospel whose meaning kept vanishing into thin air. But at this point in life I was simply complaining about insomnia and how much it bothered me. Usually I sleep four or five hours and then awaken, and at that time I would lie in bed and stew, angry because I could not go back to sleep. When I told my psychologist friend this, he smiled, almost as if amused, and then asked, "Has it ever occurred to you, Morton, that someone might be trying to get through to you? Don't you remember how God called Samuel in the night?"

From then on I began to get up in the night and write down my dreams and then try to listen. I soon discovered that this was prime time for me. It was a time when the telephone did not ring, and the children had no more questions for that day, and parishioners' problems were safely bedded down. I found that I could listen to God during this time and tell him about my fears and anxieties, and what I had dreamed. After about thirty minutes to an hour, with everything written down as best I could in a journal, I would go back to bed and soon be asleep, my inner business in better order. I also found that praying the Lord's Prayer in the rhythmical way which St. Ignatius suggests quieted me and prepared me for sleep.[2]

Later I extended this time of meditating another fifteen minutes or so, and even on those rare occasions when I cannot go back to sleep the time is anything but wasted. It is usually at these times that the best insights about my life and the world around me (both physical and spiritual) come to me. Insomnia can be a calling from the depth of oneself that we have unfinished spiritual business, that there are things we need to look at, dimensions, shadows and lights, even entities that we have overlooked.

For a morning person it may seem like a radical procedure to get up in the middle of the night in order to be found by God. It all depends on how important it is to us. So often people give God only the tag end of the day, when they no longer want to focus on the newspaper or the column of figures they have to add. It is no wonder they find so little when they give Him some time only when they are good for nothing else. It makes no difference *when* the time is, but only that it is the hour when one is most alert, most aware and conscious. This may be early or late, for an evening person just before retiring, or for a mother after the children have left for school or during their nap time. I have one friend who found her best time from nine to ten in the morning and if the phone rang, she would answer it and simply say that she was busy and would call back. Usually a way can be found, *if one chooses*.

Morning people might set the alarm thirty or forty minutes early and take their time while the house is quiet and before they have to rush off to their offices. They have a chance then to bring things together and see their way ahead for the day. Taking this much time out of a day does not seem so much to ask when we remember that the purpose is to meet One who offers us eternal meaning and a companionship of love we can scarcely imagine, and even guidance on how to spend the day. Most of us would do more than this in order to go fishing or to meet a relative at the plane. To see the importance of taking the time to let God into our lives we need mostly to stop and discover how hungry we are for Him.

Thousands of Americans, young people and old, take a regular time for quiet because Transcendental Meditation tells them to sit quietly saying a mantra for twenty minutes twice a day. Others take the time for the less formal meditation of Zen or some other sect of Eastern religion. These people have learned that they can expect positive physical and mental effects from the practice. The strains of the day are relieved, and there is a centering down. They find they are able to concentrate better; often they are able to use more of their physical and mental potential.

People find excellent reasons for turning to these Eastern practices since the Church makes almost no effort to offer instruction about such practices, or even to suggest that finding God is an even more vitally important reason for meditating. Are we afraid to ask this much of people, or has Western religion been so brainwashed by our emphasis on the material world that we really don't think there is value in taking time to turn inward? Or has Christianity lost its understanding that spirit can restore both body and mind?

Daily Prayer—Past and Present

For a long time the Church was sure of the value of time for meditation. The early Church simply assumed that all Christians would have their daily times of meeting the Risen Lord. When Christians lived with the knowledge that at any moment they might be apprehended and condemned to death for the treasonous act of supporting an illegal religion, they had reason to seek this presence. I doubt if they could have survived the tensions of that world and changed it as thoroughly as they did without the vivid consciousness of God's presence. In many communities there was a daily Eucharist and also times of praying, as well as working, together. Fellowship with others who knew the Risen Christ was their very life, and they risked everything for it—property, family and life itself. This was the atmosphere in which the Christian Church was most vital and grew most vigorously.

As the Empire accepted Christianity, this ardor cooled. In an atmosphere where it became not only legal but the politic thing to be a Christian, the Church developed its monastic communities in order to keep a more rigorous spirituality alive. In the East there were anchorites who spent most of their time alone and praying, while community groups grew up in the West. Here one could leave the crumbling world and enter a community with others who were finding a substance and reality that even the collapsing civilization could not obscure. Besides the regular gathering for prayer in the Eucharist, the seven hours of divine office daily were basic to monastic life. These specified times and forms were set aside, sometimes for private prayer, more often as a gathering together in quiet for readings from the Bible and other works and for prayer and meditation.

In the rest of the Church, on the other hand, a tragic dilution of real Christian faith had begun with the baptism of whole tribes and nations along with their kings and leaders. The result was a two-class system in which only the monks and nuns tried to follow a fully Christian way, while the ordinary Christians slipped into heaven by the skin of their teeth. It became only natural to think that the priest, the pastor, and the monks and nuns, those who follow the religious way, have the responsibility of doing the praying for the rest of us. The idea that ordinary Christians have no need to take time for turning inward and finding out what is there took hold so strongly that it is next to impossible to break into.

In the Protestant Reformation there was an attempt to provide some sense of responsibility for the average Christian. In some sects there was a measure of success, but when religion for most people was a matter legislated for them, it was hard to persuade many of them to take the religious life seriously. In the end the theologians of most of the major Protestant groups concluded that humankind was caught in a totally physical world, shut off from any experience except the physical one. In the long run most people are more consistent than we generally realize, and Protestants of almost every brand fell in line with the understanding that it is silly to think of stopping to get in touch with another dimension or realm of reality. Thus there is little understanding of the practice of meditation among the standard Protestant groups. I remember how it worried one of my professors in the seminary that some of us were always in chapel before the rest. He considered us a little too intense and thought it might well represent some psychological imbalance. As a result of this attitude more and more Christians have turned to TM or Zen or Hare Krishna.

Before Vatican II most Catholic priests said their breviary daily, keeping up the same forms of the monastic hours, but in private, perhaps on the train or alone in one's oratory. However, with the flush of freedom that came with the decisions of this historic council, the practice of daily hours has fallen off even in most Catholic religious communities, and many priests ignore the breviary entirely. One is hard put to find a Christian professional, Catholic or Protestant, who could introduce anyone to a Christian way of meditation that would make sense to people with some comprehension of the totality of life. Where would you send someone who asked for instructions in Christian meditation? Can you imagine the look of an average Protestant minister if a long-haired youth came up and asked: "Sir, how can I go about Christian meditation?"

There is good reason for letting go of enforced routines of prayer and imposed periods of silence in the religious Orders. No one can force another person to take the inner way. Turning inward is a venture that each of us must assent to and pursue on our own, because we desire it. It turns sour if another tries to take me by the hand and pull me along against my will. Unless I ask for these experiences out of my own need or for my own reasons, I can receive little spiritual insight or guidance from them, and I am likely to feel put upon, or even tyrannized in the most devastating way.

This leaves the responsibility directly on each of us as individuals, and I doubt if development is possible through meditation without some daily stopping, some daily turning inward. It is the key which unlocks the door. Then one must take hold of the handle and open the door. This is just where much of the present-day imageless meditation shortchanges people; it unlocks the door but does not open it. I shall say more about this when we come to consider the use of images. Let us look now at those weekly times of quiet that are essentially times of summing up or re-collecting and relating our lives to what we have found.

Re-collecting Time

One of the most positive of the ten commandments stresses the need for a weekly time of reflection. The commandment to keep holy the Sabbath requires that once a week we stop every kind of active endeavor, that we rest and turn to our Creator and to our fellow creatures. We meet together for worship. It makes little difference whether the time of rest is Saturday or the Christian first day of the week; the principle is the same. We need both the activity of worship and the time for preparation, time for a little spiritual housecleaning beyond the daily tidying up and dusting. We need to take out the trash in ourselves and perhaps straighten up the deepest closet or file away some of the things on top of an inner desk.

I find that I need a couple of hours each week for this, to see what I have been doing, how I have been doing, and what I need to be doing. This is a time for centering and getting my perspective back, in which my daily times of quiet are brought together and come to fruition. This time can be used in various ways, perhaps to read more in the Bible, or to take a longer look at either a problem or a project in one's spiritual life. It may be needed to probe deeper, to get at the roots of things and unravel those too complex for the daily times of quiet. Sometimes these hours are needed just to become really still, to let the rush within one die down. Or again, they can be used to check one's life and action against the priorities one has set for oneself.

About once a year, and sometimes oftener if life is changing rapidly, one needs a day or two alone, with no family or friends or tasks to interrupt. Anne Morrow Lindbergh has shown as clearly as any writer today the value of having such time by herself, a time at the beach cottage described in her *Gifts from the Sea*. This is the purpose of the retreats that have been so meaningful in many religious communities. It was out of a ten-month retreat that St. Ignatius planned and set down the insights for *The Spiritual Exercises* used by so many leaders.

This yearly time alone allows a reevaluation of one's life, asking which things are really valuable, and which ones are simply done out of meaningless habit. In these retreats of at least a day or more we can meditate upon the message of the Gospel, letting the figures and stories speak a meaning for our own lives. We may go deeper into ourselves and try to let the reality of the spiritual world play upon the deepest, least known levels of our being. Some of us may realize how often we live from day to day without asking what our existence is supposed to mean, and we may want to set specific goals for ourselves. There may even be a major breakthrough, perhaps in a dream, which puts one's life in a whole new perspective. Almost everyone finds some breakthrough from this much time alone and in quiet.

After such an experience, the importance of a daily time of stopping and listening usually becomes crystal clear. St. Ignatius understood this. Because of an extended time alone he had realized the futility of the ordinary world of unconscious secular life and the importance of the saving and transforming love and power of Jesus Christ. He went on developing the *Exercises* primarily to help others find such a new beginning. Most of us need new beginnings at least once a year. We need a few days, at least a long weekend, for a yearly spiritual checkup, a time to redirect and refocus our goals. If a person has an eternal soul, it is probably worth this much time to help get it on the right track.

When these longer periods of stopping have borne fruit, they carry over into ordinary life. We become aware of this deeper level of reality in the midst of ordinary preoccupations, and strangely it does not make us less efficient, but more so. It is almost as if, even when we sleep, we become conscious of the presence of God touching us. Thomas Kelly's *A Testament of Devotion* speaks of how the awareness of one's quiet time carries over into all other aspects of life. Frank Laubach's *Game with Minutes* and Brother Lawrence's *The Practice of the Presence of God* tell the same story. Brother Lawrence found that even picking up a straw from the kitchen floor became an act done for, and with, the Risen Christ.

I find the same thing in my own work; it goes best when I am not trying to do it just on my own. I spend a lot of time talking with people. When I am conscious of another wisdom listening through me, I often let words come from my lips that are wiser and hit the mark far more creatively than any of my own ideas. I have learned to try to check with this deeper insight and when I do, the best intuitions come. They are purely given, striking like an arrow with a message hanging from it that passes before the inner eye. Even in public when I am speaking from a prepared talk. I find that if only I can hang loose, often a new idea inserts itself into my outline and I say something unexpected that gets through to people. This is just a sample of the ways in which one can catch momentary reflections of the spiritual dimension and find oneself looking both horizontally—at the physical world—and vertically at the same time.

The same thing happens when people use the Eastern Orthodox technique that has become so widely known as the "Jesus prayer." As a person says this brief prayer over and over again—"Lord Jesus Christ, Son of God, have mercy on me, a sinner"—gradually the entreaty becomes the undercurrent, the very foundation of life and action. Somewhere deep within, a person becomes aware of contact with another reality. The classic story of this devotional practice, *The Way of a Pilgrim*, describes the growth of this awareness and some of the effects on the world of people and matter. This kind of sustained concentration on another level of reality can go on while one is at work mowing a lawn, or even while adding a column of figures or writing a letter. It is possible to live on two different levels at once, and even to increase one's efficiency in the outer world at the same time.

Any of us can start with this kind of short, ejaculatory prayer that seeks to establish our reconnection with this realm little by little. This practice doesn't even take time, but rather redeems time and gives it a new depth and meaning. As the connection gradually deepens, one will find the time of quiet meditation infinitely valuable and the whole day suffused with the same quality. As one then discovers actions and reactions, feelings and ideas in oneself which do not fit with this quality, they should be brought into one's quiet time and examined carefully.

One of the best ways I have found of keeping myself reminded of the importance of these times alone is to keep a list of things that are important to me in order to see just how I do use my time. Generally I put them down like this:

My family—my wife, children, and their families.

Those toward whom I have special responsibility.

My friends.

My students and counselees—time spent in meetings with students.

My religious practice, my time for God, for the Eucharist.

My teaching, the reading that keeps me current, and research.

My writing, organizing what I have learned to share with a larger group.

My lecturing.

My recreation, time to rest and to play, to enjoy life and be recreated.

My sleep.

Periodically I review this list and ask whether I am actually spending my time in the way I think it should be spent. Sometimes I see with a shock how easy it is to fritter my time away, and I realize that I have let my activities run me instead of keeping my real priorities in view.

More often, however, I feel bewildered by the number of conflicting loyalties that face every last one of us in today's world. How is it possible for any of us to decide what is really best and allocate our time as we should? At that point, if I have been too busy, too preoccupied to take time, I have a choice. Either I must stop and check my direction or I am caught living mindlessly, unconsciously driven by the tyranny of time. And this, as I well know, is sin *par excellence*; to continue unconsciously may well be the primal sin. I am not wise enough to arbitrate among the demands. Only by bringing them into my daily, weekly and yearly times alone can these priorities be gradually sorted out. In the presence of the Other, they assume their proper perspective and value, and I then rank them in better order. The fact that this order changes in different periods of my life makes it even more necessary to have yearly times of review and reconsideration.

Someone has said that the lives of most persons are like jewelry stores where some trickster has mixed up the price tags. The diamonds are priced at next to nothing and some worthless baubles at thousands of dollars. Unless we stop business as usual and take stock, we are likely to end up in bankruptcy. So long as the store is crowded with people, there is no chance of taking inventory and putting things to rights. We must close the doors and take the time alone. Then we can check with the stock list, our list of priorities, and give the right value to the right object. If we truly believe that God is a loving Father, there need be no fear He will take away what we need (or think we need). He wants us to find Him so that He can bring us to our deepest and most lasting satisfactions.

Still, life has a way of keeping our priorities or price tags shuffled, and to bring order and harmony into life, to find meaning in it, requires stopping and redeeming time by reflection in quiet and silence. The next question, then, is: How does one find the value and use of silence?

10
Silence: Discovering
the Way Inward

The idea of linking silence with prayer may sound like an out-and-out contradiction to many Christians. We are accustomed to thinking of the familiar forms of prayer that people use when they join together to worship or ask God for something. These forms almost always follow a lead given in the past. They are shaped by words set down in the Bible, particularly the psalms, or by other poetry and by the liturgy. They can vary from the words that come spontaneously in the simplest service to the most elaborate prayers that have grown up around the Eucharist and other sacraments, and either may be used in private devotions.* Of course, there is no question about the value and importance of this way of turning to God, but it is not the only kind of prayer that we need.

There is another, equally important way of praying in which a person becomes silent and tries to listen instead of speaking. Instead of picking up a familiar lead and speaking about the things that all of us feel are needed, one tries to become still. One's effort is to be silent enough to hear, first, the deepest needs of one's own heart, and then the prompting of the creative Spirit in whatever direction it may indicate. In this second kind of prayer, which we call meditation, one is trying to follow one's own inner road as it is opened.

Each of these ways of praying is needed and each supports the other. Through corporate prayer we are able to reach for the goals we have in common. If one's meditation leads away from these goals, it will be clear that one is off course and needs to back up and check directions. On the other hand, corporate prayer has a way of losing its vitality and its touch with reality. If it becomes no longer vital and creative to pray together, we can be quite sure that our formal prayers need the nourishment of individual fellowship with God. Unless the members of a group are finding some encounter of their own with the Other, their act of joining together for religious services usually becomes one more meaningless activity, merely the ritual indulgence of a nice habit. One can

---

*Some religious groups question whether an individual may legitimately use the Eucharist in private devotions, but this does not exclude the use of prayers that are similar to the sacramental ones.

sense the difference in a congregation where a considerable number are finding an inner contact with God.

The first step in finding such a contact with God is learning to be alone and quiet. This is the beginning of silence, of the process of introversion. There is just one aim to start with, to still the tumult of activity in mind and body and center down in a state of recollection. And this means shutting out the invading noises from both the outside world and the inner psychic one. To become really silent one has to come to a halt outwardly and inwardly at the same time. It is very much like thinking about getting a car tuned up while roaring down the freeway. One cannot do much about it until one slows down, pulls into a service station and turns the motor off. In reality this idea of stopping the wheels of progress periodically for silence is common in religious practice.

Religious Traditions of Silence

No one in Eastern religions doubts the value of silence. The practice of being alone in stillness is certainly central in Hindu religion. Yoga and also various forms of Buddhist meditation begin and end in silence. Throughout Zen the value of utter stillness is emphasized; the goal of *satori* is to reach this ultimate peace, and the novice begins searching while sitting still in the lotus position. There is a strong tradition in Chinese religious thought that the way of coming into harmony with tao, which is the ultimate principle of reality, is by inner quiet, by stilling the inner confusion so that one comes to peace and harmony within. Almost the same approach is found in certain sects of Islamic religion.

The whole tradition of shamanism springs from the shaman's experience of initiation in absolute solitude. A shaman is a religious leader who makes direct contact with the religious realm and then mediates these realities to the people. This religious expression is one of the most interesting because it is found in nearly every corner of the world with much the same experiences, and yet its spread can be explained only to a small extent by cultural contacts. Shamanism has been known in Greece and India, in Africa and Australia, and among the American Indians the visionary quest for revelation is seen as an initiation into adulthood. It is this way of going into oneself or into the desert alone in order to find the nature of the spiritual world which Carlos Castaneda has described so well in his books.

We forget that silence is equally important in the Christian tradition, starting with the long history of experiences of the Hebrew people. These experiences go back to the solitude of Abraham when God's covenant was first given. They are found in the lonely receptivity of Moses on Mt. Sinai and Isaiah's willingness to listen alone in the temple, and also in the fact that one day out of every seven was set aside as the Sabbath, which was a day of quiet and rest for all Hebrews. Still, we do not always see how many similar experiences there were in the life of Jesus of Nazareth. As I found when I went back to the New Testament after some experiences of my own, it is very easy for us to overlook things about Jesus which do not fit with the kind of life we are accustomed to living.

Many of the major events of Jesus's life took place when He went off by Himself. After His baptism He went alone into the desert for forty days to meet and deal with Himself. There in silence, where Satan appeared to Him, He was prepared for His ministry (Matt. 4:1-11, Mark 1:12-13, Luke 4:1-13). It was in the silence of a lonely mountain that the experience of the transfiguration was shown to Jesus and three of His disciples (Matt. 17:1-9, Mark 9:2-10, Luke 9:28-36). After the last supper together, Jesus prepared for the ordeal ahead by taking His followers into the Garden of Gethsemane where He prayed alone and in quiet while the disciples slept (Matt. 26:36-46, Mark 14:32-42, Luke 22:41-46).

Again and again He went away to some solitary place, away from the activity of people. These times are mentioned so often in the gospels that there is but little question that this was Jesus's regular practice, and several of the references show that these were times of prayer (Matt. 14:23, Mark 1:35, 6:46, Luke 5:16, 6:12, 9:18, John 6:15). He told His followers to go into the closet and shut the door to pray (Matt. 6:6-13). He understood and supported Mary, the sister of Martha, in her quiet attention to Him (Luke 10:39-42), and He commended her for not getting involved in household business. In Luke's version, the Lord's Prayer was given after the disciples had watched Jesus apparently praying in silence and asked Him to teach them how to pray (Luke 11:1-4). Evidently Jesus, even though He was the Son of God, tried to keep His relationship with the Father in good order, and wanted His followers to know how their own channels to God can be kept open through silence.

The Church has never really lost this understanding. In both Eastern and Western monasticism the tradition of returning to times of quiet and stillness has remained strong. The practice of Hesychasm (which is simply a form of the Greek world for quiet) continues today in the isolated Greek communities on Mt. Athos, and there is a new appreciation of the Greek fathers whose writings in the *Philokalia* have recently been translated into English. The same tradition is found among all the mystics from Origen to St. John of the Cross and among the Quakers like John Woolman. It has been kept very much alive by the Quietism and Pietism of many Protestant sects as well as by many religious Orders in the Catholic tradition.

Many different people, often as different from each other as Bishop Fénelon and Søren Kierkegaard, have spoken of the religious value of silence. Fénelon held that one should not speak if it is possible to remain silent, while Kierkegaard in one of his most telling passages wrote that a real Christian

> often feels a need of solitude, which for him is a vital necessity—some-
> times like breathing, at other times like sleeping. The fact that he feels
> this vital necessity more than other men is also a sign that he has a
> deeper nature. Generally the need of solitude is a sign that there is
> spirit in a man after all, and it is a measure for what spirit there is.[1]

The same view was offered to the literary world by Thomas Carlyle in *Sartor Resartus* (and Maurice Maeterlinck later expanded upon these words):

> Silence and Secrecy! Altars might still be raised to them (were this an
> altar-building time) for universal worship. Silence is the element in
> which great things fashion themselves together, that at length they
> may emerge, full-formed and majestic, into the daylight of Life, which
> they are thenceforth to rule. . . . Nay, in thy own mean perplexities,
> do thou thyself but *hold thy tongue for one day:* on the morrow, how
> much clearer are thy purposes and duties; what wreck and rubbish
> have those mute workmen within thee swept away, when intrusive
> noises were shut out! . . . As the Swiss Inscription says: *Sprechen ist
> silbern, Schweigen ist golden* (Speech is silvern, Silence is golden); or
> as I might rather express it: Speech is of Time, Silence is of Eternity.[2]

In our time there are writers from Thomas Merton and Agnes Sanford to Dag Hammarskjöld who put the same emphasis on silence. Merton speaks of silence as necessary to contemplation, while in *Markings*, Hammarskjöld tells how his times of inner quiet made it possible for him to endure the constant turmoil of political conflict. In *Sealed Orders*, Agnes Sanford recounts how necessary her daily times of quiet and silence have been in making her ministry of healing such an effective one.

For the most part, however, modern man sees no place for silence among the realities of life, and so finds little time for it. In another place I have spoken about life in our urbanized and industrial society in these words:

> Most modern life is a studied attempt to avoid ever being alone,
> faced with the reality of the inner world. Just imagine how a line-ar-
> tist like Steinberg might sketch the day of the average man, beginning
> with the moment a disc jockey connects with him to awake him in the
> morning. He may stay wrapped in gentle music while his razor
> whirrs, and then the news bombardment begins. He gets his breakfast
> in between skeins of words—headlines, box scores, political phrases,
> and a running commentary from his wife probably like a cartoon out-

side. He drives to work joined to the radio again, and switching over to concentration on a job even requires the help of pipeline music. With lunch he is fed conversation and business problems like spaghetti, and there is only one difference at dinner. He chops the family threads off to change over to TV or perhaps a meeting. Only when he drops into bed, too tired even to dream, do the conscious lines stop radiating, and if he cannot sleep there is the ever present sleeping pill or tranquilizer to remove the necessity of a night-time encounter with silence. The next day the routine starts over, and if there should be any interstices, the picture is quickly finished by simply adding squiggles to the lines and calling them recreation.[3]

Obviously to find the way of silence one needs to disconnect, to unhook from much of the activity and even turn off some of the light that seems so necessary to modern living. In a very real sense the way of meditation is a way of detachment. Let us look at what this means.

Silence and Detachment—Becoming Unhooked

Almost every approach to religious practice suggests ways of human growth and development that depend on separating from one's ordinary round of activity. In most religions the understanding is found that people must nearly always let go of reactions and ideas that are simply customary or habitual before another level of life and meaning can break through to them. As long as one is like a ping-pong ball, bounced back and forth by every emotion and outer relationship, it is hardly possible to enter the meditative process. At the same time it is all too easy to overemphasize detachment as if this were the only route to God, and this often results in a pathological and distorted denial of life. When any such aspect of religious life—tongue speaking, for instance—becomes the *end in itself*, the real search for God comes to a halt, and the door is opened to one-sidedness and evil.

William Johnston has written with depth and understanding about the place of detachment in Christian religious experience. In *The Still Point* he compares Christian practices with those of Zen and shows how similar they are, and also how both of them work toward psychological maturity as it is understood in depth psychology. From a psychological point of view, detachment from habitual, unthinking activity is part of the process of growing up. It is the first step in learning to live as a separate individual and trying to stand on one's own two feet.

So long as a person thinks that life cannot be lived without some*one* or some*thing*, perhaps father or mother or parental substitute, or that life will fall apart without the accustomed indulgences or the round of activity, that person has not approached psychological maturity, but is living a dependent existence rather than becoming a self-contained individual, a person in his own right who can give love without any strings attached. The ability to give love without expecting anything in return is one expression of maturity. The mature person is also able to be alone and silent, and the effort to turn inward in silence leads toward this detachment and the maturity that goes with it.

Becoming inner-directed, of course, does not guarantee maturity. Unless the individual takes the inner direction out into the world around him and tries to put it to use, this inner-directedness can become just as one-sided as today's total emphasis on outer direction. It can even be schizophrenic. What maturity requires is a balance between the two.

One basic difference between Eastern and Western religion is this matter of balance between detachment and *attachment*. In both East and West the immediate goal is the same, to help the individual achieve self-containment through detachment. But in Eastern religion this is final as there is nothing further to become attached to. Buddhism sees no God at the end of the process, and so one of the central themes is *escaping from*. The final goal is to become detached from this miserable wheel of existence. Zen, springing from the soil of Buddhism, also seeks detachment as an end in itself. Yoga is based on a similar principle of freeing one's self physically, emotionally and spiritually from entanglement in the world.

In Western religion detachment is equally important, but not as an end in itself. Instead the aim is freedom which will allow the individual to find new and richer attachments to God and to other human beings. Christian devotional practice stresses this goal of freedom from relationships of actual dependency. It is mainly in this way that we can come to the inner wholeness that allows us to give ourselves freely to God and to our fellow men.

So much of the time our lives are scattered in unconscious reactions to the demands of one attachment or another. Often we are not even aware of their strength, and only in silence can we begin to seek detachment from them. As one begins to withdraw and feels the surge of emotion of losing something, self-knowledge begins. By discovering this lack of freedom, one becomes able to loosen the ties that need to come unbound. Then one can gradually discover how the bits and pieces, fragments of responses and reactions and emotions, can be gathered together into a whole personality.

Neither freedom nor inner-directedness is a final goal. Instead, each is a valuable tool in moving toward wholeness. They are steps on the way to learning the meaning of God's love for us. As one finds the reality of that love, it becomes possible to offer oneself to God in a mature way and to give some of the same love and understanding to others, self-giving love without strings attached. This way of wholeness and love is central to the life and teaching of Jesus, and to most Christians who have caught the inner meaning of His life and words. Whatever else it involves, one finds in this process of detachment and reattachment the meaning of being born again, of giving up an old life and being given a new one.

This is not an easy way to follow, however. Detachment is a tricky process, and the word itself can be twisted into all sorts of meanings. By a simple shift of emphasis, detachment can be twisted to mean denial and a practice of devaluing and rejecting anything that is stamped "worldly." Anything not purely from God, or leading directly to God, may be seen as evil and harmful to the religious way. This is the kind of attitude that rejects and hates all that is natural and human in this world, and it can lead to the most extreme and dangerous asceticism.

When matter or the body or the human spirit are seen as either valueless or evil, then one has no choice but to beat down these obstacles to the religious way. Whether this view results in wearing hair shirts and spiked chains, in sitting for years on a pillar, or eating only cabbage leaves, or in simply refusing to participate in life *as it is* in this world, it is equally dangerous. The person glories in asceticism and forgets love. It is all too easy to be heroic about a belief like this and to forget how much heroism it takes to give real love.

The trouble is that others who are not so strong are attracted by these psychic athletes. They mistake feats of ascetic discipline for a way of following Jesus of Nazareth, and they learn not detachment from the world but fear of the world. Most people overlook the fact that fear can produce just as strong an attachment as love. A young man, for instance, can keep himself just as firmly tied to the mother's apron strings by opposing her at every turn as by doing whatever she wants. Either reaction is nearly always a form of dependent and unconscious attachment. The same thing is true of our relations with the world at large. Either too much involvement with or too much contempt for worldly affairs may show that we are handcuffed to them at a deep level.

St. John of the Cross believed in the value of detachment and asceticism, but he warned again and again of the danger of exaggerated personal penance. This was almost his theme song in *The Ascent of Mount Carmel*, even though this saint did not always follow his own advice and sometimes engaged in personal practices that would be hard to accept today. There is danger in mixing detachment with asceticism in this way because it may be prompted by masochistic self-hatred rather than by a search for relationship with God. It is one thing to start with a judgment on the body, or the psyche or the world, with two strikes against them, and quite another to try to stand off from these things so that they can be put into a proper perspective of value. They can then become allies in training for the true freedom of a life of service to God.

This takes effort. Detachment in this sense demands as much discipline as either Western asceticism or Eastern separation for its own sake. There is no shortcut that leads to instant wholeness or mature attachment. Meaningful relationship is born out of detachment, which is usually first quickened by reflection in silence. The importance of detachment for the religious way, and its dependence on silence, can hardly be overemphasized. One reason for the power of the social action of Martin Luther King was the way it sprang out of his wholeness which was the wholeness of a person recollected in silence and the presence of God. Almost all Christian reform of any significance which in the end healed rather than destroyed, has sprung out of the same source.

Silence can be a mini-experience of death and resurrection. It is a temporary cessation of one's doing and planning and desires. When we actually die, we give up the possessions that have mattered to us and entrust them to the care of others. Much the same thing happens when one stops in silence. Action, planning, desiring are all suspended, entrusted to the Other in silence, while the thoughts and emotions and realities that surround them are given a chance to regroup.

Most of the time we go spinning along like a top, without wondering where the momentum comes from. It is almost impossible to imagine the mechanism of life slowing down to a wobble until it topples over. Yet this is the way of new beginnings, and the function of silence is to slow the mechanism down so that it can be rewound and started out again on a new course. This is a process of slowing the ego down, of letting self-centeredness fade out so that the larger self can take over and be moved by God's grace.

There are people, of course, who are already too withdrawn from the world for their own good. Besides learning to use introversion wisely, the extreme introvert needs to be nudged into the outer world to find a way in it, particularly among people. There is also the danger of mental illness. The illness of the schizophrenic, for instance, and that of the autistic child is the inability of that individual to reach out for relationships in the outer world, and the signs of danger in introversion are not always so clear. For many it is important to have the help of a counselor who can tell whether detachment and silence represent fear and avoidance of life, or whether they are bringing one to participate more fully in it. The need is increasing today for people who are trained to offer this combination of psychological and spiritual discernment.

It is much easier for introverts to turn inward than for extraverts. The introvert feels at home in the silence for such a person's interest is already there. For the extravert this means an about-face or turning away from all that seems valuable and familiar. The difficulty for the introvert is in stepping out of the self, in reaching out, say, to a stranger in church or at the swimming pool. Turning towards the inner world is just as difficult for the extravert, and also just as necessary and valuable. Both are as vital to the Christian life as the two halves of a beating heart. But today's world applauds our efforts to reach out and tries to forget that those efforts require an inner basis which is found in silence. It is silence, and the fact that something happens in the silence, which needs to be stressed today.

It has never been easy to become really silent, and now when our technology makes it even more difficult, the Church has little to suggest to ordinary Christians about centering down. They are welcome to try Transcendental Meditation or some other Eastern practice which does offer specific methods, but the Christian wisdom developed by so many spiritual leaders in the past has been largely forgotten in the Western Church, and particularly in most seminaries. How then does a sensible, well-organized modern individual start on this way to find the meaning of silence and hopefully within it an encounter with a reality beyond the tangible, immediate world?

A Quiet Place

The first problem is to find a place where the outer confusion can be shut off, where the bright lights and the telephone cannot break in, and where even religious discussion is stilled. The purpose is not to create, or make something happen, but to allow it to happen, and *where* it takes place is an individual matter. Some people find it easy to quiet down in a church where the rule of silence is observed. For others it may be in one's own room, or in a garden or near the water, or on a mountain top. I even find that one excellent place for me is riding in a car with my wife, who does not talk while she is driving; nothing can interrupt and I become still very quickly.

There is mana in certain places that can draw a person to silence,* for instance in a room which has known the silence and listening of many people. This was the kind of power that Jacob felt when he awoke from dreaming of the ladder to heaven and cried out, "Truly, Yahweh is in this place and I never knew it!" Then he was afraid and said, "How awe-inspiring this place is! This is nothing less than a house of God; this is the gate of heaven!" And he made a sacred monument of the stone on which he had lain and poured oil on top of it, and he named the place Bethel (Genesis 28:10-19). We in the Western tradition are often reluctant to admit that there is reality behind an experience like this.

Such experiences have been known among many peoples. In our own country the Sioux sent their young men alone to a mountain where many others had gone to await a vision. Even today Carlos Castaneda has written of being told by Don Juan to find one particular spot in front of the Indian shanty, a spot that had mana or power for him. Each of us can have a place like this, where stillness can take over and one becomes open to a reality beyond oneself. Many people find the quiet of an empty church the ideal place for recollection. Besides

---

*There are people who find themselves drawn to silence by the pageantry of formal worship or by the Hare Krishna chant. Although some people are helped to center down in ways like this, they also need a time to use the silence, and most formal worship does not provide this.

the religious art that awakens associations, the very atmosphere helps to bring one to silence. There is good reason for churches to be open twenty-four hours a day.

At certain times and perhaps especially for certain people, silence may best be found among a group who are seeking it together. As I have mentioned, my own understanding of meditation began among individuals who gathered because they wanted quiet before the chapel services began. One of the central reasons for informal prayer groups is to initiate people into the use of silence, as we shall consider later on. There is also power which inheres simply in the presence of certain individuals and gives others the inspiration to turn inward. The guru and often the minister fulfill an archetypal role which meets an inner psychic need of people, who seem to have a religious need that is often projected upon the religious person.* By reflecting upon one's relationship with such figures one can sometimes see the nature of this religious need and the reality of the spiritual world which creates that need. Through this contact people may be brought to their own still point of discovery.

In the beginning, however, most of us need a place that eliminates practically all outer sensations. It is hard enough to forget one's own body, and until a person learns how to cut consciousness off from the usual sensory barrage, one needs—figuratively at least—to shut the outer door. Wherever the place, it should be free of personal clutter, no letters to answer or papers to read or clothes to mend. Any position is right which relaxes the body's control over our thoughts and feelings. It may be quite natural for one person to assume a yoga position, or for another to stretch out on a bed or on the ground, or just to sit in a comfortable chair with eyes closed or open.

Becoming Quiet

Sometimes after every whisper of activity has ceased, the body is still too tense to let go. It communicates in jerks and twitches, even cramps. Of course, the tension may be caused simply by a hyperactive day, but even this is usually a sign of emotions and desires which we have not faced and which have dropped into the unconscious. From there they are sending up messages to the body to be vigilant and ready to act. As human beings, however, our first task is to get the

---

*This is one reason it is so upsetting to a congregation to discover that the minister has clay feet. Their representation of the archetype of spiritual leader is taken from them, and the trouble is that most people lose sight of any archetypal reality unless they have some outer picture of it. Those who do not enter the silence themselves seldom have a way of realizing that these same realities can make contact with the psyche of any individual who is open to them. Archetypes are typical patrons of mental activity which enter into the individual's psychic make-up. They point to realities beyond the individual as hearing points to sound and eyes to seeing something visible. For a further understanding see my *Myth, History and Faith* (New York: Paulist Press, 1974).

psyche alert and vigilant so that it can take direction of our actions, and to do this, the body must be taught to be still and wait. The simplest way—the one to try first—is to let go as best one can and quietly tell one part of the body after another to relax, waiting patiently. Or for those who have learned Yoga, there are other specific methods of quieting the body.

Besides this there are visual aids to settling down which may be helpful at one time or another. One can fix the eyes on a single object, perhaps on the sanctuary lamp in a church, on a distant vista in a picture or a rock in the bubbling water of a stream. At other times one may find that the only way to stop thinking and sensing is to close the eyes and focus on a black dot in the center of nothingness. Some people are able to concentrate on sound as a more or less meaningless object, one that brings up few associations, so that the sensory world dies away into stillness. At times music may be quieting to start with, but this is true only in settling down. In the silence itself music is a distraction, and the greater its impact the greater the distraction. I find music a spur to creativity, particularly in writing, but this is very different from silence.

It may seem superfluous to remind any human being that talking puts an end to silence, but this is such an effortless activity for most of us that we are hardly aware of the constant flow of words. Obviously silence cannot begin until the outer flow of talk has ceased, but something more than the mere sound of words must also die away. Words themselves can be used rhythmically to help produce silence. Practices like the Jesus prayer, the mantra in Transcendental Meditation, and the chanting of Hare Krishna are aimed at bringing the ego to a halt, rather than adding to the stream of already conscious ideas and plots and plans. Certain repetitive actions, such as knitting or whittling or even drumming, can have much the same effect. Talking, however, is something else again.

Our talking does not end with articulated words. It goes on a mile a minute inside the individual. Much of our thinking is actually an inner dialogue. Our minds are full of ideas and pictured desires and purposes that we talk and think and discourse about to ourselves. One can almost feel the tension in mouth and throat in this kind of thinking and inner talking. If one is to lay it aside, the approach must be cautious, like a policeman stepping into the intersection, first motioning traffic to slow down, and then holding up a hand that means "Stop!" This must be done without words, without adding to the disturbance when one more item of unfinished business slips in demanding to be considered.

Just as the silence seems complete, a noise or other sensation may intrude. Or an interruption may come purely from within, perhaps an idea about tomorrow's plans or a worry about a foolish remark or something one has forgotten to do. It does no good at all to get angry. This only adds to the activity that is trying to break in. With good-natured patience, one puts the cares of yesterday and tomorrow into the suspense file, much as St. Teresa told of doing. One day, trying to become still in the chapel, the saint noticed that the altar hangings were crooked. "How careless the sacristan is!" she said to herself. "I must. . . . No, I am here to pray, not to tell the sacristan what to do." With a smile she quieted down again, only to hear a sharp noise on the roof where some tiles were being replaced. "That careless workman!" she thought. "I had better get out there. No mere man could do it right. . . . *No*, not now." And once more, she turned to rebuild the silence.

Out of nowhere daydreams may pop up. One may see the Little League team becoming national champions, or a new book turning out to be a best seller. We may find appetites and desires we scarcely recognize as our own. Perhaps we see ourselves handling millions of dollars, or as movie stars giving autographs, or as kings and queens. Daydreams are the partially conscious spinning out of desires and hopes in a pictorial fashion. They are an extension of our ego consciousness. Even when they reveal more than we have guessed about ourselves, they are the ordinary stuff of private fantasies which anyone can discover with a little imaginative play. These Walter Mitty "B" movies, which seldom unlock any real secrets, need to be stilled. Gently one turns them aside and watches them disappear.

This kind of silence cannot be hurried or forced; it does not come through effort. Instead, it must be allowed to happen. This is like eating an artichoke. It must be done a leaf at a time, down to the heart. If one tries to take it in a single bite, all he gets is a mouthful of thistles. One has to set aside time for silence and then turn toward it with composure, letting go of immediate things a little at a time in order to enter a world where dreams and also the energy for life are born.

This is the point at which something in the silence takes over and becomes active on its own. One is no longer involved just in a world of personal experiences or even private daydreams. There is contact with a flow of images of a different nature, images which have a life and power of their own. Some may find themselves powerfully moved as they act out scenes of a drama within their own psyches. The images are charged with emotion, and they have the same autonomous life as dreams and the same psychic significance.

The masters of both Yoga and Zen, as well as the Christian mystics, speak of encountering such images in the silence. In general the writers agree in referring to powerful experiences quite different from daydreams or casual encounters with fantasy. But when it comes to the value of these images and what to do with them, we find the ideas of classic Christian meditation often opposed to those of Zen and similar religious approaches.

As we shall see, there are even ways of influencing the images that are encountered, thus affecting the forces they represent, but this requires a deep understanding of the psyche. It is very difficult to deal with these basic psychic realities that we meet in the form of autonomous images. Most of us are afraid of experiencing the emotions they arouse, which underlie our human behavior, and with good reason. Yet these archetypal images and forces do not remain dormant simply because we keep out of touch with them. They go right on working, hidden from our conscious minds so that we often fail to understand them and either react negatively or become possessed by them, causing untold difficulties. The worst difficulties people get themselves into are generally the result of their failure to respond in the right way to these universal forces of the spiritual world which we meet as images in the silence.

Silence and Emotion

Out of silence disturbing emotions often come to the surface which are difficult to control. They can range from vague apprehension to terror and panic, or they may vary from bitterness and indignation to aggressive hatred and rage. Usually we attach these feelings to some object in the outer world, something we do not really need to fear or someone who deserves our compassion rather than our anger. Most of our lives are constricted by half-conscious fears of some kind that keep us from dealing adequately with the world around us. They can cause extreme reactions like becoming rigid at the thought of seeing the doctor or the fear of losing a job, or exploding with anger over some imagined slight. One person withdraws from being hurt because everything seems hopeless, while another strikes back in anger at whatever seems to be causing the hurt.

It is not easy to accept that these violent and disturbing emotions are a part of our being and not caused just by some situation in the outer world. Realizing this, however, is not the end of the difficulty. Since these feelings do arise essentially within us, it seems on the surface that we should be able to still them to the point of extinction. And once they are under control, why should we let human passions disturb our meditation at all? The idea is very attractive that we should be able to reach a state of perfect relation to God that will free us from any disruption in our emotional life.

We forget that the real task is to bring the totality of our psychic being to God and not just to repress and split off those parts of ourselves that we cannot change. If we deny our emotions, we do one of two things. We may successfully repress them and so cut ourselves off from one vital source of energy, becoming zombis, half dead. Or else we dam these emotions up to the point where they break loose on their own and use up that valuable energy, usually in the most destructive ways. Easterners deny the value of the physical world and so there is little legitimate reason for emotion.

The difficulty lies in making these reserves of psychic energy available for our best use. This is possible through meditation and the effort to grow up spiritually and emotionally. In the silence one can allow feelings to arise, disconnected from their ordinary targets in the outer world, and learn to deal with the depth of the psyche directly. Meditation requires silence, and silence opens a person to the direct impact of emotions and to knowing the autonomous images that arise along with them.

Dr. Jung discovered how overwhelming one's emotions are when they are faced nakedly and separated from objects in the outer world. He realized the necessity of learning to deal with them, and also the danger that mental illness can result from this contact with emotions and the images that lie behind them. Jung wrote of the difficult period of his own discoveries following his break with Freud:

> I was frequently so wrought up that I had to do certain yoga exercises in order to hold my emotions in check. But since it was my purpose to know what was going on within myself, I would do these exercises only until I had calmed myself enough to resume my work with the unconscious. As soon as I had the feeling that I was myself again, I abandoned this restraint upon the emotions and allowed the images and inner voices to speak afresh. The Indian, on the other hand, does yoga exercises in order to obliterate completely the multitude of pyschic contents and images.[4]

Anger and fear are not the only disturbing emotions that can appear. There is also guilt, which is related to fear and condemnation, and can even cause death by reaction to a taboo[5] or by the sense of being so morally or willfully wrong that one loses all hope. In some people depression is a similar emotion but does not have the moral overtone. These people feel hopeless and lost often because they find no meaning in either human or divine relationships. In depression like this there is an "abscess on the soul" which leaves an aching, consuming void. It seems to swallow all meaning, leaving one sure that no meaning can be found in life. Boredom can be equally devastating because this loss-of-soul feeling reveals that there is no support at all for meaning or value or love.

Sometimes a person is absorbed by an emotion which—for lack of a better word—I call psychic pain. The inner being, the psyche, feels as if it has been pommeled, often beaten almost to death. The trouble can begin with physical suffering, or frequently the death of a loved one, or simply by having no outlook on the world except a feeling like staring out one window onto a blank and meaningless wall. Finally there is the reaction of a sense-of-drive where the ego feels pushed. This is an emotional hunger for power or control that drives one to do something and to become something. Although this response is related to aggression, it does not have the hostile overtones of anger because the person is not conscious of being fearful or angry.

These responses are all emotional reactions to life that, to say the least, are difficult to sort out and confront. They are not separate from us and distinct from everything else, but are tangled together in us and support each part of us like the fibers of a piece of felt. In the silence, however, if images are allowed to appear, one by one the situations that stir up these emotions will usually turn up. Sometimes they are expressed symbolically, sometimes directly in words or pictures. Each of these emotions can then be taken off the hook that seems to attach it so firmly to some person or situation in the outer world, the hook that keeps it just out of our reach. As our feelings and our personal responses to the world are taken down, examined, and brought into relationship with the rest of our being and the Center of Meaning, we have a chance of directing our reactions. Only then can we begin to realize our full value to God, as well as to others around us.

People who have tested the use of silence in this way often speak of finding the transforming power of God. By making an effort to bring as much of themselves as they can to the encounter, they almost always find a plan for their lives. They often emphasize their realization that God's greatest desire for the individual is to find wholeness, the integration of every aspect of personality into a whole. This work of redemption and salvation goes on in the silence when one is free to allow something besides ordinary occupations and ordinary levels of being to have an effect. The net result is spiritually mature individuals who have something to give to God, as well as taking something from Him.

Sometimes people have a profound experience of God and then fail to realize its full meaning for their lives because they do not stop long enough to listen. Unless such an experience is brought into relationship with one's desires and fears and angers, it inevitably loses most of its force. An experience of God can begin to change our old feelings into new strengths—for instance, our desire for power over our children or employees, or our fear of the government or of a hostile universe, or our hostility toward our neighbors or people in the club— but only if we will bring these feelings into relationship with that experience of God. Few people find this way of integration until they try to be still.

In my years of listening to people from all walks of life, I have found most of them suffering from one failure or another in trying to control the emotions bubbling up within them. Most people, when they take their masks down, are hurting, or else they are causing hurt to others. Ian Maclaren touched the reality of people's lives when he said, "Be kind, for everyone is carrying a heavy burden." People today are looking for direction in their lives. They are lost in the mazes of their own psyches, and they are looking for some way through to hope and creative activity, to freedom from fear. This is one task of Christian spiritual direction, to lead people on this way toward a sense of fulfillment and wholeness, and a realization that there is more fulfillment to come in the life beyond death. It is difficult to do this if one has not yet tangled with one's own inner maze and learned the value of stillness.

A reminder is needed that this process of inner encounter is not always pleasant. Some people start and make real progress in learning this inner way of stillness, only to break it off. One man of whom I have been told did just this. He found a spiritual director and made great steps forward. He found the way meaningful. He disentangled his life and the director was delighted. Then the director had to be away for a time, and it was about six months before they saw each other again. When they did meet and the director wanted to know how he was doing, the man replied that he had stopped all religious practice and was not trying to follow any regime of the inner way. To the astonished "Why?" he replied, "I saw a little light and I didn't like it." The light made too many demands on him.

The light often requires us to hand over more of ourselves than we are prepared to give up. Some of us do not have enough grasp of the Christian way to realize that the Father is there with open arms and with gifts. Others, like this man, do not want to let go of their ego control of life. There are some, of course, who are unable to handle any more light and should not go this way. The spiritual director must be prepared to realize how much light another person can handle. There is a point at which one has to make a decision and if the inner way is not for me, then I need to find some other way of religious practice.

Realizing the dividends of silence is like eating. Few of us quibble about our need to keep on eating. We can even sense the dangers of starvation. In much the same way, the life of the soul in most people needs to be sustained by the regular practice of silence, day after day, month after month, year after year. One cannot go in for silence in a big way, make a pile and then retire. It would be better to settle for a more modest undertaking so that one could stay in business and keep at it. Otherwise the profits soon dry up. One loses the capacity to have a sustained relationship with the world of the Holy Spirit and with the Father. Silence, for many people, allows the soul to grow and develop in its spiritual dimension. In fact, the more one finds the reality of silence, the more significant it becomes. While this in itself is a danger, the same is true of anything else we touch which has such real value.

11
Aids in the Practice of Silence

There are some ways of coming to silence and starting on the inner journey besides the ones we have been considering. While certain of them may seem too far out for some people to try, these are suggestions that may prove helpful to one individual or another, and at least one of them is probably vital for almost everyone who seeks the inner silence. This is the use of a journal which prepares a person to slow down and helps to direct the inner processes of thought, feeling, sensation, and intuition. In a different way controlled breathing may be almost as important for many ·people because it reinforces and deepens the stillness in one's own body.

Then there are several practices of Eastern religion that may be helpful. Because we are more free to show an interest in the religious quest of other peoples, the East and West have begun to share religious understanding and learn from one another. This exchange is bringing us new understanding of the religious way. While some of the Eastern practices are almost impossible to separate from the theoretical background in which they developed, there are others which can be used along with the Christian tradition. Yoga, which has been used since ancient times in India, is now valued by many Christians. The repetition of a mantra and concentration ·on a mandala can also be used as ways of turning inward. Some people find that the use of an illogical question, which is called a *kōan* in Zen practice, puts one's analytical mind at rest and offers freedom and a new source of insight.

For some people a small group of like-minded individuals, a prayer group, opens the way into silence and beyond. For others relation with a spiritual director, which resembles the prayer group in many ways, is a necessity. Often the dream gives people a re-entry to the stillness from which it came. Meditative reading and the use of images are further aids in entering silence and drawing out the meaning that arises. These particular practices require special discussion, and in this chapter we shall consider mainly those that are aids just for getting into the silence. Let us start with the journal which is important both at the beginning and later on.

Making a Record

It is difficult for many people to quiet their minds. As soon as they begin to center down, ideas start to come up that jar them out of the silence. Perhaps one has been thinking about some problem, and in the quiet right away a new solution pops into mind. Or there is suddenly a picture of some vitally needed new project. One part of the mind tries to hold onto the problem or the good idea and get it worked through. For such people it is helpful to have a notebook at hand. If one quietly records the thought—and it may be a very valuable one— one can let it go and return to stillness. If the thought keeps on returning, one can then push it aside and say to it: You are taken care of. Stop bothering me.

Sometimes if one has been involved in a trying emotional situation, he or she may be so flooded with ideas and experiences that it seems futile to even think about settling down. One seems to be caught in a squirrel cage, running as hard as possible and getting nowhere. At times like this almost anyone will find real help in writing the feelings and thoughts down in a journal or notebook. Putting down in a list all the things that are flooding in upon one, without bothering about order or logic, puts them at a little distance and separates them from oneself. The ideas and the fears are still there, but they can be put off for the moment. Again one can speak firmly within oneself, saying to them: For right now you are taken care of. Leave me alone; I don't have to be tyrannized by you.

Simply the fact of setting down these thoughts, fears, other emotions gives them body and makes them distinct. The more concrete they become the easier it is to separate them from one's soul. The most difficult reality to deal with is the kind that appears like a grey amorphous cloud. One cannot understand it or get a picture of it. There is no way to get a handle on it. In a later section I shall suggest some methods of allowing a vague mood to be turned into images, but at this point we are considering only things that are already clear enough to identify and write down. Pushing these things out of the way only makes them worse. We can usually deal with the reality if we will look at it and bring it into the silence.

There is a great difference between avoiding a thought or emotion and laying it aside after taking the trouble to look at it. In the first instance a person is pretending that there is nothing there, and so repressing these things and later on they can rise up from the depth and harass one. The other is simply a way of marking out one's inner place of stillness and putting these calls on hold, asking them to wait until one is better prepared to take care of them.

My own experience is that it is difficult to come to silence until I have paid these aspects of myself their due. With a journal and pencil ready, I start by looking at the circumstances that have been bothering me. As I write down whatever comes to mind about them, often bubbling up helter-skelter, they begin to lose their power over me. The concerns are no less important. They will be there when I get back to regular activity, but I know by experience that I will have a fresh outlook about them because of touching a level beyond my ordinary ego life. Keeping a record that gives a before and after look is a tremendous help to me in slowing down and ceasing activity. In one way it is a symbol reminding me that I have an appointment with stillness. Later on we shall look at other ways in which a journal record is important.

Breathing

No other function of the body is as sensitive to our inner state as our breathing. The slightest excitement produces a noticeable change. If one is worried about making a plane, rapt in watching a sunset or a new puppy, in communion with a loved one, or waking out of a peaceful sleep, the breathing is quite different. The idea of controlling it sounds strange to most Christian ears. Control of breathing seems like an esoteric or Eastern practice out of step with Christian ideas.

Our "Christian" religious practice has been largely cerebral for so long that we have built up a sizeable tradition which scorns and rejects the body. We have almost lost any understanding of the relation of the body to the religious encounter. Yet our bodies actually have nearly as much effect on our personalities as the other way around, and of all its parts the breathing apparatus can probably have the most effect on a person's ability to become quiet and open to hear a voice within.

I was introduced to the idea of using controlled breathing by a man who had used it in a very practical way. The practice of deep breathing had helped this man survive the agonies of a German concentration camp. He found that breathing in this way not only steadied his will, but kept his blood enriched with oxygen and flowing so that he did not suffer so much from the cold or from sickness as most of the others in the camp. Many more of them died from mistreatment, from lack of nutrition and exposure to cold, than the Nazis killed outright in the gas ovens. My friend felt that knowing how to breathe had saved his life.

Breathing is one internal function which the conscious mind can control with comparative ease. With a little attention one can learn to use certain muscles, making the breathing more rapid or slow, more shallow or deep, quite at will. Then by taking careful note of the muscle action when awakening from peaceful sleep, one can learn to produce almost the same effect by directing it consciously. This kind of breathing comes from the diaphragm. The chest barely moves, while the impetus comes from below in a slow rhythm of the abdominal muscles. This takes practice and discipline, but it is effective in quieting both mind and body. It is one way, for instance, of finding relief from insomnia. Even if the person does not sleep, most of the physiological benefits of sleep are received if one spends the night breathing in this way, and so insomnia loses its terror.

The effect of controlled breathing is almost like communication with the less conscious parts of one's being, saying to them: Simmer down and listen; there is something beyond this turmoil. It is communication in action that often works when words merely go in one ear and out the other, not even changing the cognitive mind. In essence the effect is to turn all the elements of one's will toward stillness and waiting. The fact that so many languages use a word for "spirit" which comes from "breath" or "wind" is not by chance. There is even evidence, as suggested by Thomas Mann in *The Magic Mountain*, that problems of the spirit are often expressed directly by the body in diseases of the lungs like tuberculosis and pneumonia. The word pneumonia itself comes directly from the Greek word for spirit, or *pneuma*. Learning how to use our lungs is one way of opening our spirits to new life and stilling the turmoil of our minds and emotions.

Deep rhythmical breathing can also *result* from religious practice in which there was no thought of changing breathing habits. A friend who has been consistent in the practice of prayer for years told me of suddenly realizing that she had begun to breathe in exactly the way that is so often spoken of in Hindu circles. It happened just as she reached a new level of prayer, a level which is described in the charismatic movement as prayer in the Spirit or as being baptized in the Spirit. Researchers in brain activity have learned that this breathing pattern goes along with alpha and theta wave activity in the brain, which is characteristic of our mental state in meditation. Again, simply learning to breathe in this way will often help a person to reach this state.

In *Christian Zen*, William Johnston, who has considered so wisely the similarities of Zen to Chrisianity, suggests the value of similar breathing techniques for modern Christians.[1] One practice is to count slowly and rhythmically, "one," inhale; "two," exhale, "three," . . . and so on until a rhythm of breathing takes over. Once such a rhythm will start on its own, the practice of counting is usually dropped. Alternative methods are to allow the rhythm of the heart to establish the count, or sometimes even the ebb and flow of the waves if one is at a lake or the ocean. This kind of concentration on breathing not only quiets the body and emotions, but also helps to banish thought and reasoning for the moment. It can lead one away from the outer world to find a new point of beginning out of silence.

There is also a specific background of tradition for such a practice in Christianity. As I have mentioned, St. Ignatius spoke of rhythmical breathing while saying the Lord's Prayer or the Hail Mary.[2] He considered it one of three important methods of praying, one that can also be used with a rosary in order to join the rhythm of life with a religious symbol and meaning. In the ancient traditions of Eastern Orthodoxy there is even more extensive consideration of a similar devotional practice associated with the use of the Jesus prayer. Some of these suggestions are found in the *Philokalia*, a book of devotional instruction which comes from the thirteenth and fourteenth centuries when the Byzantine

Empire still existed and the monasteries on Mount Athos were at their height. In this work a *staret*, or master of the prayer life who collected and passed on earlier teachings, wrote:

> You know that our breathing is the inhaling and exhaling of air. The organ which serves for this is the lungs which lie round the heart, so that the air passing through them thereby envelops the heart. Thus breathing is a natural way to the heart. And so, having collected your mind within you, lead it into the channel of breathing through which air reaches the heart and, together with this inhaled air, force your mind to descend into the heart and to remain there. Accustom it, brother, not to come out of the heart too soon, for at first it feels very lonely in that inner seclusion and imprisonment.[3]

In the fourteenth century two monks who were so close that they were thought by some to have one soul between them produced a set of *Directions to Hesychasts* which developed this idea further. The following directions deal particularly with breathing:

> 19. *The natural method of entering the heart by attention through breathing, together with saying the prayer: Lord Jesus Christ, Son of God, have mercy upon me. This method contributes greatly to the concentration of thoughts*
> You know, brother, how we breathe: we breathe the air in and out. On this is based the life of the body and on this depends its warmth. So, sitting down in your cell, collect your mind, lead it into the path of the breath along which the air enters in, constrain it to enter the heart together with the inhaled air, and keep it there. Keep it there, but do not leave it silent and idle; instead give it the following prayer: "Lord, Jesus Christ, Son of God, have mercy upon me." Let this be its constant occupation, never to be abandoned. For this work, by keeping the mind free from dreaming, renders it unassailable to suggestions of the enemy and leads it to Divine desire and love. . . . Another father filled with Divine wisdom, and experienced in this sacred doing, says the following in explanation of what has been said:
>
> 20. *More about the natural method of calling on Lord Jesus Christ in conjunction with breathing*
> A man who wishes to learn this doing should know that, when we have accustomed our mind to enter within while inhaling, we shall have learnt in practice that at the moment when the mind is

about to descend within, it forthwith rejects every thought and becomes single and naked, freed from all memory but that of calling on our Lord Jesus Christ. Conversely, when it comes out and turns towards the external, it immediately becomes distracted by varied memories.[4]

Experimenting with ideas like this may be extremely valuable for someone who finds it difficult to be still and to quiet thoughts. Many people have found that some such control of breathing draws the body itself into prayer, as well as just the mind. There is ample tradition, Christian and otherwise, to support such a practice, and once one makes up one's mind to try it, then it is mostly a matter of discipline to find out whether it is beneficial or not.

The Jesus Prayer and the "Practice of the Presence of God"

The ancient Christian traditions of Hesychasm stressed the use of the Jesus prayer and an imageless sense of God's presence as well as awareness of breathing. The essential element linking these practices was the search for silence, for inward stillness. For centuries one form or another of the Jesus prayer has been used for this purpose. One form is simply to invoke the name of Jesus, using it almost as a mantra. Usually the longer form—"Lord, Jesus Christ, Son of God, have mercy on me, a sinner"—is used, and not only at times of meditation. The goal is to repeat this prayer until it can be heard within oneself at all times, until it becomes an unconscious or subliminal turning toward the Christ. Beginning in the silence, constant repetition makes this prayer the underlying theme of all one's activity.

Although such prayer was central in Eastern Christianity for centuries, hardly anyone in the West was aware of the practice, except for a few scholars, until a little manual called *The Way of a Pilgrim* was translated for Western readers in 1930.* The original manuscript, in Russian, had somehow come into the hands of an abbot on Mount Athos who copied it and had one printing made at his monastery in 1884. It was a story told by an anonymous pilgrim, an itinerant who was taught to use the Jesus prayer. His story describes the things that happened because of using this prayer, and it presents this practice in a charming and understandable way.

This little book puts the ideas of the *Philokalia* into the hands of the ordinary person, showing how they can be made part of one's devotional practice while going about life in the ordinary, secular world. Using the Jesus prayer is something nearly anyone can do. As one awakens and goes to sleep, one repeats

---

*Many people in our country first heard of the Jesus prayer in the 1950s when J. D. Salinger published his short novel *Franny and Zooey* in *The New Yorker* magazine, telling about the experiences of a Jewish brother and sister with the prayer.

this prayer; working on the job or playing, one repeats it; and in times of pleasure or of personal struggle, one keeps repeating the prayer over and over within oneself, like the beating of the heart. The hope is that not only the words but the presence and spiritual reality of Jesus will permeate every aspect of one's being. The underlying idea of this prayer is that somehow the reality of Jesus is tied to the name. Much the same understanding is found in shamanism and the belief that knowing a person's name gives other people power over that person. For this reason, in many societies each child is given a secret name so that only the child's closest acquaintances will know it and thus have access to the child's being.

Although there are reasons for criticizing the practice of this kind of prayer, most of the problems start basically with matters of individual emphasis. Many people in the West are impatient with the whole idea of Hesychastic prayer because it sometimes leads to a greater interest in quiet, in basking undisturbed in God's favor, than in reaching out to others to share the love that God has given. Sometimes there is a demand for power or personal cleansing rather than an effort to serve and to create through love. These are ways, however, in which a person expresses individual immediate needs, and the best of the Christian Fathers speak of the need for both moral and individual development.

What is more important, the method of prayer practiced in Hesychasm offers little or no approach to our human darkness. Almost any kind of spontaneous image is feared, whether arising in dreams or otherwise. A person's own imagination can lead into temptation, and so the leaders of this movement have seen no reason for such direct contact with the hidden depths of our being. The idea of integration is foreign to them; they do not grasp the idea of using the images at hand to learn how to deal with things that are dark within us, or the possibility of redeeming the parts that turn out not to be so evil. Because Hesychasm avoids so much that is a part of being human, many writers consider that this inner way lacks the concern for others that is the genius of Christ and of classical Christianity.[5]

If this kind of prayer can be used as a way of becoming quiet so that the individual is able to find a relationship with God and be reshaped by it, then this way has much to recommend it. Otherwise, using the Jesus prayer becomes an end in itself, often more like the devotional practices of Eastern religions than a truly Christian practice.

There are some similar forms of prayer found in the West, but without concentration on the name of Jesus or on any particular words. One of them which has had an influence halfway around the world was developed by a lay brother who remained a cook and servant. In *The Practice of the Presence of God* Brother Lawrence told how he tried to make the least thought or the meanest task an offering in the presence of Jesus, even to picking up a straw from the scullery floor as he went about his job of cleaning up after others.

Prayer as expressed in the life of this unsung saint of the Western Church has much the same distinctive character found in the life of the Russian pilgrim in *The Way of a Pilgrim.*

There is no finer description of this way of quiet, of realizing the presence of God, than the writing of Thomas Kelly, another Westerner who practiced this kind of prayer. Kelly died as a relatively young man, and his writings were brought together by Douglas Steere. *A Testament of Devotion* tells essentially of living on two levels at the same time, being aware of the outer world of business and people and at the same time being in touch with a deeper level and with a quiet, living presence. In it Kelly clearly suggests that this joining of awareness does not make one less adequate in dealing with outer things, but more responsive and able to act. Many years ago Frank Laubach worked out specific ways of developing this inner consciousness of God's presence; these instructions are set down in his pamphlet, *The Game with Minutes.*

There are others like Thomas Merton and Jacques Maritain who discuss a similar understanding that is very real in their own lives. It is often expressed with great depth of imagination by these writers and sometimes by poets. Something of the genius of the Jesus prayer is found in all of these approaches. But when it comes to how to do it or how one can find this way of prayer, Eastern Christianity has it all over us in the West. The Hesychast tradition is different from Western thinking, but these Fathers of the Eastern Church offer practical understanding and instruction which can be integrated with Western thought and are not really difficult for Western Christians to use.

Our understanding of the Holy Spirit or the actual presence of the Christ Spirit forms a bridge to the use of the Jesus prayer. This prayer can then become a way of entering and reinforcing our inner stillness so that this Spirit can be heard and given leeway to accomplish two things in us. First, we can allow it to work upon the images of divided parts of our own personalities, helping us to become integrated or whole. Second, we can then allow it to form a deep pool of quiet within to which we can return again and again for refreshment, renewal, regeneration.

Ways of Eastern Religion

Finding an opening to silence to begin with, however, is the biggest problem for most Westerners, and the gap in practical devotional instruction in the West is filled to some extent by teachings from the Far East.* The masters of Yoga, for one, have found a following all over the Western world. This practice

---

*The use of a mandala is similar to the idea we have mentioned of concentrating, for instance, on a sanctuary lamp. The Eastern practice, however, is more directive. The mandala is usually a symmetrical figure, circular or square in form, representing wholeness and often using the figures of gods to form the pattern.

goes back to the beginnings of Hindu religion. The essential idea is that certain exercises of the body and ways of breathing restrain the spirit and mind so that one is freed from the world and comes to a still point within, which gives one some power over oneself. Many Christians have found Yoga a real help in their practice of Christian meditation. This technique, which helps to bring the psyche together, can be readily separated from the religious theory which underlies it.

While Yoga must usually be learned through a teacher, there are several good sources of information about the practice. Jean M. Dechanet's *Yoga in Ten Lessons* gives a clear idea of the technique, while Baba Ram Dass in his book *Be Here Now* suggests more of the underlying attitude. Tapes are available of talks by Swami Satchidananda on this Eastern method of prayer which he describes as the scientific means to harmonious development of physical, mental and spiritual peace.[6] In most larger cities, of course, teachers of Yoga can be found.

In some ways Zen Buddhism is quite similar to Yoga, but the practices of Zen allow more room for individual variation and the need for instruction by a master teacher is perhaps even greater. The basic technique involves meditation in the modified lotus position so familiar in the East, along with concentration on a *kōan* or seemingly meaningless question that, in effect, brings the person's conscious mind to a halt. This and various other elements of this discipline are described by William Johnston in *Christian Zen* which is an excellent introduction to the subject. In the last few years more and more people in this country have sought instruction and become followers of Zen.

In both Yoga and Zen meditation the activity of the brain changes. Alpha and sometimes theta waves are produced, and in both of these states the capacity of the mind changes. As certain psychics in Russia and experimenters in our own country have discovered, psychic gifts often depend upon a state of relaxation like this.[7] The most gifted psychics often have to relax to the point where silence begins to take over before they can tune in on these gifts.

These Eastern forms of meditation appear to have a very similar effect, bringing a person to a deeper level of brain functioning and perhaps of psychic functioning as well.* Capacities often develop which are beyond our ordinary sensory functioning. A person may become open to telepathy and so know what is going on in other peoples' minds, or to precognition (seeing into the future, or in postcognition into the past), to clairvoyance (seeing events going on at a distance), or to psychokinesis (one's thoughts have some kind of direct effect upon physical objects). These capacities are often found among Hindu gurus and Zen masters. They appear to be simply one of the results of continued meditation. There is danger, of course, if a person enters meditation just to find these capacities. They can do just as much harm when used for personal power as the good

---

*Some authorities believe that during meditation the right side of the brain, which is ordinarily used only in a limited way, is tapped and put to use.

they achieve when used for self-development.

Transcendental Meditation offers to help its followers find the same alpha wave state in just a few lessons instead of the many years it usually takes to become proficient in either Yoga or Zen. In general the initiate is taught a certain position and practice of meditation, is given a mantra—a set of words or syllables that are peculiar to the individual—to recite, and then is taught how the mantra brings one into tune with the cosmic rhythm of the universe and how, by reciting it, one comes to share in the recreative source of cosmic energy. The initiate learns to sit quietly for twenty minutes morning and evening, breathing regularly and reciting the mantra, and in a relatively short time is ready to do it individually.

There are remarkable psychological effects from this practice. Alpha waves are apparently induced in the brain. A person's alertness and perceptual ability may increase. Physical reactions like blood pressure and heart rate that are directly affected by the psyche may become slower or steadier. Many people have found helpful effects like these. In addition, although TM is closely related to its founder, Maharishi Mahesh Yogi, it does not require followers to subscribe to any belief beyond the most general theoretical framework. Instead the movement apparently relies on the fact that its teachings work. There are classes on many college campuses and in cities all over the country.

Beyond these general facts, however, the way of Transcendental Meditation is a closely held secret. The only way of learning the practice is to be taught it by someone who has been initiated in the same way. There is little hint of what kind of initiation to expect. Since a set fee is charged, and this is the only way that one can acquire a mantra and learn how to use it, these facts have caused some skepticism on the part of outsiders.

Scientific and Other Experiments with Meditation

In recent years science has discovered a whole new understanding of the way our bodies and minds relate to each other. It has been found that meditation has profound and largely positive effects upon both brain and body, as TM so often claims in its sales campaign. In all kinds of psychic research there is also a growing interest in the altered states of consciousness that result from meditative practices. At the same time the traditional distinction between voluntary and involuntary bodily functions has been overturned, and it is now realized that through the process of biofeedback the average person can learn to control body functions that at one time were considered beyond conscious direction. Among other things, one can learn to shift brain waves and even produce the alpha rhythm that is characteristic of the meditational state.

Charles Panati introduces his superb survey of the field in the book, *Supersenses*, by suggesting that the fifties will become known as the computer age, the sixties as the space age, and the seventies as the age of psychic discovery. Only now it is not religious groups that are primarily interested in meditational techniques, but laboratory researchers, medical men, and even business men.

In the *Harvard Business Review* for July-August 1974, an article called "Your Innate Asset for Combating Stress" advocates offering a demystified version of TM as an alternative to the ordinary coffee break. The author is Herbert Benson, a professor in the Harvard Medical School. He suggests that companies adopt a twice-a-day "relaxation response" break* as a means of counteracting the flight-fight patterns that are such common reactions to the day-to-day stress in modern business. Dr. Benson offers his idea as a way of increasing creativity and helping individuals resist the many diseases that result from these ordinary physical reactions to stress.

The advocates of biofeedback suggest the somewhat simpler technique of learning through a monitoring device to influence or control certain bodily processes and reactions at will. The process of altering one's brain waves or his blood pressure is somewhat like watching the scales to control one's weight. The ease of learning in a few sessions to produce, say, alpha waves in the brain is often compared with Zen or Yoga which can offer similar results but only after years of practice, or with TM which takes several months for full proficiency. As the leading researcher in biofeedback, Barbara Brown, points out in *New Mind, New Body*, we do not understand how the process operates. Of course, we do not know much about the true significance of brain waves either, and it is probably a good idea to remember that triggering a certain brain wave will not necessarily provide the same effects as meditation.

Various studies have been made of the effect on consciousness of certain experimental practices similar to meditation. These studies of how changes in perception are produced are most interesting. For instance, a fixed image is played upon the retina of the eye by mounting tiny projectors on contact lenses which move with the eyes; very soon the image disappears and alpha waves appear in the brain. Another way to produce much the same effect is by sense deprivation which consists of shutting out all sight and sound and, as far as possible, all tactile sense. After a period of "blankness" the tell-tale alpha waves and their images often begin to appear, apparently unrelated to the external world, thus producing a state similar to dreaming.

Many of the modern students of consciousness have come to believe that the comfortably stable world of consciousness is really something one makes up to shield oneself from the constant bombardment of outer sensation and inner imagination. As Henri Bergson once suggested, the main function of our sense

---

*Dr. Benson proposes the use of twenty-minute periods, on the ground that such methods of relaxation have practically no negative side effects when they are practiced in short stretches. He cautions about the dangers of disorientation and withdrawal from reality which can result from extending the periods for too long a time, say over a matter of hours. He has recently published a full-length book on this technique, *The Relaxation Response*.

organs and brain and nervous system does not seem to be involved so much in producing perceptions, as in restricting them.* The purpose seems to be to select those particular perceptions that promise to be of practical use at the moment.

Breaking out of this world of outer space and time, one begins to appreciate how great a mass of other sensations can get through. At the same time imagination begins to function in a new way and one also is open to a vast new group of inner images. The experiments which support this view of consciousness are described by Robert Ornstein in the second section of *On the Psychology of Meditation*, and also in his larger work, *The Psychology of Consciousness*.

Such altered states of consciousness are usually marked by alpha waves in the brain, a sense of relaxation, and by the inner awareness of images which do not seem to come from ordinary waking consciousness. But that is not all. It is in this state that the psychic phenomena of extrasensory perception and psychokinesis appear. Until just a few years ago the idea of investigating these phenomena scientifically was almost unthinkable. They appeared to lie outside the magic circle that bounded "reality," but they are now being studied in many of the major hospitals and universities throughout the country.

Researchers have demonstrated that people have the capacity to receive information from other minds without ordinary communication (telepathy), and to be in touch with both the future and the past (pre- and postcognition). Other students are working on psychokinesis (the capacity to influence objects by mind power alone) and psychic healing. Each of these capacities has been verified by research using careful scientific controls. Almost overnight we are being forced to realize that we have the ability to receive knowledge which does not come through ordinary perception and consciousness, and that the way this happens most often is in a relaxed condition of mind and body, either in the natural state of dreaming or in a meditational state.

The implications for religion are breathtaking. If our ability to perceive extends beyond the ordinary methods limited by space and time (and this much is

---

*The English philosopher C. D. Broad commented that "we should do well to consider much more seriously than we have hitherto been inclined to do the type of theory which Bergson put forward in connection with memory and sense perception. The suggestion is that the function of the brain and nervous system and sense organs is in the main *eliminative* and not productive. Each person is at each moment capable of remembering all that has ever happened to him and of perceiving everything that is happening everywhere in the universe. The function of the brain and nervous system is to protect us from being overwhelmed and confused by this mass of largely useless and irrelevant knowledge, by shutting out most of what we should otherwise perceive or remember at any moment, and leaving only that very small and special selection which is likely to be practically useful." Quoted by Aldous Huxley in *Doors of Perception*. Huxley goes on to suggest that the brain and central nervous system are like a reducing valve, filtering out the information which is not related to practical living.[8]

demonstrated in the laboratories), then the possibility that we are able to per-ceive religious objects or contents is no longer beyond belief. Of course these studies are not very often made by theologians, who usually leave one with a bewildered feeling of having said something juvenile and unenlightened if one expresses an interest in these phenomena. The Church doubts and fears these ex-periences that are associated with the religious ideas and practices of the past. Instead, it has been left to a troubled and enquiring secular community, par-ticularly to medical men and scientists, to investigate them and to discover that reason does not replace the need for meditation but, if anything, increases it.

There are various techniques for opening up the tight capsule of space and time. Zen and Yoga, Transcendental Meditation, paying attention to dreams, the use of biofeedback—all can be helpful for some people in reaching stillness and opening themselves to new experiences within. What is important is to real-ize that there is a goal beyond this stillness, beyond the peace and relaxation or beyond the interest in extrasensory perception. There is a real danger in much of Eastern thought and in our own scientific probing into the mind, but it is not because there is something dark and evil lurking in either of them.

The danger lies in the fact that Eastern ways of prayer and scientific inter-est in altered states of consciousness do not go far enough. The road stops once the relaxation, the peace or detachment or extrasensory perception is achieved, and then one is left to wander. Even as thorough a book as Charles Panati's *Supersenses* offers no hint that there might be something more. It is all too easy today to overlook the Christian hypothesis that there is an object (God or cre-ative principle) to be sought and found which is infinitely more important than the expanded human state. From a Christian point of view—the view of clas-sical, traditional Christianity—a person who stops with the peace and quiet is then in real danger of losing the way because such a state is only the *first step* on the journey of meditation.

The way of avoiding this danger is suggested by the practice of one Trap-pist monastery in this country, where it was found that novices needed help in learning to become quiet. Training in Transcendental Meditation was chosen to offer them this help. TM is not used, however, to replace Biblical meditation or any of the ordinary services, but in addition to them. The novice learns that it is used simply because people raised in our secular culture find it difficult to leave the tension and stresses behind. Any of the techniques that are available can be used in this way so that Christian meditation can then become effective to open one to the influence of Love (or God).

The Purposes of Aids to Silence

Each of the ways toward silence that we have considered is an external device, a method meant to help the individual find a way to seek an individual experience of God through silence. Any of these practices can be helpful so long as one is fairly sure that this is a method that fills one's own personal need, and then follows it consistently and sincerely toward the goal of being silent. Christianity suggests there is more to life than silence and detachment and if this is clear to us, we can make use of these practices without becoming lost.

It is crucial, however, to know the goal well enough to distinguish it from the means. In our earlier discussion of the climate of Christian meditation, I have sketched out ways of knowing the goal that we seek. When we are clear enough about our own point of view we can find help in the methods of Eastern Christianity or in the ways of the Far East, perhaps by consulting the *I Ching* or through mandala contemplation, or even in the ways of shamanism or Islam. If we are clear about where we stand and the direction we must take, such methods may be useful in order to follow our own way to the end.

Those who lack such a goal and standpoint may have some reason to fear other ways like those of Zen or Yoga. They have no way to relate these unusual methods except as a kind of method for finding instant religious satisfaction. They often treat the religious ways of other peoples like a fad, more like vitamins and organic foods or acupuncture than a way of approaching God. Perhaps they expect that someday these experiences will be regulated in the same way that we test vitamins today.

The practices we have touched on, however superficially, make one insight clear.' Prayer is more than words, meditation far more than a rational or cognitive process. It involves the whole person, the entire being—breathing, moving, acting, rising up and lying down, entire days and nights. Only as the whole person is turned toward the meditative process does the experience of God in Jesus Christ become a reality. This is the same deep experience it was for Origen or Gregory of Nyssa. This reality can be as full for us today, as great and complete as it was for those men in the third and fourth centuries.

PART FOUR

The Use of Images
in
Meditation

12

Silence, Mysticism and Religious Experience

It's easy to suggest that we Westerners need to adjust our sights on the world and learn to deal with it better. The hard part comes in stopping our ordinary world so that we can get off of it, look back at our preconceptions, and find a new outlook. To most people the idea of stopping the world seems almost ludicrous. There is even a sad and funny song called "Stop the World—I Want to Get Off" that makes people laugh. Yet this is just what silence can do for us. Silence unbinds a person from ordinary perceptions and attitudes and offers a fresh look at life and reality. By giving us in the West a new perspective on the ideas we have inherited, it can bring us a vision of the world and humanity as more than just materialistic.

Silence can open a door on a new dimension of reality. It is like finding a trap door or a secret passage, giving a way out of our usual, ego-dominated existence. Where there seemed to be only an endless, gray alley of concrete and mortar, or a prison of velvet walls with scarcely air to breathe, in silence suddenly we find ourselves in open country.* It may be a rolling and verdant land or a frightening world of great chasms and strange creatures. In either case we step into a realm of being quite different from the one we respond to daily in the outer physical world.

What I am describing is much like the darkness in a theatre just before the curtain goes up. As the lights dim, we turn from our companions to wait expectantly. We are not waiting for darkness or semiconsciousness but for the activity on stage, tragic or comic, and whatever it awakens in us. As I shall show later, I believe that this has a similarity to the way final meaning is provided in our lives. In silence we often find such meaning on the stage of our psyche (or soul) with its scenes and action.

Sleep often has somewhat the same effect. Sleep can separate us from the

---

*Metaphorically, of course, for the inner scene often resembles our own lives very closely and yet is very different.

world of space and time in two different ways. Sleep can provide a dreamless rest which releases tension and recharges life and this in itself is a tremendous gift, bringing courage and energy to start on a new day. Then there is the sleep which leads one into dreaming and so into an existence which is experienced as outside of space and time.

Here the rules of our ordinary existence do not apply. The dreamer can be two different people at the same time, expanding or contracting time to fit the circumstances of the dream, merging one place into another or changing locations as if space were no problem. Logic and rationality no longer apply. And yet there is so much meaning in this strange movement of images that it can even show us the very meaning of our lives. In the fourth century the great saint and mystic, Gregory of Nyssa, recognized that there was a close relation between the art of Christian meditation and the experience of dreaming in sleep.[1]

In sleep one automatically goes from outer physical sensations to a peaceful state. What happens in sleep seems so easy and natural that the person who has trouble sleeping is even considered sick. Yet one can also go from the outer physical world to the peaceful, quiet state while awake, by consciously deciding to enter into it in meditation. There are much the same physiological effects in both sleep and the meditative state, as well as almost the same sense of a person's losing life in order to gain it. Then there is the flood of images that well up in the same way in the psyche whenever one becomes completely still, whether in sleep or through a conscious, directed movement into the inner realm in meditation. Mystics of every tradition speak of the images that flood in upon one during silence, and in sleep much the same thing happens at least four to seven times a night in dreams.

Every one of us dreams at least that often, but we are so accustomed to sleep that few of us pay enough attention to realize what a strange new land we encounter in dreams. It is easy to ignore these natural productions of the psyche. Whether a person is willing to look at them at all depends upon whether one can see any meaning in them or not. In meditation one also has a choice—to pay attention to the images that arise within and see where they lead, or to dismiss them as meaningless, or as a dangerous distraction, and then return to utter and undisturbed stillness. In the latter case, one steps into a state which no words or images seem to describe.

Are the images of sleep and meditation a snare and a delusion, or do they lead us further and further into meaning? This is one basic question which faces the individual who learns to be silent, and the answer will determine the kind of religious practice that person takes up and follows. It is my suggestion that few things are much more important for the development of our religious life—no matter how extraordinary it becomes—than knowing the images that arise within us and meditating upon them. This understanding has been almost forgotten by most religious groups, both Eastern and Christian. Before we go on to consider how images are actually used in meditation, we need to see how it is possible for two such different points of view as the Eastern and the earlier Christian traditions to exist side by side. This means distinguishing and clarifying some of our ideas about psychology, philosophy and theology, first of all in relation to mysticism.

Understanding Mysticism

Ask ten different people to define the word mysticism and you will probably get ten different answers, some of them none too friendly. There is so much hazy thinking and misunderstanding about the idea of mystical experience that I have purposely avoided the subject as long as possible. Other writers take the same tack as William Johnston does in his excellent study, *The Still Point*, in which he compares Zen with Christian devotional practice. Most thinkers find it wise to lay some groundwork before tackling the problem of mysticism.

Whatever else the word means, the experiences of mysticism are supposed to be different from those of sense experience and to be able to take a person beyond the world of space and time. One of the problems with understanding mysticism is simply the fact that this is too big a field for one word to cover. "Mysticism" conveys all kinds of meanings to various people, and too often a term that carries too much meaning ends up meaning little or nothing at all. The Greeks, for instance, had twelve different words to describe other ways of encountering reality besides sense experience,[2] while we have only this one overworked, moth-eaten term that arouses more controversy than understanding.

It is hard to be specific about something when one lacks words to describe it. Usually such a poverty of vocabulary reflects poverty of experience and lack of discrimination. In this case it reveals the failure of Western thinking for several centuries to provide a spiritual or intellectual climate congenial to this kind of experience. In recent years most Western philosophers and psychologists have maintained that mysticism is only a subjective experience, a layer a person adds to our sandwich of sense experience which is all concocted from the world of space and time. This view was first stated with sophistication by Immanuel Kant, and it was later assumed by all positivism and most existentialism. Many psychologists have even come to view mysticism as a sign of mental imbalance and disorientation.

A great many religious writers have followed the same thinking. I remember at Cincinnati in 1941 how the School of Applied Religion reacted to Joseph Fletcher's* remark that mysticism is something that begins in mist and

---

*Of *Situation Ethics* fame.

ends in schism. For many Christians mysticism is either illusion or delusion, and
that is that. It is a flight from reality and, even worse, a flight from Christian
morality and responsibility. This is the view of Protestant theologians like Bultmann, Barth, Bishop Robinson, and the early James Pike. From the Catholic
point of view the very careful theologian Karl Rahner writes in his book *Visions
and Prophecies* that there is little place for mystical experience in modern
scholastic theology, and there is little knowledge of what to do with it. Few of
the schools training people to minister to our Western world make any real effort to present a different point of view.

Yet those who call themselves mystics speak of finding the goal and fulfillment of the religious quest in their experiences. They suggest that the meaning
of religion lies in the reality which they encounter through this inner realm and,
in particular, that the inspiration and power of Christianity come from this reality. It is just such experiences, they find, which open us to the source of love
(God) and bring us its creative and heroic energies.

What are the reasons for this almost total disagreement about the value
and reality of mysticism? There is not much question about the main reason.
The idea that one has no access to any realm of experience besides the material
and rational leaves the mystic with no place for inner experience to come from.
If this be so, the mystic must be suffering from delusion, or something worse.
This idea itself is based upon *faith*—in the sense of believing something one has
no evidence for—a faith that all knowledge ultimately comes from reason and
sense experience. As I have shown in my book, *Encounter with God*, there is no
good reason to maintain such a scientific faith when scientists like Oppenheimer
and Heisenberg have abandoned it.

Baron Friedrich von Hügel has shown how superficial most criticisms of
mysticism are within such a framework.[3] One cannot expect to understand the
mystical experience (or meditation) by approaching it with the naïve philosophical outlook so common in Western religion since the Enlightment. Baron
von Hügel's magnificent study, *The Mystical Element of Religion*, opens up a
far more mature view of the subject. While it is not exactly light reading, this
work can bring the discussion of mysticism to an entirely different level. The
student who will take the time and effort to read it will find that it provides the
philosophical base which is indispensable to any serious study of religious experience in our time.

The understanding of the psychologist also depends upon the philosophical
point of view, even when such a view is not acknowledged. While this makes it
easy for many psychologists to be contemptuous of religious experience, some of
the most important modern studies indicate that people do have experiences
from outside the space-time world and that these do not represent regression or
mental deterioration. Instead these studies suggest that some such religious expe-

rience is probably needed for the fullest development of personality.*

Even if the validity of religious experience were admitted by everyone, however, there are still other things to cause disagreement about these experiences. In the first place, religious experiences are not as alike as peas in a pod. There are at least three main kinds: sacramental experiences, those usually called contemplative experiences, and ones arising through meditative use of images. These are all elements of mysticism which I shall discuss. At the moment what is important is that they are very different experiences; each has its own value, and each needs the support and balance of the others. Yet they also merge with one another so that it is often hard to see how they differ.

At the same time, human beings are not all alike. Different types of individuals can usually find communication with the Other more easily through one or another of these religious experiences. One may have to experiment to find which way is suited to one's own personality type. But it is difficult for us to look at these experiences carefully and realize that they are basically different ways of approaching the same reality.

This makes it difficult to understand what those who have lived the mystical life are talking about. If one is to discover their meaning, it is necessary to enter the laboratory of one's own experience, and this usually involves a "dark night of the soul" or a sense of depression, dryness and lostness which few people seek unless they are impelled to. Therefore many theologians who write about these things are like geologists who have never been in the field. Since they have had no taste of their own inner experience, seeking out their opinion is about like consulting a wine expert who is a teetotaler or a cheese fancier who has tasted only one kind.

Another sort of problem has arisen within mysticism. Among people who did have experiences, a theory of mysticism and prayer developed which presumes that religious experiences are arranged in hierarchies or levels, and that there is a truly sophisticated encounter which has nothing to do with images, while other kinds of experiences are more primitive. The growth of rationalism reinforced this conclusion. Since imagination is essentially irrational, its use came to be feared and experiences involving images were avoided. In the end, one

---

*Henri Bergson's *The Two Sources of Morality and Religion*, William James' *The Varieties of Religious Experience*, as well as the twenty volumes of C. G. Jung's studies and the work of Dr. Roberto Assagioli in *Psychosynthesis*, are all based on this understanding. One of the best recent studies of religious experience and human growth is found in the 800-page work edited by Merton Strommen, *Research on Religious Development*. "Religion and Psychological Health" by Russell Becker,⁴ which is one of several excellent and relevant articles, draws the conclusion that *there is simply no objective study to support the theory that religious experience is connected with questionable mental health*. To maintain this connection is to be influenced by pure prejudice.

kind of mysticism was seen as the only true religious experience, the only real mystical state. Merging into the "infinite" at least makes rational sense. The term *mysticism* came to mean only the "final" stage of development, while the value of other experiences was denied. Later on I shall have more to say about this thinking and the difficulties it has caused.

Obviously there are not many people who have imageless experiences of such force, and so mysticism became reserved only for the select few. The idea that inner images, which can appear spontaneously to any of us, might lead beyond one's personal psyche was never considered. Therefore, mysticism was no longer seen as something which ordinary people might hope to experience. Unless one was ready to make a full-time project of the religious life it was considered impossible to get very far.

Then since, for some, the value of images was never quite lost, a rigid and enforced kind of image prayer developed in many religious communities. It was taught by authoritarian methods so that many people felt caught in a forced and mechanical practice which often seemed superstitious. This kind of prayer was already thoroughly misunderstood by the secular world and now it became associated with people's experience of being forced upon the religious way, which does not work very well for any of us. Thus when the time was right, it was easy to throw the baby out with the bath water. The use of images was discarded almost wholesale, without reflecting that what was needed was to get rid of the regimentation without getting rid of the practices it had been trying to enforce.

It is hard to lay aside a prejudice like this, particularly if one was damaged by a practice that became meaningless to one. The use of images in prayer, however, has a rich and powerful history, as psychologists have discovered. My introduction to this kind of prayer came through the studies and practices of C. G. Jung, who discovered that images and imagination have a healing effect on a person. Although this idea has been rejected and forgotten by the Church, my hope is that readers whose background has alienated them from this tradition will wrestle with their prejudices and try to hear what is written in the pages that follow.

As a result of these various problems, Western Christians came to emphasize just one aspect of religious experience, which was called mysticism, or else none at all. The trouble with putting one part of anything into the driver's seat to run the whole show is that the experiences tend to become distorted or even misrepresented. The essence of evil seems to consist in making a part of something appear as the whole thing, and so evil is a valuing of a part more than of the whole. Religious experience is no exception to this. When one element of religious experience is viewed as the whole of one's experience of God, in the end that experience often goes sour or it can become actually evil and destructive. It is no wonder that mysticism has come to be viewed so dubiously today.

From this point on I shall use the word *mysticism* very little, because it has so many negative connotations and it covers so many different experiences that it can hardly be used without causing confusion. I shall speak instead of *religious experience*, which is not quite so charged with negative overtones. Since my interest is primarily in practice rather than theory, I shall consider these experiences only in enough detail to be clear about the practices I am trying to present. A certain amount of theory, of course, is unavoidable in order to be sure that you and I are thinking about approximately the same thing. With this background let me go over the territory once again from a different perspective even at the risk of some repetition.

Three Varieties of Religious Experience

A person's religious experiences can probably be understood best in terms of the way that person perceives the divine, and allows it to work in his/her life. As I have suggested, there are three main kinds of these experiences—the sacramental, the contemplative, and those giving an inner perception of the divine in images.[5] The most common and widespread of these experiences are the sacramental ones in which the divine comes into focus directly through some element of the outer, physical world. In the Mass or Communion, for instance, a person has the outer experience of receiving the bread and wine, and at the same time may experience receiving Christ inwardly. Outside of the Christian tradition there are various experiences of the sacramental that may use some natural element like the Black Stone of Mecca, or a statue or sacred building like the temple of Diana in Ephesus, or some activity such as the Hopi snake dance or Navajo sandpainting. Originally people believed that the divine power seemed to flow from the object or act itself, and the less conscious the individual or group, the less distinction is made between the inner and outer realities. Nearly every religion known to man has used this approach in some form that brings the sacred or the holy into intimate relationship with the material realm and the human realm, blending places and times, objects and attitudes with the divine. So long as people remain largely within the collective framework, accepting the ideas and understanding of the culture as final and all-inclusive, the outer symbols of that group remain alive and carry divine power, so that people are not forced to seek other ways of finding that power.

This kind of experience makes for a very conservative religion, one that is stable and very difficult to change. The mores of such a group are absolutely accepted, and the religious institution is inflexible. Its laws and rituals are to be observed without question. This is the kind of stability and religious attitude found in the priestly religion of the Old Testament and expressed with great feeling in Psalm 119.

It is easy to look down on the original forms of sacramental experience as primitive, and consider it quite unconscious to project the inner, spiritual reality upon outer things. Of course, in ancient times people saw nymphs in streams and spirits in trees, and later the alchemists projected their growth process into the retorts and crucibles with which they worked. Yet this is one way in which all people find some of their meaning. The ancient Greeks used their projections to develop as fine a philosophical relation with the world as we have known. The medieval alchemists set down luminous ideas about psychological and spiritual growth in those strange writings which only make sense when we understand that their "philosopher's stone" was a spiritual reality and goal, not a physical one. The ancient Hebrews used their own sacramental experiences to bring an understanding of divine order into human moral life and thinking.

The great Christian sacraments, beginning with baptism, have offered a further step of breaking off from one's old life and entering into a new relation with God. For Catholics and also many liturgical Protestants the Communion or Eucharist is the continuing place of renewal where the divine touches humanity. The bread and wine become the body and blood of Christ; in partaking of them one actually shares the life of the Risen Christ. Within this tradition there are other sacramental experiences—confession and absolution, saying the rosary, the stations of the cross, the forty hours—which are alive and have power to open people up to the divine. And as Jung has shown, the dogmatic structure of the Church meets nearly all the psychological needs of those who follow its way.[6]

For the average Protestant the Bible itself has some of the same sacramental power. While most nonliturgical Protestants have shied away from the obviously sacramental, the Bible is literally seen as the congealed thought of God, and if this is accepted, one may then be in touch with God Himself. Total and absolute authority are often given to the words and ideas of the Bible, and thus authority is sometimes projected upon the one who preaches them, which sometimes causes explosive situations. In these churches there is an absence of sacramental action and this gap is only partly filled by services of prayer and great music.

Human beings do not outgrow their need to use sacramental experience. This should be clear to anyone who has ever fallen in love and known the power of projection. Suddenly to one in love another person appears luminous and carries all value and meaning. Poetry often flows, even from those who never before wrote poetry. As Plato originally pointed out, physical love can lead to an appreciation of the beauty of spirit of another human being, and then on to worship of God Himself. Thus falling in love can in a sense be a sacramental experience of the divine.

Equally, anyone who has nursed a full-blown hatred or anger can understand how well projection works. Another person seems to become the very devil. One need not even know the person to feel the revulsion. I recall one friend, the owner of a jewelry shop, who said that certain people she did not even know made her angry just by the way they walked in and approached the counter. Massacres and wars, lynchings and pogroms are only the ultimate result of this spirit. When its energy is channeled and directed against a whole group, then this group of people, whether they are black or white, German or Jewish, European or Oriental, become carriers of everything evil. People who project this evil onto others believe that the worst that can be done to them is fully justified, because the purpose of harming them is only to eliminate evil in the world.

Even so, projection is an important function of the human psyche. So long as we do not think that what we are projecting is necessarily real in the outer world, this is one way of coming into contact with the forces that work from within, so that we can tap some of their power and even begin to learn about these forces. This is the principle on which projective tests in clinical psychology are based. Both the ambiguous picture in the Thematic Apperception test and the ink blot of the Rorschach test are used to bring out the inner attitudes and feelings of the individual, even attitudes and feelings that are not realized. Religious symbols that have been used over the ages have the same power and effect.

Even the most conscious people find that some of their meaning and power comes to them through projection. There is great value in these religious experiences, in which spiritual reality is projected upon seemingly inanimate matter. By providing the religious community with its rituals, they offer continuity and stability to religious life. The group itself is held together and given energy by their experiences in common. Psychologically a person is safer in this experience than in many of the others because it is a religious experience that is brought down to a power level that humans can manage easily. Yet there are some real dangers when sacramental experience is seen as the only valid kind of religious expression. In *The Memoirs and Confessions of a Justified Sinner*, the Scotch writer James Hogg turned one possibility into a delightful satire. His single-minded hero found himself among the elect of God and proceeded to act as God's instrument to eliminate the nonelect by murder, beginning with his step-mother. We shall come back to this problem after considering the other experiences.

Union with the Imageless State

The second kind of religious experience is at the opposite pole from the one I have been discussing. This is an experience of union with the divine in which no outside elements are involved. Physical matter, symbols, ritual are all forgotten, and the only things that matter are the person and the immediate perception of the divine. There is also quite a difference in the origins of this approach to God. Instead of tracing back to the beginnings of religion, or even of Christianity, the search for this experience in the Western world began in the third century on the eastern fringes of the Christian world, along with the new doctrines of Neo-Platonism.

It began with the philosopher Plotinus and whatever impelled him to seek an immediate merging of himself into God. Perhaps Plotinus had had some early contact with Christian belief.* Whatever the reason, his ideas were stated quite well, and they soon flowed into Orthodox thinking and practice through Evagrius and the early Hesychasts. Later the followers of Plotinus became deeply involved in pagan speculations, and about the year 500 A.D. their influence was strongly felt in the Christian writings of "Dionysius the Areopagite." Although the source of these documents never became known, their ideas were incredibly influential. Beginning with Gregory the Great, through various medieval writers they were handed down to leaders like St. John of the Cross and St. Teresa, and finally with Adolphe Tanquerey they left their mark on much of the devotional practice of modern Christianity.

There is good reason for this historical note. Much that is thought to be central to Christian devotional practice has little or nothing to do with the New Testament or the practice of the early Fathers and Doctors of the Church. There is an element in today's practice of meditation that comes from the thinking of Plotinus. And this is not only different from historical Christianity but, as we shall see later on, may actually be opposed to the early Christian thinking and experience.

This kind of union with God is an experience of losing one's ego, of dissolving into the very marrow of the universe. It gives a sense of identity, oneness, ecstasy and bliss. Since it comes like a thunderbolt, and all the human soul can do is receive it as a pure gift; it is marked by passivity, openness and waiting. This usually is achieved only as the result of strenuous intellectual discipline. The experience is that of the pure and almost inexpressible joy of being one with the center of all things, of having found one's end and meaning and goal, and this is then seen as the goal of the religious undertaking.

In this understanding, God is seen as so far above and so far removed from humanity, that no words or images or concepts can begin to express the experience. Thus, according to this point of view, when a person has achieved this state of contemplation, the ultimate—where images and descriptions and material forms themselves are of no further use—has been reached. The logical result is withdrawal into a state of quietism. Of course, the great Christian proponents of this view, like St. John of the Cross and St. Teresa, do not follow it to any such logical conclusion. Instead they blend it with ordinary popular devotion, such as receiving the sacrament and saying one's offices and also with charitable action and love for others.

In some traditions, however, this kind of meditation aims at detachment from all emotion as well as from any images. The will and desires are extin-

---

*Plotinus kept his early life a dark secret, and apparently not even his followers knew where he was born or what had happened to him before he came to Alexandria to study and then to teach.

guished and one is said to merge unconsciously with the quiet rhythm at the core of all "being." From this point of view there is neither good nor evil, for if evil is recognized at all, it is most often seen merely as the absence of perfection or the result of still being caught in the illusion of emotion and of physical reality. Thus, everything moves unalterably toward its goal in the heart of the universe, and all actions and beings are moving in that direction whether they know it or not. Therefore, all one can do is try consciously to yield to the inevitable process and become part of it in meditative experience. One can further it only by ceasing to resist and accepting whatever comes in quiet and silence, thus entering into the process itself. This is the way to nirvana, satori, union.[7]

From this point of view the important thing is to be cut off from any positive or negative tie to what is considered the phenomenal world of illusion, both physical and psychic. The person can begin the task of separation, then must learn, usually through a guru (or teacher), to let go of all will and all desire. Gradually this way of self-perfection and self-attainment is realized, and with its completion the ego, the sense of personal identity, dissolves. Ultimately, according to those who practice this, as one comes to the central peace at the heart of all things, one finds the meaning of life.

It is not hard to see how this idea took hold in India where human life seems to have been dominated by misery almost from the start. Detachment is probably the only attitude sensitive people can take to live alongside the hunger and poverty and sickness that are commonplace even today among the masses in India.* Western Europe in the seventh century was not much better. The ideas of the followers of Plotinus made sense in that time when people saw little hope of eliminating evil which often made human life nearly unbearable. Sensible people simply got off the world and escaped.

The great mystic saints of the Middle Ages also lived with misery and dangers that are hard for us to believe. Men and women were stalked by plague and famine and marauding hordes, and they forgot the idea of a God who came to heal and restore this life. Instead they looked for a God who would mercifully lift them out of the world into a bliss that would make up for all the misery. They turned to ascetic communities and rejected bodily life and the flesh in order to arrive at this experience of another world. Even though the great saints of this time balanced their other-worldliness by emphasizing charity and reaching out to people in the world, they were convinced that the main goal of the human soul was a blissful union with God. The point of existing was to reach a relationship with God in which nothing of this world interfered. They tried to reach a state uncluttered by emotions or images or ideas.

For three centuries or more there has been almost no other thinking in

---

*This also helps to explain how an Indian spiritual leader today can promote meditation so widely simply as a way of making people feel better.

Western Christianity about the human experiences of God. Many of us have actually forgotten that there was once another understanding of these experiences, a very different Christian view of them. In this older tradition it was understood that people could come face to face with the divine reality at the center of all things, but this experience did not deprive them of the ego necessary to relate to the world. This encounter with another reality brought freedom, but in the process the ego itself was changed. By being found and touched by divine reality, the ego was purged and purified and given some of the infinite substance of that reality; like ore, it went into the smelter and was melted and molded into something new. This was the preparation for action in the world, for acting in accordance with the reality one encountered. As von Hügel has suggested, the essence of these experiences is growth, harmony, action (as distinguished from activity), while the idea of simply a blissful union with God is marked by passivity, fixedness, and oneness.[8]

Meditation in Images

The third type of religious experience is found by turning inward and using one's imagination as a tool with which to contact the reality of the spiritual world. This practice, which can be learned by most people with a little determination,* opens up various levels and depths of reality in the inner realm that can be met and explored as one deals with the images that rise. At first it is difficult to keep from bobbing back and forth between ideas and images and desires. Then things that are very real begin to appear. Within this realm one finds images, often dark and threatening ones, revealing bits and pieces of the self, or at times one is shown images that refer to universal symbols or those shared by all of humanity. These levels merge and mingle with each other, so that a description of the human soul like Plato's chariot pulled by one white and one black steed—by will and passion—seems deceptively simple. Instead one may feel tied to a wagon pulled by a team of twenty mules balkier than the Borax ad portrays.

At the same time realities from beyond the psyche appear, sometimes in symbols that have to be studied in order to understand them, or sometimes in clairvoyant or precognitive experiences—which are possible since there is no time or space in this realm. There are times when the very substance of evil and destructiveness is revealed, perhaps on the heels of an experience of great good. And finally there are experiences of the reconciling One (or God), in which one finds the center of all things and the point of rest and of meaning. I shall describe these various levels in detail in the next chapter.

---

*It is probably easiest for persons who are introverted and intuitive to allow spontaneous images to arise and move within the psyche. But this can be learned, in part in ways I have already suggested and shall consider further later on.

As I come to discuss these experiences, it will be helpful to understand three things. First, this kind of meditation is based on a framework in which the journey is valued more than the harbor. This way and the growth and development which come from it are themselves one of the final values. The practice of meditation helps people to keep on "the way." Since we thus come close to God and participate in His nature, we share in His pure, energizing love. We are moved—to use Dante's words—by "the love which moves the sun and other stars." Of course we find moments of rest and peace and bliss, but these are like stopovers on a journey rather than the end of the road.

In the second place, the determination to give this kind of practice a try depends on the way a person views the world. Few of us, except for some very simple souls, will stay with this kind of meditation unless we have a world view which recognizes the reality of our inner psychic world and how it overlaps a world of spiritual realities. Yet for the most part religious thinkers do not seem very interested in the soul or psyche and whether or not it has access to such a spiritual (or psychoid) world. Most of them, including both Barth and Bultmann, have spent all their efforts trying to persuade people that we have only our rationality and rational moral sense to rely on in dealing with this purely material universe which they believe is all that exists. And this probably does more to keep people from productive religious practice than any kind of anti-religious thinking. Thus it is left to ordinary people like you and me to try to understand the interplay between psyche (or soul), spirit (the realm of spiritual realities), and matter.

The third thing to understand is that each of the levels of experience I have suggested merges into the others. While each has a value of its own and a place in the life of each individual, they are not sharply defined or separated from one another, but are gradually merged into each other. We are dealing with life in both its organic oneness and its complexity, and these things need to be considered not as one thing or the other, but on a many-pointed scale that keeps both the oneness and the rich variety in perspective. There are no hard and fast lines in the meditative process any more than elsewhere in real life.

From the Christian point of view this way of meditation came from God Himself through the incarnation of Jesus Christ. Instead of God's being completely transcendent and utterly removed from humanity, He became Himself a member of the human race. He became a specific man, Jesus of Nazareth, in whom God's reality is found fully and deeply. The theological controversies of the first five Christian centuries show how central this idea was to early Christianity. We have already touched on the difficulty that is created in Biblical criticism because the early Christians considered that their experiences of the Risen Christ had just as much authority as anything said or done by Jesus during His life on earth. The early Christians spoke of both experiences as if they had happened during His lifetime. This understanding of access to the Risen Christ through inner images is also found in the devotional works of Christians like Origen, Gregory of Nyssa and Augustine, and it continued to be central to Christian practice at the time of the Middle Ages.

Père Jean Leclercq once discussed this with a group of us. He said that the practice of the high medieval time consisted of reading the Bible, meditation in which one entered into the reality of what had been read, relating it to oneself and one's world, and then going out to do something about it in actions which produced results within oneself as well as in the world outside. In *The Spiritual Exercises* of Ignatius of Loyola, this way of using the New Testament images was brought to a highly developed form in which traditional religious images were used most effectively, but in a way that sometimes lost touch with the spontaneous images awakened within the individual.

In recent history one small group of Protestants has probably embodied the creativity of this kind of prayer more effectively than any other religious group. The Society of Friends or Quakers, in their three plus centuries of existence, have kept alive the conviction that in silence one meets the reality of that inner voice from God which gives inspiration, guidance and direction, and transformation. They have practiced this conviction, becoming silent not just for bliss, but for relationship with this reality and for the content that comes out of the relationship. Although there are fewer members in this denomination than in many a Catholic diocese, what these few have accomplished for others is literally astounding. From George Fox and William Penn to John Woolman and right up to the present, this group of Friends has listened to the inner voice of God and then acted—with vital social impact. And the world is ever so much better because of their listening and then acting upon their own inner contact with God.

Meditational practices like these often make use of images connected with the incarnate Christ and His life and parables. In following this method one pictures himself in relationship with a particular image, perhaps identifying with the prodigal son returning from tending swine, or with the man who was set upon by thieves. Or one may see and hear oneself talking with the Risen Christ and bringing all parts of the self to the encounter, a virtually never-ending process. It was the contention of early Christianity that this kind of practice actually brought the person into relation with the reality that the image represented.

It is ironic that after I had three years in seminary and several more studying the devotional masters, it took a Swiss psychiatrist to suggest this possibility to me. It was C. G. Jung who showed me that such practices can work today, and that images not only open one to the depth of oneself, but also beyond to the world of psychoid realities where one is able to come into contact with the realm of God Himself. These realities are called "psychoid" because the one thing we know that resembles them closely is the psyche or soul itself. In the twenty volumes of his collected works Dr. Jung develops a "language of the soul" in order to discuss the reality that is found through inner being.

Perhaps even stranger, I first learned about using Dante's images in *The Divine Comedy* in meditation not from any theologian or devotional writer, but from a wise psychological counselor, Helen Luke, in her remarkable book *Dark Wood to White Rose*—and then from the writings of an Italian psychiatrist, Roberto Assagioli, who speaks of talking with the inner Christ in an unabashed way that would make most Christian ministers blush. He finds that this kind of meditation, which he calls psychosynthesis, often produces profound changes in both the inner and outer lives of his patients, and he tries to help them achieve spiritual psychosynthesis as well as personal development.[9]

The Goals of this Experience

For these medical practitioners, as in the basic Christian view, the ultimate goal of meditation is love. In both the Christian framework and its Platonic philosophy, this must be understood as love between the person* and God, or a real relationship, and not as a union which absorbs and merges the person into God. There is a great difference between Plato and Plotinus in this matter, as Paul Friedländer has shown with penetrating insight in his critical study *Plato*. Plotinus looked for a union with the Divine in which one's own dim light was absorbed by the center of light. Plato, on the other hand, saw love as the final process, and this takes two, a person and God. Love means relationship with another, and there can be no love where the ego on one side is dissolved or annihilated.

There is a basic difference between those who see the universe as ultimately characterized by impersonal MIND and those who see it as principally LOVER. There is a great gulf fixed between this aspect of the East and the West as Joseph Campbell points out so well in *Myths to Live By*. One can merge into ultimate Mind and be lost in imagelessness. One must encounter and relate to the divine Lover, and one will find that images are needed to describe that experience.

This idea of love between human beings and God is based on the understanding that God is so deeply interested in the real physical world that He became incarnate in it, and that He is so deeply concerned about real human beings that He died for them. He wants us to become fellow workers with Him and so He makes His power—which we discover in psychoid reality—available to us in the physical world. The individual who meets these realities in the inner self is constantly renewed, transformed and changed. There is suffering, but this is only part of the growing process and not the end of it. There seem to be no limits to the possible growth of the human psyche in its fellowship with God.

---

*A new term is needed to denote the transformed and expanded ego that results from this kind of experience.

One probability is that life in the hereafter is a continuation of the same growth process begun within the world of space and time.

At the same time there is another, almost equally important goal related to evil. While it is not popular these days to consider evil, particularly as a psychic, spiritual or metaphysical principle, not believing in it provides practically no insurance against its activity in our lives. Evil can often be dealt with, however, at its point of entry into the world if we will stop and become aware of the images that come unbidden into the psyche. It may come as a shock to find how often within ourselves overwhelming images and overwhelming emotions go along together. One may be driven by a mood that seems related only to some outer circumstance, and then suddenly become aware of an image within. Perhaps one sees himself or herself drowning in a swamp, or infected by a vampire's bite, or even turned to stone by a glimpse of the Medusa. Strangely enough, when such an image is glimpsed one is then no longer helpless in the power of the mood. The individual can then turn to the image of the Christ who has met and defeated Evil and find the only One who can lift us out of lostness or destructiveness or imprisonment. Even the best of us need His help, not only against petty and self-seeking egotism, but in dealing with the Evil One or the very source of Evil.

Again, in this tradition, the purpose of meditating must be understood in terms of God's interest in this world and His desire to have us become free to relate to Him. He also offers to pay a ransom to help people become free from the destructive force that runs through all of reality. He offers this in the same way that the father offered his prodigal son acceptance and reconciliation in the story told by Jesus of Nazareth. I could use either "redemption" or "salvation" to express this, but these words have been so loosely used that they have become part of a religious jargon which no longer has much meaning for the average person. The important thing is to know our purpose in entering the inner world, and to know that *we are looking for the Risen Christ and a relationship with Him*.

Jung in particular warns against entering the inner world lightly out of curiosity, or wandering aimlessly among the images in it. In his "Psychological Commentary on 'The Tibetan Book of the Dead'," he suggests that invoking such experiences lightly is like "meddling with fate, which strikes at the very roots of human existence and can let loose a flood of sufferings of which no sane person ever dreamed."[10] In another article, addressed to the clergy, Jung noted that

The opening up of the unconscious* always means the outbreak

---

*Another term for the inner or spiritual world is the world of the unconscious.

of intense spiritual suffering; it is as when a flourishing civilization is abandoned to invading hordes of barbarians, or when fertile fields are exposed by the bursting of a dam to a raging torrent. The World War was such an invasion which showed, as nothing else could, how thin are the walls which separate a well-ordered world from lurking chaos. But it is the same with the individual and his rationally ordered world. Seeking revenge for the violence his reason has done to her, outraged Nature only awaits the moment when the partition falls so as to overwhelm the conscious life with destruction.[11]

Carlos Castaneda speaks in much the same way about the incredible power of the "allies" one encounters on the inner journey. This overwhelming negative influence is proverbial in the drug culture where wandering out of light into the source of Evil is known as a "bad trip."

At the same time students like Jung are very much aware of our need for contact with the inner world. Jung in particular realizes that this is the source of humanity's creative power and energy, as well as the cause of many of our difficulties. We find contact with God in the inner world, as well as finding contact with the power of Evil, and in both cases our way of learning about the contact and what it demands of us is through images. Yet in much of religion today the only thing that is stressed about images is the danger or folly of trying to work with them.

Both Zen and Hindu thought warn against dealing with the images that rise spontaneously out of silence. Zen calls this stage of the process *makyō*, which means literally the world of the devil. It is considered a totally chaotic world of experience from which no meaning at all can be obtained. Much the same idea is found in the thinking of St. Teresa and St. John of the Cross, which flows from the late Middle Ages into modern thought. As William Johnston puts it, St. Teresa described the prayer of quiet by saying "that the *will* is lovingly fixed on God; the *memory* is occupied with His love too; the *understanding* is in darkness; the *imagination* (the fool of the house) romps and frolics wildly where it wishes."[12]

In *Dark Night of the Soul* St. John of the Cross spoke plainly about the importance of disregarding images from within:

> The third sign whereby this purgation of sense may be recognized is that the soul can no longer meditate or reflect in the imaginative sphere of sense as it was wont, however much it may of itself endeavor to do so. For God now begins to communicate Himself to it, no longer through sense, as He did aforetime, by means of reflections which joined and sundered its knowledge, but by pure spirit, into

which consecutive reflections enter not; but He communicates Himself to it by an act of simple contemplation, to which neither the ex-
terior nor the interior senses of the lower part of the soul can attain.
From this time forward, therefore, imagination and fancy can find no
support in any meditation, and can gain no foothold by means
thereof.[13]

In spite of this thinking, St. John of the Cross continued to listen to his inner
promptings all through his life, and his superb religious poetry contains some of
the most sensual imagery.[14] The thinking he represents, however, arose just
when the rest of the Christian world was beginning to deny the inner value of
religious images.

   At this same time the teaching of John Calvin was taking hold, which persuaded most Protestants that almost any religious use of images could lead only
to error.[15] And on the other side of the fence secular thinkers were developing
the idea that the only valid images are ones that give an accurate picture of
outer physical reality. It became easy to question the way the New Testament
and the Church Fathers had used images inwardly. It is no wonder that by the
time the ideas of Ignatius of Loyola became popular, his tremendously valuable
suggestions for using images in prayer were gradually turned into a rigid and
often sterile system which touched a few people, but left only a bad taste in a
great many mouths.

   As a result most of us are at a loss when it comes to approaching these
realities that are beyond our immediate grasp. We who are living today have
never known a world that placed a religious value on the human psyche or soul
and the way it experiences realities from that other realm that are similar to it.
These psychoid realities even bring us into direct contact with God through
images. It is time to ask what is so different about our approach to religious experience, and how we can understand the religious experiences of other people
and of other times. Let us see how these questions can be answered.

Understanding Religious Experience

   What people experience as religious content depends largely on two factors.
It is determined first by people's psychological development, and second by their
understanding of the structure of the world, or their world view, and the kind of
experience it allows them to be open to. As I have already suggested, there is no
question about the importance of our view of the world. We human beings have
a way of tuning out or thinking impossible any experience that does not fit into
some accepted category in our model of the world. For instance, until the theory
of nuclear physics was proven at Hiroshima, most people marveled at Mme.
Curie's strange new atomic discovery and dismissed it more or less as a freak of
nature.

People's strange experiences of the nonphysical world are often met by much the same attitude. It is exciting to hear about them, but unless one has an understanding of the world which allows for such experiences, they are swept into a corner and forgotten. What we are consciously aware of becomes more and more selective as our awareness works with sensations that we build into our concept of the world. My book *Encounter with God* is an attempt to show some of the facts that open up the world so that there is a place in our view of the world for religious experience.

The matter of psychological development makes this even more complex. Most of us are aware of the way primitive peoples and children generally approach their experiences. They do not make a very clear distinction between what comes from the outer physical world and what comes from their inner experiences. In fact it worries many parents to find that children see so little reason for distinguishing between the inner world and the outer one. This is not considered "normal" at the present time in our society. It was all right for archaic mankind to see a god in the lightning and spirits in trees, but there is something dangerous about the child's having an imaginary playmate and using this kind of play to project inner realities onto people and things that belong in the "real" outer world.*

There is some justification for this fear. One sign of mental illness is just this inability to make distinctions between the two worlds. In certain forms of psychosis the person is so absorbed in what is going on inside that it becomes impossible to deal with outer reality, and few things frighten people today more than this kind of "madness." Moderns have learned to fear the inner world. Yet some psychiatrists see this retreat from outer reality into the inner world as healing; they see it as a retreat from some intolerable condition so that the psyche can heal itself and be able to cope with outer reality.

In truth the line between "normality" and "abnormality" is not a Berlin Wall between inner contents and outer reality, but the ability to distinguish which is inner and which is outer. The sick person hallucinates, while the normal person realizes this is a projection of some vision of an inner reality onto the outer world, and recognizes the difference between physical realities and psychic or psychoid ones.

What is hard to realize is that this kind of undifferentiated consciousness, which is primitive or childlike, is part of all of us. It is a stage of development,

---

*Even sophisticated moderns, however, still do things like knocking on wood, but without stopping to think about summoning the aid of the spirit dwelling there. Both Mircea Eliade's *Shamanism* and the four books by Carlos Castaneda give a clear picture of this kind of reality.

and yet one that we never entirely pass beyond. This attitude might be diagramed in the following way:

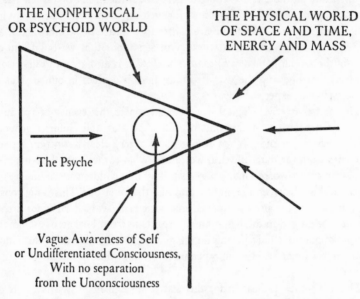

THE NONPHYSICAL
OR PSYCHOID WORLD

THE PHYSICAL WORLD
OF SPACE AND TIME,
ENERGY AND MASS

The Psyche

Vague Awareness of Self
or Undifferentiated Consciousness,
With no separation
from the Unconsciousness

The psyche is represented by the triangle lying between the world of psychoid or
psyche-like reality and that of space and time, energy and mass. Its vague
awareness* of self is suggested by the small circle, contained entirely within. No
clear line is drawn separating data received from outside and from within, dividing inner unconscious experiences from those experiences that come or are
sought from a distinct physical world. In dealing with this outer reality the person has little way of knowing whether one is seeing what is there or projecting
an inner image—which may or may not be true—upon it.

For several reasons, including the development of science, Western peoples
felt a need to distinguish between the two kinds of experience. Bit by bit they
directed their consciousness outwardly, even insisting that children conform and
forget their inner perceptions. Most of us, however, no matter how sophisticated
we are, do not discriminate very fully between these two worlds. We project all
sorts of inner realities upon the outer world, especially in our relations with
other people. The commonest ways are in the love relationship or in hate which
ends up in divorce and war and racial violence. There are also elements of
projection wherever there are closed minds which refuse to look at new facts,
whether in science or religion.

Yet the solution is not to eliminate making projections. As Freud showed so
well in *The Psychopathology of Everyday Life*, the inner world is here to stay.

---

*In this vague awareness the individual has not come to the kind of developed and
differentiated consciousness which has developed in Western thought since Descartes.

Projection is a fact of life, and the problem is to use it as creatively as possible. Religious ritual can help us to know the realities that touch us from within by giving us creative ways of expressing them sacramentally. Human beings have used these ways almost from the beginning of time. Through sacramental experience the individual is plugged into this kind of knowing. By projecting the realities found within into religious elements and activities, one can see and know these realities almost as if looking at them in a mirror. Modern people have just as much need for this way of knowing as the most primitive worshiper, and the real difference is that our mental maturity often makes it easier for us to project inner encounters into images in meditation than to know them by faith in the sacramental.

Instead, the development of consciousness in the Western world has resulted in a point of view that insists that we have outgrown any such way of getting knowledge through images and must discard that idea. According to this view, the time, space, energy, and mass realm contains the only basic realities in the universe, and a person is simply one outgrowth of them. This point of view says outright that human consciousness developed simply by chance and has no way of relating to other nonphysical realities unless they can be known through the five senses. Thus, our consciousness gives us only the ability to experience the physical world and reason about it. Those who hold this view admit that we have developed a superior brain and nervous system but, as the behaviorism of B. F. Skinner explains, the human consciousness is still only the result of physically conditioned responses. In order to know anything for sure we must depend upon facts that can be tested outwardly.

This point of view is best pictured by a box comprising the known, physical world:

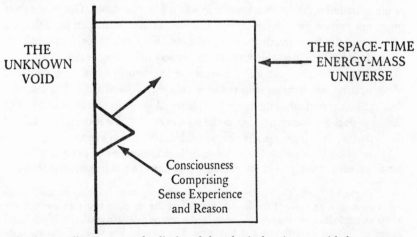

THE UNKNOWN VOID

THE SPACE-TIME ENERGY-MASS UNIVERSE

Consciousness Comprising Sense Experience and Reason

The four walls represent the limits of the physical universe, with human consciousness directed only toward external, physical stimuli. Since it is believed that this is the only source of experiences that are real and valid, there can be no direct source of religious experience. According to this point of view, one may see value in certain external events, and by reasoning may infer that God might be there in these events. But with no way of knowing any nonphysical reality, such speculation remains speculation and gives little confidence. Any idea of a direct experience of God, such as a vision that might come from the God source, is absurd. Since there is no basis for such experiences, they must be considered hallucinations or perhaps signs of mental breakdown. It is difficult in this framework to make much sense of meditation as an effort to find religious experiences.

Among many students, however, from medicine and anthropology to mathematics, there is a growing awareness that this world view rules out a lot of important data and information. According to that view science is able to produce absolute knowledge objectively, without considering the importance or necessity of values, and this new breed of thinkers has begun to consider that this causes science to become meaningless and to lose its steam. They suggest—much as I am suggesting for religion—that science needs to go back to its sources and learn how to think, and what to think about, all over again. Paul Feyerabend, for instance, says very specifically that scientific discovery will continue to disappear unless scientists learn to develop their imaginations and open up their limited view of what makes up reality. In his book *The Natural Mind* Andrew Weil offers a similar understanding of the drug culture among young people today. He shows that the drugs are an effort to open up another realm of perceptions and values that has been lost by our culture.

All of us have something of the primitive and the child within us as well as a good deal of the objective scientist. Both the child and the scientist within us give us elements of our experience, and the wisdom we need is to learn how to work with both. At present we tend to see only the data which fits and is useful to the system of thinking about reality in which we were raised. One of the most important reasons for developing meditative techniques is to open us so that we can see realities from which we have been cut off by today's single-minded, intellectual objectivity. And this suggests a third way of viewing reality.

This third view of the world accepts our Western stress on the importance of physical reality. It starts with the view that the physical world has independent reality that demands the clearest, most conscious effort to understand it. But this view does not therefore jump to the conclusion that this is the whole story of the universe. It rejects equally the one-sidedness of the West, and the one-sidedness of the East which finds illusion in both the inner and outer worlds. Instead it takes a fresh look at the archaic* understanding of human experience in

---

*The word "archaic" does not imply anything derogatory. It simply means belonging or relating to an earlier time, and in this case we are speaking about a view of reality which was primitive (in the sense of being the earliest or most original), and which lasted almost unchanged until the time of Descartes. The rational line which Descartes drew between consciousness and other kinds of less conscious experience may have been one of the greatest blunders of all time, as L. L. Whyte has pointed out in *The Unconscious Before Freud*.

the light of present-day discoveries, and finds more than one reason for believing that we are in touch with two kinds of reality. This understanding is supported by the findings of medicine and parapsychology, and by the physicists' questions about matter and energy and space and time and whether sharp distinctions can be made among them.

As a result, this view sees humanity in touch, first, with a physical world that is experienced in forms that become more and more mysterious the more we learn about them. At the same tine it finds human beings open to an objective psychic or spiritual world which appears to be independent of the individual psyche and apparently extends beyond it. The experiences of this world often come in dreams and visions, sometimes accompanied by strange outer events that appear to be meaningful coincidences and make both worlds seem even more mysterious. If we are to learn much about the meaning of either world, we need to distinguish these experiences from ones that are limited just to the physical world, and then study both kinds by the same analytical methods. Although at some time in the future we may discover that these two realms are actually parts of a single realm, at present they appear to be separate and independent, and those who insist that there can be only a physical world do so on a basis of faith, not of known fact.

This point of view can be diagramed in much the same way as that of vague awareness with two main differences:

THE NONPHYSICAL, PSYCHOID OR SPIRITUAL WORLD

THE PHYSICAL WORLD OF SPACE AND TIME, ENERGY AND MASS

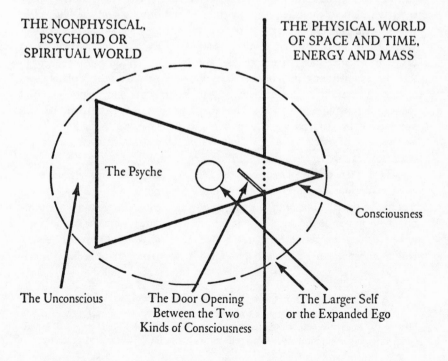

The Psyche

Consciousness

The Unconscious

The Door Opening Between the Two Kinds of Consciousness

The Larger Self or the Expanded Ego

The circle around the psyche and the small one like a hub inside it represent a new center of personality different from the ego, which I call the larger self or the expanded ego. It includes experience from both the inner and outer worlds. Within the psyche there is a line separating clear analytical awareness from the aspects of psychic experience that are less distinct and harder to grasp. This line suggests how well the emphasis of Descartes and the Enlightenment on total clarity and clear awareness has been accepted within our psyches. But the short-cut of eliminating this division by simply ridding oneself of consciousness—found in the drug culture and in so much Eastern thought—is rejected. Consciousness is accepted as a significant part of the whole. With an effort to find a way through the barrier between conscious and unconscious, one discovers that the line between them is not so clear-cut. There is even a door that can be broken open, leading to the discovery of new contents and their integration on a new level.

As I have suggsted, this is one of the main reasons for learning to use medi-tation. With a different valuation of our psyches and some hope of finding con-tact with another realm of reality within ourselves, and with at least some inner experiences of our own, most of us will find an entirely new appreciation of religious experience of all kinds. One may find such an experience in any of four basically different ways.

There are first those numinous* visions of another reality, that are experi-enced as entirely different from ordinary outer experiences. These are big experi-ences which may come once in a lifetime. They come out of the blue, often without being sought, or they may come at the end of a long period of seeking as happened in the case of St. Thomas Aquinas. Very often the person has no desire for another such experience and wonders if it is possible to live through such an experience again. There is such numinous power that it is plainly seen as coming from the divine and is often considered as the most important event that can happen in a human life. The importance of such inner experiences was pointed out by Andrew Greeley in a recent article in the *New York Times Magazine*.[16] In *The Idea of the Holy* Rudolf Otto describes their power and fascination as coming from the *mysterium tremendum*.

Then there are great religious experiences which seem to come from some event in the outside world. For example, as St. Francis was praying before a crucifix, he saw the lips of the corpus move. Experiences like this have the same numinous power as the ones that are described as "inner," but the divine seems to be touching the person through the outer physical world. Often the "outer" reality carries an inner emotional power and is sacramental.** In addition, some-

---

*A numinous experience is an overwhelming experience of the Holy.

**This is the kind of experience which dominated the thinking of Schleiermacher and became the normative experience for those who followed his lead. Religion was experi-enced when outer, physical reality was suffused with a feeling of absolute dependence.

times a significant outer event actually coincides with an inner experience which joins the two so that the world around us suddenly appears to become in tune with another level of being.

Experiences such as these that bring the outer and the inner together at the same time in a meaningful way have a deep emotional effect on human beings, filling them with pulsating new life. For the Hebrews the crossing of the Red Sea was such an event, while the early Christians found this reality in their experiences of the Risen Christ. The way Christ appeared to the early Christians "in the Spirit" was as real to them as their experiences of Him before the crucifixion. These experiences could come either to an individual or to a whole group of people as the handful of disciples knew when they had the experience of Jesus's transfiguration (Matthew 17:1-9, Mark 9:2-13, Luke 9:28-36). The feeling of awe that came over all of Jesus's followers as He turned His face to Jerusalem was a similar experience (Mark 10:32). This experience of the Christ's power in both the inner and outer worlds at the same time is what led to the doctrine of the incarnation and the atonement.

Although the popular world view in the West has made it difficult to imagine how psychoid (or spiritual) events can influence events in the space-time world, this is the experience that underlies Christianity and it is experiences of these meaningfully connected events that make a broader world view necessary. The modern experiments in parapsychology and the practical understanding of Dr. Jung show that there is a closer connection between the physical world and the inner psychoid or spiritual world than we have believed.[17] Thus it is not necessary any more to deny the basic Christian belief in the interworking of these two worlds or realms. Today's world no longer considers their interaction impossible or absurd.

The third kind of experience gives a sense of being one with the physical world. In this experience it seems as though one's outer husk dissolves, bringing an immediate experience of a connection between the inner reality and the pulsing life of the physical world. The strict limits of space and materiality seem to disappear so that one may sometimes see a world of shifting forms and images of matter, or sometimes everything dissolves leaving one with simply a sense of participating in the reality of all things physical. Such an experience is described by Teilhard de Chardin in *The Hymn of the Universe*. Something of the same sort is often spoken of by drug users, and the same kind of experience of a union with the physical world can also come in dreams. The difference between the inner and outer worlds dissolves and one finds oneself merged into the very essence of the whole.

Finally, there is a fourth way of coming to an experience of inner meaning by meditating on one's own inner experiences. Withdrawing in silence, one can go back into the images found in dreams or fantasies by imagining them. At first one must do the imagining consciously in order to recall them. Then they can be allowed to take over and go as they will. One is then able to take part in the play of these images, partly by listening and partly by directing them. At this point the person receives directions from within, and that meaning comes through from the inner world as alive and as clear as it often is in the outer world. Sometimes one has an imageless experience of sensing or knowing the meaning of this psychoid world. More often specific meaning or direction for life is found by participating actively with the images as they arise from this inner world.

All of these experiences can be called religious experiences. It is not a matter of certain experiences being religious while others are completely secular. Any experience, entered into to its depth, reveals a religious quality. The real question is one of relative value and realizing that experiences fall along a many-point scale. While some experiences have very little religious significance, there are others that have tremendous religious value, sometimes enough to give meaning to the whole of a person's life. There is a continuous many-pointed scale from experiences that are the least religious and the most secular, to the less secular and the most completely religious.*

One main purpose of meditation is to break the individual out of the ordinary secular way of perceiving or looking at both the inner and outer worlds. This is one way of breaking open the categories and models or views of the universe with which we try to make our world of sensation both understandable and secure. Some of the religious traditions seem satisfied to stop there and find a vague union with the "formless void," which eliminates the need for images. Christianity suggests, however, that if we will allow the model and its categories of the world of sensation to be broken, and if we will then remain open and searching, a new model or view of the universe is often given. In the last lines of *The Divine Comedy* Dante sums this up, stating his own experience of finding meaning in the heart of the celestial and divine white rose in these words:

Yet, as a wheel moves smoothly, free from jars,
My will and my desire were turned by love,
The love that moves the sun and other stars.

The Cyclical Process

Finding this meaning does not happen overnight, however. In the classical Christian view the process of meditation is like a wheel that is going somewhere. The purpose is to lead the person to an inner reality which can be called Love. Once we are aware of the model of this Love, which is the same as was given in the incarnation of Christ, then our desire will be to allow that Love to guide our

---

*The difficulty of pinning down the source of meaning is shown by Arthur O. Lovejoy in *The Revolt Against Dualism*. He concludes this monumental study of human knowing with a myth as the way to account for the mystery of man's knowing.

outer lives. It is as though we ourselves become the wheel and seek to move all we are and do toward the goal. This process takes real awareness on our part. It is important for us in meditation to hold onto the sense of consciousness and to keep it from being flooded by a sense of total union with the unknown. Instead, we withdraw our consciousness from all the outer distractions in order to know more about the *source* of this love as something or someone who wishes relationship with us. We human beings, who fall in and out of love so easily, should realize that an overwhelming experience of the source of this love is only the first step toward a real relationship with this source or, as I prefer to call it, with Love.

The meaning or experience that one finds in this inner relationship to Love then has to be taken back into the outer world and expressed toward others in loving action. One detaches oneself from Love to bring more love back into conscious relationship. Both aspects of the cycle are essential for as long as we live and perhaps even throughout eternity. In fact, there would not be much to say about meditation if it had no outer and observable effects. Baron von Hügel's description of this process is the best I know. He says:

> . . . the movement of the specifically Christian life and conviction is not a circle round a single centre,—detachment; but an ellipse round two centres,—detachment and attachment. And precisely in this difficult, but immensely fruitful, oscillation and rhythm between, as it were, the two poles of the spiritual life; in this fleeing and seeking, in the recollection back and away from the visible (so as to allay the dust and fever of growing distraction, and to reharmonize the soul and its new gains according to the intrinsic requirements and ideals of the spirit), and in the subsequent, renewed immersion in the visible (in view both of gaining fresh concrete stimulation and content for the spiritual life, and of gradually shaping and permeating the visible according to and with spiritual ends and forces): in this combination, and not in either of these two movements taken alone, consists the completeness and culmination of Christianity.[18]

Such a process is meaningless except in terms of images, both outer images and inner ones.

If there is an encounter with Love rather than absorption into it, then one has the experience of meeting someone or something concretely. There is therefore content to this experience and being able to express it is terribly important. For instance, by describing God as the loving father of the returning prodigal, Jesus was able to make it quite clear to whom we are to pray. If there is a reality to be found in the silence of meditation and one has no way to express the contents of this reality, it is easy to become just as lost as in a dark wood of shifting images. If there is no way to bring these contents into view and see where they are leading, it is even possible for one to follow the wrong goal without realizing it.

Ordinary concepts and rational ideas are not very helpful. Even scientists find that they are not really adequate to describe matter. The rational and carefully defined concepts of science simply will not stretch far enough to make complete sense of subatomic physics and quantum mechanics, as Werner Heisenberg shows in his book, *Physics and Philosophy*. Today's scientists keep on trying to learn what they can from their images about what is going on inside of matter itself. Yet, when it comes to the most important of all realities, God, most people either turn to rational concepts or talk about experiences that are beyond verbal communication.

I must confess that I get annoyed with the sloppy thinking of people who talk about how unknowable God is, and how inexpressible their contemplation of Him or their union with Him is. It is as hard to describe the taste of deliciously ripe bleu cheese or to explain to someone who has never tasted a dry soda cracker what this tastes like. But some description is possible if one will use comparisons with other images. The real problem is to get people to take a taste and find out for themselves. There is also a way of communicating about the encounter with love or God that injects meaning and value into one's life so that people will want to taste this reality for themselves. If it is important not to keep God incommunicado, how then can we approach this reality without shutting it up in one conceptual category or another?

The Language of Images

Human beings have other tools besides rational language for describing what they feel and know and value in the inner world.* For as long as we have records, men have used images to tell about these inner things, and about the world they meet on the other side of silence. Practically every religion on the globe has used such images as the basis of its myths and rituals. As I have detailed in my book, *Myth, History and Faith*, the stories which these images weave make up the myths that are central to the religious life of nearly all people. Myths give a picture of the reality encountered from beyond the world

---

*Even this nonrational language of the soul can be critically analyzed and described using careful theological precision if one believes that it refers to something and has some inner experiences of it one's self. David Burell has provided a superb analysis of Jung's language in *Exercises in Religious Understanding*. Using this language of images does not deny rationality. It is not a question of rationality or image, rationality or myth, rationality or emotion, but a matter of rationality and image, myth and emotion. With this note and a clear understanding that my description which follows is simplistic and inadequate, I go on to suggest that this language is worth learning. Like learning any other language, this one takes experience and time.

which we normally experience, and we develop its meaning through the creative, religious use of ritual. Sometimes, like the Christian myth, the reality first enters the life of one exceptional individual and thus is translated directly into history. The rituals are then based upon the outer facts of this individual's life as with Christ.

The range and variety of images found in inner experiences are almost unlimited. Besides sharing in the elements of a society's collective myths, whether they are religious and otherwise, one also finds images of one's own that are part of a personal myth. These images are the ones used in the language of drama and poetry and story, and this is also the way that dreams usually speak to us. Although dreams can sometimes use rational thought and abstract the logical meaning out of a situation, the way they touch and move us most often is through symbols and stories which appear as pictures and myths.

Over the ages nearly every religious group has developed a tradition about the value of listening to dreams. As a result, people in every kind of culture, from the most primitive to the most highly developed, once realized that dreams were a way, not only of learning about themselves, but of coming into direct contact with God or the spiritual world which pushes in upon the inner depth. Christianity was no exception to this. During the most vital years of our own religion, most Christians were as deeply involved in following the images in dreams as almost any modern-day psychologist. When I discovered that this was true, it was almost like a detective story for me. The facts about Christianity and dreams, except for those in the Bible, are hidden away in documents that often seem musty from disuse. Yet the facts that are there are as important to our Christian belief and understanding of the world today as they were centuries ago.*

People in the West, however, are afraid to trust this kind of image. We are taught to use logic and to rely on pictures of sense experience that can be refined and analyzed. Then we are almost hypnotized into believing that this is the only way of learning anything significant or communicating about it. But when so many scientists are questioning whether we can even learn about the ultimate nature of matter in this way, there is good reason to ask if this kind of thinking alone can bring us much knowledge about God and spiritual reality.

If we want most of all to learn about God as best we can and to communicate something of that experience to others, our best bet is to use the images that are given to us. Of course these images need to be related one to another and to the rest of life, logical and sensory. Communication is possible so long as there is a reality that can be savored and recalled in imagination, whether it is that taste

---

*The results of this search are found in my book *God, Dreams, and Revelation*, which was originally published as *Dreams: The Dark Speech of the Spirit* with an appendix containing some of the most important materials from the Fathers of the Church.

of bleu cheese or a taste of God. Perhaps our greatest difficulty is that the language is not so limited in the case of God. The whole language of images that can be written or spoken, drawn or chiseled, danced or acted, is available to be used.

The fact that this language is not "scientific" or conveniently logical is not a good reason for avoiding it. We tend to forget the problems scientists have with their pictures of sense experience. Mathematical logic and precision tools do not protect science from having to use guesswork, and as we see more and more clearly today, the bigger the bite of knowledge, the less dogmatic science becomes. In the far-out fields of astrophysics and nuclear physics scientists must turn to imagination to describe what they see as their total picture of the physical world.

There is no percentage in pretending that it is easier to give a picture of the divine encounter than it is of the encounter with the particles described in nuclear physics. The images that are given are not static or dead like a statement of pure logic. They are very much alive, and they shift and change and vary in their meaning and impact. In fact, using images is like managing a school of talented artists. One does not pull a lever and watch them turn out landscapes like robots. A person would try to get to know each of them and then guide and protect them as individuals. Artists can be dealt with mechanically only if one is satisfied with copy work rather than art. Even so, there are times when dealing with images seems like facing stalking beasts or an armed robber in the night, and one no longer feels master in one's own house. At such times there is even more need for patient give and take with whatever is appearing.

In some strange way this seems to happen quite naturally in the silence. One asks questions of God or some other image of the psychoid realm and hears answers given in the most unexpected way. This is exactly like a dream state in which unexpected figures and images appear out of the unconscious depth. But in this case one's conscious mind is awake and enters into the situation without, however, stopping the flow of images. The important thing is not the images themselves, but what they symbolize. These images point beyond themselves, perhaps to some emotion or desire the individual has neglected. Or they may point to a realm of reality other than the ordinary space-time world. Images from this depth can even bring a direct encounter with the creative, victorious Risen Christ, whom we also seek in the outer physical world, but whose self-sacrificing love is found in a unique and creative way in the inner world.

In the encounter with one's own depth, a person comes to know, in images, the realities in that inner world that all human beings share. These realities have an effect on all human beings by pushing them into action or by holding them back (perhaps in anger or by some other emotion). One learns to work with the language of dreams and visions which is often poetic and expresses deep, unexplained feelings. By using this kind of language one can touch another's despair, or share another's delight. It is like the language of love poetry, which expresses something almost everyone has known and touched. And one often finds that this same language can express the even more intense and burning love of God from whom love springs.

It is true that we can encounter this creative Spirit or God without silence and outside of the directed process of meditation. God can break in upon a person no matter where one is or what one is doing. Such an experience remade the life of John Newton, sending him from slave trading into the priesthood and inspiring the hymn "Amazing Grace." This rarely happens, however, to a person who has developed a strong ego, which includes many of us. In addition, God is a Father who is usually too polite to break in upon a person unless one stops and turns to Him. While there are always exceptions in the inner world, it is not wise just to sit back and wait for a crisis when there are other ways of opening oneself to this reality. And in the end, if one is given an unasked-for experience, that person will get the most out of it only by turning inward in silence, considering what it was and wondering how it can be found again or learned from.

There are dangers, however, in this way of seeking images in meditation, and there are also dangers in religious practice which avoids such an encounter. Before we go on to consider the actual practice of meditation let us look at what happens when religion goes overboard on either side.

The Dangers of One-sided Religious Practice

A complete religious life involves more than one element. It needs to be rooted in the traditional practices and beliefs and morality of the Church. At the same time it also needs to seek the bliss and contemplation of God that provides the essential meaning to these traditional practices and the motive to share that meaning with others. Finally, the whole structure depends upon the individual's continual growth and ability to bring all parts of the being into the religious process and keep integrating them so that more and more of the love of God is brought into himself and then into the world. This last process, in particular, involves the use of images and imagination. Use any of these three elements by itself and religion becomes a mere shell, with the result that the single element itself becomes warped and even demonic. We need balance in our religious life.

When people limit religion only to the historical institution, without even trying to understand how the institution was originally shaped by the other elements, then religion can become mere superstition. It may even seem that nothing is left but a set of hand-me-down beliefs that must have dropped out of the sky. As von Hügel remarks, there is

> a ruinous belief in the direct transferableness of religious conviction;
> and a predominance of political, legal, physically coercive concepts

and practices with regard to those most interior, strong yet delicate . . . springs of all moral and religious character. . . . We thus
get too great a preponderance of the "Objective," of Law and Thing,
as against Conviction and Person; of Priest as against Prophet; of the
movement from without inwards, as against the movements from
within outwards.[19]

Von Hügel calls attention to the rigid organization and obsession with detail,
and to the almost military demand for blind obedience, that often dominate the
Church when this attitude takes over. The Spanish Inquisition and Calvin's betrayal of Michael Servetus to be burned at the stake probably represent the low
point of this one-sidedness.

When authority takes over, the Church pays the piper. People lose interest
and turn away from the sterile dogma and enforced morality, and finally from
the institution itself. Its symbols often lose their life for most people and its rituals seem to become formulas to work magic. One is left with no way back to the
former faith short of accepting the whole cultural and institutional package with
all of its regulations and rules. In addition, the Church is left with only authority
as a basis for teaching or communicating its message.

There are equal dangers in a one-sided search for direct religious experience, whether the emphasis is simply on contemplation, or on the further step of
Quietism, or on seeking God as Infinite Mind. When the emphasis on contemplative experience is dominated by the ideas of Plotinus, the result is almost a
caste system. The individual must pass through fixed stages of meditative life in
order finally to "arrive." One starts with confessional prayer (the purgative
stage), moves on to meditating with images (the illuminative stage), and finally
comes to imageless union with God (the unitive stage). Only the last stage is
considered to have enduring value.

This attitude makes it possible to devalue institutional religion and its sacraments, and also the kind of individual growth toward God that comes through
opening oneself to images in meditation. By passing from meditation to contemplation, and finally to union with God, one can believe that one's spirit has
grown beyond any need for the other stages. This person then waits upon God
purely passively and is valued for doing so. In this method the only mature kind
of prayer is seen as one in which a person unites with God in an imageless way.
Images are discarded as something childish and outgrown, and the plastic and
fluid nature of the human psyche is overlooked, as well as its boundless potential
for growth in depth found through the unconscious.

Many less than fully developed souls (and who among us wants to admit
this?) assume that they are already past the stage of meditation. Therefore they
repress any images or anything rising up from the depths. The result is too often
a "saint" who is petty and bad-tempered and suffers from spiritual pride by believing that he or she has "arrived." The repression of vital energies can also

result in far worse difficulties, as we shall see.

A similar emphasis is found in Quietism with its belief that the individual is above social religion and does not need to do anything about all the ordinary religious practices and morality.* As this movement spread, many people became so possessed by the idea of the total value of silence that they avoided any activity, whether saying their beads, or making the sign of the cross, or taking part in the Eucharist. They shied away from any inner image, even removing outer images like crucifixes because they were felt to hinder devotion. Among the early Protestants the effort to get rid of images in every form took a reverse twist. Out of touch with the historical Church, Protestant beliefs became increasingly rigid and concerned with order in their outer lives. The individual who tried to live up to these beliefs had no inner images to show what was going on within, and so the result was an uncontrolled release of emotions that reached a high point in the wild orgies of the Munster Anabaptists.

It is also dangerous to see God as Infinite Mind with which one may merge, sloughing off one's emotional life. Although this kind of meditation is found in Christian devotion from the fourth century on, it became a major strand only in the late Middle Ages. As one Benedictine abbot remarked to me, "This is more like the religion of the East than the religion of Jesus Christ." In Eastern thought the truly adept person comes to the point of passionlessness, even apathy, and is thus cut off from the pain and agony of this world, and also from the effort to redeem it.

Seeking this goal of merging with God as Infinite Mind cuts one off from sharing in the goal expressed by Jesus, who loved so much that He suffered human agony and desolation to the fullest in order to deliver humanity from it. The early Christians viewed God as all-encompassing love which one encounters and then tries to share with other human beings, and they lived and loved and died trying to redeem the ancient world. That view of God as the source of all love requires images and individuals who stay fully alive to express its reality. Mind, on the other hand, can be met through concepts and ideals, and without emotions or images.**

---

*Hare Krishna chanting provides another totally unitive experience. When the leader of one group was asked why there is so much misery in India where the practice began, he replied that those people had abandoned the right way and were being punished for their sins. There were further questions about what their group does to try to help people, and he indicated that they tried to get people to come to their headquarters by providing a free meal once a week. As von Hügel shows in his thorough description of the Quietist controversy, Quietism offered just such a totally unitive and vertical religion.[20]

**For a concise and typical statement about the value of imageless prayer see "Images are necessary in the beginning of our relation with God in prayer" by the Rev. Thomas Schultz, O.H.C., in *The Beacon*, Vol. 29, October 1974, Diocese of Northern Indiana (Episcopal).

While there is a place in Christian thought for the experience of merging with divine Mind or the cosmos, this is not seen or experienced as the end of the process. But like most such ideas, this idea of prayer had far-reaching effects. Human beings came to be viewed as essentially rational mind, like the creator God. This is still the attitude of most Catholic and Protestant thought which is rooted in the scholastic reverence for mind alone. In this belief, if one brings the mind to the right point of view, then the rest of the human being will come around, including our emotions and our behavior, which is largely influenced by emotion. Unfortunately this is simply not true, as the crisis in education reveals. A human being is bigger than just rational consciousness. Unless one deals in images and rituals—which are images in action—only a small part of one is touched, and that person goes on without finding a religious point of view.*

Each of these efforts to contemplate God without images leads people to believe that an irruption of images into one's life is a regression, and a dangerous split occurs. One is separated from the emotional life which often returns to attack in depression or neurosis, sometimes even in a complete mental breakdown. When natural sexual or other vital energies are so fully repressed that not even images of them can arise in the soul, they build up pressure to the point of breaking out with fury in mental illness. One acquaintance who has lived for twenty-five years in a contemplative order has told me how many of the sisters found it necessary to seek psychiatric help in order to accept their humanness. These sisters had to learn to deal with the images that arose in dreams and fantasy before they became well again.

The danger is even greater if one tries to move directly into imageless contemplation, or simply into living by rationality alone. The Easterner does not attempt to get along without images before going through a long, long period of training and development in which the body is taken very seriously and brought under control. This practice is far more balanced than its Western counterpart. Even so, there are inherent dangers.

The idea that images are only for beginners assumes that one can come to such a state of rational control and conscious perfection that the inner life is in perfect order—dreams, emotions, relations with others, sexual impulses and the rest of instinctual life all in harmony. Perhaps one would then no longer need images bubbling up from the unconscious in order to deal with these things and grow. The problem is that many people think that they have achieved real per-

---

*Joseph Campbell speaks to this problem in his work, *Myths to Live By*. Modern people who fail to use images and myths are alienated from their religious heritage. Again, *the use of images and emotions does not deny the value of mind and rationality. It is not a question of either/or, but of both/and. Rationality has a place and so do myth and image.* So often when this irrational aspect of religion is emphasized, one is accused of attacking the rationalistic establishment.

fection when all they have done is to repress these things into the unconscious where they are perfectly obvious to everyone but the individual concerned. This may be the reason one Trappist monk asked an analyst friend of mine, "Why is it so much harder to love those in the cloister than people outside?" The person who reaches consciously for perfection often by-passes wholeness and becomes impossible to live with. This happens so easily in religious communities where perfection and rationality are seen as the prime virtues, rather than wholeness and love.*

C. G. Jung tells a story about a Christian leader who appeared to be very holy indeed. Jung could find no chink in his armor and was so impressed that he decided he might have to follow the man. But then he met the man's wife and saw who bore his darkness. And Jung realized that he had been taken in by a masquerade.

We have the ability to shut ourselves off from the depth of our own being and avoid knowing our real selves, but this is not the religion of Jesus Christ. He spoke of welcoming home the prodigal, being saved by the outcast Samaritan, finding the lost sheep and coin. This was an inner accepting was well as an outer one, as John Sanford shows so well in his book *The Kingdom Within*. I have never known anyone who did not need this kind of self-knowledge. We are none of us in such control of our lives that we no longer need to listen to the images that come in dreams and meditations, and to keep on seeking ways of turning our moods into images.

It is reassuring to read the lives of the saints and see how often they spoke of being imperfect. In spiritual things one is always a beginner, and the more advanced one becomes, the more such a one admits the distance to the goal. Human beings seem to have infinite perfectibility which is achieved only in the life to come, and this may be one of the reasons eternity is granted to us. Our undeveloped qualities, our sins and imperfections keep coming to light through images so that we can deal with them and suffer and grow. Christian devotional life is never entirely removed from suffering nor from images. There are moments of pure illumination, but then we move back into the fray. Imagination and the body are not to be treated like first-class offenders as St. John of the

---

*There are other dangers in withdrawing into total contemplation or Quietism. This produces an experience which is practically incommunicable. The practice is considered the private possession of a small group, and often it is believed that only a chosen few are privileged to have such experiences. Thus the caste system usually extends to people as well as to hierarchies of prayer.

In addition, Quietism has sometimes been linked with the most extreme asceticism and mortification of the body in an effort to cut off all physical influences. For instance, one wonders what value St. Simeon found in sitting for years on top of his pillar; this comes close to sickness. In fact, if the prayer of quiet is to have results, it needs the balancing effect of the other elements.

Cross and St. Teresa suggest in their less careful passages. None of us is really filled with the Spirit of the loving God until both imagination and body are cooperating and at one with that love as in Jesus Christ. No wonder Christianity was called "the way." It is the process of becoming, again and again, forever. And in this process images are the recurring guideposts upon the way.

One purpose of meditation is to help the psyche (or soul) know the images that can be tapped within our own being and that reveal the soul's condition. They not only give us clear indications of what is affecting us in hidden ways, but some of them offer exactly the guidance that is lacking in our ordinary life. If we repress these images and even forget those that come in sleep, we exclude from our consciousness the very influences and ideas that help with our development and direction. Encouraging the psyche to become imageless can lead us away from ourselves and stop the transformation process by which we grow into the fullness of the children of God.

It is just as dangerous, however, to go overboard about using images as it is to be gullible about anything else. Like particular statues, images can become idols for people. One may see power in the object itself, not realizing that the object only symbolizes a reality of a very different nature. Simple people can sometimes see inner psychic images (which in part they have created) and then think they are gazing upon ultimate reality rather than upon an image. The same person may worship a plaster statue or an icon, and when falling in love, believe the love-object to be a god or goddess. It is no wonder that St. John of the Cross worried so much about people using inner images, particularly in that romantic and half-conscious time when Don Quixote went forth to joust with windmills. The making of images is one thing that authority cannot easily control, and so it tries to do away with them.

Still this is probably the least of the dangers. We have already discussed some of the greater perils of this inner way of meditation. In particular, the person who does not have a strong ego can become so fascinated by the kaleidoscopic movement within as to lose interest in the outer world of men and cities and hunger and pain. By piling up images the individual can escape from real life. This escape leads nowhere except to traveling in circles like being lost in a dark wood. If the ego is weak enough, the fascination with inner images may become so great that the person cannot distinguish them from outer realities and finds the inner world the only real one; the result is then psychosis. The Western advocates of Zen do not talk much about the number of people in Japan who try the way of quietness and get lost in *makyō*, or the morass of wild images. What happens to them is called Zen madness. They leave outer reality and seldom come back.

Before one goes about dealing with images, it is important to be sure that one has a relatively stable ego and a good contact with outer reality. One also needs the support of other human beings, as well as the check and the testing which only human fellowship can provide. And finally, it is important to be sure that one has a genuine need, of one kind or another, to find contact with this other reality, and that it is not being done just out of curiosity or because someone else is doing it. The inner way is not a path strewn only with rose petals; there are dark and demonic forces that have to be encountered, and there are times when even the most self-reliant of us must be willing to seek help.

In addition, we need the balance of other religious practices in order to remain in healthy contact with the spiritual realm. A partial spirituality becomes one-sided and often destructive, and so we need the sacramental and institutional life of the Church, the unitive experience of quiet contemplation, and conscious rational understanding and reflection, as well as meditation with images or directed meditation. But this, of course, is the heart of the problem.

It is difficult for people inside the Church to take image meditation seriously. Christian thinking has discounted this kind of inner experience for so long that it seems to have little or no value. From the beginnings of modern philosophy and theology right down to the present leaders—to Barth and Bultmann, Robinson and Bishop Pike, and those who follow them—there has been little place in the thinking of the Church for inner religious experience. Therefore there has been no real reason to take meditation very seriously. It is not emphasized, and so Christians ignore it and the theologians see no reason to change their minds.

Yet as I have said, the whole structure of religion, its traditions and morality, its convictions about God, its hope of finding Him and bringing more of His love into the world, depend upon persons who are growing inwardly as well as outwardly. By this I mean that we are all affected by the forces that work in the unconscious, in the inner world. We thus have a choice. We can grow and keep learning to deal with these forces by developing the vast creativity and power that is found there, or we can let them operate through us without our knowledge. When this happens they interfere with our best efforts to believe and to act like Christians. As Jung remarked, "People no longer feel redeemed by the death of Christ."[21] It is time to look within and find this experience, which is one way of developing and deepening our inner lives.

In this way we can well enrich our religion and our relations with other human beings. At the same time we can safeguard our own psychological well-being, as well as that of our immortal souls. If we wish to allow God to become the leaven which raises the whole of our being, then we must allow all that we are to arise in images and be met and refined by this encounter.

And so most of the rest of this book will be instructions on how to find this way through using images in meditation. I shall try to suggest how one learns to use images and the imagination, showing how this relates to dreams. I shall then take up various meditative practices, from meditating on the Bible and its images to turning a mood into images and using images in intercessory and healing prayer. After giving several examples of meditations, I shall conclude with a consideration of the most profound and satisfactory instruction ever given for using images in prayer—the Lord's Prayer.

Summation

Few people have summed up what I have been trying to say in these last chapters any better than T. S. Eliot in his *Four Quartets*. In this work art intersects with the meditational way, using images to describe the inner way and lead one further upon it. Twenty years ago when I first read these lines I did not understand them. My experience had not grown up to them. Now they sing with meaning and speak so well what I have experienced. What a summary they offer:

> At the still point of the turning world. Neither flesh nor fleshless;
> Neither from nor towards; at the still point, there the dance is,
> But neither arrest nor movement. And do not call it fixity,
> Where past and future are gathered. Neither movement from nor towards,
> Neither ascent nor decline. Except for the point, the still point,
> There would be no dance, and there is only the dance.
> I can only say, *there* we have been: but I cannot say where.
> And I cannot say, how long, for that is to place it in time.
>
> *Burnt Norton*, Section II[22]

13
Exploring the Nature of the Spiritual World

People do not set out to explore new territory unless they are convinced something is there to set foot on. So long as people like Magellan and Christopher Columbus believed that the earth was flat and that there was no land beyond the horizon, they could not dream of sailing out into the Atlantic to search for Cathay, and end up finding a new world. Navigators had forgotten what the ancient Greek mathematicians knew, that the earth is a sphere and one could even calculate the distance around it very accurately.* Before they could go out looking for new territory, people had to get over the belief that their ships would sail off the edge of the earth and that they would probably meet horrors beyond description.

Exploring the inner world is not very different. In ancient times humankind knew that there was a spiritual world as complete in all its elements and wider in possibilities than the outer world. But once a little foothold of consciousness was revealed in this territory, the idea of exploring further was gradually forgotten. People came to believe that there is only a flat land of consciousness that will support man from within, and that it is utter folly to go beyond these known horizons. One would come to the edge and find only a void, or else a place of horror, of demons and madness. The only safe thing to do is to wall off this forbidden territory and try to forget that it exists. In the end scarcely a trace is left of the things religion once tried to say about this realm.

In almost every religion there are ideas about communication with the world of spiritual realities. They are found all through the New Testament and in many of the greatest Christian writings almost to the present time.** Besides depicting humanity's relation with God, Jesus spoke about angels and demons as actual beings. He showed people how the spiritual world influences them, and

---

*This was done in Alexandria about 200 B.C., using the careful notations of certain travelers of the angle of the sun in various places, and also the duration of eclipses.

**In a booklet entitled *The Reality of the Spiritual World* (Pecos, New Mexico: Dove Publications, 1974), I have tried to show how some of these ideas are related to our present-day experiences and our understanding of them.

that they themselves can have an effect upon these realities. But these ideas are hard to understand today, even though they were tested over and over by the followers of Jesus.

It sometimes seems that the earlier Christians had a view of the world that we are scarcely able to glimpse. The early Church found in the philosophy of Plato an almost ready-made vehicle to share their ideas and experiences with the pagan world.* By developing and building upon that thought, they were able to offer quite a clear picture of reality—one that was not too different from the thinking of many people of the time. On this basis Augustine and Ambrose in the West and Basil the Great and Gregory of Nyssa in the East developed a comprehensive view of humanity and its relationship with both the spiritual and physical environments. Yet our modern experience in the outer world seems to be so different that we find no relation to this view of the world.

Even the careful restatement of that point of view by St. Thomas Aquinas did not bring the idea of the spiritual realm any closer for modern people. The Aristotelian outlook that it provided is more familiar to us, and in St. Thomas's writing the realities of religious experience and love are also apparent. But it is hard for us to grasp the fact that the writers of that time were talking about the meeting of two kinds of reality. Dante probably reached the height of symbolic expression of this idea in The Divine Comedy. It tells of a visionary experience in which Dante is led through hell and purgatory to the highest level of heaven, finally to behold God Himself in the heart of the celestial white rose. As Helen Luke shows in Dark Wood to White Rose,[1] The Divine Comedy makes sense today if it is understood, with the help of depth psychology, as Dante's experience of one's inner journey. It is perhaps the greatest of religious poetry and one of the most profound and moving expressions of the human spirit. Instead, it is often seen merely as a quaint picture of early religious belief.

In these two great Christian eras it was easy to believe in the reality of the spiritual world. People were convinced that they knew the spiritual world as well as the physical one. In a practical way they were certain about its nature and that we have access to it. Both the early Fathers** and the later Latin Church held this view. By the year 1300 this was the point of view held by peasant and philosopher, by king, priest and scholar alike.

Few moderns, however, are able to see the world exactly as it is described by either of these great theological systems, and the problem is that modern theologians offer no other comprehensive view of the world that can attract acceptance and belief. Most of us must play a take-it-or-leave-it game, and it is

---

*In their practices, however, the early Christians rejected the Platonic understanding that matter is intractable, chaotic, and opposed to the influence of the divine ideas.

**This point of view has continued in the Greek Orthodox tradition.

time to ask if there is any way of finding another realm of reality without accepting one of these total world views. Can people today find some experience of a spiritual realm in a way that will stand up under modern critical evaluation? The one way that I know of is by the experience and study of dreams. While it is not very likely that modern theology will blaze this trail, the consideration of dreams is one method that is open to every one of us to find out what the inner world is like. Those of us who become aware of our dreams will realize that we are sometimes immersed in a world in which angels and demons, and even God, might speak.

Dreams as a Gateway to the Inner World

In my own experience with ministers and lay people, with agnostics and confirmed believers, I have found that dreams offer the best evidence for the existence of another level of reality and the best introduction to its nature. There is good reason why this is so. There is nothing thought out, contrived or invented about a dream. It happens naturally to every person almost like clockwork, from four to seven times a night. A dream can carry its own message and conviction; it has power.

Most dreams also seem to have a healing effect. They are being studied medically and psychologically almost continuously today, and a great deal has been learned about what they do and the need for them. But the best modern techniques provide only guesses as to how they are produced. The real suggestion comes from religion and from the long and powerful history of the religious understanding of dreams. Even Christians, for nearly fifteen hundred years, considered dreams to be a natural way in which spiritual reality reaches out and touches us. With this understanding the dream can be seen as the most natural way for God to give His revelation to people today.

This idea was neglected for so long in the West that people forgot the importance of dreams in their lives. As Freud and his followers began to pay attention to dreams once more, their interest was centered almost entirely on mental illness. They had found the tool that helped in diagnosing and treating the fearful seizures and hysterias that afflicted so many people. Gradually, however, they began to investigate the psyche in greater depth. After considering the histories of a great number of patients, Jung realized that sickness can be caused simply by the fact that a person has been cut off from those realities of which all the great religions have spoken. He saw the dream as the most readily accessible means of discovering the nature and intention of these nonphysical or spiritual realities. Coming back into touch with this reality often had a profound effect on a person's mental and physical health.

The big impetus in the current study of dreams began just about twenty years ago when a young doctor in Chicago, William Dement, discovered that periods of vivid dreaming can be detected by a sleeper's rapid eye movements, and also by brain waves that are more like a waking state. As he tested sleepers in various ways, Dr. Dement found that these strange intrusions into our lives while we sleep have important implications for our mental health. When either people or animals were deprived of dreams, they became very disturbed. Even the U. S. Navy established a laboratory to study the effects of dream deprivation on the ability to give and to carry out orders.

In a very different experiment at Maimonides Hospital in New York, Montague Ullman has shown that certain individuals, selected for their sensitivity, can pick up images from other minds in their dreams. Sixty feet away from the sleepers, separated by walls of brick and glass and lead, other persons studied certain pictures. By simply concentrating on the picture *and* the dreamer, they were able to transmit very specific images into the dreams which these sleepers reported, although no known physical energy could have passed between them. There is also some work on modern dream incubation in which the researcher found that young people experienced a level of religious dreams that were far beyond their personal experience and knowledge.[2] Their dreams opened a door which they were not looking for and could not have expected.

On the other hand, I have worked with several young people who were definitely seeking meaning and had turned to the use of psychedelic drugs to try to find it. I remember particularly one young man who had used dangerous amounts of LSD. I suggested that instead he try recording his dreams. The first time he came in again he could hardly wait to tell me that he had followed my advice. When he really looked at his dreams, he told me, he found that they were better than any trip he had ever had on LSD. The experiences that came to him out of sleep—without being demanded or forced and without the dangers of drugs—provided exactly the experience and meaning he had been hoping to find. One's own dreams can reveal a world that is not as narrow and restricted in possibilities as we usually believe the physical world to be.

More recently, working with groups of students at Notre Dame, I have seen almost the same story repeated again and again, usually without the drugs. The upperclassmen are often agnostic. Sometimes the influence of science, sometimes of existentialism, makes these students throw over their traditional religious beliefs. They lose confidence in authority, and they feel caught, as if the physical world were a strait jacket which confines them and allows them no room for the special experiences of religion.

When these students keep a log of their dream experiences for at least a few months, I have found that most of them begin to realize that they are in contact with a level of reality which cannot be stuffed into only rational and physical categories. They come to see that there is more in traditional religion than they had thought. Their own dreams open them to the possibility of religious experience and faith and to the need for religious practice once again. By working with dreams they become aware of dimensions of reality which they do not usually wish to ignore, dimensions which lead to a religious attitude and an integration of their entire lives around it.

There are always dangers in looking toward the inner world, as I have stated in the last chapter. One's experience of the world can be thrown into confusion; an old frame of reference may be shaken until it no longer seems stable enough to stand on. However when one has already lost a grasp on understanding the world, then it may be necessary to turn to inner experience. Probably the least dangerous way of coming to the inner world is by opening oneself to dreams. The dream provides a natural safeguard; a person tends to forget things that one is not ready to look at in dream life. If unacceptable pressures build up too much, the dream lets off steam on its own like a built-in safety valve. If there are dangers in a conscious interest in one's dreams, they are usually less than the dangers in having no religious point of view at all, and they are certainly far less than the danger in turning to drugs to find religious meaning or experience.

The Christian View of Dreams

In nearly all religions the dream has been seen as one way the spiritual world speaks to people. Sometimes dreams are understood as individual journeys into the spiritual realm. When I first began to take them seriously, some twenty-five years ago, I realized that there was a lot about the subject in both the Old and New Testaments, and I began to wonder how long this "primitive and unsophisticated thinking" had lasted. First I read the entire Bible again looking for references to dreams and visions. They were scattered all through it. As I studied these passages and the Greek and Hebrew words, I found that in both languages the words for "dream" and "vision" were used so interchangeably that it was hard to tell them apart.

I found hundreds of references to dreams and dreaming and only one or two that were negative to dream interpretation. Ultimately this evidence was set down in the book which is now entitled *God, Dreams, and Revelation*. It was begun partly out of curiosity—because I had caught sight of a new vision of reality and wanted to see what my own religious tradition had to say about it— and partly out of irritation with one rather arrogant analyst who informed me that no one but a trained analyst had any business fooling around with dreams. But I was not prepared for what I found as I went on to study the records of the early Church.

I discovered that every major Father in the early Church, from Justin Martyr to Irenaeus, from Clement and Tertullian to Origen and Cyprian, believed that dreams were a means of revelation. The same view was held by Athanasius who stood like a wall against one effort after another to sidetrack or derail the faith. Ambrose, Augustine, all of the Doctors of the Church, both East and West, considered the dream a source of revelation, as the Eastern tradition still does. These men all believed that dreams gave access to the same realm of reality which one could penetrate in meditation. That realm in which God was found could be revealed either spontaneously in a dream or vision, or by opening oneself consciously to it in meditation.

The Latin jurist Tertullian, who became an enthusiastic advocate of the Christian cause, wrote at length in Latin about dreams, stating that nearly everyone on earth knows that God reveals himself to people most often in this way. The story of Sts. Perpetua and Felicitas, whose martyrdoms were foretold by dreams, may have also been written by Tertullian. The briefer references in other Christian writings were piling up, and three hundred years later Synesius, the Bishop of Cyrene, set himself the task of organizing the complete understanding of dreams at that time. The treatise he wrote* is one of the most careful and detailed studies produced before the work of Freud and Jung. For the next thousand years the Byzantine writers drew upon these ideas in one commentary after another.

It is clear that all of these men held basically the same idea. There were two worlds, physical and spiritual, and humanity was a bridge between them. In dreams the realities of the nonphysical world were at work autonomously; acting on their own and governed by their own rules, they intruded into the ordinary lives and experience of human beings. And at times dreams were also the instrument by which God spoke to men and women.

The same tradition continued in the West until scholasticism became more sensitive to the thinking of Aristotle than to the life of the early Church. Even then people continued to speak of the visions and dreams that touched and transformed them. It was reported that St. Thomas himself had a vision of overwhelming power just before he stopped writing on the *Summa Theologica*. St. Theresa of the Little Flower told of the dream that sustained and strengthened her during her last years. Although many Christians told of experiences like these, the official theology of the Catholic Church has left no place for understanding dreams or seeing any way of immediate and natural intercourse between the individual and a nonphysical world.

The Enlightenment had an even more thorough and destructive effect on Protestant circles. Its ideas were sparked by Descartes, and even though his insights came in two famous dreams on the night of November 10, 1619, Descartes did not stop to consider that he was spawning a system of ideas that had no place for anything as irrational as dreams. He stressed only one-sided consciousness and clarity of thought. As Protestant thinking came to accept this framework, it began to throw out any belief in dreams, which are certainly dif-

---

*This work is called *Concerning Dreams*. In the original edition of *God, Dreams, and Revelation (Dreams: The Dark Speech of the Spirit)*, I included a summary of Synesius's understanding of dreams in an appendix.

ficult to pin down with clarity. For the same reason it rejected any idea of communication with God or the spiritual world. There was simply no way that God or anything of Spirit could reach us, or that we could communicate directly with either of them.

Occasionally a person of spirit and courage—a person like the great Baptist minister, A. J. Gordon, in the nineteenth century or John Newton a century earlier—would speak of God breaking into his life in a dream. But for most Western Christians, particularly for sophisticated ones, the curtain was drawn on this kind of communication in dreams or visions. My friend John Sanford and I both published books on the Christian interpretation of dreams in 1968. So far as I can discover this was the first time since 1791 that a serious Christian study had been made on the subject. When David Simpson wrote in that year, he mentioned his fear that the message he was offering would fall on deaf ears. Apparently this English clergyman sensed the temper of the times.

The times are changing when an influential and popular Christian writer like Catherine Marshall shows she believes that God speaks through dreams. In *Something More*, published in 1974, Mrs. Marshall included a chapter on her own experience with the Christian interpretation of dreams. Christians need to ask why the Church has rejected this understanding of dreams and experiences of spiritual reality. Does the rejection spring from a one-sided cultural bias, or from what Christians actually find when they examine their own experiences in the light of their Christian heritage? Let us take a look at the way dreams express meaning so that we can decide for ourselves.

Dreams and the Levels of Reality

For most of us the first hurdle in understanding dreams is to lay aside our notions about them. As long as one tries to make every dream fit some particular idea, it will be difficult to make much sense of them. The idea that every dream will predict the future, or direct one's love life, makes it almost as hard to understand dreams as insisting that they are only chaotic and irrational. If one tries to find deep significance or a great revelation of God in every dream, one will end up making nonsense of most of them. The same thing is true of trying to make every dream about a familiar person reveal some fact about that individual.

Instead, these images that flood in upon us in sleep are as complicated as life itself, and the best and easiest way to begin to understand them is to realize that different dreams refer to different kinds of human experience. Over the centuries we have learned to accept the variations in physical reality. For example, we recognize that radioactive uranium has more implications for the nature of physical matter than a piece of granite. In much the same way, certain dreams and psychic experiences have greater significance in revealing to us the secrets of nonphysical reality.

Over the last twenty-five years, working with dreams and with the ideas of
C. G. Jung, I have had reason to learn again and again how complex the
human psyche is. The psyche is able to gather and use experience and knowledge from many different levels of the physical and spiritual worlds in ways we
do not begin to understand. Each of these levels is represented in dreams which
offer us a deeper and deeper understanding of ourselves and our universe. Let us
try to see these various levels with the help of a diagram.

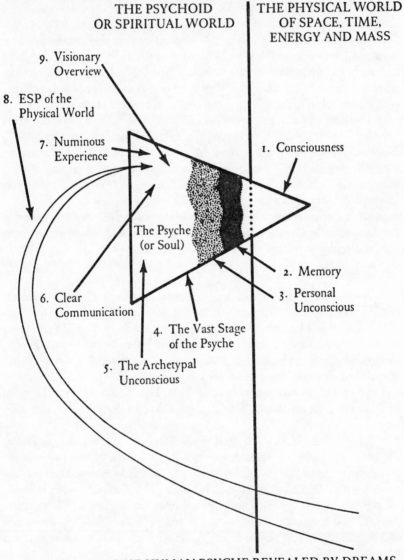

THE HUMAN PSYCHE REVEALED BY DREAMS

The diagram again is divided between two worlds, the outer or physical one, and the world found within, which is like the human psyche and so is called psychoid or nonphysical or spiritual. The triangle represents the psyche, with the following areas and levels of experience numbered around it:

1. The tip of the triangle shows how human consciousness extends into the physical world, picking up experiences that give direct information about that world, and at the same time filtering a whole series of other experiences (through the dotted line) into conscious awareness.

2. The closest level is memory, which allows us to probe deeply into the physical world by storing experiences of it from far and near, and then comparing and analyzing them. Memory also allows us to keep learning about the inner world in the same way, starting with those very common dreams that come from this level and seem to be only a rehash of some previous experience. At first glance these dreams seem purely accidental, but if they are examined closely, two very interesting questions can usually be asked. Why did the dream pick out this one event and ignore others that might have been more interesting? And why did it make certain little changes in the action? These questions usually raise points of such significance that one begins to realize there is a wisdom in the psyche that produces the dream, and this wisdom seems to have a purpose in selecting and editing even the most common level of dreams.

3. There are more startling dreams that come now and then from the third level of the psyche which is like a locked box in which certain kinds of experiences are filed away and forgotten. Suddenly a dream may bring up the girl who sat next to one in the third grade and, perhaps forgotten for forty years, she emerges complete with name and identifiable personality. Often things come up that have been forgotten because they were so unpleasant. One of the clearest examples I recall happened with a minister who was counseling with me. He had talked about certain actions, carefully remarking that he had never done them. One day he brought a dream about friend of his from years before. When I asked what it meant to him, he was embarrassed. Then the story came out. As a childish prank, he and his friend had once done the very things he had forgotten about. Once he was able to talk about this incident, his repression was broken. But until the dream had penetrated his personal unconscious and presented a figure from the past, he could not remember the incident or even admit the story to himself.

4. Then there is a level of personal dreams that seem to come out of nowhere—showing a person situations never known and almost certainly never to be met. One finds whole dramas enacted within oneself. Sometimes in these dramas there are characters who are known and others that are unknown, and one is involved in events like scenes from a three-act play. These dreams command attention, and if one will take the trouble to relate them to one's life, they often will open up insights that are seldom found in other ways. The scenes are carefully laid, using people who can be recognized as symbols of parts of oneself,

and in this way we are given a picture of ourselves that is quite different from the one we ordinarily experience. The dreams from this level often work to compensate for something that is one-sided in a person's conscious attitude. Thus they are truly revelations that make our deepest motives stand out clearly and show us the direction our lives are taking.

I will never forget one very gentle woman in her mid-sixties who came to me because she was deeply troubled by a recurring dream of this kind. She told me with horror how she dreamed of murdering her mother. She had been raised with the idea of caring for her parents in their old age, and her anger over this restriction of her life had been repressed so completely that she could not bring herself to see this side of her feelings. Had she been younger, she might have been able to face this unconscious anger and begin to live fully. But tragically, as the dreams revealed, the tension within her was too great and she died of a stroke not long after. I have known people at war with themselves who dreamed of being prisoners of war in North Vietnam or in Germany. Our unconscious feelings about the usual or collective attitude of our society are sometimes revealed, for example, by dreaming of a collision in the railroad yards, or of walking improperly clothed through the lobby of a big hotel.

In these dreams we find a wisdom speaking from within us trying to point the way toward integration and this wisdom often suggests how we can find wholeness and meaning. The dreams are often unpleasant because they must first show us parts of ourselves which we do not want to see. As Dr. Alan McGlashan has described in his superb study of the psyche, *The Savage and Beautiful Country*, there is a strange, purposeful dreamer within each of us, busy arranging the details of these dramas to show what is needed without any knowledge or help from the conscious ego.

5. Coming out of an even deeper level, there are dreams which speak in universal or archetypal symbols that appear to be common to all peoples and belong to the very structure of the human psyche. No amount of digging into one's own personal life will reveal their meaning. These images speak of humanity's ways of relating to the spiritual world, and we understand them only as we study the myths and fairy tales and stories of various peoples. I have never worked with anyone who did not dream at some time of some of these symbols like the ocean, the man or woman who cannot be recognized, the snake, a fish or fire or whirlwind, a mass of molten metal contained in a dish, a horse that drops dead, or in this day a car that is stuck. After one has exhausted all personal associations there is still meaning—a meaning that one knows is right when it is discovered. As Jung found in listening to the dreams of many hundreds of patients, people in the twentieth century still bring up the same strange symbols that the alchemists, for instance, worked with in the Middle Ages.

Jung's interest in how the human psyche is shaped by realities from this archetypal area, and from some of the next levels, is well known. It has been described by Aniela Jaffé in her fascinating and factual study, *From the Life and Work of C. G. Jung*. Yet it is difficult for modern people to accept these deeper levels of reality, particularly the next four, even when their own dreams present them with the evidence.

6. Most of us have had some experience of clear communication. If not in a dream, then one may have had the experience of going to bed with a problem and waking to find that a clear solution has been worked out in the night. In much the same way it is sometimes possible to ask for some answer in a dream and suddenly to wake up while dreaming of a perfectly clear and sensible reply. It is as if God had actually spoken in our own language and with good grammar. These communications generally seem so important to us that I sometimes wonder why the deepest meaning does not speak in this way more often. Edgar Cayce has suggested, however, that God is not too interested in giving us ready-made solutions to immediate problems. What He really seems to want is relationship with us. Since the very first requirement for relationship is to get acquainted, God perhaps prefers to use the language of symbols and images with us because through our working with them we come to know the One who gave them to us. The Hebrew prophets, St. Paul and others believed that God could communicate in words we know, but often used symbolic language.

7. There are several kinds of numinous dreams which all have one thing in common. They are all frightening. Almost every time an angel appeared in the New Testament, the first reaction was fear, and the angel's first words were: "Do not be afraid." There is an excellent description of this kind of experience in Rudolf Otto's *The Idea of the Holy*. It is so overwhelming to meet with the numinous, the holy, that one's spine tingles, but with more than ordinary fear. There is a sense of awe at stupendous power, like standing on the platform just under the brink of Niagara Falls. Or in a dream one may face a power that seems to be the very center of malice. It appears so destructive that the dreamer feels paralyzed, and feels no more able to move than a rabbit caught rigid with fear by a snake.

It is no less awesome or frightening to come face to face in this way with the creative and upbuilding force of the angelic or even the divine. Many people have had significant dreams of the Risen Christ that had a central effect on their religious development for the rest of their lives. In addition, one may seem to meet a friend leaving this life at the actual moment of his or her death, and this sometimes happens in dreams when the dreamer has no knowledge of the person's expected death. A recent survey showed that 40 percent of those questioned believed that they had had experiences of this kind, usually in dreams.*

---

*In order to obtain answers that were freely given and true, the questions had to be phrased so that they would not betray any negative attitude of the researcher, nor make the person feel that he might be belittled for telling the truth. In surveys like this it is difficult for people to be open if they feel any chance of being criticized for what they say.³

8. Through a dream a person is sometimes given knowledge of something happening in the physical world that did not come by any direct means. Experiences from this level reveal a strange capacity within the psyche, a power that now and then frees us from space and time. Throughout history people in every culture have reported such experiences, and today the same kind of reports are coming from modern laboratories in our own country. Once in a while, as happened to the chemist Kekulé, a scientist is given some key fact about the nature of the physical world in a dream. Even so, there is so much stress on the analytical process today that science is in danger of forgetting what these strange happenings tell us about the source of our knowledge. Reminders keep coming from the philosophers of science about the necessity of staying in touch with our sensitive, imaginative capacity if we want to keep on making discoveries and developing a creative relationship with the physical universe.

9. The last level produces those rare dreams that usually come once in a lifetime. One seems to stand on a high spiritual mountain from which is seen a view of the actual nature of things, a view of the reality of Christ's victory over evil and of the ultimate power and substance of love. Jung had such a dream-vision at a time when he came close to dying. It occurred long before his death, however, and in it he was told to return to the place he had come from. In his book *Dreams: God's Forgotten Language* John Sanford tells how his father, shortly before he died, was given a flash-back dream that went on to show the hands of the mantelpiece clock stopped, and through it a path of light on which he walked out into the garden; in the weeks that remained he knew peace. Arthur Ford also tells of an experience very much like Jung's in which he was told to return to this world. In each case these experiences leave an abiding sense of fulfillment and purpose and peace.

From this brief review of the kinds of experiences expressed by dreams, it appears that there are four quite different ways of human knowing. There is first of all knowledge of the world and of ourselves that comes directly or through memories. On one hand this includes sensory experiences of the physical world, either immediate or by recall. And on the other hand, experiences of dreams give us knowledge of the human psyche (or soul) by showing us in symbols and images what lies within and beyond ourselves. These experiences help us to know levels and depths in the psyche or soul, ranging from things remembered and those long forgotten to aspects one never knew about oneself, and even blueprints, in more or less clear detail, of the structure of the soul or psyche.

Second, there is knowledge of the physical world which comes, not through the five senses or memory of sensory experiences, but through these same depths of the psyche. And third in the same way we are given knowledge of another dimension of reality similar to the human psyche but different from and independent of it. In these experiences we find a world with an evil as well as a creative side, a world that can speak either in symbols or in straight English—or

Arabic or Japanese; and out of which experiences of the dead sometimes rise. Finally, in probably the clearest of visionary experiences, some find knowledge of the central harmony and creative power of the universe, as Dante described it so beautifully in the closing cantos of *The Divine Comedy*. This knowledge or meeting is given by God Himself and is often experienced as meeting with the Risen Christ.

Each of us has some taste of most of these nine levels, and through meditation one can often step into any one of them. By learning to meditate on the images and symbols that are given, one's dreams and even the course of one's inner life are changed. The goal of Christian meditation is to bring the creative power of the Risen Christ to bear upon the totality of our confused inner being. In this way growth can begin and one can keep moving toward wholeness which is one of the marks of the sons of God.

The dream presents pictures of what needs to be done, and sometimes it even shows the solution that is required. But work has to be done through meditation so that the negative possibilities revealed by the dream are avoided, and the positive and creative possibilities may be brought to actuality. Meditation is not a simple process to be learned in a few lessons. It is rather an exploration of a whole limitless territory. In the act of meditation one consciously enters this territory with all of oneself and starts an adventure which very likely pauses only for an intermission and then continues after this present life.

A Personal Dream History

The idea of finding the deepest religious meaning in dreams is still strange to most people, however, and an example may be helpful. My own record of dreams goes back more than twenty-five years, with two or three dreams written down on most nights of every week. Although it was never much of a problem to see that they were leading into new terrain, there were times at the beginning when I devoutly wished I had never started considering them and could forget what they were telling me. One of these times was on the night when I woke up to the picture of myself as a clergyman struggling with vestments that had been thrown on the floor, and then trying to take up an offering through the branches of a dead tree which had fallen across the church and cut the main body of it completely in two. But it was obvious that the dreamer within me had no intention of letting me forget what a state of deadness, confusion and chaos I had gotten myself into.

Only a few nights later I awoke to see myself doing nothing but staring in fascination at a pink peach pit. There was nothing else that I remembered in the dream, but this much was about as prophetic a vision as one could have. I had to reflect on it, and as I did I was led back twenty years to a trip to Georgia and to some things that had happened there that I had never been able to speak of to anyone before. As a result I began to learn two lessons quite clearly. I had to deal with something in the depths that seemed to know my problems fairly well, but from a different angle from my own. And talking over my dreams with another person certainly opened up possibilities in them that I had never considered before.

In the next brief snatch I saw myself as a student in a military academy in a situation that finally suggested, as I considered it, that I needed more discipline. There could not be much progress until I developed discipline both outwardly and in my inner life, particularly in meditation, Bible reading, and sticking to the religious life. This was followed by a dream about earth-moving equipment so vivid that I almost jumped up to see where the trucks were. But I remembered that I was camping in the San Bernardino mountains where it would be a tight squeeze to get even small equipment in. The heavy reconstruction was taking place inside me, and it behooved me to stay out of the way of the equipment. Besides the actual danger of being run over, my ego concerns would also delay the work that had to be done before the new roadway would be much use to me.

Another dream that was no less vivid was about burning with anger at a dictatorial forest ranger who, appropriately enough, was nicknamed Red. I was rather proud of myself for being able to express anger in the dream. But the person who was helping me understand these dreams suggested that my anger was really directed at the "Red" inside me, that there was a bureaucratic, authoritarian, unbending dictator in me who kept blowing off steam at the wrong time and the wrong people. I simply did not know that there was a part of me like that and could hardly believe it. I considered myself more of a Caspar Milquetoast. Then I went home and told my wife. She smiled and said that she had been living with that dictator for years. Still not convinced, I asked the children, and they burst out laughing at my innocent air. They knew this side only too well.

Then there was a night when I dreamed that I was driving hell-bent with a ghoulish witch holding fast to the hood of my car. She emanated the worst evils one could imagine, and I could not shake her loose. Finally I simply stopped the car and faced her attack. As I did, I suddenly realized that I did not have to be destroyed by her. There was a bucket of water beside me, and I picked it up and baptized her in the name of the Father . . . of the Son . . . of the Holy Ghost . . . only to see the figure slowly melt away. I was ready to know that there is a power far greater than evil, and that one does not ultimately have to fear evil if one will face it and use that power.

The climax of this series of dreams came after a long effort to carry out the suggestions that had come out of them. On that night I was celebrating the Eucharist on Pentecost. I dreamed that I was wearing a brilliant red chasuble, and the reality of the Spirit touched everyone and everything around me. At that moment I knew the presence of the Holy Spirit. It was there as a living reality.

This dream did not need interpretation, but only the willingness on my part to let it be lived out in my life.

In these dreams from one quite unexceptional psyche, several of the different levels of reality were expressed. First, the stage was carefully set in the context of my outer life, using the symbols of my profession to show the utter barrenness and chaos of my situation. The next two dreams pointed to personal levels that had to be dealt with, first to a memory and the fears associated with it, and then to the need for discipline that had been buried in the personal unconscious. At that point the stage of the psyche was set and shored up for the heavy reconstruction work. Then the personal unconscious and the archetypal level erupted together in the figures of Red the ranger and the evil witch. The latter was possibly a numinous experience, and it laid the ground for what was certainly an experience of that level in my dream of celebrating the Eucharist. The change in my life and attitude had taken hold and would continue to develop.

This did not happen without my cooperation. It took place as I learned something of the way of meditation, and as I learned to bring my new feelings and ideas into the world around me and give them a chance to work. As I have suggested, dreams will reveal the problems and give solutions, and a great deal of the hard work goes on below the surface. But one has to learn, by working with images in meditation, how to help the process, sometimes directing it and sometimes understanding when to keep hands off. In my case it took place over ten years. It was an exciting journey into a savage and beautiful country, searching for the loving Father who waited for this one prodigal to return.

14
Developing Imagination:
Stepping into the Inner World

The key that unlocks the door to the inner world is imagination. Most of us can allow images to arise from the unconscious that will tell us about our inner being and how it is affected by forces from the spiritual or psychoid world. One can even learn unknown things about the outer world in this way, but this kind of imagination does far more than simply provide information. Images give us a way of thinking that brings us closer to actual experiences of the spiritual world than any concept or merely verbal idea about that realm.

The powers of the spiritual realm seldom deal with people just on a conscious, rational level. God, of course, can reach an individual by a rational conversion experience, but such an experience is only the *beginning* of a journey into deeper and deeper relationship with God. God seems to want the whole person and to be willing to work with our ego consciousness as though it were a slender life line that will grow stronger with deeper inner experiences. When prayer and meditation concentrate only on concepts, they do not touch the most profound part of our being except when it happens accidentally. Conceptual thought does not have the same power as the ability to think in images.

We are so aware of the importance of logical, conceptual thinking, however, that it seems strange to speak of imagination in the same way. Every one of us needs logical, purposeful thought to direct us in any area. We need it to analyze problems and set up goals, and then to review our methods and results and find out if we are getting anywhere. This means studying things like Euclid's geometry, philosophy and logic and basic science in order to learn how to use words and concepts and ideas logically. This kind of thinking is hard work. It develops later than our imagination does. Logical thinking follows different rules and is used for very different purposes than imagination is.

Images come from the inner world where we have the most intimate contact with realities that are usually hidden from view in the outer world. They have the power to contact these realities and offer us ways of relating to them so that we gain the insight and drive and energy which they hold potentially for our use. Images also help us work with the emotions that are generated by these highly charged experiences of the spiritual world. When one is overwhelmed by a negative experience of this realm, it is almost impossible to get at the root of the problem without images that will show us what the negative force is, and then enable us to bring God or the Risen Christ into the picture by the use of the imagination.

Even so we may have trouble appreciating the value of this process. It cannot be measured by the same standards that are applied to logical thought. Logical reasoning can be directed toward specific results. Once a person learns the rules and can make the effort to stay within them, that person is in control. One is then master of one's thoughts, able to tell them what to do, particularly if keeping to the rules of deductive reasoning. Imaginative thinking seems more like a game that many people consider suitable only for primitive people and artists. Many people even fear its use; they worry about letting imagination interfere with the hard work of rational, conceptual thinking.

It is true that imagination requires a very different capacity. With imagination one does not have conscious control of the images worked with. They cannot be called up or stopped at will like concepts can. Images are more like living beings with a life and purpose of their own. Often they take the individual into strange territory where he or she does not know the terrain well enough to take direction and has trouble enough simply trying to follow where the images lead. Relating to the inner world takes as much time and effort as it does to know the outer world. The part of ourselves that we find within is usually just as complex to know and relate to as anyone in the outside world, and learning about an inner event or a symbolic object is nearly as difficult as trying to peek inside an atom of uranium and understand how it works. If it were as simple to work with images as many people seem to believe, people would make fewer excuses for not doing it and perhaps make more effort to discover these creative experiences within themselves.

The difficulty is that so many intuitive people keep logic at arm's length in order to protect their insights, while people who work with rational ideas are trained to avoid intuition or imagination for fear of hampering their ability to deal with hard, cold facts. Only a few of the most creative thinkers today seem to realize that our ability to understand and deal with the world around us depends upon both capacities. As scientists have studied the source of their knowledge and ideas, they have come to realize that even the most carefully developed concepts rest originally on images which first came up from someone's unconscious as a flash of insight does. Far from stopping each other, logic and imagination go hand in hand with each other. Imagination is needed by logical thinkers fully as much as logical reasoning is needed by intuitive people in order for both to know the world, and to realize and share the full value of the experiences that are available to us.

For generations our training in Western culture has put logic on a pedestal and neglected the value of imagination. Thanks to imaginative thinkers like Einstein, science has continued to grow. But the inner world, where human growth takes place, has been cut off and denied the benefit of logical understanding. Our first task is to learn how to use images again in order to open up the depths of the psyche that have been closed for so long to modern man. We can then look to the more difficult job of trying to understand the experiences that are found there. It will make very little difference what name we give to this venture. Some people will call it *active imagination*, like C. G. Jung and his followers. Others may speak of a process of *psychosynthesis* as Roberto Assagioli does. And still others will use the religious term *meditation*. But in each case the meaning is the same. Each one speaks of seeking that part of the real world that can be explored by turning inward and using the images found within.

The Exploration—How One Goes about It

There are many older descriptions of this venture, but these accounts are often expressed in terms that are difficult for modern people to follow. In addition, these experiences do not follow set patterns. They vary almost as much as the individuals who seek them, and the only rules that come close to being inflexible are, first, that one must believe in the importance of thinking and experiencing in images, and second, that the individual must take enough time in quiet to break away from immediate concern with the outer space-time realm. Aside from that, each person has to follow an individual technique and find a way of awakening imagination, guided largely by the demands of one's own personality type.

Therefore, we shall consider a number of different suggestions, drawn mainly from present-day writers. They are offered in the hope that various individuals will find that one or another of them strikes fire within and shows the way. These are possibilities to pick and choose from, and only someone who is guiding others on the inner way would be interested in all of them. One of the most helpful examples was given by C. G. Jung in 1935 during a series of lectures to a medical group in London. Jung was speaking in English, and in the transcript of these talks his ideas seem to come through with particular clarity for us. Let us look first at some of the ideas he presented and then at the case story he told in answer to a request by one of the doctors to explain the technique of active imagination.

Jung took care to point out that he did not mean playing with the foolish inventions of daydreams. Perhaps it is possible to learn something about oneself by drowsing away a summer afternoon picturing what life might be if one were surrounded by wealth and servants and important personages. But these movie-like episodes are already half conscious. And when they take over the full screen of consciousness, it is only for a few fleeting moments, and then one comes back to the harsher realities of the actual world with a dull thud. The essence of active imagination, on the other hand, lies in the fact "that the images have a life of their own and that the symbolic events develop according to their own logic—that is, of course, if your conscious reason does not interfere."[1] And Jung even told a little story from his own childhood to bring out his point.

When he was quite young he often visited an aunt whose house was full of interesting pictures. One of them showed his grandfather, who had been a bishop, standing on the steps of his house looking down a pathway leading to the door of the cathedral. Often, Jung said, he would kneel on a chair looking at the picture until his grandfather came down the steps onto the path. His aunt always told him that he was mistaken; his grandfather was still standing in the same place. But the child knew perfectly well what he had seen. "In the same way," Jung went on, "when you concentrate on a mental picture, it begins to stir, the image becomes enriched by details, it moves and develops. Each time, naturally, you mistrust it and have the idea that you have just made it up, that it is merely your own invention."[2]

It is usually not too difficult for most people to start the process by concentrating on something graphic. The hard part comes in realizing that something could move unexpectedly inside us without our conscious direction. This is why it is so vital in developing imagination or meditation to realize that the ego is not the only force operating within one. As Jung proceeded to suggest, anyone who writes or lectures knows that the writer is not the creator of the ideas. This lesson was hard for me to admit. I had to learn that consciousness is not so much in charge as we like to think, and that we need contact with forces that are at work at deeper levels of our being. Even walking or raising an arm is done more *through* than *by* a person. In writing or lecturing, the ideas come popping out on their own. If I do not have the support of the unconscious, I am stymied. It may be as small a thing as not being able to remember a name, or the whole thread of ideas may be broken.

The same thing is true of the level from which real imagination comes, except that the flow does not consist of memories. Imagination reveals a new level of inner reality. It does not create these elements. Imagination is a source of knowledge, a means of cognition which can dry up if it is ignored. If one pays attention to it, however, one finds a spontaneous creative process working within. One can observe the forces at work, can relate to and even influence them, but one cannot create what they do by use of ego power. A person can accept what they offer and act upon it, as scientists accept and act upon their intuitions from this level of reality. Very much as the scientist uses this way to find new levels of reality in the physical world, one is then given access to many levels of the world from which dreams come.

Dr. Jung's Example

The story Jung told the group of physicians gave a delightful illustration of how a young artist learned to use his imagination in this way. Jung began by remarking that this case was especially interesting to physicians because of the difficulty the patient had in using active imagination to learn about himself psychologically. He went on:

I was treating a young artist, and he had the greatest trouble in understanding what I meant by active imagination. He tried all sorts of things but he could not get at it. The difficulty with him was that he could not think. Musicians, painters, artists of all kinds, often can't think at all, because they never intentionally use their brain. This man's brain too was always working for itself; it had its artistic imaginations and he couldn't use it psychologically, so he couldn't understand. I gave him every chance to try, and he tried all sorts of stunts. I cannot tell you all the things he did, but I will tell you how he finally succeeded in using his imagination psychologically.

I live outside the town, and he had to take the train to get to my place. It starts from a small station, and on the wall of that station was a poster. Each time he waited for his train he looked at that poster. The poster was an advertisement for Mürren in the Bernese Alps, a colourful picture of the waterfalls, of a green meadow and a hill in the center, and on that hill were several cows. So he sat there staring at that poster and thinking that he could not find out what I meant by active imagination. And then one day he thought: "Perhaps I could start by having a fantasy about that poster. I might for instance imagine that I am myself in the poster, that the scenery is real and that I could walk up the hill among the cows and then look down on the other side, and then I might see what there is behind that hill."

So he went to the station for that purpose and imagined that he was in the poster. He saw the meadow and the road and walked up the hill among the cows, and then he came up to the top and looked down, and there was the meadow again, sloping down, and below was a hedge with a stile. So he walked down and over the stile, and there was a little footpath that ran round a ravine, and a rock, and when he came round that rock, there was a small chapel, with its door standing a little ajar. He thought he would like to enter, and so he pushed the door open and went in, and there upon an altar decorated with pretty flowers stood a wooden figure of the Mother of God. He looked up at her face, and in that exact moment something with pointed ears disappeared behind the altar. He thought, "Well, that's all nonsense," and instantly the whole fantasy was gone.

He went away and said, "Now again I haven't understood what active imagination is." And then, suddenly, the thought struck him: "Well, perhaps that really *was* there; perhaps that thing behind the

Mother of God, with the pointed ears, that disappeared like a flash, really happened." Therefore he said to himself: "I will just try it all over as a test." So he imagined that he was back in the station looking at the poster, and again he fantasied that he was walking up the hill. And when he came to the top of the hill, he wondered what he would see on the other side. And there was the hedge and the stile and the hill sloping down. He said, "Well, so far so good. Things haven't moved since, apparently." And he went round the rock, and there was the chapel. He said: "There is the chapel, that at least is no illusion. It is all quite in order." The door stood ajar and he was quite pleased. He hesitated a moment and said: "Now, when I push that door open and I see the Madonna on the altar, then that thing with the pointed ears should jump down behind the Madonna, and if it doesn't, then the whole thing is bunk!" And so he pushed the door open and looked—and there it all was and the thing jumped down, as before, and then he was convinced. From then on he had the key and knew he could rely on his imagination, and so he learned to use it.[3]

It is possible to learn a lot about this technique of meditation by reflecting upon what we are told of the young man's actions and reactions. In the first place, he really wanted to discover this other dimension of reality. This is the first step. Very few people ever learn to meditate until they want to enough to work at it. The young artist tried and tried again. His first venture was an effort to enter the poster from outside; this act was essentially sacramental in nature. The second time he started with an inner image.

Almost any representation of outer reality can be a starting point. A picture, a statue, a myth or story, a crucifix can be brought into the psyche and encountered within. Many people find that great art stimulates their imagination. Archetypal religious symbols can also start the imagination working. But it is equally possible to start from within the imagination. One can begin with a dream that has bubbled up out of the unconscious, or the memory of a story. Or, one can simply wait in the stillness until an image appears and then follow it as it moves. These are some of the vehicles that can carry one to the gateway of imagination.

Of course, in the case of Jung's young artist, the moment he went over the hill he entered the inner world, the unconscious. He left the outer physical world behind and entered one of the many levels of reality found within. If he had been taking a Rorschach or "ink blot" test, or a Thematic Apperception test, he probably would not have been so surprised. When a psychologist asks, "What do you see?" one would feel foolish just to give the sensible answer, "An ink blot," or "An unfinished sketch." One lets the vague forms stir the imagination so that it brings up images from the deep recesses of mind, or tells a story with an outcome that suddenly seems to fit the neutral outline of a picture. In this way the unconscious is touched and revealed. By giving one's imagination freedom in these tests, to move as it wishes, one suddenly finds oneself in a world of limitless possibilities no longer restricted by the material outline of an ink blot or a half-finished picture. This person has stepped into the inner world where the laws of physical matter do not apply. The only real difference from meditation is that in these tests one is interested in learning about the depth and psychic structure of the individual, while creative meditation is aimed at learning about both the individual and the world that individual has entered.

This young man, however, was not sitting across from Dr. Jung. His first reaction was that his experience was all bunk, and the whole process dissolved. If one tries to enforce the rules and ideas of the outer physical world to make the inner world conform to what we are accustomed to, one is quickly jolted out of it. The inner world can be investigated in depth only when it is taken seriously and not subjected to logical and sensory doubt.

The artist did not start out with any religious venture in mind, but imagination led him right to religious images. If religion matters to a person, imagination will produce religious images regardless of the original intent. In this story the realities of the divine mother and then of the evil, furtive creature lurking behind the altar hold our interest so that one wishes Jung would go on and not leave us wondering what happened next. But most likely Dr. Jung would smile and remind us that we all have access to this world and to experiences of our own that are just as interesting and usually just as directed toward religious meaning.

Other Ways of Awakening Imagination

There are dozens of ways of helping people get back into the imaginative realm which they knew so well when they were children. But most adults have to learn first of all that there is nothing wrong with imagining and becoming as little children again.* We have looked at the way parents usually react to their children's experiences of the inner world. They are afraid that a child's imaginary playmate—or even the angels that William Blake saw—is a dangerous sign that the child is not adjusting to the ordinary, outer world. It is upsetting to them to see the child actually at home in both worlds; they are afraid the child will not be able to tell inner reality from outer.

The problem in growing up, however, is not to reject the inner world, but to learn to distinguish between inner and outer realities. The child is not yet able to tell the difference clearly. In fact, children's responses to a Rorschach test are sometimes hard to tell from those of a psychotic person. But, as Laurens van der Post has shown with such depth in his novel *The Face Beside the Fire*, it takes

---

*Mark 10:15.

years of restoring to undo the damage that is caused by punishing a child for inability to distinguish between inner and outer realities. Since the Enlightenment
generations of people have grown up trying to avoid imagination and the inner
world, and when a faculty like this is repressed, its power for us usually turns
negative. The way we treat mentally ill people, quickly isolating them from the
rest of us, shows how afraid we are of being gobbled up by the inner powers.

Just as children have to begin learning to think logically and to know the
world outside—and children must do this in order to develop a strong ego so
that the inner realm may be easier for them to handle—adults need to find the
magical reality within once more and know that it can be terrifying or comforting, and begin to understand how it differs from the physical world. In this way
our lives will become less restricted. We will come to know the reality of the
spiritual world, and we will also find ways of being a little more sure whether
we are dealing with the physical world as it is, or with an idea we have constructed about it without recognizing that the idea was based on inner reality
rather than outer.

Rix Weaver's book *The Wise Old Woman* offers a good explanation and
many illustrations of finding the inner way, while Roberto Assagioli's
Psychosynthesis: A Manual of Principles and Techniques is packed with suggestions for developing imagination.[4] He starts with simple exercises like imagining
a blank blackboard and seeing a series of numbers gradually appear on it, and
goes on to increasingly sophisticated techniques, even for evoking auditory or ol-
factory imagination. One contributor to this book suggests a therapeutic technique in which the patient imagines being in a meadow and then reports to the
therapist what has been observed. At another session the patient is told to imagine being on a mountain, and later visiting a chapel, and to bring back reports
of what happened. Archetypal symbols of this kind will often stimulate deep
levels of the psyche and help the meditative process take off. Sometimes it helps
imagination to share the images with another person. This is one advantage of a
prayer group or having a prayer partner.

By inventing stories one also reveals the depth of oneself, and far more
than that, and the more naturally the story flows on its own, the more it reveals.
This technique has been used in English classes to have students make up their
own fairy tales, and it is surprising how much they are stimulated and how
much they disclose almost unintentionally. Great literature reveals not only the
depth of the writer, but also what is happening in the collective psyche (the part
of the psyche that all people share together). and sometimes even the nature of
reality itself. Robert Louis Stevenson, for instance, expanded the images of a
dream into his best selling novelette, *The Strange Case of Dr. Jekyll and Mr.
Hyde*, thus revealing his own split and the split of Victorian England grown
rich and cultured on imperialism and the slave trade. Herman Melville wrote at
an even deeper level, so deep that his contemporaries hardly understood his
masterpiece *Moby Dick* at all.

The greatest literature speaks of the nature of the spiritual world and of God, and about humanity's relation to them. In *Faust*, which was his life work and probably the greatest work in Germanic literature, Goethe depicted the height and depth of spiritual reality and its incredibly redemptive and compassionate structure. Shakespeare left an equal heritage. Jung is reported to have said of him, "Here was a man who knew God." Shakespeare's plays deal with more than human nature; they tell us about humankind's interaction with all of reality, and in this way they reveal the very nature of God Himself.

One's own efforts at insight can start with dream images like Stevenson's, or by looking at a picture as the young Jung did, or by walking into a new scene like the young man who worked with Jung. One can begin with images of one's own meaninglessness, as Dante did in *The Divine Comedy*, or by visualizing a Bible story (and I shall say a lot more about this in a later chapter), or by simply waiting for the right image to appear, and then concentrating on it until it begins to move. Some people are able to sit down at the typewriter once the action has begun and record it as if they were watching from a press box. My own imagination has led me in this way through three long sequences. One of them lasted off and on over nearly two years, and I had set down about eighty thousand words before it came to an end. Some of the scenes which occurred were as real and vivid as any outer or physical experiences I have had.

Of course this is not the way to creative images for everyone. Many people find that drawing or painting or modeling will open up imagination to them far better than storytelling. There are a number of interesting studies of the spontaneous drawings of children that show how much the child reflects the inner life in this way, and the same thing is true of adults, as psychologists find when they use the "Draw-a-Person" test. I have seen hundreds of reports of this test, and it is still amazing to me how much one reveals about the self when simply asked to draw a person and then to sketch a person of the opposite sex. Drawing ability has practically nothing to do with the results.

Many of Dr. Jung's patients used painting to see more deeply into the images that came to them, particularly their dream images, and Jung illustrated some of his works with his patients' pictures. This way of bringing out images has been adapted for children by asking them to draw an island including everything they would want to make it their very own. A similar technique of "sandplay" is used by many therapists, even with adults. The person plays with a large assortment of miniatures of all kinds, placing them in the sand to create whatever scene comes to mind. When Dr. Jung was struggling to understand the materials that were rising from the unconscious, he used a similar kind of play with stones to build a model village in his backyard. In his autobiography, *Memories, Dreams, Reflections*, Jung describes his initial feeling of humiliation at going back to child's play, and then the great value of doing just that. He also describes the work he did in stone in later years at his retreat in Bollingen.

The important thing is to find whatever activity will help one to develop imagination. Many people find an activity like building or sculpturing most helpful because it involves them more completely. For myself I find few things that release and spur my imagination more than building sand castles on the beach, seeing whole cities before me complete with castles and towers and temples. One time a few years ago I spent several days alone at the beach making a mandala* of different colored shells, and the memory of this is still important. Making the mandala brought something together in me. Children and adults alike need to have plastic materials available to bring concrete touch to a realm of existence which can slip away all too easily and be forgotten.

For some individuals weaving or gardening may bring out this contact with the depth of imagination, while others find the key in dancing or acting. Dance therapy helps the person let out the deepest feelings in dramatic movement, and this may well be the reason primitive religions have given so much place to the dance. Even today's formal church procession has something of this element, which is sometimes given free rein in the more enthusiastic churches. Drama itself also has a place in present-day therapy and in at least one ancient religion. Psychodrama, as developed by J. L. Moreno, uses role playing to help patients know and accept the forces at work within them, very much as religious ritual seeks to do. The greatest dramas of the ancient world, those of Greece, arose out of religious rites, and even in classical Greece drama was still a religious observance.[5]

The relation among dance and drama, religious ritual, worship, creative play, imaginative writing, painting, and meditation is very deep in human life. Johan Huizinga, the great Dutch historian, has suggested in his book *Homo Ludens* that it may be real misnomer to call ourselves *homo sapiens*, and that the term *homo ludens*, or man the player, seems to be closer to the truth. It is the human's ability to play creatively, rather than to think, that apparently sets humankind apart from other species. In fact, it may well be our imaginative capacity, which is always characterized by a sense of play, that really makes us human. This capacity keeps us in touch with the roots of reality so that we are able to keep our bearings and find meaning and purpose. Our sense of the sacred, which provides our direction in life, undoubtedly springs from the merger of the playful with the imaginative.

The Symbols that Awaken Imagination

If ordinary meadows and mountains and fairy tales can awaken a response from the depth of people, there is likely to be far more power in the symbols

---

*A mandala is a design like a rose window in which all the parts relate to the center. I shall say more about it later on.

that originally came from that depth and have been hallowed by people's actions at sacred times and in holy places, by their sacraments and rituals, and in their sacred writings and religious art. Some of these symbols are well known. We are all familiar with water that has been blessed, particularly for baptism, or with the whole image of the sacred stable at Christmas time. But when we look up at the heavens at night, how many of us stop to think that the familiar constellations of stars speak to us of the beginnings of religion? Even their names came to us from the ancient Greeks who looked into the clear Aegean skies and peopled the heavens with gods who sent blessing or misfortune into one's life. Out of the depth of these ancients came their deepest concerns, not very different from the way Abraham was doing farther to the East, except that the Greeks allowed these yearnings to illuminate the heavens. No wonder men are drawn by astrology. There in the stars was one of the first places that people pictured their gods.

One of the principal symbols of Eastern religion is the mandala or circular design that is used in meditation as a way of gathering the elements of one's being around a center into wholeness. As Dr. Jung discovered, people have a natural tendency to form mandala designs, often making them of images from their own lives and from their dreams, and this leads them towards wholeness and to look for religious meaning in life.

In Christianity this meaning is developed in almost a tapestry of symbols that reveal God's concern for human beings. The whole Bible is a moving story of how God works with people and finally overcomes the evil that affects their lives. It is told mostly in images from history and in teachings that are anything but abstract. The Bible does not try to show us how to put this message logically in neat propositions. Instead it is deeply concerned with giving us a picture of how we can find the reality of the victory over evil, and one way to do it is to use the images that are given.

Using the imagination, one can step into the events recorded in the New Testament or into the stories told by Jesus. One can be present at the birth in Bethlehem, at the stilling of the sea or the feeding of the five thousand, at the foot washing, the crucifixion or at the various resurrection appearances. In this way any of us can participate in the eternal reality that broke through in history in the person of Jesus of Nazareth, and continues to break through whenever someone becomes truly open to the Holy Spirit. Basically, what we are asked to do is to let the images speak to us, and then to share in the victory and power and allow them to show through in our outer lives in service to others.

The tragedy is that so many modern churches have tried to become intellectual and eliminate this rich and meaningful symbolism from their Christianity. They are so worried about reaching people's minds that they leave no way to touch a person where it counts, in the heart and soul. Of course, much of the symbolism that could reach to the depth of the psyche became surrounded by superstition, and it was sometimes expressed in atrocious art forms. But the remedy for that is to throw out the superstition and some of the art, not the symbols. Jung has pointed out in unmistakable terms how much the stripped-down Protestantism of the recent era has contributed to the neurosis of our time. The Church in Switzerland was almost as good an example of this as our New England Meeting Houses.

Only a few of the great geniuses, men like Lewis and Eliot, Tolkien and Jung, have been able to discover enough symbols within themselves to begin making up for the rich imagery which took centuries to develop fully and can be found in the traditional Catholic Churches. For instance, the best modern presentation of the central Christian idea of the atonement is not found in some carefully thought-out volume on theology. It is in *The Lion, the Witch, and the Wardrobe*, written by C. S. Lewis for children. In this simple but powerfully moving story he brings out the majesty and compassion of the Christ, through the figure of the magnificent lion, Aslan, better than any theological discourse. If people can learn how to step into symbolism, the stained glass windows and statues and images of the Church can do more to feed the soul than all the concepts that could be put into a sermon.

Meditation and Psychotherapy—Learning from Each Other

The practice of using images in meditation has been rediscovered by modern psychiatrists trying to bring sick people to health again. Because they had nearly the same passion for healing as the first Christians, they were willing to try something that even looked silly to many people. They realized that the excessive rationalism of modern times had cut us off from the inner world, and that this separation was a main cause of mental anguish, neurosis, and physical illness as well. The human body cannot sustain a divided mind without suffering illness also.[6] A number of depth psychologists began to teach patients to use imagination through techniques very similar to the early practices of Christian meditation.

The results were surprising. By learning about their own psychic depths, using dreams and symbols and imagination, patients recovered their health and they found religious meaning as well. Jung's experience with patient after patient made him quite certain that a neurosis could never be totally resolved until the individual came into touch, usually through imagination, with the reality of which all the great religions speak. Thus in recent years in Western countries the use of imagination in meditation became mainly a therapeutic tool used by the healing professions.

This has raised doubts about whether the practice is safe for religious people to use. Psychiatrists had to get into the act for just one reason: people with Christian backgrounds had backed out, and God will apparently raise up sons of Abraham from stones when it is necessary. Both religion and people badly need psychiatrists who understand the religious depth of human beings and religious educators, pastors and spiritual directors who understand how the human psyche functions. Humankind (and also God) pays a severe penalty when people do not stay in touch with the whole of themselves. What is *not* saf is to keep on treating individuals a part at a time. The person is a whole and can function well only when treated as a whole.

Dr. Assagioli sums the problem up well when he writes:

> From all that has been said it is apparent that, in order to deal in a satisfactory way with the psychological troubles incident to Self-actualization, a twofold competence is required—that of the professionally trained psychotherapist and that of the serious student of, or better still, the experienced traveller along the way to Self-realization. This twofold endowment is at present only rarely found; but, considering the growing number of individuals who require such treatment, it is becoming increasingly urgent that as many as possible of those who wish to serve humanity by administering to its greatest needs should be induced to qualify for the task.[7]

Perhaps the fact that Dr. Assagioli was writing for his profession, rather than for a specifically Christian audience, suggested the use of the word Self-realization instead of a religious term. But his meaning is clear, particularly when he goes on later to develop it in relation to spiritual reality. The Church, its ministers and individual Christians have a job to do.

As Jung said a long time ago, the overwhelming need of people for a religious outlook presents the Church with a vast horizon, but few Christians seem to notice it. The attitude that the Church should deal only with "religion" and "religious ideas" and stay far away from the insights of psychology or psychiatry is still strong among Christians. The implications of this approach are frightening. It suggests a world split in two, with no bridge between the religious and the secular. It suggests fear of psychology, perhaps fear that its discoveries will deny the value of spiritual growth, and that there is no point in trying to integrate psychological knowledge into the framework of spiritual life. Perhaps it is simply fear of atheism in psychology and ignorance of the number of psychiatrists who insist that a religious outlook is imperative if their profession is to go on holding out the hope of healing people's illness.[8] Or does this attitude suggest most of all that to become spiritual one must leave behind the parts of oneself that desperately need God, the very parts which can bring one to a truly religious attitude?

If it is true that God actually became incarnate in the world in Jesus Christ, then there is no opposition between the divine and the physical, between the spiritual and the secular, the human. Jesus had observable effects on people wherever He went, not only changing their lives by conversion, but also by healing their minds and emotions and bodies. Jesus loved people so much that He exposed Himself to condemnation and real death on a cross, suffering the worst that could happen to any of us. Christians with an attitude anything like this have little to fear from atheistic doctors. The healing effects of this love and acceptance of all that is human will show through in spite of what anyone thinks or says.

It is not hard to seek God with an attitude like this. If one seeks with the whole of one's personality, not just with concepts or by gazing into an imageless void, that person will find God, even around some strange corners. There is one catch, however. To go searching in this way, Christians need to be equipped. They will want meditation to reach into the depth of themselves and touch the parts that need God—the emotions, the anger and fear, the depression and sense of being lost and hopeless, the dryness and inability to look beyond the ego. To touch these problems, Christians need to learn a great deal from the psychological professions. Psychologists have been working for nearly a century to find out what can pop out of the depth of a person, and what structure is found below the surface. It is very foolish to try to work with people without equipping ourselves with as much of this knowledge as we can.

We also need to know how to work with images. Images and emotions are so closely connected that it seems to be impossible to deal with one without working with the other.[9] By experimenting with ways that Christians once used images in meditation, we can get back to working with the real needs of people, especially their need for a contact with the center of meaning. We can stop playing around the fringes of reality, while other people do the important jobs. Those psychologists and psychiatrists who realize the need for religious reality in our lives will usually be glad to learn ways that help their patients and to share some of their own insights if we take the trouble to find them and get to know them.

Christian symbols are able to uncover the religious depth of the spiritual world very much as the Rorschach and the Thematic Apperception tests reveal the hidden things and quirks and cracks in our personalities. If the physical world were all we had to deal with, we might be able to forget these sometimes difficult depths. But what we do in the physical world is often determined for us in this other realm of reality, and our choice is whether to go blindly or to find contact with it through the images and art, the myths, stories, rituals and dramas of religion, and with the help of Christian spiritual direction. Let us look at this and one or two other problems and then consider several actual meditative practices which have helped to bring these symbols and stories alive and made them real in a number of lives.

15
A Check List for the
Venture Inward

Relating to the spiritual world may seem complex, but once one gets the hang of it, stepping into this realm in meditation is as easy as walking through a door. Do you remember how many false starts and stumbles it takes for a child to learn to walk? But once it has been mastered, the playpen has to be put away. Walking into the inner world is not very different. One tries and waits, and concentrates again and again. And suddenly one is *there* and knows that the experience can be found.

In Christianity this process begins with the realization that God broke through into human history in a unique way. We learn that there is a spiritual realm, and because of the death and resurrection of Jesus we know that His love is found in it. There is something worth the effort. And when an individual becomes ready and turns to this reality—usually because one is unable to manage by oneself—then our teaching, preaching and training of children in the basic elements of Christianity are nearly fulfilled. Probably no one is educated into a vital and personal faith. But when the need arises, a person who already has some understanding of spiritual reality and knows where to turn for guidance and spiritual direction is ahead of the game.

We have already considered why it is important to stay in touch with the Church, but there is so much misunderstanding about the psyche and the inner journey and what is found there that a concentrated reminder is advisable. Let us look briefly at this process and then see how the sacraments and rituals of the Church relate to it. Keeping a journal and finding companionship and spiritual direction will then complete this list of outer requirements.

The greatest values of this process are seldom revealed to people who make a fetish of learning about the spiritual world entirely on their own. These people would not dream of tackling mathematics by starting to count on their fingers and toes, or putting the science of physics together from their own observations. They go to school and work up from Euclid to Einstein, expecting to be taught even about things that can be seen and touched. But the same people may insist that one does not need religion to learn about the intangibles of the spiritual world because anyone can find out what is in the inner world for oneself.

It is no wonder people lose their bearings among these realities. The possibilities in the spiritual world are so incredibly rich that it is often hard to keep one's goal in sight. When religious traditions are ignored, the dangers of inflation or of unexpected encounters with dark and demonic forces are great. A person faces the same risks setting out simply to prove something one thinks is true about the spiritual world. This reality has substance and one cannot reconstruct all that has been learned about it by oneself or make it conform to one's own ideas. In approaching spiritual realities, it is only good sense to go back again and again to religious sources and check one's direction.

There is no other way, in fact, to keep the Christian goal of this process in view. In order to know and relate to the love expressed by the Christ, most of us have to learn a great deal about giving and receiving love. Once we become open to its source, we find gifts of all kinds offered without asking whether we deserve them or not. All that is required in return is that we do our best to use them to give proper love to other people. In the first flush of finding oneself touched by love, a person is often tempted to think that this presents no problems. I have yet to meet anyone at all conscious, myself included, who did not soon find plenty of problems.

Besides going back to the Bible and the sacraments, it is important to use our minds and rational ability. Even the most thoughtful individuals need to remind themselves that God gave us these abilities and that using them to come to God, as well as to deal with the world, makes good sense. By comparing our experiences with those of other people—both present-day and in the historical record of our faith—we can see what blocks our way and whether we are perhaps fooled by an evil appearing as an angel of pure light. To guard against accepting ideas that are superstitious or downright nonsense, we can examine our experience in the light of the best understanding of psychology and science. This kind of critical understanding is essential unless we just want to believe something because it is pleasant or because we wish it were so.

Finally, this process which we find through meditation is like life itself. It grows as we reach out to express love in stumbling efforts that send us back to the Church and the Bible to prepare ourselves to try again. With each cycle we become more able to love in a positive way and to bind up the wounds of people who are hurting, and also to be conscious and to bear our own conflicts and failures and inconsistencies. This process of spiritual growth is as organic as the body itself. Each aspect is equally important, and if any one of them takes over and becomes the central concern, then the whole process breaks down, and turning inward in meditation loses its meaning. It is this whole process of awakening spiritually which gives meaning to the effort of learning to meditate.

Sacrament, Ritual and History

The sacraments and ritual of the Church give an immediate contact with the historical base of Christianity in which this meaning is rooted. Even though much the same contact can be found by meditating on the events in the Bible, we cannot assume that the historical base of the Bible is really known or understood today. The aspect of rational understanding, which is equally important and must not be belittled in any way, has come to dominate our approach to this base. We tend to forget the actual experiences we are trying to understand. Studying the Bible and trying to understand the events philosophically and theologically should serve to strengthen our contact with these events, rather than replace it. In the sacraments one participates in the reality that has been revealed historically and seeks to be restored and to find new meaning from it.

The sacrament of baptism, first of all, commits the individual to a new way of life. The importance of this entry into the Christian family and fellowship cannot be stressed too much. Although churches have come to limit baptism mostly to infants, there is no mistaking the meaning for the families who present children and for the Christian community that accepts them. In baptism one dies and rises again, symbolically a new person. The past is wiped clean; by accepting that we cannot make it on our own, we are given a new beginning. This is exactly the attitude that is necessary if one is to enter the spiritual world with any safety. And this sacrament can constantly remind us of how close the divine is to our ordinary lives. One of the commonest acts of everyday life, bathing or washing, can bring back the reality of this way of new beginning. Even people who know little of Christianity often find that a dream of bathing awakens the same meaning for them. In addition the Church provides for renewal of baptismal promises in the service of confirmation, in which the laying-on-of-hands symbolizes being touched by God.

These two rituals cannot be repeated, however; outwardly they are once-and-for-all experiences. It is the Eucharist or Holy Communion which provides a method by which one may return to share most deeply in the historical events of Christianity. Here the ordinary food of Jesus's time, the bread and wine, are used to express His continuing presence among His followers. Jesus's last supper with the little group, His death, and then His resurrection and His actual presence among the worshippers are reenacted. In receiving his body and blood each worshipper can realize Christ's incredible love for us and know that He gives Himself over and over again. By imagination one can be part of the broken-hearted group of disciples who had not believed He would be resurrected until He broke bread with them at Emmaus and on the shore of Galilee.

Then, as the Quakers point out so well, one is rooted in concrete reality. Every meal becomes a reminder of what happens at the altar, of the reality of Christ's self-giving love poured out for everyone. One can come as often as desired, even daily, to renew the experience of taking Christ into one's life. Many believe that in celebrating this ritual of thanksgiving, the priest does not stand alone at the altar, but that Christ is truly present.

In providing the sacrament of penance, the early Christian community recognized that people always slip back and fail in their intentions. Sometimes they act in direct contradiction to all their plans and hopes. The opportunity to return and be forgiven offers another chance to realize God's love for us, particularly for the prodigals. For many people there is no surer way of finding new life than by accepting the forgiveness and love offered in penance.

There are three other rituals that use human touch sacramentally. Probably nothing else conveys the sense of deep relationship so well. Can you imagine living with a person you really love and never touching each other? One touch can often do more than thousands of words. In the sacrament of the laying-on-of-hands and unction for healing, in the sacrament of marriage, and in the sacrament of the conveying of holy orders, touch is used to communicate God's loving concern for persons. In each of these God touches the person in a very real sense. In the first He offers healing which comes from beyond the touch of human hands. In the second two people are joined in a sacramental union as they touch hands. And in the third an individual is given specific tasks in the service of God and empowered by the Holy Spirit to carry them out.

Here again we find a marvelous union of the spiritual with the physical, this time symbolically by means of a very common human action. By tying the earthly and the spiritual together, the person is experientially reached where our roots are, in the concrete outer physical world. At the same time the most basic needs of the psyche or soul are met in one or another of these sacramental acts. From baptism to holy orders these rites offer rebirth, transformation, renewal out of failure and guilt, physical and mental healing, joining with another in marriage, and finally bringing the spiritual into our religious practice.

The sacraments provide a base of reality for the inward journey. They keep us in touch with the historical reality of Christianity, the way God entered into the world in Christ, and also with the importance of our physical nature, both in itself and in giving God ways of continuing to break through into the outer, physical world. The sacraments make us realize how important the simplest, most physical acts can be as ways of allowing God to reveal Himself to us. Commonplace actions which we often ignore, like touching, bathing, eating, can become the most important ways of opening our lives to Him. For some people these sacramental acts alone are enough to meet their religious needs. It is important to understand that one takes the inner journey in order to enhance this sacramental life, *not to replace it.* One of the main purposes of turning inward is to revitalize and enhance these living symbols. When they have lost their meaning, they must be revitalized or religion dies.

To start the inner journey without some such base of religious practice, however, is almost to court disaster. I am not as sanguine as people like Ira Progoff who once told of writing in his journal: "Suppose the Nazis had burned all the Bibles in the world. What would happen? . . . Well, we'd just have to make new ones from the same place that the old ones were made."* To my way of thinking, this is an overly optimistic view of the human psyche and an underestimation of the value of history and what we have learned through it.

Recently a friend who is working in religious education in Australia came to quite a different conclusion. She had written to me worrying about the number of people who feel that Christian symbols have lost their meaning since Vatican II. I made some suggestions, and later she wrote to agree. "I think I understand," she wrote. "Our job is to touch the well-springs, not so much to find new symbols or to try out those of Eastern religions, but to let the old ones come back to life. Thinking about the first Christians makes me wonder about people who are breaking away from the church today. Would many of them be willing to start off on their own if they really thought about the cross that brought the symbols of our Christian culture alive in the first place?"

We in the West have a big investment in Christianity; the best things in our life and culture have been shaped by it more than we ordinarily realize. As I have tried to show, we need the structure of a religion as firmly rooted in history as Christianity. We need what it can tell us about the symbols that are awakened, and what we *do not* need in meditation is to be carried away by every new flood of experience. If one has real knowledge of historical Christianity and is actively participating in the life of the Church, that one will find direction and guidance built in and, thus, far greater freedom. It is possible then to learn from many different practices.

If the things that are experienced take one too far from what is found in the teaching and practice of Christ, or if one is made to *feel superior* and separated from the Christian fellowship, an active Christian will know that it is time to look for counsel from someone who knows the inner way. For most Western people there is nothing that will take the place of contact with Christian rituals and a Christian group.

---

*In another place Dr. Progoff states the same idea even more clearly: "It seems to me that religious experience in our time has to be created new and fresh out of each person's symbolic experiences. Just as we don't want to dream someone else's dream, so we shouldn't follow the doctrines of last year's or the last century's ideology. Truth lives in the contact with inner reality, and we can always rely on that being there. The specific quality of the religious life in our period of history is that the spirit comes—not through prophets or rituals or doctrines or religious institutions—but through the individual. What I'm doing is providing a methodology that is self-regulating and that has no fixed structure, so as to permit that to happen."[1] It is my experience, on the contrary, that method alone is not enough to bring order out of the inner world. In fact, if Dr. Progoff were to look a little deeper, I wonder if he would not find that he is regulated by a structure from within.

The Religious Journal

Participating in the symbolic life of a religious group helps to anchor an individual in reality. This is also one purpose of keeping a record of our inner experiences. It is one thing to be caught up by an inner experience and to be swayed by it without regard for what happens next, but quite another to relate the height or depth of the event to one's life as a whole. As inadequate as written words are to express the totality of an experience, recording it is about the best way we have to consider what has happened objectively and try to see its meaning. At the same time we need to remember that the best description cannot capture the flavor of even a simple taste of bleu cheese. But the record of an experience can always be reopened imaginatively to discover more of its meaning.

One of the best ways of starting the inner journey is to begin keeping a journal, and this is more necessary once the journey is under way. In fact the two often go hand in hand. It is the inner journey which makes a journal coherent by giving it meaning beyond the personal and making it more than a mere succession of outer events. The journal itself makes the meaning available, laying one's insights out on the table and showing their power to influence action and so to transform one's whole life. This way of using a journal can reveal the implications of one's inner experiences so that they can be translated into the outer creativity and loving action that is the completion of the inner way.

In addition, simply writing these experiences down shows that they are worth recording and that the venture inward is being taken seriously, and this opens a person to further growth and inner development. Since we are dealing with personality, rather than a fixed order of things, the more we look into inner reality, the more is revealed. There is probably no limit to the value of keeping a journal for many individuals, any more than there is to the religious possibilities of human development. People who have heard me lecture sometimes come back years later to thank me for the suggestion about keeping a journal. For many people starting a journal is the religious turning point in their lives.

There is hardly a master of the religious way who could read and write who did not keep some record of this inward journey. Many of the greatest religious classics were set down originally as journals which these people kept to record their spiritual journeys. They seemed to feel that it showed lack of respect for the source they sought if they came to an encounter with Love and did not make a record of it. In the *Confessions*, St. Augustine began a new literary form by bringing together in one story the relation between his spiritual and his outer experiences. Hugh of St. Victor left an amazing dialogue between himself and his soul and St. Teresa left her autobiography, while the *Journal of John Woolman* is an inspiring document, and there are dozens of others that reveal the secret of these great lives and how they found the secret themselves.

Even today we find records like Dag Hammarskjöld's *Markings* and the selections which have been published from Thomas Merton's journals, and once in a while someone writes about the value of keeping a journal. In *The Symbolic and the Real*, for instance, Ira Progoff builds a whole religious way around keeping what he calls an intensive journal. More recently in an article in *Worship*, Edward Fischer of the University of Notre Dame presents some interesting ideas about the value of the journal as worship.[2] But I have found very few instructions for people who might want to use a journal as a means of growth in the Christian way of life. And so it has seemed a good idea to me to offer people some rather concrete suggestions. Let us consider some of these ideas which I have used in discussing the problem with various groups.

First of all, in a real sense a journal becomes a sacrament or outward and visible sign of a person's inner spiritual journey, and one way to be sure of valuing it as such is to lay out some money for the book itself. If one scribbles these innermost experiences on scraps of paper or old envelopes, it will be hard to treat them as worth very much, and generally the spiritual world responds accordingly. Instead, using a bound book like a ledger shows an expectation that something of importance will be revealed and a readiness to take care of it. I have accumulated quite a stack of these volumes in almost thirty years of keeping a journal, plus a few small notebooks from the times when I was traveling. For longer fantasies I often use the typewriter because this makes it easier to keep up with the flow of images without interrupting them, and these sheets are collected as carefully as the bound volumes.

Then there is the problem of secrecy. There is not much value in a journal unless one can be honest in it, and this is hard enough without worrying for fear someone will discover any secrets it may hold. Our inner lives are probably far less interesting to others than we might think, but one can take reasonable care and use some kind of code for anything that could damage anyone's life and reputation, our own included.

For two reasons each entry should be dated. If our purpose is to find central reality out of the great mass of experiences that touch human beings from all sides, then the first task is to see how our own experiences, inner *and* outer, relate to one another in our ordinary framework of space and time. It helps anchor us to reality, in reflecting on an inner event, to know the time sequence in relation to other things that were happening in our lives. In addition, there will inevitably be gaps in any journal. The only way of knowing for sure how long it has been since one stopped to reflect and record inner events, or perhaps even took time to meditate, is to see a date on the last entry. It is also important to set aside a regular time of day for writing. As with meditating, this should be some of one's best time, not what is left over from other activities when one is dead tired.

People often ask about content. What does one record in a journal? First of all there are dreams, which must be written down in the night or whenever one wakes up remembering a dream. Then in the morning, before jumping up to start the day, I pause and look back over what has happened during the night and try to visualize what I have encountered. If some insight about one of the dreams pops into mind, I stop right then to reflect on it and make a note. At this point, even if I do not understand much that the dreams have tried to say, at least I have set down enough facts and any thoughts so that I can go back later and ask questions. As James Hillman suggests in his book *Insearch*, this is one way to "befriend" our dreams and our inner life.

I have already spoken of recording fantasies. These are also formed of spontaneous images, but unlike dreams they come when asked, when one tunes out everything but the inner world in meditation. As one learns to observe the movement and sometimes the words of these images, this becomes an important element of the journal. This vast area of psychic life needs to be known and connected with our ordinary daily lives. But so often these spontaneous images are pushed aside and ignored, or one becomes lost in their flow and ends up merely indulging in meaningless play with them. The only way to discover their meaning for us is to make some record of dreams and other images. Then we can try to understand how to deal with them by reflecting on them or perhaps sharing them with someone else.

At the same time it is equally important to record the personal things that affect our lives and can either open up this other reality or cut us off from it. I make a point to write about my angers and fears and hurts, depressions and disappointments and anxieties, my joys and thanksgivings, my experiences of real fellowship and closeness. In short I set down the feelings and events that have mattered to me, high moments and low. It is amazing how often things that seemed negative and overwhelming shrink to manageable size when they are set down in black and white, while some of the most attractive things lose their luster when they are examined. The journal is like a little island of solid rock on which we can stand and see the waves and storms for what they really are, and realize how hard it is to be objective when one is tossed by them.

Sometimes, however, an emotion is so overwhelming that simply writing about what is disturbing us is not enough. The only thing to do is to call a halt and allow the emotion to be shaped into a new mold in meditation. It is like shutting down the machines to retool a factory. In a similar way, one turns off the production of the same old emotional reactions so that a new image can arise which can then be worked on creatively. It is difficult, however, for most of us to express anger creatively. We usually direct it toward other people, letting it out in the wrong way on the right person or in the right way on the wrong person. Some of us have to learn that it does no one any good just to turn anger loose. Instead, one can use a journal to begin to work with it. As Edward Fischer suggests:

> Martin Luther found that to rage against his enemies helped him
> to pray better. If you must rage, a journal is a safe place to do it. If the

spent anger leaves more space in the heart for prayer, that alone is a
good reason for keeping a journal.[5]

In the next chapter I shall say much more about ways of expressing anger and
the necessity of doing so if we are to get far on the inward journey.

I wonder if any of us can really answer "Who am I?" and "Where am I
going?" until we can lay out the fragments of our lives and reflect on them. Life
does not come into view all at once, but in a journal one can see parts scattered
over the pages and begin to realize the shape of a whole. In this way I begin to
see what I have avoided, the deficiencies that need to be made up, the excesses
that need to be curbed, and how all this relates to my goal. One of the amazing
things about God is that He seems to have a unique destiny for every life. The
meditative journey can help unlock this secret, showing a person possible ways
of developing toward it so that life becomes creative and valuable to oneself and
to others. But it is foolish to go looking for such a goal without ways of checking
on our experiences. Our lives are too complex to keep a direction without using
a journal or other spiritual direction.

A great deal has been written lately about the value of autobiographical
writing. By looking back over one's life, a person sees the turning points and
which events have been crucial. One glimpses how meaning and purpose have
been received into life, and sometimes how one has avoided accepting them. A
journal does much the same thing, but with an added dimension. Looking at
things past in one's journal means reflecting on the present and how past and
present work together to shape the future.

Keeping a journal is one activity on which youth has no corner. It actually
improves with age and can continue as long as one is able to hold a pencil or
speak into a tape recorder. At thirty, or even fifty, one does not have the depth
and wisdom that come in later years. The longer one writes of the depth of self,
the more that person finds to write about and the more profound the reflections.
Jung's *Memories, Dreams, Reflections*, for instance, was dictated when he was
well past eighty; it was finished only a few weeks before he died, and this is one
of the most significant books of the twentieth century.

Yet many people fear that keeping a journal of this kind will foster too
much introspection and that it may be unhealthy for certain individuals. While
this is true, these individuals who need to become more extraverted are few. As
Edward Fischer has remarked, for every person who pays too much attention to
the inner life there are ten who do not do it enough. For most of us the fear of
introspection may be just a poor excuse for not taking our lives seriously enough
to look into them. Even people who find their most creative expression in painting or sculpture or dance also find it helpful to pause and consider the total pattern of their lives. Keeping a journal can help most of us to see the meaning of a
particular activity and how to increase its meaning in a new way.

There are people, of course, whose imagination simply dries up when they sit down to write. A journal offers them no help at all in developing a flow of images. These individuals usually have to experiment in order to find ways of giving form to images, even to those that come in dreams. They can often work with paints or clay, or even miniature figures in a sand tray. At the same time it is just as necessary for them to write all that they can in a journal. The plain facts about our experiences, both inner and outer, can be set down and then let imagination play upon them. And these are the piers and girders which we build to construct a bridge between the inner and outer worlds. By using the record in a journal we are able to get down to bedrock and build on a solid foundation of reflection.

Sharing One's Inner Life

One reason for making a record of fantasies is to be able to share them with other people. This kind of sharing allows one to check on the flow and direction of the images that must be dealt with. Often we are unable to see the danger signals in our own dreams or imaginings simply because they reveal things that lie beyond the range of our consciousness. But these pitfalls may be quite apparent to someone whose consciousness has developed differently. Sharing our own inner journey also helps others learn to use imagination and gives them confidence to try it. An atmosphere is created in which fellowship grows in a way seldom found through ordinary communication.

For nineteen years I met with the same small prayer group each week. The membership changed, but over the years it remained the same group. We met after the Eucharist and almost always began with silence. We discovered that we could become silent more quickly together than any of us could alone. The members seemed to help one another, each becoming quiet for the others, as well as for ourselves. A directed meditation followed, which I usually led, drawing the subject from whatever images came to me out of the silence. After a few minutes more of quiet, we then shared any images which had come to us and discussed the attitudes and problems, the fears, hopes, joys that had been evoked by these images or by the meditation. We then concluded with a period of study aimed at trying to understand these experiences in relation to similar ones in Christian history.

Not many Christians except the Quakers have used this idea of finding meaning by being silent together. Since first borrowing it from them, I have tried it with many groups including priests, nuns, ministers, and seminarians, most of whom have told me that it was the first time they had ever had such an experience. This has been one of the most creative ways I have found of helping people who want to grow in the prayer life. Even as large a group as twenty-five or thirty can be quiet together. Usually after thirty to forty minutes I ask the group to share what has happened to them, and often each person tells of the experience. Some describe simply centering within themselves. Others tell of being assailed by ideas at first, and then of gradually quieting down until images appear unbidden. Nearly everyone, no matter what has come, speaks of a sense of restoration, of being touched by some reality. Many people in these groups, finding that others have the same problems and yet meet something real on the other side of silence, have been encouraged to take time alone to try to find the same reality.

The Jesus prayer can also be used in a similar way by groups trying to become silent together. A group using this method starts by asking each person to say the Jesus prayer silently for about half an hour. Without breaking the silence each person is then asked to write down whatever happened during that time. The recording takes about half an hour more, and this is followed by the same period of sharing the experiences. I have never been with a group like either of these where the individuals did not speak with some amazement of the fact that they could become so quiet, and then tell of the same sense of a presence, often with images appearing in a similar way.

Our whole culture looks with such doubt on the possibility that anything independent of human affairs could be found in the inner life that one needs such an experience for verification and support. For my own part, finding that other human beings react in much the same way that I do gives me courage to go further. These periods of sharing give each person a chance to express what one has known and worried about and a chance to receive support and suggestions from others.

These times of prayer and turning inward also lead naturally to thoughtful study and an attempt to understand what is experienced. In the group with whom I shared for so many years we studied various books of the Bible verse by verse. We spent a year and a half seeking to understand the Eucharist in depth. Along with the lives of St. Antony and St. Martin of Tours, we found I and II Samuel among the most interesting studies. It was as fascinating as one of Carlos Castaneda's works to see how the spiritual influenced almost everything these heroes did.

In order to understand religious literature in any true sense—certainly as a history of people and places, times, and events, but even more as an effort to show how God and other forces can influence these things—it is necessary to come to these works with the deep understanding that is often given in silence. Unless one has met something on the other side of silence, all the study in the world usually will not reveal the imprint of that reality. As one goes on to read and study alone, this becomes even more clear. The only way to understand the inward approach is to have taken it oneself. The trouble with our present-day rationalism is not that it tries to help us understand rationally and reasonably, but that it eliminates so much of our direct experience which we need to have and then to attempt to understand.

Here I feel that one reminder is necessary. There are some people who should not be in a group seeking silence in this way. Unfortunately these are often the very people who are attracted to a "prayer group." Often an effort is made to accept them out of Christian charity, but this is far from charitable. We need to understand human beings and the fact that what feeds one person can poison another. It is not good to let these people disrupt the group, and the best thing is probably to suggest that it is limited in number or in some other way. It is not wrong to close a group if this is done for truly Christian reasons.

The importance of such a group for those who have started on the inward venture cannot be emphasized too much. The need is almost universal. By sharing experiences and insights, one continues to grow and the group serves as a launching pad for continuing attempts to penetrate our inner space. The care and acceptance of each other also gives the members a home base or community to return to. It is well to remember that a group can be just two or three people and that, even in the most desolate spiritual area, one can usually find another person or two who will pause once a week to be quiet and share the reality that is found beyond silence.

Spiritual Direction

There are times, however, when one needs more than the fellowship of a group who pray together. Problems and anxieties may arise which are too personal and serious to share with and ask help from the group. After all a prayer group is not an encounter group or a therapy group, and for that matter I have grave doubts about the value of any group in which people let loose all their angers and hurts and oddities. I have seen too many people damaged by such encounters in groups where there were no restraints. There is a dark and destructive side in each of us, and in the heat of feeling it is very difficult to decide what should be expressed and what should not. Encounter groups may have therapeutic value, but *only* when a skilled leader is present to apply the needed checks. Much of the enthusiasm for these groups comes from people who simply will not face the destructive depths within themselves and other individuals.

When any of us is dealing with this depth we need another person who has met the same or similar forces of darkness, who has passed through them and who has survived. This is the widespread religious idea which Mircea Eliade has described so well in *Shamanism*. The shaman is one who knows the inner way and can guide others. Such a one has met the powers of darkness and felt their full impact. By being psychically torn apart by them, and then reconstituted and brought back together and to life, the shaman is no longer vulnerable to them or threatened by them and can lead others through the darkness and protect them from the evil spirits that constantly attack human beings. Since shamanistic societies consider sickness mostly the result of falling into disharmony with oneself and succumbing to an attack of evil, the shaman is also the healer.

The approach of early Christianity was not very different. The forces of evil were understood to be independent or autonomous. They attacked an individual's psyche directly, and they also had a foothold in the world where their attacks could be seen in sickness and in the persecution of Christians. Since Christians had been rescued from these forces by Christ who had power to deal with evil directly, in a sense every Christian was a shaman and a potential guide. When St. Perpetua was about to be thrown to the lions, she was asked why she did not revile and reproach her persecutors. Her answer was that she did not want to add to the evil which already had such a hold on these people; her suffering was not caused by these men, but by the power of evil. This is the attitude of confidence and charity which one hopes to find in a spiritual guide or a spiritual director.

For a long time the Church was the place to find such guidance. Christian leaders combined a deep understanding of the psyche and its workings with their knowledge of theology and how to use liturgy and prayer forms. Indeed many of the Church Fathers were psychological experts. They seemed to feel that God's intent in coming into the world in Jesus Christ was to help human beings work with all parts of themselves and become whole persons, starting from the inside and working out.

Gradually, however, the ideas of Christianity were hooked more and more just to events in the outer world. Its methods of prayer and meditation and joining in worship came to be used more for purposes of suppressing undesirable elements in people than as ways of putting every element to work and coming to wholeness. Almost everybody in the Church became convinced that people are supposed to live above their emotions and keep their angers, fears, lusts, and any kind of fantasies under lock and key. It became all too clear that the Church expected people to follow religious precepts and avoid getting into the psyche or soul and confusing the objectivity of religious knowledge.

Consequently it has become difficult in our society to find individuals who have both religious and psychological understanding. To add to the problem, such individuals are few and far between in the Church, while in the psychological profession it is very easy to find people who know the psyche but have only a superficial knowledge of Christian traditions and no real commitment to them. When the need for guidance arises, as it so often does on the inner journey, it is a good idea to know what to look for in a spiritual director. What qualities does one look for, then, to find someone who knows the inner journey and the pitfalls and can also see the possibilities for growth?

The most important thing to look for is the person's comfortable acceptance of himself or herself, in fact acceptance of everything that goes to make up a total human being. Spiritual direction cannot even begin unless we can share whatever is in our being, good, bad and indifferent. A counselor who makes one feel uncomfortable enough to hold things back can only give advice about surface problems, which will probably do no harm. Good advice, as Jung once remarked, seldom hurts anyone because so few people take it seriously.

In order to help us open up levels of our being which seem unacceptable but need to be understood and drawn into use, a spiritual director must be un-judging and unshockable. Even then it is hard for many people to get over the fear of revealing something shocking and being judged for the nth time. I have found that it can take years for some people to share the totality of their being with me. The more intelligent and sensitive the individual, the longer it usually takes. But when such a person does become truly open, the movement toward wholeness is ready to start.

Before anyone can help another with this process, that person must be self-accepting. Jung has commented that this is the very essence of the moral problem and that facing the prospect makes any honest person livid with fear. In a moving and almost poetic passage in *Modern Man in Search of a Soul*, Jung writes of the absolute necessity of self-acceptance before one can go a step of the way with someone else on the inner journey. He writes:

> Yet the patient does not feel himself accepted unless the very worst in him is accepted too. No one can bring this about by mere words; it comes only through the doctor's sincerity and through his attitude towards himself and his own evil side. . . . We cannot change anything unless we accept it. Condemnation does not liberate, it oppresses. I am the oppressor of the person I condemn, not his friend and fellow-sufferer.[4]

If this quality is necessary for a psychiatrist, it is ten times more needed by spiritual directors. Again and again I have talked with clergy and seminarians who had had "spiritual direction" but had never opened up the problems that were bothering them the most. Recently I talked with a nun in her middle forties who told me about her angers. She spoke of what a relief it was to talk about them and described how uncomfortable priests and other religious became if she let any of her hostility show. She had ended up trying to hide her anger, and it was really bottled up within her. It had made her sick and ruined her religious life.

Another quality needed by spiritual directors is a sense of commitment. One should be as certain as possible that there is no danger of starting to work with a particular director and then, when the going gets rough, of being dropped. This is sure disaster. One would be better off not to start a relationship at all than to find that the other person, usually because of fear, is backing out. One still has the original problem and a feeling of rejection on top of it.

So far the things we have been talking about are essentially the qualities of real Christian love, which is indispensable for spiritual direction. But this is not all that is needed. It is equally important to find a guide who understands the structure of the human psyche or soul and how it functions. We have enough trouble finding our way in the inner world without letting misunderstandings about transference or projection, about varying personality types, or depression, or fear, deflect the only compass we have. I do not see, in fact, how it is possible to help another person on this way without understanding psychology, but not in the limited sense of accepting the dictates of one school of psychology. For our purposes there is no real substitute for at least some understanding of the approach of C. G. Jung because his approach includes most others.

There are compelling reasons for seeking out a spiritual director who grasps Jung's understanding of human beings and his approach to psychological facts. In the first place, Jung did not pin himself down to one indisputable view of these facts. He succeeded in combining the best insights of various approaches, and he was usually the first to amend his own ideas. Jung's interest was in finding ways to help human beings grow, not in establishing psychological dogmas.

Second, what Jung's understanding offers is a point of view from which psychological processes and spiritual realities can be seen, and a method of working with them that keeps them alive and moving in the psyche while one learns about them. His methods often remind one of the way scientists learn what is going on inside the atom by tracking atomic particles on the move; they have more in common with such experiments than with many of the common psychological and psychiatric methods. It is rather important to keep things alive and moving in the psyche if one is trying to reach the central meaning in his life. One will not get far if the first signs of new growth are aborted every time they appear, no matter how accidentally it happens.

And finally, this is the only major psychological point of view which insists strongly on our need to approach the psyche, its development and its problems as religious matters. Jung's understanding of psychology fits naturally with the goal of religious meditation because the stress is the same. Human beings cannot become whole without a religious orientation.

There is a gradual increase today in the number of clergy and Christian lay people learning to work with the techniques of Jungian psychology. It is unquestionably becoming easier to find individuals who are familiar with the symbols found in dreams and who understand how a person's dream life shows what is going on below the surface of consciousness. This skill is needed for spiritual direction. One does not have to look for a trained therapist, but it is important to find a director who knows enough to see when therapy is indicated, and who will direct one to a therapist when the situation requires it. The director should also know quite a bit about the use of symbols in primitive mythology and rituals, as well as in Christianity.

It may seem redundant to suggest that a Christian spiritual director must know the Bible and Christian literature thoroughly. But if one has ever looked for help with a full-blown mystical experience, one may understand what I mean by *thorough*. I have met religious counselors who would back away if St. Teresa herself showed up in their offices. I was simply lucky the first time I was faced with such an experience, early in my counseling work. I had been reading Baron von Hügel and suddenly realized that this was the kind of experience he was talking about. One needs a guide who understands the possibilities of the Christian way well enough to recognize its beginnings within a person.

The last and perhaps most important credential for a spiritual director is to have taken the inner way himself or herself and still be on it. Such a director will not give the impression of having it made. If a person appears too confident about these experiences, it usually means that he or she has come to a standstill and is too blind to see the way for anyone. One can better trust a guide who admits honestly to having days of wondering about ever making it through and is still open and able to learn from experience.

Several years ago I wrote an article about the value of having the help of a spiritual director on the inner way. The response was almost overwhelming, mostly from people asking how to find a director. One of the tragedies of our time is the failure of the Church to prepare men and women for this task, which once had as important a place in Western Christianity as the guru does in the East. In the Middle Ages not even the greatest saints tried to turn inward without the help of a confessor or director. But today the Church seems to feel that it has no power to help. It tries to work with human beings just on an outer level and leaves their souls up to the psychiatrist or psychotherapist. People are left split in two, often with no way of bringing the split-off parts into touch with the center of meaning.

Nothing is more needed today than to provide people with a way of making the inner journey in order to find that meaning. And no task is more important for the Church than arranging for people to be trained in the inner way so that they can guide others on it. Providing schools for this purpose is just as important as teaching ideas about God and training ministers to preach and run churches. The spiritual reality is there to be experienced. As Andrew Greeley has shown in a sociological study of mystical experiences,⁵ people find it for themselves whether they want to or not. What the Church has to do is take a chance on believing in this reality.

Until it does most people who want to follow the inner way will have to hunt for spiritual direction on their own and hold onto their best insights if the help is not all that one would wish. Finding help is probably easier for lay people. They are usually able to listen to one another and give each other real support. But it is particularly difficult for the clergy. If they have to turn to lay people for help, it is hard to find someone able to listen openly to a minister, and sadly enough, clergy usually have trouble listening openly to one another.

The important thing in entering the inner way is to have someone with whom to share one's deepest and most personal experiences, someone who will respond when help is needed. In the sixteenth century Benedict Pererius, a Jesuit priest, suggested that to find the best interpreter of dreams we should look for a person with plenty of experience in the world and the affairs of humanity, with a wide interest in everything human, and who is open to the voice of God.⁶ This is a good summary of what one is looking for in a spiritual director.

16

Putting Imagination to Work

There are many places to cross the river of silence and enter the strange and beautiful, sometimes terrifying, territory of the inner world. Different people find many bridges, fords, paths of imagination that lead to this country where almost anything, verdant or stark, may be a potential symbol filled with meaning for our lives. Although the various entrances are not as separate as they might seem at first, we shall look at them separately in order to understand the process a little better and to get some feel for it.

I shall first of all suggest a number of these entrances to another world and then look at certain of them in detail, considering some examples. Since the ways of imagination are practically unlimited, varying almost as much as the individuals who use them, we shall not try to cover every one that comes to mind. The ones we consider will be well-tried ways of using imagination for religious purposes. Persons who have become familiar enough with ways like these can then branch out on their own. The examples I give will be just that—examples. *They are not meant as forms to be imitated,* but as ways of stimulating each individual to try out the imagination. The important thing is to work with one's own images that come in meditation, relating them to the great symbols of our religion.

One way to start is to enter a Biblical story in imagination. By stepping into an actual event or taking part in one of the stories told by Jesus, one can participate in images that are already formed and share in their deepest meaning. The opposite way is to wait for images to arise spontaneously from within and then follow them as they move. If they become too threatening or destructive, we can call upon the Risen Christ to support and save us. After all, getting into a real pickle is often the only thing that brings us human beings to find the Christ. A third method is quite similar. Instead of trying futilely to ignore a bad mood, or going right out to celebrate a good one, one can enter the mood and allow it to be expressed in images which can then be worked with, again turning to the Christ to bring renewed vitality and a sense of direction. Any of the outer expressions we have mentioned, from imaginative writing to gardening or weaving or sand play, can also be used to bring images into focus for this purpose.

Still another method is to listen to one's dreams, which are a natural expression of the inner world. They come without knocking or asking leave, and seem to vanish again into nowhere. But if their images are given quiet, meditative attention, they can be invited back and figures can even be persuaded to speak of meanings from all levels of being. By using this natural bridgehead to the inner world, one begins to discover that the ways of communicating with the Risen Christ are just as natural and actually not very different from making contact with an inner dream figure.

Some people find that the experience of tongue speaking provides just as natural a bridge to the inner world, opening up communication with the Holy Spirit and allowing images from many levels to arise. For others quiet prayer does much the same thing. Simply the act of affirmation—affirming that one centers on Christ and the love that goes both ways—will open many people to reflections and insights which are a form of imagination in action. The effort to share that love through intercessory prayer often works equally well to open some persons to the same kind of insights, and also to the value of learning to use the imagination.

One must be particularly careful, however, not to use intercessory prayer as a way of seeking insights for other people, but to trust God to manage that department. These methods of contacting the power of the spiritual realm can all be used unconsciously with damage to others. Any of them can open us to forces hidden in the ego that desire power and domination. They can also open us to destructive voices, as well as creative ones—voices potentially as destructive as those heard by Charles Manson. Even the greatest Christians have sometimes mixed up the voices that spoke to them and done things like promoting an inhuman crusade. It is hard enough to sort out the insights intended for one's own life without trying to see the way for other people.

At the same time the insights and power that are given to us have to be used or they come to naught. We have been given the yardstick of genuine concern and warmth and love for others, and we are expected to use our heads as well as our hearts to reach out to them in that way. As we enter the spiritual world it is important to keep reminding ourselves of this yardstick.

The inner world of images is altered simply by our entering it. One can change that world as much as digging or blasting or steam shovels change the outer world, and the change can be for good or for ill. That is why it is so important to find the center and meaning of this inner world so that one is working with its ultimate meaning and not against it. And then one finds the most amazing truth. As one brings the creative power of love to bear upon the events and figures that are found in the inner world of images, changing them by its power, at the very same time—synchronistically (which means by meaningful coincidences), as Jung put it—one often finds the outer world changing along with them. It appears, in fact, that any final change in the outer world must be preceded by a change in the world of spiritual reality, of images and symbols, and *vice versa*. There is a power and mystery in imagination which is beyond our comprehension. This is hard work and we can find a thousand lousy excuses for not doing it.

Entering the Biblical Events

There is good reason for starting with the images of the Bible. These images have a "mythic" reality that can be entered and shared, that changes the life of many who do so. The stories and the figures in them have power to open up and even reshape various aspects of our lives. So do the stories and figures of other religions. One can participate in the stories of the Nordic Siegfried, or those of Buddha or Shiva or Arjuna in the same way. But, for me at least and for most of us in the West, these figures all leave problems which the Christian story does something to resolve.

Before people move over to one of these other points of view, it would be wise for them, as John Dunne suggests in *The Way of All the Earth*, to know the point of view they are taking off from. Otherwise they often find themselves bogged down in the kind of psychic swamp that results when two streams become backed up in the same area. The problem of so many Westerners is that they know their Christianity only intellectually, and not even that very well. When they start looking for something new and different, it never occurs to them to ask whether the approaches can be put together. If they had really assimilated the elements of Christianity, they might stop to think before trying to pour such a hodgepodge of religious ideas into the same container.

The only way I know of to be thoroughly familiar with a religious point of view is to live with it imaginatively. For Christians this means knowing the Bible in a way that is impossible so long as we read it only with our heads, to understand the concepts in it. For a long time it was understood that the Bible is not just an intellectual exercise. As Père Jean Le Clercq makes a point of showing, well into the Middle Ages the Bible was read in the monasteries so that one could step into it, find its meaning inwardly and be transformed.

If we want to find such meaning in the Bible, we must imagine ourselves in it and moving with it. For instance, one can start at the beginning of the life of Christ, imagining what it would be like to be Mary pregnant with the Holy Spirit. How did she face village gossip, the fear of being rejected by Joseph, and then the long, hard trip to Bethlehem? One example of a great poet's meditation on the birth narrative is W. H. Auden's *For the Time Being*. The whole story obviously came alive in him, including the attitude of Herod in slaughtering the innocents, and the flight into Egypt.* One need not wait for Christmas to meditate on these events. Our purpose is to reflect on how the Christ Child can be born in each of us, and this is not seasonal. Giving oneself plenty of time

---

*My own ordinary attempt to meditate on the Christmas story is presented on pp. 239ff.

to live with the story only adds depth of meaning to Christmas when it does come.

The boyhood visit of Jesus to the temple, or the period before His ministry can be lived in this way. We can start home with Mary and Joseph after the Passover celebration in Jerusalem, turning back frightened when we find that the boy is missing. Or perhaps one stands in the temple with Jesus, as amazed as the learned men at His answers to their questions. What was in the hearts of Mary and Joseph, and how did Jesus appear in giving His answers? Or later on, what were Jesus's days like in the carpenter shop after Joseph died? Did Mary worry secretly when He decided to leave home, even though the younger children were able to take care of her now? One can follow Jesus to the Jordan and try to see the heavens open as John baptizes Him, or hear what words of approval are spoken as the Spirit descends. This kind of imaginative walking with Christ fills in the story and helps one grow with its depth. It cannot be done in a hurry. Its reality springs only out of silence.

As unpopular as the idea of fasting is to most people today, few Lenten experiences can be fully real unless one takes the trouble to watch and wait and fast with the Christ as He meets the awful reality of evil in the wilderness. The encounter with Satan is a real one. Jesus does not project the evil onto any group or individual, but meets it head-on in temptations which have not changed much from that day to this. T. S. Eliot bridges the centuries in his stirring play *Murder in the Cathedral*, showing how similar and yet contemporary the meeting with the evil one was in the death of Thomas à Becket. Evil is always tempting us to use power or good works or spiritual clout rather than love as our motivating force. I find only one way to set out living my life as Jesus lived His, fulfilling my own unique destiny. And that is to stand beside Jesus in the desert as He searched His own soul and listened to the devil's words and rejected them.

We can stand with Matthew at the customs table and listen to find out if one of us is being called to follow Jesus along with Matthew, or beside the lake with Peter and James and John. What came to their minds as they answered the call, and what comes to mine if I hear it given? How did their situation differ from that of the rich young ruler who decided that the price was too high for what could be gained, or else that he would be a lost shadow without all his customary attachments? What new step is required of me that asks, "Are you Matthew or the rich young ruler?"

In the gospels many of the healings of Jesus are described in great detail. One can pick out any of these stories and try to sense its fullest meaning. How much did the persons involved realize beyond the sense of being physically well again? What lay behind their illness, and how did life change for them after the encounter with Jesus? In *The Bible in Human Transformation*, Walter Wink uses the story of the paralytic who was carried to Jesus by his four friends to illustrate an imaginative method of using the Bible to transform human beings.[1] His purpose is to show that the Bible can and ought to be used in this way, and the method he proposes* can be used either individually or in groups. I have used it with groups and know how effective it is. In the next section I offer an example of this use of the healing stories.

One can even be present at one of the resurrection appearances recorded in the New Testament and know the restoration of life to Jesus the giver of life. In an illustration later on I try to show the meaning these stories have had for me. I can sit with the crowd at the feeding of the thousands, taking the food in imagination and perhaps questioning the boy who brings the loaves and fishes and realizing what claims it makes on me to share in it. I can follow one of the group home and see the change in that person's life, or if there was none, find out why. By following the Lord up to the Mount of Transfiguration along with Peter and James and John, one can sense the tingle in their spines as they see the Master transfigured and feel their wonder as a cloud covers them and a voice is heard. One can follow them back down, their eyes open to reality, to find the disciples working vainly to help an epileptic child, and realize how much need there is to bring this kind of glory into action in specific situations.

We can imagine ourselves on board ship with the apostles when the storm threatens to sink them and they have to awaken Jesus. By sharing the terror and then seeing the waves subside and the wind drop, we can feel the change within ourselves. I have to confess that it was hard for me to do much with this story until I ran across a similar first-hand account in the life of a Navajo medicine man. In *Hosteen Klah* Franc Newcomb has described an experience of the same reality. She and others of her family were in a car with the Navajo shaman when a tornado bore down on them. Hosteen Klah stepped out into the face of the advancing twister, spat earth towards it, and the terrified group watched it divide and pass over them.[2]

Then there is the triumphant procession with the Christ into Jerusalem when the very stones would have cried out for Him if the people hadn't. One can see the disciples bring the donkey for Him to mount and hear the shouts. I have often imagined events of that Passover week, seeing myself at the last supper, having my feet washed by the Lord Christ Himself, sharing in the meal and hearing Him say: "One of you will betray me—one who is eating with me." And then carrying torches and singing psalms we go out to Gethsemane and wait while Jesus prays. There is simply no better preparation for the Eucharist than to spend one's quiet time before it living the story this ritual expresses.

---

*Wink draws on the method used by Sheila Moon and Elizabeth Howes. These two Jungian analysts have developed it over a number of years in the groups they hold every summer at Four Springs near San Francisco. They have written widely on their work. *Man the Choicemaker* is one of their most relevant books.

Sometimes I seem to be alone with Him in the Garden as His soul is sifted and He wonders if He can go on. It almost seems that I have to see the bloody sweat and feel with Him the decision in order to know that I am not alone in my own struggle to make the hard choices, to do His will and not my own. As I stand beside Peter later on, I learn to live with the Peter in me who fails again and again and again, and yet picks up the pieces and goes on. In any time of tragedy there is help in following the events of that night. Even to watch the tauntings and floggings, to listen with Mary and John to the words of love and then of desolation and hopelessness from the cross, to see the body being taken down and placed in the tomb, gives the realization that there is One who shares our agony when all our hope is extinguished.

Thank God, then, for the resurrection which tells me that I still have reason to hope. Knowing that His pierced and broken body was brought back to life makes me see in my own agony that I can be reconstituted, that my dis-membered soul can be brought back together. I may watch with Mary as she walks into the garden to find only an empty tomb, or with the apostles huddled together in such fear that Jesus has to show them who He is. Or I may start out for Emmaus, perhaps with ones who have given up and are going home, and meet a stranger. I cannot help but find my own heart touched when He reveals Himself by breaking bread with them in the little inn that is no longer remem-bered for any other reason.

There is a strange and important truth to living with Christ not only in His defeat but also in His resurrection. Life usually forces us to live out our sor-row and agony. In this way we are brought to search for some help outside our-selves, some way of finding a new beginning. But just as this search seldom starts until one can picture the nature of the need, so we usually stop short of finding new life until we are able imaginatively to experience the resurrection as a reality, a real possibility within ourselves. Those who have not imagined the events of the resurrection again and again in concrete images can hardly know the power of the Christian message, the ability of light to conquer darkness. Without some kind of experience of Christ's rising from the dead, we can scarce-ly know the meaning of the atonement, or accept the power of the Spirit to touch and heal the gaping wounds of the world.

If one imagines only the sufferings of Christ and humanity, one can get stuck there. The door to victory over death and the evil one is opened only as people are able to realize—actualize in images—the victory of Christ over these forces. His victory and resurrection can then enter into the individual life and work transformation. Without these experiences in the beginning there would have been no dogma of the atonement, and there is very little point in it today unless people experience the reality of being rescued from the evil one and becoming one with God in Christ.

In addition, when one lives with Christ in these various experiences, Jesus becomes as real as the people with whom one sits down to eat dinner at night, or even more real. He becomes a person to whom one can turn and speak in the hours of quiet late at night or early in the morning. He becomes the friend who waits with open arms on the other side of silence.

In the same way one can relive the stories of the book of Acts and those later in Christian history. We can walk with Peter and Paul as they move through the pagan world bringing hope and release from fear, offering new meaning in life and healings of body and mind. We can step imaginatively into the healing at the Beautiful Gate or the raising of Dorcas, or the encounter of Peter with Cornelius. We can know the Paul described in Acts as well as the Paul of the letters. Reading this book meditatively, it is possible to imagine that Luke is present in the room and to ask him about a passage that is puzzling. This is possible with any document of the New Testament or, in fact, a religious work from any age of human history. The basic idea of the communion of saints and the reason for keeping this idea enshrined as a creed is that there is communication among those who are joined in Christ whether they are living or dead.

One does not have to believe in reincarnation to find the idea of the communion of saints meaningful. In the unconscious the barriers of space and time do not exist, and so there is nothing but our own desires and our view of things to keep us from being open to people in Biblical times or in any age of history. A person who enters history for ego reasons will not get far, but if there is a real desire to learn, for instance, from a saint like Francis or Teresa or from someone like George Fox or John Newton, one may find the very realities that were opened up to them become open to us also. One must be able to read with heart open, silently listening, never hurrying but waiting for the words to strike fire within. In this way one can hear realities speak out of another realm, helping to unfold the meaning of religious works and bringing amazing answers and depth of understanding. Critical intelligence is then needed, of course, to be sure that one is not being gullible or deluded by wishful thinking, but is actually finding contact with a wisdom other than one's own.

We can also step into the pages of the Old Testament with the help of imagination, particularly the Psalms which express the whole range of human emotion and every agony of dereliction. The Psalms reassure us that we can bring any pain or fear to God. One can relive Elijah's journey into the desert, or see him taken up in the chariot of fire as Elisha accepts his mantle, drawing out the meaning of this story as Teilhard de Chardin does in a moving meditation in *The Hymn of the Universe*. We can suffer with Job and out of our own agony identify with his struggle, or we can stand beside the burning bush with Moses or walk with Jacob or Joseph or Abraham. In *The Man Who Wrestled with God*, John Sanford has shown how deeply these stories of the Old Testament speak to people in the modern world when God's truth is not reduced to just an event in history. In a very real sense these stories are myth and history combined. They reveal the eternal patterns of spiritual reality, which is the particular function of myth. In a manuscript not yet published, Walter Wink has also made a wise analysis of the meaning of Jacob's wrestling with the angel at Jabbok, showing that it is a symbol of what nearly everyone faces.

Imagination is equally valuable in finding the meaning of the parables and stories told by Jesus. He used the story form as a vehicle to reveal realities to people not only because this was the best way for that time, but also because stories are timeless in the same way that the unconscious is free of the limits of time. Of course these stories speak to an outer moral situation, but they speak at the same time to an inner one. They can do both at once, and the only way to unlock the inner meaning is to let imagination play upon the story.

As I read and meditate on the story of the prodigal, I see myself first as prodigal, then as elder brother, and often as both. The story of the good Samaritan shows me that I have been set upon by thieves, that there are thieves within me, as well as a priest and a Levite who turn away from my trouble, and that I can also find a despised Samaritan in me to bring healing. All these parts of myself can be awakened in me. I am the laborer who was the last to come to the vineyard, and also the one who complained because, through the Lord's mercy, I received a full day's wage. I am the servant who received only one talent and buried it, and yet I can turn the story around and work as hard as I can to win the Lord's approval and avoid condemnation. Over and over in this way the scripture becomes a living reality in me and opens me to a deeper reality in myself.

The parables about the kingdom of heaven have ways just as amazing of speaking to us. John Sanford's study of them in *The Kingdom Within* shows how profoundly these sayings of Jesus can speak to us, and also suggests a method of finding such a deeper understanding of them. Most of us are so accustomed to these usually brief statements that we often overlook the incredible wisdom they contain and how wisely they direct us upon the way of spiritual maturity. Anyone who wants to understand the teaching of Jesus can profit from this book.

In approaching either a parable or an actual event, the secret is to become silent and concentrate on the picture or scene that is presented until it comes to life and begins to move. Then I find that there is a choice. I can stay on the outside and simply observe the action as it unfolds, or I can step onto the stage and become a part of the action. I can even become one of the characters, sometimes sharing in their joy, or often in their agony and pain and then in transformation and victory. It is amazing how the life of Jesus and the parables He told open up to reveal a living, growing meaning within us if we allow imagination to awaken them again and draw us into their reality. They speak at a deeper level than the intellect, touching the total person as intellect seldom can.

The Eastern Orthodox church, of course, continues to work with images.

This understanding among Eastern Christian Fathers like Maximus the Confessor is described by George Maloney in *The Breath of the Mystic*:

> The ordinary person reads Holy Scripture and sees nothing but the letter; he does not penetrate behind the type to the antitype. Symbols in the Old Testament fail to reveal God's true mind, but the person with the gift of contemplation sees beyond the surface images. Every word, every picture tells him something deeper about God. The same applies to man in his relation with other men; a normal man views other men only as they present themselves to him externally. The man of interior vision can see beyond to the inner *logos*; he can pierce through the phenomenal, the physical appearance of the sensible order and enter into an interior vision that allows him to see that man in God's light.[3]

The Greek Church did not come to this view of images and imagination without conflict. In the great iconoclastic struggle in the eighth century, the idea of perceiving the Spirit of God through images was strongly opposed. Those who feared that allowing the use of images would lead only to superstition and lack of reverence finally lost out on the ground that denying the use of images would deny the incarnation. If images could not carry the imprint of the divine, how could Christ have become incarnate so as to secure the salvation of mankind now? The final resounding victory was reflected in the words of the "Synodicon" decreeing:

> . . . so we believe, so we say, so we proclaim, honoring Christ, our true God, and his saints, in our words, writings, ideas, sacrifices, temples, and images . . . [and in conclusion] . . . This is the faith of the fathers, this is the faith of the orthodox, this is the faith that has sustained the ecumene.[4]

Thus Eastern Christians continued to develop the understanding that by using imagination to reveal the meaning in scripture, we find the meaning and direction of the universe and come to understand the world around us. Meanwhile Western Christendom began to concentrate mainly on images that represent the physical world directly, and neither side seemed to sense its need for the other. We in the West have been shortchanged because our failure to respond to Jesus by using His stories and His scripture imaginatively keeps us from threading our way through the maze of realities that touch our lives from all sides. Once we take this primary step, the other ways of using images from within usually become meaningful and valuable.

Spontaneous Images and Spiritual Reality

One of the natural ways of getting into the spiritual realm is to allow images to appear like a waking dream or vision. When one has become quite still, with all inner activity quieted so that alpha rhythms take over in the brain, images will usually appear spontaneously and unplanned. In this way one enters the realm from which dreams arise, a realm of spiritual reality partly personal, partly archetypal, and partly coming from objective reality separate from any individual psyche. These images sometimes tell a story, and sometimes they tumble out in confusion. We have a choice of either dismissing them or trying to find meanings in them.

The first choice of dismissing the images is common in Eastern religions, while the other way of finding meaning in them is the way of the West and Christianity. In Christianity the person as an individual has supreme value, and it is crucial for each of us to integrate our inner life into a meaningful pattern. especially since we expect it to continue after death. Unless the images that tell of our inner life are undersood and made a part of our inner structure, we may end up split and faced wih the prospect of dealing with our conflicts in eternity where it may be more difficult. At least we know there are chances of working at our problems in this life and we don't know what they will be in the next. In the East there is no such stress on individual development. Individuality is seen more as an ill-fitting coat which a person must shed in order to escape from illusion and reach the goal of perfection. There is no encouragement, therefore, to pay attention to one's dreams and spontaneous images; this leads to individuality which is a barrier to the Eastern goal of merging with the perfect oneness of all things.

This Eastern idea goes against the grain of Western culture. And yet we usually avoid spontaneous images because so often they call attention to parts of our lives that were so unpleasant we repressed them. When one enters the inner world in this way, the first thing encountered is oneself, and there is no escape from this home-place no matter how many angers or poisonous fears or destructive impulses are hidden in the woodwork. We cannot start to grow toward the meaning that is intended for each of us until we will face whatever shows up within us however unacceptable it may seem.

Of course if existential thinkers like Sartre and Becket and religious leaders who follow them are right, there may be no point in struggling in this way to grow and bring ourselves to wholeness. These men believe that we are in a spot with no way out of absurdity and despair and destruction, and if this is so then perhaps the Eastern solution is the better one. In a meaningless universe with no concern for the individual, no center to offer itself as a source of love, why would anyone with good sense try to awaken parts of the personality that are sure to prove troublesome? The Zen masters have reason to warn people about the danger of madness in working with images. Images can reveal these less desirable human traits, and if there is no reality such as God to offer us help in dealing with them, we have little choice. In that case we had better keep them buried as well as we can and try to live above them. And if this is the only alternative, the Eastern way offers more help than an attitude of stoic heroism.

There is good evidence, however, that the New Testament is right in indicating that help is found in inner experiences like dreams and visions and, as Jesus instructed in the Sermon on the Mount, by *praying in secret* to One who *sees in secret*. Anyone who actually tries to find the experiences of God, the Spirit, or the Risen Christ that the New Testament writers took the trouble to record is sure to learn about the depth of human nature at the outset. The images that offer contact with the center of all reality and those that dredge up all kinds of things about ourselves both spring up from the inner world in dreams and spontaneous images during meditation.

Someone who does not dream very often may wonder how images can reveal things we do not know about ourselves. Suppose one sees the image of oneself attacked by an animal or struggling in a swamp. It does not take much intuition to realize that one picture speaks of the violence and amorality of our animal nature, and the other image of the despair that eats away at our hearts so much of the time. When we visualize images like these and record them, most of us find ourselves faced with an enormous task. We are shown the rejected memories of childhood, the hostility and anger lurking deep in our souls—sometimes even against those we love the most—our sexuality and the fears it arouses, our cowardice and despair and even unconscious lack of faith. If we are seeking God or the love that desires us to grow and become whole and care for others, then if these images are emerging within us they have to be dealt with. Otherwise they keep blocking the path. One cannot seek God with a self that has value without dealing with that self.

It sometimes seems that God has made us half angel and half beast, asking us to bring the two together to work in fellowship, so that we will know our need for His help. He provides the wealth of imagination which gives us contact with all parts of our being, and far beyond our individual being. Our task is to learn to use these images which tell us about ourselves, integrating what we can in order to grow toward our full potential, toward God.

Understanding the Images from Within

Whatever else one can say about the images that arise spontaneously or in meditation, they are seldom meaningless. In *Symbols of Transformation* Jung has shown, for instance, how the images coming to a woman on the edge of mental breakdown explained her problems and tried to give her a solution although she could not understand it. The spontaneous images that speak to us in our need will usually do as much if we will listen to them, mull them over and try to understand them. They can give correction and directions on the inner way, providing balance and opening up new vistas in the same way that dreams often do for people who are having psychological problems.* They are as much a part of our lives as dreams, and they can be understood in much the same way that dreams are understood.

The important thing is to take the images that come in meditation seriously and spend time with them, realizing that they are given to us to be *used* like building materials in our lives. They do no good if they lie around and are forgotten, but neither can they be allowed to dictate what shape our lives are to take. Our job is to use these images without being possessed by them, rejecting any that would damage or weaken our lives or souls. There is often a temptation to let dream images do our thinking for us so that we lose ourselves in them. But as Zen emphasizes, such images also reveal a destructive tendency in the inner world that can pull one into psychosis. The neat trick is to distinguish between things that will add to our lives in areas we have not yet dealt with, and things that must be put aside because we cannot handle them at all, let alone integrate them.

The images that come in either dreams or fantasies can sometimes be so clear that they do not need to be interpreted. They are individual revelations to us which make their meaning clear. Later I shall give an example of a series of such dreams. But not all inner images are so obliging in their effort to communicate. Some of them play a game of follow-the-leader, and one can only follow them into the territory within and go where they lead. This is hard work. It requires complete attention to the images while taking care not to break their flow. Usually this is worth the trouble. Images like these often reveal more about our inner life and the various levels of spiritual reality that touch it than almost any other activity.

At the same time, the first thing to understand about these images is how to tell the signs of danger. Not every peril, of course, is a signal for us to run for cover. Finding oneself hanging onto the edge of a cliff, for example, very likely suggests that one needs to find a way down that cliff and discover what lies below. Or, robbers who attack us may represent some rejected part of our being that has been denied and is trying to take its rightful place. Any part of oneself that is denied can turn hostile and destructive. But if some element in the inner world appears determined to possess one's life completely, it is almost certain to be evil. One of the main characteristics of evil is its effort to take over the whole human being and exclude everything else. Evil is usually a partial good that insists on being the whole good.

---

*There are also images of joy and fulfillment and celebration which need to be met and brought to reality in our lives. But images speaking of our problems almost always come first, and we shall consider those of joy and celebration later.

Sometimes a figure of great light and power appears and the only way to tell whether it comes from the Christ or from the evil one is to test it and see if it contains this possessive quality. The Christ never seeks to dominate, but to free, and since the goal we seek is to relate to the Christ, our task is to avoid being taken over by *any* element of the spiritual world. There are elements in that world that try to take us back into the dark and destructive unconscious, and none of us can handle these possessive elements on our own.

But if one is able, in imagination, to call out to the Christ for protection, the Christ who has defeated evil at its very heart will come and stand against whatever force seeks to possess the individual. Sometimes we meet forces that tear us apart, or we may find so many parts of our personality scattered that it seems to us the same as being destroyed. We do not need to remain shattered. By calling out to the Risen Christ we will come to know that He is present with us, and we can thus come to know the reality of the resurrection and the power of His continuing presence. As He gathers the fragments that have been scattered in our imagination and restores our brokenness, we often find that our outer lives also tend to come together. One can also learn to recognize the signs of dangerous personal inflation through images that are usually only too clear, and then we can deal with them in the same way. No figure or image that I know of other than the Christ gives such protection from destructive evil and from the despair that can otherwise swallow us.

We do not deny this saving power of Christ by recognizing a need to seek counseling and turning to someone for additional help and guidance. It is most important to take this step when it is needed and reinforce the imaginative contact with Christ. On the other hand, existential thinking and Eastern religion, both so popular today, do deny this power of images in our lives. Existentialism simply stops with man's fragmentation and despair; it is all crucifixion and no resurrection, while Eastern religions suggest that nothing can redeem the world. These two approaches keep many people from using meditation as a way of finding victory over evil. They see no point in encountering images and the emotions and reactions associated with them, and then asking Christ to redeem these things and turn them to good use. Instead, meditation becomes a way of calling a temporary truce. One gets a breather through detachment and then returns to the fray to meet the same old problems in the same old way.

Until we can realize how important it is to work with images in the inner world, there is not much chance of making headway with our approach to this life or to the realities beyond. In more ways than one we are dependent upon imagination because it is seldom possible for something to take place, particularly in the outer world, until someone has imagined it spiritually within.

If the images that arise have been recorded and reflected on and are still not understood, however, one can bring them before the creative spirit within and ask for their meaning. This was the way Joseph and Daniel learned the meaning of the prophecies that were given in their dreams. The One who gives us the images can also interpret them. In addition, when one calls upon the Risen Christ for help, in giving us help He may interpret the images for us as well.

I remember vividly the time I saw myself at the altar rail facing an idiot-like figure who turned his back on me when I was about to give him communion. In imagination I went to him and asked him why he rejected me. He told me that I was the one doing the rejecting. I let this figure lead me through all sorts of darkness and evil until together we returned to the church. This took many hours, but it helped me integrate much I had neglected and rejected.

Sometimes we are presented with images which recall some Biblical story. One sees oneself caught in a storm at sea, or condemned and executed, or lying beaten by thieves beside a road, or in a tomb like Lazarus. One can then approach the Biblical image in meditation and bring its meaning to the actual situation. An image of betrayal or of being lost and despairing can take one back to the Psalms and their continued trust in the midst of pain and agony. There is hardly an image of any kind that does not have a parallel in the Bible stories. From images of fire and whirlwind, despair and death to those of resurrection and hope, of great banquets and of the heavenly Jerusalem, one can find in this book almost every imaginative avenue to victory over evil and a creative, fulfilling life.

Even so, there are many images which require study. Perhaps one sees a great white bull at the center of a labyrinth, or finds a strange blue crystal placed in one's hand. It may be necessary to go back to mythology or the images of alchemy, to the indexes in the books of Jung and to encyclopedias, as well as to the Bible. There is no reason why the inner world should be easier to understand than the outer one. It may even be a good idea to get some professional help if a set of images seems important enough to one's life. Images can even be worth spending money on.

Turning a Mood into Images

Sometimes instead of finding images in the silence, one is overwhelmed by a mood, by anger and fear, or boredom, a sense of going to pieces or of personal inflation, or even by joy and victory. If a mood persists, we feel as if we have no handle on our lives. Under our own steam there is no way to direct it toward meaning, and we become the subject of the mood, completely at its mercy. The only way we can begin to take control again is to pause and try to see what image the mood seems to remind us of. Then we begin to comprehend what has to be faced and see how to manage it.

Those who allow moods to run them are generally men and women who have not yet integrated the full saving power of Christ and His atonement into their lives. They have further to go on the inner way. We know very well that saying one has faith in Christ is not meaningful if one does not show love and forgiveness to others. But the idea that forgiveness must extend to one's own self, bringing love into one's inner life, seems harder to grasp. The first step in dealing with a mood is to realize that something is wrong with our faith if the healing of Christ does not touch us within and bring freedom from the moods that can disturb our best efforts.

Once again, it takes imagination to open up these tender spots that need to be touched by Christ. The only way to do it is to enter into the mood and allow it to express itself in images and pictures and stories. This is impossible if one stays busy and avoids the mood or pretends that it isn't there. In fact busy-ness is usually our best excuse for avoiding the responsibility of inner growth. But as one sinks into the mood, it can be pinned down enough to bring another reality into the picture.

I remember the first time I did this. I was feeling oppressed and discouraged, and went into the church alone and sank into the mood. The same image came again and again: Grayness, grayness. I seemed to be in a gray cloud, or under it, out of touch with any value or meaning, enclosed within my own dull, meaningless grayness. I sat in that grayness, just waiting, for about fifteen minutes. Then the thought, the image, came all on its own. "At least it is not black. How happy you ought to be that it is only gray and not black. At least in grayness there is a suggestion that somewhere the sun is shining and trying to break through." After a few minutes of absorbing this image of the sun, the grayness disappeared, the sun did shine within, and I found that the oppressing mood was gone.

Some moods are so overwhelming, however, that they defeat any attempt to be quiet. I have a friend who suffers black and ugly depressions like this, so painful that suicide often seems the only way out. On one occasion her mood was oppressive beyond words. It seemed to consume her. I asked her what it was like, what it felt like. She replied that it was like a claw which tore at her skin and even deep into her heart. Then I asked her to picture the claw, and she spoke of the coarse black hair, the fierce curved nails, and finally of the whole monstrous creature that was attacking her. But mental images were not enough. She found that as she drew this figure, and then drew herself opposite it and the Christ between, her feelings of agony and pain abated, and she regained composure and control and could go on. This was an extreme situation, but useful because it outlines the basic idea in sharp contrast.

There is a natural attraction between images and emotions* which makes them affect each other mutually. It is almost impossible to speak of emotions

---

*For instance, if one passes a fight going on in the street and notices it enough to take in a memory image, there is very likely to be emotional involvement. Later one may find the picture of the fight popping into mind unexpectedly at times of being upset, or the same feelings aroused if there is some actual reminder of what was happening in the street at that time. There may be even more impact from an experience of love, and sometimes far more from an experience of some inner image apart from anything outer.

without using images. Emotions give rise to images, and by the same token images trigger emotions. This makes it possible to learn how to manage emotions, but at the same time this is exactly what makes them so unmanageable and difficult for most people to deal with. The fear of using images to arouse emotion is quite reasonable, but it avoids the issue. We are in contact with images whether we like it or not, and they keep right on awakening emotions in all of us. And since religion has become guarded about using images to describe meaning in this universe, this has given free rein to all the images arousing fear that there is no meaning. This is not a matter that is generally treated with indifference.

The direct images of our own actions keep reminding us of how impermanent love can be. We are afraid that there is nothing that can be really counted on, and the more fearful we become, the easier it is to turn our fear loose in anger and make the problem worse. This creates real difficulty for people who are sensitive enough to want to control their moods and emotions and not fly off the handle at themselves or others. If one truly sees nothing one can depend on or no meaning, at least in this world, then as I have suggested, the only sensible thing to do is to detach oneself from images and the emotions they ordinarily awaken and hope that meaning will come from some place beyond all that.

If there is meaning at the heart and center of things, however, then all kinds of emotions have meaning. Even the most distressing emotions are reasonable reactions when we find lack of meaning and hurt and pain in a world where we believe there is something else to be found. Understood in this way emotions can lead one toward the most central of all goals. Certain emotions also indicate whether one has gotten off the path or not and help us in the search for inner meaning. There is no cure for terror or rage except that we find Love. Then one finds that the energy of every emotion, either destructive or not, can be put to use by Love. Augustine expressed a profound truth when he spoke of our hearts being restless until we find fulfillment in God. We are emotionally torn until we find meaning that is truly worth going to bat for. This understanding that emotion is placed in us and has a meaning of its own contrasts sharply with most of the Far Eastern thinking which finds emotion a handicap to be overcome by mature individuals who will simply rise above it.

This basic Christian understanding also contrasts rather sharply with the puritanism of more recent times which made Christians do their best to bury anger and hatred once and for all. Since most of us are influenced by this attitude, we have to learn from scratch how the emotions that bring on moods can reveal themselves in images. This is done primarily by asking what the fear or resentment, the lust, or hunger for power, feels and looks like. Each time the emotion rises up it may produce a different image. Fear might show an icy hand squeezing one's heart, or reveal the world as an endless waste of boiling mud pots and desert crags, or a torture chamber run by a madman. Anger might show oneself as a black-mailed warrior charging to destroy everything in the way, or ramming one's car through a crowd; it may be revealed as a volcano pouring molten lava over everything green, or a madman thrusting an atomic bomb into the furnace in one's own basement.

Hundreds of more subtle images may seem easy to ignore, and everything in us usually tries to push the nightmare pictures back into oblivion. Little that we have been taught suggests any way of dealing with these images and it seems like the ultimate blasphemy to turn to God and tell Him that this is the way one feels about His creation. Often one fears being struck down like Uzzah when he accidentally touched the ark.* But when such a mood and such an emotion become concrete enough to work with, one can see the alternatives better and learn that there is a choice to make.

Whether To Open Pandora's Box?

In this century we have seen more than one vision of madness translated into reality, mostly by men like Stalin or Hitler who thought that they were dealing only with the world as it is. They would have vigorously denied that their own emotions and the images that were awakened played any part. But when fear takes hold of a gun, or anger invents a napalm bomb or builds a concentration camp or a "tiger cage" for prisoners of war, people's egos have already become deeply involved in accomplishing a goal, and they no longer have power to choose between facing the reality within or inflicting it on the intended victims. They become convinced that it is right to destroy. Mature reflection, however, suggests that God would prefer people to turn to Him instead of taking their feelings out on His handiwork.

Many people turn their negative emotions upon those around them in ways that are less dramatic but very nearly as destructive for anyone who gets in the way. In addition there are probably almost as many who force their emotions underground to fester and break out in psychosomatic illness or depression. In Chapter Ten of my book *Healing and Christianity* I have described the devastating effects on the body from tension caused by fear and anger. Tension in one's body and nervous system usually speaks of emotions that have not been faced and so are being converted into bodily ailments. These diseases, among them some of the leading causes of death today, show that the body itself is weeping. The mouth, because of our ignorance, may lie, but the body and its symptoms reveal the truth. In today's tension-filled world, we cannot afford not to listen when there are ways of turning and finding the healing which God wants to give.

---

*2 Samuel 6:3-11. As in much of the Old Testament, this story projects the anger entirely upon God, leaving fear as the only proper human reaction.

There is just as little need to allow depression to take over and control one's life, even though this illness, which is the common cold of modern psychiatry, keeps on afflicting more and more people in spite of the most enlightened efforts to deal with it. Depression expresses in unmistakable terms our need to break out of the rationalistic prison that has been built up around us, and come to know first ourselves and then the meaning which can be found in Christ, in Love. Depression puts the alternative squarely before us because it seldom responds very much to ordinary treatment. And if it goes far enough so that the reason for living is gone, one's body will respond with sickness and even death. We shall look at depression further in this chapter because it represents almost the sum total of all our negative moods and thus illustrates the possibility of a choice very clearly.

Then there are the emotional problems of our sexuality which were increased severalfold by the Puritanical and Jansenistic brands of Christianity. The failure to face and understand our physical desire often contributes to our moods. Even worse, people who avoid these emotions often cut themselves off from their physical being like leaves that dry up and wither and blow away, or else they quietly store up the dynamite of desire in the unconscious until it gains power enough to blow up and shoot them into a new orbit. This seems to be particularly true of religious professionals; my experience has been that they are often more frightened of their desire and ability to love than they are of their hostile destructiveness. We Christians need to know how to use our emotions in order to love. There is probably no other reason so important for electing to know and work with our moods and emotions.

If we will once live through the betrayal and crucifixion of Christ in our imaginations, we will realize that there is no reason to fear showing the worst of our images of violence and defeat and pain to Him. Our images of fear and anger and lust are no worse than the reality He experienced and defeated. The Risen Christ can take an image of fear, perhaps the image of a person cringing under an attack of burning arrows, and turn these burning arrows into arrows of love and hope. He can deal with any of our emotions in similar ways if we will make the effort to get to know those emotions and understand them and then ask Christ for help in handling them.

In addition, God is far better equipped to take our anger than we have been taught to believe. I believe that He would far rather be the target for our anger Himself than to have us turn it upon ourselves and others. Letting anger loose on ourselves generally causes such emotional upset that we become of little use to God, and when we make others the target, we often destroy them. We forget that God is a loving Father who knows a child will rage sometimes and scream, "I hate you!" If we let Him know our actual feelings, no matter how inappropriate or wrong or stupid they may seem to us, I believe He will look for what is wrong and where the hurt is, just as any of us would try to do for our own child. God cares enough to help us understand our distress and to help us turn our rage away from destructive reactions, perhaps even to something creative.

How then do we who have been trained to keep our distance from God and from ourselves begin to find the reality of this contact? Let us take depression, the most difficult of moods, as an example.

Finding Contact with Meaning

The first problem in depression is to admit that there might be some meaning in the universe and that one needs to be touched by this meaning to bear the agony of feeling hardly able to stay alive. The next step is to stop identifying with this mood and realize that there is another part of oneself that has been silenced by the feelings of worthlessness and self-hatred (or in other moods, of anger or fear or lust). Instead of repeating endlessly, "I am no good. There is no hope because I have nothing to offer," one becomes silent and listens. One allows the "I" to become a "you" and then one often hears a voice saying, "You stupid creature, you are no good. . . . Nobody loves you. . . . You have no morals. . . . It's no use; you botch everything. Why don't you just pull the plug and get rid of yourself. . . ?" By hearing words come from somewhere and writing down whatever is said, it may begin to dawn on a person that this is *only one voice, a* voice which speaks for only a part of one's total self.

Many times this gives one a kind of handle on the feelings. At least one can no longer try to deny these feelings. It is clear that they must come from somewhere, and perhaps they come from something that is trying to destroy one's selfhood or real sense of being. This realization—whatever our ideas about the source of the voice and what created the mood—makes it possible for us to start resisting the mood. One cannot fight a mood so long as one is identified with it or believes that it is coming from oneself. Fighting oneself only ends up in a draw. But once the destructive feelings can be seen as coming from a source that is not really oneself, we can begin to fight off these feelings. If one has written this down in the evening and comes back to look it over in the morning, then it is easier to see that the voice has overstated one's worthlessness, or anger or other feelings.

I know because I have done this, and by doing it I have suddenly realized that, as bad as I am, I am not that bad. In this way we come to learn that the evil one and his allies are always liars. They have been shut out of heaven and they will do anything to separate human beings from God and draw them into their camp. They will use depression, or any destructive emotion or mood. One has to learn, of course, to sort the feelings out. There is even a very normal kind of depression that results when one has done something wrong and needs to feel contrite. As long as one is on the inner way, or has to deal with moods, it is necessary to distinguish the out-of-proportion moods which try to possess the person completely from the normal kind which should not be avoided but used as an avenue to growth.

Allowing a mood to speak with its own voice is one primary step in using imagination, and sometimes this is enough to make the mood loosen its iron grip on a person. But if not, the next step—if one is able to do it—is to use imagination and to allow the figure behind the voice to appear. Perhaps one imagines it as a criminal who has one tied down or locked in a cell, or perhaps it seems that one has been thrown into a pit and is being trampled and prodded and poked by a dozen demons' underlings. Whether the image is of a monster or a taunting figure, one seems to be helpless, with no way out except to allow help to appear through one's imagination. Often the inner cry for help brings a strong power from God or Christ into the scene. One will recognize the Christ because He expresses the image of the One who struggled against these very forces on the cross and defeated them. As the demons retreat before Christ's steady gaze, He leans over and lifts one out of the mire with a warm embrace.

We can work with any mood in this way if we will enter the mood with the imagination and turn to the figure of the Christ. One can go on with the image and follow Him, perhaps to a mountain valley where a spring flows out of the hillside and there be washed and cleansed and healed. Sitting there beside the water, one can know the reality and closeness and love of Christ in practically the same experiences that St. John of the Cross described so beautifully in his poetic works. Even our angers and fears can be turned to good account, and one can often be released from the sickness of body that they sometimes cause.

Sometimes in imagination I bring my hurt—and there is seldom hurt without some response of anger—before God and ask Him why He has made this universe so that I must hurt so. I also ask why it is that others have such pain that they are brought to disintegration in psychosis and suicide. I then tell Him that He has made the universe. It is His fault, and only He can give the answer. He listens, and I am reminded to turn back to the book of Job. No one ever spoke out more courageously and honestly than Job did in his complaint in the third chapter of that book. In the end it was the honest and angry Job who was justified, not the "friends" who tried to discourage him and treated God as if He needed the support of their theological nonsense. Honesty *always* pays with God.

One of the most magnificent sequels to the book of Job in modern literature is Jung's *Answer to Job*. In it Jung, recovering from a brush with death and months of physical agony, identified with Job and turned toward God with bitter anger. This work is often misunderstood by people who see it as a work of theology because they do not understand the need for using honesty and active imagination in communicating with God, or the surprising results of this kind of believing anger. As one student from a pietistic Lutheran background expressed it, "Nothing ever made God so real to me. Here was a God who could bear

Jung's wrath and transform it." Yet how few of us have enough faith in ourselves, or in a loving Father, to bear the emotion of anger toward Him long enough to let anything happen.

When people are willing to take off their kid gloves in dealing with themselves and with God, they have a chance of bringing their anger to God who is the source of all things, and having this anger transformed into creative energy. Facing God in anger shows far more faith in the redeeming, self-sacrificing Christ than backing away for fear of being irreverent. As I have suggested, God does not seem to be interested in having us cringe before Him and then take out the tension of our anger on other human beings, or in having us destroy ourselves with sickness which comes from the repressed anger. For some people a ritual is helpful to let out this destructiveness in a creative way. Perhaps one way to do this is to keep the children's broken toys, and when one needs to work out the anger take them out to the desert with a rifle and cherry bombs and blow up these broken toy houses and cars and lead soldiers and so release hostility in a creative playful way. Or if one is not yet able to face the images of one's own anger, it may be helpful to open the book of Psalms and find some of the images of pain and suffering and anger that were addressed to God.

The notion that Christians are required to lay aside all images of sexuality in order to approach God is just as damaging as burying anger. It often turns our religion of love into one of chastity, and it helps to make the modern problem almost the opposite of the ancient one. In the ancient world there were few restraints and people had to learn to control sexual and other appetites so that they were no longer slaves to any and all desires that popped up. Today the problem is to learn that there are two sides to both love and sex and to learn about using the less-known sides.

In the first place, as Berdyaev has pointed out so well in *The Meaning of the Creative Act*, love that avoids the physical component entirely is merely a cerebral exercise and not the real thing at all. But equally important, one's physical and emotional desire for another generally has a side far beyond animal instinct. In loving another, one may be projecting onto that person some content from the depth of one's own psyche or beyond it, and this is often a most attractive and creative element either of oneself or of the spiritual world. Coming to know this element from within may be the most important reason for the attraction. Yet people have a strange idea that the only way to live out an emotional attachment is to enter into a physical relationship. And this, as Rollo May develops in *Love and Will*, involves many people in sexual relations that have no more depth than a handshake.

The deeper aspects in intense attraction can be found only by allowing imagination, rather than physical desire, to guide one's actions. Sexual desire often gives one an image that has power and that even carries the divine. It is not easy to deal with physical desire in this way, but the results are more productive than the usual consequences of either living out or burying every impulse that comes along. Still, it may seem that one would only be courting these desires by trying to work with them in images. In some cases this may be true, but it does not necessarily follow. While the images can always be used to daydream over the object of one's affections and get up heat for action, one can also use them to deal with the situation in imagination. In this way one can discern the nature of the attraction and be prepared not to be taken over by passion when the time becomes ripe for it. Sometimes the object of desire can lead one to heaven itself as Beatrice led Dante in the *Divine Comedy*.

Dealing with human sexuality and its attractions in this manner is far more creative than wearing a hair shirt or a chain with spikes around one's middle, even figuratively, to mortify the flesh. Indeed anyone who listens to the depth of one's own being, the fear and anxieties, angers and despair and lusts, need not mortify the body in order to remain humble. Such mortification may well be an escape from dealing with darkness of the soul and then doing something about it. Anyone who reaches down within, will find more than enough darkness to ward off inflation and pride for years to come, maybe forever.

It is also important to realize one's moments of peace and joy, of centeredness and thanksgiving, celebration and victory, in active images. In fact, one of the great aspects of the Eucharist is that it portrays the victory of Christ in the world and also in each of us. The Eucharist allows us to share in the emotions and power of the action so that we are made a part of the victory and celebration and absorb them within our being. This is similar to the dramas of ancient Greece—which, after all, were religious celebrations and sacrifices to the gods.

For many generations there has been an overemphasis on penitence, the cross, suffering, and mortification. At present the needed reaction to this one-sidedness is in full swing, and we need to remember that it is just as wrong to emphasize only the celebration. Unless one has faced the darkness which is in most human beings and has come to terms with it, celebrating will probably be hollow, or even phoney and insincere. Unless I have been rescued from something, and have a picture of something for which I am truly thankful, my act of celebrating the crucifixion and resurrection seems superficial and just doesn't come off.

It is good to celebrate and to help others share in the joy. But the individual who celebrates with no personal reason for celebration has probably missed coming to full potential, and very likely is still in darkness and perhaps in turmoil and confusion. If we do not allow the darkness to be expressed and overcome, then our lives are often filled with emotional, moral or physical distress. Yet the Church goes on emphasizing nominal penance and immediate thanksgiving in the Eucharist without realizing the agony right at hand, even though there is no secret about the vast problem of mental illness or the number of people who pay psychiatrists to listen to them. When the clergy and religious professionals learn to use images to deal with their own suffering, they will be able to listen to others and instruct them so that they can begin to repair the deep hurt of modern humanity. The Eastern Christian Church offers pointers in its emphasis on inward weeping for one's powerlessness and failures and sins as the preparation for God's gift of Himself, the real occasion for celebration.

If one keeps celebrating without first looking within, there is danger. One may be meeting a partial image of the Christ and trying to let one's life be run by that piece, instead of seeking to relate to the whole reality. One is then giving up one's own life merely in order to lose it, not for the real purpose of regaining it and becoming a real helper of Christ in the struggle and the victory.

Even worse, one may be in danger of inflation. Inflation happens when we hold ideas that always lead to seeing ourselves as victorious and powerful and in control of every situation, and when this happens it shows that something is wrong. Most human beings just do not have that kind of power in either the inner or the outer world. Dreams of flying or of being praised and earning honor and respect are generally a signal to look deep within. The power that we have is not the property of the personality. It is given. When a person thinks that his or her own wisdom or love or creativity is necessary in order to save the world, then pride and egotism have taken over. Whenever I get to thinking that I am indispensable to the scheme of things, I usually get sick. I have a friend who can tell when I get in that frame of mind, who usually says to me, "Relax. You don't have to save the world. Jesus Christ has already done it." When I feel a task is just too demanding, I often find by listening in meditation that I am trying to carry God and His Church on my back. What a relief it is to realize that I have no such burden. I breathe much more easily when I take this realization in and integrate it once more into my being.

Poetry and Story as Maps of the Inner Territory

In recent years a great deal has been written about the use of stories in theological study. In addition, people who are trying to describe their experiences of God have begun to find that categories of rationalistic thought are not adequate for sharing what they have experienced, and so they turn to poetry or story, to fairy tale or fantasy. In all of these ways, emotions and experiences are expressed in images rather than in pure concepts.

In poetry the heart pours out the whole gamut of its feelings, from fears and hurts and pain to joy and restoration and renewal. All through the history of the Church no part of the Bible except the gospels has had more use than the book of Psalms, which expresses the most universal feelings of the human heart. Not everyone has the ability to pour out feelings in words, but most of us probably made a good stab at it when we were first in love. This makes it easy to see why poetry is such a good vehicle for sharing the reality of Christianity, which is essentially a love affair with God in Christ. In using poetry in this way, one is not trying to break into print. The important thing is to express as much as possible of one's own experience of being touched by the love of God. In the final section I shall share some of my own outpourings, as well as including two examples of the greatest religious poetry.

In telling a story one reveals the self. Many of the great storytellers from Shakespeare and John Bunyan to Robert Louis Stevenson have been studied by individuals who work with the insights and wisdom of depth psychology. These studies show that at the deepest levels a writer often reveals not only himself or herself but things about the general structure of reality itself. One thing which makes the plays of Shakespeare so incredibly powerful is that they make clear in story form Shakespeare's struggle against darkness and his ultimate victory with God's help. Martin Lings and James Kirsch have both written studies of Shakespeare's plays showing how deftly the great dramatist integrated a religious point of view into them.[5]

There are few better examples of the Christian faith than the stories of C. S. Lewis, including *The Great Divorce* and *The Screwtape Letters*, his space trilogy, his seven-volume fantasy adventures in Narnia, and his story *'Til We Have Faces*. Story seems to be one way in which it is natural for man to express his striving for growth and individuation and meaning. Rosemary Haughton has shown in her many books how often a fairy tale or story gives some deep hint of the same meaning that is revealed so dramatically and clearly by the events described in the New Testament.

Of course it is helpful to read the stories of others, particularly ones like those of C. S. Lewis, to get a fresh slant on the message of the gospel when familiar ways of saying it seem to go stale. But besides this, writing stories of one's own, just letting them flow, reveals where a person is and where one can be taken. Not long ago one of my students at Notre Dame tried this idea. His life had fallen apart in an existential neurosis, and he thought he was dying. What was really dying was his old ego adaptation, and that feels just as bad as physical death, maybe worse. I suggested that he tell what he was experiencing in a story, looking at it as if it were happening to someone else. The effect was startling. As he wrote, he gained a sense of objectivity, realized his need for meaning, and let the story develop ways of finding it. With this background he read the New Testament and proceeded to pay as high a compliment as I have ever heard a modern young person give to Christ. He told me with amazement, "I wouldn't have believed it, but Jesus was a real freak-out."

The direction of such a story can pinpoint where one is within. If one's stories end with absurdity and a sense of being cast away and meaningless, it probably shows that the author has found no meaning worth integrating into his life. One cannot make such a story express, convincingly, more than what one is, or is trying to become. But gradually a series of stories can be expanded toward meaning, opening a person's life to hope and victory. There is a tremendous difference between making up sweet, sentimental episodes that have no depth and writing from a gut level of meaning. By writing in this way, out of existential lostness and a desperate need for victory, one actually becomes open for the victory to take place. This does not happen to people who are satisfied with playing out their days over an empty abyss. Hope and victory almost always have to be imagined in order to be born.

Speaking with the Christ

A number of creative thinkers have written lately about the idea of bringing dream images to life and acting them out or speaking with them. These images are a real part of each individual, and they will go on revealing themselves if one allows them to. Contact with them can lead to self-discovery and also to discovery of contents from the spiritual world. Fritz Perls has written a good bit about this kind of imaginative discourse with one's inner images. His effort is to tie them to the here and now, to the present situation and the feelings and attitudes of the moment. This is valuable, of course; it is wise to know who one is and where one is heading before venturing further, but the process can open up much more than that.

If one does not shut the door by disbelief, dream images can bring contact with other realities of psychic power beyond oneself. E. L. Rossi has described in some detail the process of encouraging them to speak. In *Dreams and the Growth of Personality* he uses Jung's basic approach, particularly what Jung described as active imagination, and incorporates Perls's ideas and what Assagioli calls psychosynthesis. He shows how it is possible to interact with these images, listening to them not just to understand one's problems, but even more to seek the help of those realities that show us how to grow toward wholeness.

Christ can be approached in the same way if He is the one whom Christians say He is, the true image of the loving God. If we can communicate with other elements of the spiritual world through dream images, then we can also interact with the image of Christ and the reality which He incorporates and expresses. Of all the processes of imagination which have helped me, none has offered half as much value as this approach to Christ. Several times a week I simply stop and wait before Him, sometimes picturing Him at the time of the resurrection, rising victorious from the tomb, or perhaps knocking at the door of my soul, as William Hunt's picture, "The Light of the World," suggests. And then in the quiet I say, "Here I am. Tell me what you wish of me."

At first the interchange may seem forced and unreal. Often I wonder if I am making up the answers that come out of the silence. And then within me something clicks. There is a change, and suddenly I know that I am not talking to myself. There is a voice other than my own, the voice of someone who cares about me, one who speaks to my deepest problems and fears, one who heals my wounds and restores my courage. Often I ask Him why He bothers to come and be with someone like me. Each time He tells me that He is Love and that it is the nature of Love to give of itself, that He cares for every human being and comes whenever we will allow Him to enter and share Himself with us. This experience is one that is never exhausted. It returns each time as fresh and real and autonomous as a magnificent sunset or an encounter with a truly loving human being. One can never predict what the meeting will bring.

It is out of these encounters that most of my growth in understanding and personality have come. I have brought before Him my fears and doubts, my attachments and angers. Each problem has been dealt with lovingly and with skill, and I have learned to accept and make better use of many elements of myself and my situation. From these experiences of fellowship have come the best ideas that I have had, the most effective sermons, my best attempts at reconciliation and caring for others. In these meetings with Love, He has conversed with me and told me of His defeats in the world and of His victories. Out of this sense of sharing as well as being cared for, I find encouragement to keep on trying to grow and become what He wants me to become, and I also find directions about what to do and to work on next.

Many less sophisticated Christians center their religious lives around this practice. They disregard the materialism and rationalism which surrounds them and firmly believe that the meeting with Christ is a vital and urgent necessity. In the way that Rosalind Rinker describes in *Teaching Conversational Prayer*, they find a presence with whom they can interact, a presence which opens their eyes to themselves, to the world around them, and to the words of scripture. It is easy to ridicule such people because they are naïve. And often they do say some rather silly things because, once they begin this practice, they tend to let go of their critical capacity. Those who keep at the practice, however, come to know reality better than the general run of the people who criticize them.

Quietly approaching the reality of Christ over and over again gradually brings confidence that there is something beyond the limit of our space-time world. Experiences open up which we often tune out when they come in other ways. One is no longer closed to the possibility that there may be a perfectly acceptable view of the world which admits the reality of a God who cared enough to become man and dwell among us, who still cares enough to communicate with us today. Like the first "giant stride" on the moon, it is then only a step to realize that one need not be gullible and uncritical about every experience that comes from across the boundary of space and time. After all, there *is* a view of reality that insists upon testing these experiences and demands that we bring the best of our critical and analytical abilities to these encounters.

When one's prayer experience is based on a world view which has room for this kind of communion between God and human beings, then meditation is no longer a peripheral issue in life, but a central reality to those who wish to go the religious way. Religion then becomes real and very practical. Religious practice gives us ways of finding a loving Lord who has conquered death and evil, and who is ready to enter our lives whenever we will unlock the door of the soul and let Him know that the latch is off. If we can find the best that life offers in this way, it would be foolish for us to refuse to admit that there could be such a reality and shut out the experiences that point to it.

Intercession

Once we have found the reality of such a Lord, it becomes important to share Him with those we love and with those who seem to need Him the most. Intercession is one real way of helping others find His love and power in their own way. Even outside of prayer we have far more unconscious influence on one another than we often realize,[6] and when we are seeking the objective reality of love, this unavoidable psychic influence can be directed to help open others to that reality. Thus intercession becomes a powerful instrument for God to use through us. Bringing others into the presence of the risen, victorious, loving Christ can be a special vocation for some people. And it is needed by all of us, along with other ways of reaching out, to keep our meditative life from becoming too self-centered and introspective.

Nearly every one of the suggestions I have offered for meditating about oneself and one's own problems applies to intercession. It is fine to pray over a list of people and mention each problem and each special concern. But too often this kind of prayer is only a mental exercise which does not get outside of one's head. In order to pray for others one must first of all be silent. Then in images one finds oneself before Christ, perhaps in some Biblical setting, and then sees oneself bringing the other person to that spot where Christ is healing or bringing insight or consolation. Obviously we are not trying to bring the person into *our* presence, unless we have a rather exalted idea of our own power. When we pray for people, we are trying to help them be open to finding contact with God, and the best way to do this is imaginatively to see them in contact with Christ. We can then share some of their pain or sorrow or lostness and help them carry it before the Christ. We already know Christ's love, and the most that we can do is to try to be adequate channels of imagination so that the reality of His loving, transforming power can move in and through others and bring them to new life.

This takes time, and the results may also take time. In intercession patience is a virtue which is sometimes needed beyond all others. So often when we pray for another, we want action immediately, and when it doesn't happen we get discouraged and give up. We forget the examples in Christian history such as St. Monica, the mother of St. Augustine. For twenty years she kept on praying for his conversion while he wandered about the cesspools of the ancient world. When Augustine finally came to himself, he fulfilled exactly the image of the dream she had had years before; she had seen herself standing on a wooden rule, and looked up to see her son standing there beside her.

I find it helpful to keep a list in my journal of people who are particularly important to me, whose needs I should remember in prayer. I have on the list the members of my immediate family and my close friends, and also those with whom I am in a counseling relationship, students with whom I work closely, and my colleagues. In addition, I list those who have offended me and whom it is hard for me to love. I also keep there the names of some of the dead who have been very close to me. But when the problem of one person or another seems to be particularly important, perhaps someone in trouble or sick, I may spend most of the time trying to bring that person into the relationship I have suggested. Each of us has certain people who are our responsibility, often in both outer action and meditative prayer, and if one has such a list, they will not be forgotten.

The opportunities for imaginative intercession in meditation are almost limitless. We find the reality of this way of touching others when our relationship with the living and communicating Christ is present and real, and when we keep up our end by continuing to grow. This is the only sure basis for finding the reality and power of either meditation or intercession. Intercession, of course, does not take the place of action on our part. We also need to take direct responsibility for others, as well as for our own growth.

Again and Again. . . Reaching toward the Forever . . .

Some people seem to wish that the psyche and its relations were like algebra. Once a problem in algebra is solved, it stays solved. But algebra is a conceptual system, while the psyche is an organic reality that grows and changes through relationships. Once a concept is worked out and expressed, it is over and done with. But not so with the psyche. It needs to be exercised with problems that need solving over and over again. The psyche is like a muscle that atrophies when it is not used.

Any dynamic, living reality needs constant exercise in order to grow and develop. The images and insights that the human soul receives about itself and about the world are like its muscles. The image or insight which I receive today needs to be reintegrated tomorrow, and next week, and the week after. This is why we come to the Eucharist week after week, and sometimes more often. Victory and growth need constant reaffirmation, constant development, reintegration. The growth available is like an endless spiral staircase. If one stops climbing, where is there to go?

Thus the work of meditation is not a single action or an accomplishment leading into a harbor, but a way of life. It is a way of assimilating victory and defeating the constant attacks of the evil one. This is never done once and for all, but has to be done again and again, leading us a step at a time toward eternal life.

One of the most telling expressions of this fact in modern literature was written by the well-known playwright Arthur Miller. It is actually a personal meditation written into the action of his play *After the Fall*, in which he reflected on the tragedy of his inability to love, his failure to touch and rescue his former wife, Marilyn Monroe, with love. On a stage representing the human mind, with characters that come and go like ideas, Miller plays out the life story of his autobiographical hero, Quentin. Quentin has met a woman who had gone through the bombings and horrors of the concentration camp, and who still hopes. He wonders how she can hope, and then she speaks:

> HOLGA: Quentin, I think it's a mistake to ever look for hope out-
> side one's self. One day the house smells of fresh bread, the next of
> smoke and blood. One day you faint because the gardener cut his
> finger off, within a week you're climbing over the corpses of children
> bombed in a subway. What hope can there be if that is so? I tried to
> die near the end of the war. The same dream returned each night
> until I dared not go to sleep and grew quite ill. I dreamed I had a
> child, and even in the dream I saw it was my life, and it was an idiot,
> and I ran away. But it always crept onto my lap again, clutched at my
> clothes. Until I thought, if I could kiss it, whatever in it was my own,
> perhaps I could sleep. And I bent to its broken face, and it was horri-
> ble . . . but I kissed it. I think one must finally take one's life in
> one's arms, Quentin.[7]

Toward the end of the play Quentin realizes that Holga can hope just because she does know the worst about life and herself and has accepted it. He then speaks Arthur Miller's own affirmation of this truth: that he too can hope because he has come to face the reality of the world and humanity's struggle in it.

> QUENTIN: To know, and even happily, that we meet unblessed;
> not in some garden of wax fruit and painted trees, that lie of Eden,
> but after, after the Fall, after many, many deaths. Is the knowing all?
> And the wish to kill is never killed, but with some gift of courage one
> may look into its face when it appears, and with a stroke of love—as
> to an idiot in the house—forgive it; again and again . . . forever?[8]

PART FIVE

Adventures
on the
Other Side of Silence

17
Windows Inward

To a Russian or a Greek of the old faith an icon is a window into eternity. They believe that it is a true vision of the eternal captured out of an instant in time. The pictures and stories I present in this section have opened similar windows for me or for others. They may awaken the same pictures in your imagination, or perhaps they will stir enough imagination in you to open such a window of your own.

The first group includes mostly stories from the gospels. They include some of the greatest of these stories retold as the images originally spoke to me of the power and victory of Jesus. They suggest how we can share in and experience the amazement of the first Christians at that love and power which then sent these early Christians out to outlive, outthink and outdie the ancient world.

It is much easier to express the defeat and suffering of Jesus than to express His joy and resurrection. His agony can be tasted to the full in imagination, and even when the pain and distress are overplayed, the sense of reality still remains. But it is hard to express joy and restoration without becoming sentimental, usually sickenly so. In today's world where the idea of crucifixion is so often played to the hilt that people lose any hope of the real victory, there is need to free our imagination and allow it to lead the way toward resurrection and victory. To start with, let us picture the beginning of this one story which brings us real hope that victory is possible.

I

THE BIRTH OF THE CHRIST CHILD: THE IMAGE BECOMES MAN

Birth is never easy. I know it is difficult to let the Christ be born within me. I wonder if I have the courage and strength to stand against the world. I am not even sure how to handle the ordinary problems that have to be faced this morning. What will I do about. . . ? I let the question die and try to put away all the other thoughts and concerns that slip in, and just be still.

I concentrate on Mary and Joseph and the problems they had to face so that the child could be born. First in Nazareth, and then the long trip to Bethlehem. . . . When another concern of my own breaks through, I try not to get upset. I simply tell it to wait and focus again on the images I am trying to awaken.

The image of Mary in Nazareth, the perfect image of the human soul . . . Mary, young, alive, obedient, open . . . standing by the village well, dressed in the garb of that time, a long embroidered dress, a veil covering her head. . . . As the pictures begin to flow, I see her standing there thinking back to the garden and the strange appearance of the angel with the startling news that the power of the Highest is to overshadow her and that she is to bear a child. . . . She is remembering her own words in reply: *I am the handmaid of the Lord, . . . let what you have said be done to me.*

How can the Christ child be born in me until I am as willing as Mary . . . as open and as ready to take whatever comes? Lord, how is it possible for me to be accepting in the way that Mary was? She knew that the people of Nazareth wouldn't understand.

Now that I have actually entered the scene I can see the village gossips standing near the corner of the synagogue. They glance toward Mary knowingly and cluck to themselves. I can tell that she hears their voices murmuring away: "She always thought that she was so holy, and look at her now. Pregnant . . . poor Joseph . . . And her parents. . . ."

Even Joseph had doubted. She is feeling the pain of being doubted by those closest to her. How hard it is to withstand this pain. So often the doubters and the gossips have their way. We open ourselves to the spirit and find new life, and then we back away because we cannot bear the criticism, the misunderstanding and derision and condemnation. Wondering how Mary can take it, I follow her back to the little dwelling where she lives with Joseph. It is a simple place with a dirt floor and few furnishings but a straw pallet. Even the poorest today have more. She prepares a simple meal, placing small loaves to bake on the open hearth. . . .

I watch as Joseph swings open the door and comes over to embrace Mary. His face is troubled and Mary senses that something is wrong. . . . He tells her right away: "An edict from the Emperor. Everyone must go to their own birthplace for an Imperial census. You know what this means. . . . We have seventy-five miles to travel to get to Bethlehem, and with you about to bear your child. How can we do it?" . . . How can any of us face the trip we have to make to our spiritual home where we can allow the Christ to enter?

It was not easy to bear the Christ child then, but Mary and Joseph make their plans. The donkey that usually carries the carpenter's heavy beams will carry her. They will gather enough food together and start out in two days so as to avoid the Sabbath restrictions. They plan to wear their heaviest clothes, in fact the only warm things they have, because the winters can be cold. . . .

Bright and early they start out, leaving the little home locked expecting to return. The sky is overcast and a cold wind blows . . . they trudge the dusty road hour after hour, hour after hour. They pause at noontime by a ravine with a spring and eat some cheese and dry bread and then go on . . . there is rain and the dust turns to mud. Evening and darkness are coming when they find a mill and knock on the door . . . wet and tired, and Mary only a few days from childbirth. The millers let them in and they sleep on the bags of grain in a corner of the cold mill. Outside the wind howls and the rain beats against the roof. . . .

During the night the rain stops and the next day they go on another thirty miles under the broken clouds. It is cold, bitter cold. They meet others traveling from their homes, huddled in heavy cloaks, who barely nod. Hour by hour, they go on; they break at high noon for rest and then go on again. It is no easy thing to bear the Christ child . . . the sheer drudgery must be tasted to the full if one would bear the Christ child and bring Him to birth. . . .

This night an old villager and his wife let them sleep in a corner of their hut. It is good, they say, to welcome strangers. One may entertain God in so doing, and once we were all strangers when we left Egypt and wandered through a new land. . . .

Another long day . . . cold wind, and snow on the mountains, but ahead the lights of Bethlehem . . . their destination. They had enough money for the inn. They had taken all their savings just for this . . . with the time of birth so near. . . . In hope and expectation Joseph knocks on the great door of the inn. The innkeeper opens the door. He is a hulk of a man, larger than life-size, framed by the light of a fire blazing on the hearth. . . . "Sorry, no room." "No, not even a corner." And, "No, I don't know what you will do. The villagers have all locked their doors and gone to bed . . . too bad. . . ." The heavy door clangs shut and the dark is even more penetrating. . . .

Joseph stumbles down a little hill. The time is very close. There is a cave in the hillside with a shelter built in front of it . . . some straw in the back, and standing in the shadows a donkey and some oxen. . . .

It is an oriental stable . . . the dung is thick on the dirt floor of the cave . . . the manger in the center gleams with the saliva of the oxen that have eaten there. It is better than nothing. . . .

Not a likely place for the birth of God, but perhaps the less likely the better. Then no one can say that his life is a less probable place. A runaway child sleeps on a pile of straw at the very back, a frightened child who has run away from the beatings of a stepfather and is now recovering. . . . The stable turns no one away. . . .

The child is born.

The Christ is born. They have some cloths to wrap him in. Some straw laid in the manger makes a crib for him, and the oxen are lowing softly in the background.

And so the Christ child is born. . . .

It is no easy thing to bear this child . . . and if He can be born in this stable He can be born even in me. . . .

The star is shining . . . and there is a heavenly song breaking through the cold night air. Peace on earth to men of good will. . . .

II

AN ADVENTURE INWARD: THE SOUL-ROOM AND THE KINGDOM

Let us go on an imaginative journey from the marketplace to the sanctuary, from the crowded streets to the deep aloneness of the soul room, to see what we may find there. Let us trace a path in our imagination which any of us might follow and try to understand.

First of all let us turn into the silence . . . not hurriedly or violently, but quietly, like pulling off the leaves of an artichoke one by one. It is so much easier to be still when we are together as we are today. There is something in our common desire for silence that we do not always have alone.

First of all let us be comfortable. . . . Then let us still the inner voices which scream and blast away. Let us put away our longings and desires. Let us lie fallow, inert. . . . Then it is that our imagination, which is our forgotten faculty, is allowed to come to life. Let us put away all our critical and analytical abilities and be just passive.

What is this silence like? It is like coming into a quiet sanctuary set off in a garden away from the marketplace, insulated from the busy-ness and confusion, the anger and desire outside. It is entering this sanctuary which can be found within each of us.

The marketplace . . . the busy streets, people coming and going, never stopping . . . never knowing where one is going or why, but always busy, working until exhaustion takes over . . . then the television, and afterwards sleep in which we forget our dreams . . . and then more busy-ness, day after day, and for what. . . . ? Even a home can be filled with this kind of busy-ness, even our time of recreation . . . even the ministry. . . .

The marketplace . . . everyone trying to take advantage of each other, intent on one's own gain, making the good bargain, the good deal. . . . The bright lights and mechanical voices trying to sell and convince . . . keeping us busy. . . . Everyone struggling and contending in the marketplace, each wearing a mask to be unknowable. Everyone afraid and expecting the worst from others, always on guard. . . .

Judging, criticizing, and being judged and criticized . . . no peace and little fellowship. Almost none . . . only brief spasms of love, and then even within families judging and criticism, hostility, anger, fear. Many families live in the marketplace.

We seek to leave the marketplace, and automatically a voice booms out: THERE IS NO PLACE TO GO! YOU CANNOT ESCAPE THE MARKETPLACE BECAUSE THERE IS NOTHING BUT SLEEP AND NOTHINGNESS BEYOND IT. JUST STAY BUSY. KEEP JUDGING AS BEST YOU CAN, FIGHTING TO GAIN WHAT YOU WANT. DON'T THINK TOO MUCH ABOUT IT. YOU CANNOT MOVE OUT OF IT. Yet within there is another voice which speaks without saying a word and tries to draw us out of the fleeing crowd . . . tries to let us know that the marketplace is only a place of flight, a way of blind headlong flight in which we pray for a quick death and then a nice funeral and nothingness . . . .

Something, at any rate, draws us out of the heady, maddening confusion that is the totality of life for so many people . . . something draws us aside and suggests that we pause and look and see the black void ahead. . . . Wouldn't it be better to go into our own shabby, little soul-room where we can be still and think? Yet we fear to go there . . . we fear our shabbiness. It is hard to decide, and several times the crowd surges around us and would engulf us again, but we finally turn away from it. . . .

We find the entry way to our little dwelling. It is dirty and ill lighted. Inside the room is gloomy . . . oatmeal wallpaper hangs in shreds from the walls . . . the curtains are dirty and tattered . . . except for a sagging sofa and a desk piled high with clutter, most of the furniture lies in broken pieces about the room. There is an odor coming from the corner where the sink is filled with dirty dishes and a heap of rubbish and garbage pours out onto the floor. Obviously we have not spent much time here. This is a room no one has cared for, a stop-over when there is no other place to go.

Even here the television is turned on and a radio blares in the background. We dare not be alone. We carry the marketplace into the very soul-room via the television so that we have no time to remember and see ourselves.

We are afraid of our own company . . . we fear that we cannot stand ourselves and our own nothingness. . . . We are afraid of our helplessness . . . better to hurry and do something than to be still and face our helplessness before the god of the marketplace . . . THE PAIN OF NOT BEING GOD!

We are afraid of the pain that has been locked deep in our hearts, hidden under books and piles of clothing and china and useless things . . . we are afraid of our failures, follies, our sins . . . the monsters of our desires and feelings . . . the old beast within us, the old angry ego that wills never to give in. . . .

No wonder it is too hard to leave the marketplace. No wonder we seek each other with masks on . . . in order to forget and not have to look within ourselves . . . Then each of us is alone in our own soul-room . . . .

And now I turn off the television and the radio and let stillness reign. At first I wonder if I can endure it. A million terrors afflict me. . . . Then through the silence comes a strange noise, and I am more petrified. . . . What is it? A branch brushing against the roof, or a night-flying bird at the window? Or is it some malignant creature trying to break in, perhaps a thief ready to do me in. . . ? I expect the worst, programmed as I am to fear. . . .

Listening intently, I realize that even before the stillness began the noise was there, but mingled with the other sounds of life, it was indistinguishable from the rest. I can tell that the noise has been there as long as I can remember. . . . It is a soft, persistent, gentle noise . . . it almost calms my fears. It is a knocking, determined and persistent, but kindly, patient. Amazing how much the sound of a knock reveals about the one who is knocking. It comes from the other side of the room. I have heard that there was a door there, but that it led nowhere. I was warned to stay away from it or I might go mad. . . .

The sound draws me . . . I go toward the door. . . . Caught between fear and curiosity and hope, I call out: "Come in." A voice replies softly: "I cannot. The door is bolted from within."

The bolt is rusty and so are the hinges. I finally draw it back and tug at the door. At first it will not budge and then it springs open . . . and there . . . right before me . . . there He stands . . . lantern in hand, the other hand raised to knock . . . a crown of thorns upon His head, but worn with richer dignity than any jewels . . . a rich cloak with a ruby for a clasp . . . the hands are scarred. He speaks:

"Behold, I stand at the door and knock; if any man hear my voice, and open the door, I will come in to him, and will sup with him, and he with me."*

I fall to my knees and cry out: "I am not worthy that you should come under my roof." Then He speaks again, and there is a note of harshness in His words: "Who are you to call him for whom I died unworthy? Who are you to call unworthy him at whose door I have stood from the beginning of time and knocked." He takes me by the hand and lifts me up and steps into my little soul-room. The light of His presence transforms the dull shabbiness.

Swiftly His hand clears the confusion. In the twinkling of an eye what was torn, dirty, littered is cleared as if a river had run through it, or a legion of angels had come to cleanse and renew my soul. . . . I am fresh, clean, renewed, redeemed, transformed . . . the broken in me is mended, the illness healed.

For a long time we sit and talk. I pour out my anguish, my hopes, my joys, my fears, all of me. He listens, an arm around my shoulder. I weep, and the tears themselves are cleansing. Then He takes bread and breaks it and gives it to me, saying: "This is my body." He also takes wine and blesses it and hands me the cup and says: "This is my blood. . . ." What wonderful things we speak

---

*Revelation 3:20.

of . . . great mysteries which make my heart burn within me. Then He takes me by the hand and leads me to the door. . . .

I protest. I cannot go out there, but He laughs, and His laughter is the music of the spheres . . . and He takes me out into a land of such beauty that I cannot believe my eyes. . . .

The room from which we came is but a basement chamber, a cellar cell of a vast mansion. Before us is a great green meadow leading down to an azure lake. Flowers are everywhere, of every color and shape. In the distance lie range upon range of snow-capped mountains. Childlike we roll on the grass, as happy as a child on a perfect day in May. Then He points to the great stairway near the door of the soul-room. . . .

He takes me toward it and says: "Come, my child, and inherit the kingdom prepared for you from the foundation of the world. . . . Come, this is your home . . . inherit it. Accept your sonhood." We enter the great palace, and there are angels to wait on me and such magnificence as to defy description.

I am led down a long corridor to a room that has been waiting just for me, marked with my name. He opens the door, and there I find things just as I would have wished had I known enough about myself to understand what I really wanted. . . . The colors, the furnishings fit me as perfectly as the clothes which are laid out for me to wear.

There is a beautiful pool of sparkling water behind each room . . . and there I wash and am made clean. So much dirt and grime are washed away that I am much lighter than I had thought. I am better looking than I had dreamed was possible. The rolls of fat and scars and boney joints are not really me . . . not really. . . .

And then I am clothed in my wedding garments by attending friends and brought with others to a great banquet hall. There is a feast such as I had never dreamed of . . . the banquet of the kingdom of heaven, and music and gaiety and laughter. And we are filled, with just the right amount not to be stuffed. There is fellowship with the best of friends . . . those who will be friends forever . . . who will never betray, but will bring out the best in us and give us companionship that is filled with joy.

A great curtain is pulled aside, and there, before us sitting on a throne, is the Lord Himself . . . the one who rescued me and brought me here. He is the creator, the one who made all things. He is the one who cared enough for me that He would have died if I had been the only one. He speaks as a voice within me. . . .

At first I am dazzled, but then He tells me to stand beside Him. As I step close, His presence becomes humble so that I can know His love and fellowship even better. When I am with Him it is as if I were the only one. He speaks to each of us individually, and our hearts are full of joy. Then He leads us to the great treasure vault. . . .

He selects gifts of the greatest value for each of us . . . jewels of every kind and precious metals. There is more than we can carry, and He tells us that we can come back for more at any time. Then He tells us: "It is time to go back into the marketplace and tell others what inheritance awaits them." We protest: "They will not believe us!" But He smiles and says: "Do you not believe me? . . . I am with you even unto the end of the world. I am giving you my love to go with you. Bring that love to others, that it may cover the earth as the waters cover the sea beds. . . ."

He does not hurry us. . . . As we talk we bring those who are especially dear to us, our loved ones, the sick, our friends, our enemies, into His presence, and they are transformed, every one of them, by the light which radiates from Him. . . . He waits until I am ready to return. . . .

I step back into my soul-room. It is a joy to be there. I feel at home, and I can't wait to go out and share what I have found. Bursting with joy, I step out into the street, into the marketplace. I see the men and women as they really are. Behind their masks, they are like me, frightened, seeking love, lonely. They need what I have found, and the light is ready to break through into one dark corner after another. . . .

III

THE PARALYTIC

I see myself in Capernaum. It is business that brings me here, and I am still waiting to see the Roman centurion who wants me to provide supplies. I was raised in this town, and it has been fun to wander through these streets again.

Jesus of Nazareth has just come here, and the news has spread like wildfire. A healer has arisen among my people, and they need a healer. There is so much agony and sickness. When people are prisoners politically it seems to poison their minds and also their bodies, and we have been prisoners of the Romans now for decades. I think of how interesting it would be to see this man. . . . On every street corner there are little knots of people talking excitedly. Some are frowning, and others look happy, insisting that Jesus may be the sign that the kingdom is on the way and the Romans will be thrown out. And then there are those whose eyes are full of pain, who ask how to find the way to where He is. . . .

Walking down an alleyway I see three men looking worried and shaking their heads. I hear one of them say: "We can't possibly get him there, just the three of us. He is too heavy, and he will have to be carried. He doesn't even want to go. He has no hope that he could be healed."

At this moment another of the three glances in my direction and suddenly points at me, saying: "What about asking that man? It won't hurt to ask." As the other two turn to look at me, he explains: "We have a friend here who has been lying paralyzed in his little room for five years now. We want to take him to Jesus, but it takes four to carry a man his size on a litter. Would you be willing to help us? We think this prophet can heal him. At least it's worth a try, and stranger things than that have been happening around this Jesus. Demons have been cast out and lepers healed. This man has power."

I am silent a moment thinking, yes, it would be a friendly thing to give these men a hand, and I could kill two birds with one stone . . . see the healer myself and perhaps help a poor, paralyzed man be healed. I say to them: "Why not? I have the day to kill." We exchange names and greet each other. Then the tall man, John, who is apparently the leader, fills me in.

Their friend, whose name is Obadiah, seems to be a sad case for sure. These men had been good friends of his since childhood, and had watched everything go wrong for him. He had grown up a handsome and powerful man and had been an excellent stone mason. The Romans had kept him busy on all sorts of buildings . . . there was more work than he could do. He was planning to be married when the accident happened. The Roman contractor was trying to meet a deadline and scheduled work on the Sabbath. Obadiah didn't want to, but felt he had to be on the job. He was tired, and lifting a big rock, he slipped and it fell back on him. He was pinned to the ground and passed out. When he came to, they found he was paralyzed from the waist down. The girl would have nothing more to do with him. There was no work that he could learn, and he was too proud to beg. His friends kept him alive, just barely.

As John finished the recital, the others nodded in agreement. One of them chimed in: "He's so angry and bitter I think he wishes he could die, and he probably would if it weren't for us. He'll growl at us when we tell him what we're going to do."

We had come to the little room where he lived, and the four of us ducked through the doorway. The place was dirty and smelled sour. Obadiah looked at us and said: "What are you three doing here at this time of day? And who's the stranger? One of you is enough at a time. . . . Why don't you just let me die? There's nothing to live for. . . ." His expression was bitter and ugly, but I could see that he had been a handsome man. He had probably been almost six feet tall, and his arms and chest still looked strong, but his legs were only withered poles.

John told him the plan and his reaction was instantaneous. "Why bother with me? What hope is there? Maybe this great healer can fix backaches and stomach cramps, but you know very well that no one can mend a broken back. Have you brought this stranger here to play a trick on me?"

The three seemed to pay no attention to his ugly mood. John told the rest of us what to do. They had brought enough rope to tie to each corner of the litter, and he showed us how to wind it around our shoulders. Once we started, Obadiah didn't seem to object. Something told me that underneath his complaining was a hurting, sensitive soul.

I was thinking to myself. . . . How much of me is like him? . . . I don't let the world know, but there's a part of me just as paralyzed and just as bitter and angry. I don't seem to be able to control it. And that's the way most people seem to act today. I guess everybody has some part that is paralyzed . . . only his shows more. Maybe it's important for me to know just where the paralysis is that is keeping me stuck in a rut. . . .

As I groaned under the load, I couldn't stop thinking about the strange situation I was in. We couldn't talk. It took all the energy we had just to carry him. And every time someone missed a step and jolted him, he started all over about wanting to be left alone and wanting to die. Later I really had time to reflect on the whole thing. . . . If there really is something paralyzed in me, and I believe there is because I certainly seem to be unable to keep at the things that are most important, are there also some parts of me as determined as these fellows to get help for the paralyzed one? Is there something in me that would even go up to a stranger on the street. . . ? Obadiah would have been a goner for sure if John weren't so strong and persistent, and if the other two weren't just as patient and loyal. Are there, just possibly, some friends like that in me who could rescue whatever is paralyzed and help me get on the right track again? . . . Well, perhaps.

When the five of us came up to the house where Jesus was supposed to be, we could see that it was crowded, even outside. We had expected some people, but nothing like this. Obadiah kept growling that most of them were probably just curious like the ones that were always gaping at him. I figured I was the best dressed and a little older, so I spoke, asking the closest people if they would please move a little so that we could take our friend in to the healer. Nobody budged an inch. So I tried it again, a little louder, and a few people who were obviously sick muttered: "No. We got here first." Most of the others pretended not to hear.

Once again I was brought up short, thinking to myself. . . well, that's you in a nutshell. How often had I stood around gawking at something important, exactly like many of these people . . . getting in everyone's way and not really caring at all? Even now part of me was as indifferent as if my ego hadn't gotten involved. I wouldn't have been too surprised to see myself go up and kick a couple of sick people in the shins and try to force my way in. I shuddered a little at how much I was seeing of myself. We may think we are different from any ordinary so-and-so . . . but that's the time to look again. . . .

But now the litter was getting heavier by the minute, and we couldn't keep Obadiah lying in the sun much longer. Three of us were about ready to give up and go home when the smallest of the friends spoke up. "Wait a minute," he said. "I have an idea. . . . What about the stairs to the roof? You know I've worked on roofs. The beams in this kind of house are far apart. We could go up there, I could take off a few tile and some boards, and we could let him down from above." Obadiah was even amused by the idea. "OK! Let's let me down through the roof!" It was the first time I had seen him smile. He hadn't lost all his sense of humor.

We all began to feel different as we started up the stairs. We were light-hearted, as if bent on a prank. We laughed as we stacked the tiles neatly in one corner. The undercurrent of thoughts about myself kept coming and going in the background. . . . One thing I could say for myself . . . I do have a sense of humor. That's one of my best qualities, and a person certainly needs it to face all the pain and suffering we run into in this world . . . things like paralysis and, yes, even callousness and selfishness. Seeing the funny side of things is often the only thing that keeps one from giving up. . . .

No one seemed to notice us until we began to lower the litter. They were all so intent on watching Jesus that they didn't realize how the light increased around Him until the last board was off and Obadiah was swaying gently over their heads. People moved back as the litter came down in front of Jesus. He looked at Obadiah and then at us peering over the edge of the roof. He nodded at us. We could tell that He knew what we hoped. His look said as clearly as words: Thank you for bringing him. His hurt needs healing. Thank you for your concern and care and faith. I had never known a look like that before. It caused something to change in me. In that instant my own paralysis was healed, even before He did anything for the man lying motionless on the floor.

Even Obadiah had been infected with some of our faith and hope. He was actually expecting something now, and I saw his bitter look of disappointment when all he heard were the words, "My son, your sins are forgiven." Later Obadiah told us how disappointed he had been. He couldn't have cared less about forgiveness. All he wanted was to walk again, to live as a normal man, at least able to get up and go to work in the morning. What kind of bad joke was this man pulling on him? He was hurting too much to care about forgiveness. . . .

But Jesus knew what He was doing. The stuffy teachers of the law had heard His words and were ready. They had been looking for an occasion. Jesus knew that they were thinking: "How does he dare to treat God that way? No man can forgive sins; only God can." Forgiving sins was a far bigger thing than healing, far more difficult. They believed in a God who kept a strict tally on how we keep the law. After all the man before Jesus had broken the law of the Sabbath. The accident had happened because he was working on the Sabbath, and obviously he had gotten what he deserved. Instead of being resigned to his fate, or at least looking to the synagogue for help, here he was seeking help from the man Jesus. It proved that he was no good, unredeemed.

Then Jesus spoke to their thoughts, and the look on their faces showed that He had hit the nail on the head. "Why do you think such things?" He said. "Is it easier to say to this paralyzed man, 'Your sins are forgiven,' or to say to him, 'Get up, pick up your mat and walk?' "

At first I was angry . . . mostly at their apparent attitude toward Obadiah, even though it was to be expected. We all knew what these religious leaders would think of him. He had no importance to them as a person, because he was a miserable sinner. I knew this attitude in myself . . . the inner voice like theirs which sometimes tells me: You don't deserve forgiveness or healing; you're hopeless. Nothing can heal you. Nobody but God could forgive you, and He won't because you are so vile. God wants perfection, and a sinner like you hasn't a chance with Him. . . . These are the voices that can keep me from knowing the love that is there . . . that can keep me from being healed.

Jesus then rose to His full height, and a power, a numinous power, seemed to flow from Him. He looked at the teachers and said: "I will prove to you, then, that the Son of Man has authority on earth to forgive sins." So He turned to Obadiah, reached out a hand toward him and said: "I tell you, get up, pick up your mat, and go home!" The whole place was electric. I will never forget those words or the way He said them. Everyone was watching. Obadiah looked around. He rolled over on one side and found he could move his legs. Then he turned all the way over, got up on his knees, and then stood up. Without a word he went over and threw his arms around Jesus and wept. He couldn't talk enough to say thank you. Jesus nodded to him that he could go. The crowd . . . those people who had almost kept him from getting in . . . backed away, half in wonder, half in fear. He picked up his mat and walked out.

We met him outside as he came out, and he hugged each of us. We wanted to give him a hand, but he wanted to go it alone. We were all speechless. . . . There was nothing left to say. Later when we did talk, we realized that all of us had been thinking the same thing. We had seen the breakthrough of love into our sordid world of Romans and selfishness and judging. This was a love that could break down any barrier, even bitterness, a love that could heal any brokenness of mind and soul. We talked most of that night. And the next day we went to find Jesus again, and as long as He was in Capernaum we followed him. I missed seeing the centurion, but I found other buyers. Obadiah had no trouble finding work, and soon he fell in love and was married. I always visit him and his wife when I come to Capernaum, and I am always welcome. What a friend he is. Being with him reminds me that there is a love always reaching out to me if I don't push it away.

IV

Our Last Supper Together

Jesus told us to meet Him in the room that two of us would find and make ready. The way we found the room was strange. Even though we have lived with Him long enough to take His instructions seriously, this time they sounded absurd. He told us to go into the city, and there we would see a man carrying a jar of water. We were to follow him into a house and say to the owner of the house: "The teacher asks: Where is my room where my disciples and I are to eat the Passover supper?" The owner would then show us a large upstairs room, fixed up and furnished. There we were to get things ready for the sacred meal.

Carrying water jars is simply not a thing that men do, and yet we had not gone far into the city when we saw a tall young man carrying a jar still wet from being dipped into the well. We were amazed. . . . This master of ours had strange powers. Now and then there was something about Him which frightened us, an unearthly, holy power. Yet instead of making Him less human, it seemed to bring us closer to Him. It made us love Him more and enabled us to feel His love for us. I wish I could explain it.

Everything happened exactly as He said it would. The man carrying the jar went into a large house. We did not dare to speak to him until he was greeted at the door by an older man, the owner of the house. A young servant took the jar, and then my companion spoke the words Jesus had told him. He told us later that he felt like a fool. "The teacher asks: Where is my room where my disciples and I are to eat the Passover supper?" The owner smiled as my companion stammered out the words. He was a large man, about fifty-five, a man of refinement. I thought I had seen him sometimes among the crowds who listen to the Teacher. His reply showed how gracious he was. "I am so glad that Jesus will come and use my place. I have a large room upstairs where you can be quite private and secluded. Come and see it."

When the younger man heard the name of Jesus, he turned and said: "You are His followers, aren't you?" As the four of us went upstairs together, he continued: "If there is anything I can do to help you, please let me know." So we asked him to help with our preparations, arranging the couches and tables, and while we were doing this he asked all sorts of questions about the Master and what He said. He even asked us how we had happened to follow him home, and we told the story. He laughed and said that he had felt foolish going for water but the girl who did this chore had been sent on another errand.

As the sun was setting the twelve began to gather. We found the room perfect, and there was an air of expectancy among us. We sensed that something was about to happen. Of course we thought that Jesus might be ready to bring

His kingdom into being. We gathered in knots of three or four talking about what we would be doing when the kingdom became a reality. We thought with relish of the power we might have, what part of the world we might rule, how the Romans would have to serve us.

Jesus came in. We greeted Him with warmth. Wondering what He would do, we gathered around the table and took our places. The moment we were all sitting in our places Jesus rose from the table, took off His outer garment and tied a towel around His waist. Can you imagine our astonishment? He took a basin, a common wash basin, poured some water in it, and began to wash our feet and then dry them with the towel around His waist. Here was our Teacher, our Master, acting like the lowest servant in the house. But there was no condescension in His action. He was not playacting. It was as if this were what He did every day. The first two were caught speechless by having Him wash their feet.

Then He came to Peter. Jesus was already kneeling before him when Peter blurted out: "Are you going to wash my feet?" And Jesus replied: "You don't know what I am doing now, but you will know later." This was too much for Peter. He pulled away and cried out in horror: "You shall never, *never* wash my feet! You are my Master. I am not worthy to have you wash my feet. I am your servant. I should be washing your feet. No, Master! No!"

Then Jesus spoke directly and forcefully, looking right into Peter's face. "If I do not wash your feet, you will no longer be my disciple." Jesus seldom spoke like that. A hush came over all of us. All eyes were on Peter. He was shaken. He did not know what to say. He was silent for a moment, and then he said in a frightened, pleading voice: "Lord, if that is so, then don't wash just my feet, but wash my head and my hands, all of me." The stern look vanished from the Master's face, and He went about washing Peter's feet, saying something about the fact that people who have bathed in the morning don't need to be washed all over, but only to get rid of the dirt of the road on their feet. As He wiped Peter's second foot and set it on the floor, He added something about all of us being clean, all except one.

When He came to me, the third after Peter, and took my feet in His hands, I felt just what Peter had expressed, but I held my tongue. Can you imagine what it was like to have your guru, your Master, the one whose every word you relied on . . . to have this person kneeling before you and doing the most menial of tasks? This was the one who might, before the night was out, order legions of angels to appear. This was the one who had healed the demon possessed, the paralyzed, who had even raised the dead. Yet here He was on His knees at my feet, washing them. It blew my mind. I couldn't understand. With His hands he had taken off my sandals and washed away the filth of the street which clung to my feet. He was not afraid of any filth. But I felt something more there with His hands on my feet. It was as if He were trying to touch me more deeply, as if His hands were saying something. I watched Him go from one to another in dazed silence.

When He had finished, Jesus then washed His hands, put His garments on and came back to His place at the center of the table. No one said a word. No one was talking now about what position he might have in the power of the kingdom. Then He began to talk to us. I was not too surprised at what He said. Something in me had sensed it from the touch of His hands. "Do you know what I have done?" He asked, and then went on: "You call me Lord and Teacher, and it is right that you do so, because I *am* your Lord and Teacher. Yet I have just washed your feet. I have been your servant, the lowest servant. I have given you an example. I have been a parable so that you will know what to do toward others. It is up to you to wash one another's feet. No slave is greater than his master. No messenger is greater than the one who sent him. Don't try to lord it over others. Act as servants to one another and you will know what I am about."

As He talked Jesus became more and more moved and troubled. He seemed to feel the pain of the world. He looked from one to another of us. And then these words came out like great waves crashing on a cliff: "I tell you, one of you will betray me . . . one who is eating with me. It will be one of the twelve who dips his bread in the dish with me. How terrible for that man to betray the Son of Man. It would have been better for him if he had never been born."

Every one of us was terrified and shaken. It would have been bad enough to betray any ordinary person, but to betray one who has shared his food with you, to betray your master . . . who would do such a thing? A murmur arose from us, like the sound of bees swarming. Like the rest, I had come expecting great things. . . . And what had happened? . . . First my Master washed my feet, and now He strikes terror in me. I know that there is a weak side in me which might try to betray someone, and also a power-driven side which seeks only my own gain. . . . Each of us present speaks out and asks, "Lord, is it I?"

I couldn't believe that I could be the one. I didn't think myself capable of it. . . . But then I think of all the little ways that I have let Him down. I have not always listened carefully. I've grumbled when the way was hard. I tried to push away the mothers who brought their children. I haven't always understood Him. I wondered how He could let that prostitute touch His feet. Even tonight I was talking about hoping for a place of glory. I haven't understood the depth of love, nor practiced it even among the twelve, let alone outside.

There was something even stranger to come. . . . After all this we were watching His every movement, straining for every word. As we were dipping our sops in the dish, Jesus took a fresh, round loaf of bread. He said a prayer of thanks, broke the bread and gave it to us. We stopped eating and waited in silence to watch what He would do. As we each took a piece of the bread, He said: "Take, eat it; this is my body." My mind reeled at this. Did I hear correctly? He was giving us His body to eat. What is this strange paganism, I wondered. And then came something even more startling. He took the cup of wine, the cup of blessing, in His hands. Again He gave thanks to God. And then He handed this cup to us, and as we all drank of it, our Master said to us: "This is my blood which is poured out for many, my blood which seals God's contract with men. I tell you, I will never drink this wine again until the day I drink the new wine in the Kingdom. Continue to share this cup and bread in my memory."

Do you have any idea what these words did to me and to the rest of us loyal Jews. The very idea of touching a dead human body was defilement of the worst kind. It made one unclean for weeks. But the idea of drinking human blood was beyond imagination. The blood had to be properly drained from any meat or it was not kosher, and eating it made one unclean. Blood was the very life of any living thing. One could not eat it. It was unthinkable to eat it purposely. But human blood, our Master's blood. . . . I wondered if He had gone mad. Or had He, perhaps, used this image to drive it home so that we could never forget? Reflecting later, I am sure it was the latter reason. He wanted us to remember, wanted us to have a way of knowing that He shared his very life with us . . . the reality of His being, His body and His blood.

As I took the cup I was closer to Him than I had ever been before. I was part of Him and He was part of me. I can't explain it. It just happened. He had shared Himself as never before, and He did it not only in words and actions, but with His very inner being. Slowly the broken bread and the sacred wine were passed around. No one said anything. There was nothing left to say. Judas got up quietly and went out. As we looked out through the open door we saw that it was night.

Then Jesus spoke again. I had never heard Him speak more directly. Looking back, I can see that it was His last attempt to let us know the meaning of His life and teaching. His words were comparable to the body and blood that He gave us. They were the body and blood of His thoughts. His voice was clear and deep. The words almost sang themselves: "I give you now a new commandment. Love one another. As I have loved you, so must you love one another. If you have love for one another, then all will know that you are my disciples." Then we sang a hymn and went out to the Mount of Olives.

Every time we share the mysteries I see that night again. It is burned into my heart. And when we pass the cup and share the bread, I can sense His presence. Jesus is there. It is the only thing that has kept me going as the way has gotten rougher. The followers of the way are persecuted more and more often. People seem to be afraid of love. But when we gather early in the morning and share the cup and break the bread, the reality of the whole message comes back . . . He is there. His body and blood give me an infusion of new life. There is nothing else like it.

V

THE GARDEN OF THE TOMB

I met her at the tomb. She was weeping as though her heart would break, and I was crying too. My eyes had been filled with tears for two days, and I knew how Mary felt as she stood beside the tomb. She had come to give her last service to her Lord. She carried spices to embalm Him . . . the last thing she could do for Him. He had done so much for her, given her back her self-respect, her hope, her life. . . .

This man had done the same for me. Everyone had given up on me when I met Him. I was lost in drugs and wine and lust. He was speaking in Capernaum when He looked at me and I knew that He knew, and that He loved me none the less. He reached out His hand and touched me and it was the beginning of new life. I followed Him from then on. And then the Passover. . . . There was a strange power in Him. He threw all caution to the wind. They took Him in the garden where we had gone after supper. My God, the pain and agony He bore until He gave up the ghost upon that cross.

What was there to do but weep? . . . I thought I had found meaning. I believed that He was God's Son. He was like God Himself to me. And I was a fool again. . . . It was all illusion, all a sham. I had been deceived, had seen in Him more than He really was. He was just a noble man. The world and its hurting people can't stand nobility. They destroy it. They destroyed Him, and this had destroyed me too . . . but still, I decided to go to the tomb. I knew that after the Sabbath the women would anoint His body. There had barely been time to put it in the tomb before the Sabbath began, and I would like to see Him once again. I could share my tears with Mary. She understood because she had received as much from Him as I. Her grief was just as deep and real as mine. When one is truly in despair, only one who has known such despair can be a comfort. Others usually don't understand.

Peter and John had been there, had looked in the tomb and silently gone away. I came just as they left. I greeted Mary, but she hardly noticed that I was there. She was still crying as she bent over and peered into the tomb. I kneeled down beside her and looked in too . . . Jesus was not there. His graveclothes were neatly folded, the shroud and the napkin from His head piled separately. . . .

But two people were there, majestic figures, one sitting where His head had been, another at the foot of the slab. . . . Ordinarily such figures would have sent chills of terror through me. But now we were too full of grief to be any more frightened . . . if they had destroyed me at that moment, it would have only been relief. We looked at them dumbly until they asked Mary: "Woman, why are you weeping?"

At this a fresh flood of tears poured out of Mary's eyes. But she caught her breath and explained: "They have taken my Lord away, and I do not know where they have put Him." It is bad enough to lose the one you have loved. It is worse to see life crash in because everything that He stood for appears to have been unreal. But now they have even stolen away His body . . . the only thing that seemed to be left to touch once more. . . . Mary had felt that this last service of anointing the body of her friend and master might somehow ease the pain. There is a reason why we have our customs and rituals of taking leave of the dead. . . . Taking away His body was the final desecration. Not being able to perform the last ritual was the end of the road, the last indignity, a final stab at her heart. No wonder that she wept, wept so much that she was not sure what she had seen within the tomb.

Mary had numbly held herself together during the actual nailing to the cross and the hours that He hung there. She had helped take Him from the cross and carry Him to the tomb . . . but now that she found His body stolen away, she was nearly hysterical with pain and anguish. . . .

She did not know what to make of these creatures in the tomb. She felt a chill of awe about them. They only asked a silly question about why she was weeping. She stood up and turned around. I stood close by her. . . . She nearly bumped into a man standing there whom she did not know. He wore peasant clothes, and we both thought that He was a gardener come early after the Sabbath to tend the garden. . . .

It was no wonder that he spoke to her rather than to me. I have never seen a person's face express more agony. . . . He also asked her: "Why are you weeping? Who is it that you are looking for?" They seemed like matter-of-fact questions at the time. Only later did the memory of them reveal to both of us the touch of divine irony. For moments her only answer was another deluge of tears. Finally she controlled herself enough to speak. In a pleading voice she asked him: "If you took Him away, sir, tell me where you have put Him, and I will go and get Him." Although she was looking right at the man, she was separated from him by a veil of tears. . . . She turned away.

And then He spoke one simple word: "Mary." He called her by her own name. She knew His voice. He had spoken that name with warmth and care, when others spoke it with derision. It was His voice which first broke through the wall around her heart. She had determined that no one would ever enter there again. . . .

But His voice had knocked so quietly that she had let Him in, and then there was the agony of coming back to life again, like stepping on a leg that has gone to sleep. He spoke her name again, and this time the voice brought only joy and peace. The tears dried up . . . a smile of transcendent joy lit up her whole face. She beamed with joy. I wish you could have seen it. . . . From darkest night to sunny noonday in one moment . . . it was the most amazing transformation I have ever seen. I don't know what I looked like, but I know what I felt. I felt like she looked. I hope I showed something of how moved I felt. He spoke my name after hers . . . and He has gone on speaking the intimate names of those who wait in such a garden from that day to this. Those who meet Him there are never the same again.

I wish you could have heard the way she cried out: "Rabboni!" Each syllable had a new quality. It was like a bird song. She had always called him Rabboni or Teacher. She wiped the rest of the tears from her face with one quick gesture and stretched out her arms to take hold of Him. The body that she had come to anoint in death was standing there before her, radiant in health, almost glowing in the rays of the rising sun.

Then Jesus spoke softly to her. "Not yet, Mary. Do not hold on to me, because I have not yet gone back up to my Father. But go to my brothers and tell them for me what you have experienced, and tell them that I go back to Him who is my Father and your Father, my God and your God." Then he vanished from our sight.

And Mary threw back her head and sang, and almost danced down the hill. I went with her. She kept singing again and again . . . Rabboni, Rabboni. . . . We knew that He was the Teacher, the Master, the Lord, the Conquerer. She had been right to let that voice break into the sealed chamber of her heart. There was now meaning and hope and love. . . . People did not just use one another. The universe did not just use people and cast them off. What a beautiful morning it was! The flowers were blooming in the garden . . . primrose and wild lilies, roses, red and white. How green the grass, how much a part of this new life we felt.

We found the disciples huddled together with some of the others. Cleopas and a friend of his were there. We told them what we had seen, but they only smiled indulgent smiles. They were thinking to themselves that pain works in strange ways on some people's minds. They were courteous. They did not say that we had dreamed, but we could tell that they thought we had.

But it didn't bother us because we knew, we really knew. We knew He was alive and that there was nothing left for us to fear, not even death or grief or pain or anything. . . . I'm so grateful that I was there with Mary to share her grief and her joy, her agony and her transformation. . . . And I tell this story so that others might know what it was like. I stood on the still point, the point upon which the whole world rests. I would like to share this place with you. . . . I think that's why Jesus let me be with Mary as Eternal Love broke through and showed itself in time. . . .

VI

THE ROAD TO EMMAUS

It was a magnificent spring day, and that only made the pain worse, the pain of utter lostness. Everything I cared about was gone, lost. . . . We had gone to Jerusalem for the Passover and to be with Jesus. Both Cleopas and I were convinced that this was going to be the time that Jesus would show that He was no mere mortal man.

I wasn't sure how it would happen, but I was sure that some marvel would take place. . . . The Romans would flee in terror, thrown out. The Temple would be purified, and the kingdom of God would be ushered in. We had decided to follow Him no matter what happened. If this was not the time, then it would come soon, and we would remain with Him until He was ready for the new age to begin. . . .

We had often been with Jesus and His friends. He had healed my brother and one of Cleopas's cousins. There was no one else like Him. . . . Before He came, there had been no hope. I worked from day to day. With all the taxes, I hardly had enough to live on. It is hard to live in an occupied country. One's soul is never one's own. There is always the temptation to join the underground, but it looked so hopeless . . . and then the crosses and the bodies hanging there would remind us what Romans do to rebellious slaves and plotters.

Instead He gave us a new vision of what life could be. . . . He knew my faults and loved me even more because of the struggle that I was having. He was so kind, so warm and forgiving and loving. And there was a power about Him too. It was a strange mixture, that love and power. I had never thought that I would see such a combination. He seemed to live within the world and yet beyond it . . . and a thing like that just didn't occur within the reach of ordinary people.

But we had been wrong . . . He was dead. He never raised a finger to avoid it. We watched Him die, hoping until the very end for some miracle. But then they took His body down and carried it away. He had died on Friday. Now it was Sunday, and we were going home to Emmaus to see if we could find some reason to go on, a way to pick up the pieces and want to go on living. Earlier today, while we were with His followers, Mary and a friend came from the garden tomb and told a silly story of having seen Him. . . . What fragile minds we have!

I resented the beautiful day. It was out of keeping with the world. We trudged on talking about the things that we had just been through, wondering if there could have been something else that we could have done. We were half way home when a stranger caught up with us. I don't know where he came from, but we were so deep in our own thoughts that it was no wonder we didn't see him until he was alongside.

We stopped talking as he fell in step with us. We walked along silent for a while, and then he spoke: "What on earth were you talking about so earnestly back there? Apparently it was something sad. You look as though you'd lost everything. What has happened?" We all stood still and the two of us looked at him. Our faces betrayed our inner agony.

Cleopas asked him: "Are you the only man coming from Jerusalem who does not know what has been happening these last few days?" Shaking his head, he asked us: "What things are you talking about?" And then the whole story poured out of us. ... It seemed kind of him to listen to our grief and bear the burden with us. It helps to talk about one's tears.

We told him about the man whom we thought would bring some hope and peace again to Israel. He was a prophet and all the common people worshipped Him. And He was as dear to God as He was to the people . . . the things that He did . . . the miracles and the way He spoke with power. . . . Some close to us were healed by Him. We had known Him. He had changed our lives and fed our hopes. He had given us light and joy. This Passover was to have been the time when something happened.

But our chief priests were jealous of His appeal to all the people. The Romans feared that He might start a riot or revolt. They did not know the man. They sentenced Him to death and nailed Him to a cross. And to make it worse, this is the third day since He died. Some of the women from our group came with a likely story. They had gone to the grave at dawn, but they could not find the body. They came back talking about angels who told them that He is alive. Some of the rest of our group went to the grave and found it exactly as the women had said, but they did not see Him. It is bad enough to grieve without being told stories of that kind. It's better to face the awful truth that love never wins in this world . . . or maybe even in the next . . . and just grind on until you die. . . .

And then the stranger began to talk about the scriptures. I could hardly believe my ears. This man knew the writings better than anyone I ever heard except one. My heart simply burned, hearing the way he talked. I had only heard one other person talk like that ever before, and He was dead. This man had the same kind of fresh point of view. He said that we had misunderstood the prophets, and that one never really wins through strength, but through weakness. The Messiah, he said, would naturally have to die before He could be glorified. It made such sense. He spoke of the suffering servant, of dying to rise again. He showed us how this theme kept occurring through the books of scripture from Moses right through the prophets.

The three and a half miles to Emmaus simply vanished while we listened to him. He gave us a vision of the world where love finally conquers even though it dies . . . no, a vision of love that conquers just because it dies willingly. . . . The whole of the law and the prophets became luminous. My spine tingled as I listened. Then we started to turn off the road toward a little village inn, but the stranger seemed about to walk on. I called to him . . . "Sir!" . . . in our confusion we had never asked his name ... "Sir, why don't you stay here at the inn with us. The day's almost over. It's getting dark, and we're hungry. You must be, also. Come and stay with us." He seemed happy to be invited . . . He nodded in agreement and came in with us.

The innkeeper showed us where to wash and then fixed a table for us. The servant brought loaves of bread and set a jug of wine and cups on the table. The stranger sat down quite casually at the table. He reached over and took some bread. It was unusual for a guest and stranger to reach for food or drink first, but somehow I did not think it strange . . . the order of things just seemed to be different. Then he said a blessing. Somewhere I had heard a blessing like that once before. Then he broke the bread and gave it to us.

I was looking at His hands and suddenly I saw them. . . . There was the print of a nail in each hand. A shudder of joy, of incredible hope passed through me. . . . My eyes traveled from the hands to the face . . . and the man was a stranger no longer. It was Jesus, the very one that I had loved so much, who had accepted and understood me when no one else had ever tried. He looked at me with an expression that I wish I could describe . . . it was a mixture of joy and confidence, of compassion and friendship. There was a touch of humor in the slight smile upon his lips. I reached out my hands in amazement, with joy and yet bewilderment, and then He vanished.

Suddenly the joy burst through me as if a dam had broken. I felt as though I had truly been carried to the heart of love. It was strange that His disappearance did not make me sad. His disappearing was part of His victory, victory over space and time and everything. His vanishing meant that He was always present, always there. I looked at Cleopas, and he looked at me. Without words I could tell that he had experienced the same thing . . . we both knew. Then we cried out together: "We must return and let the others know so that they don't suffer any longer." This was our first thought. We wanted them to know that Jesus had risen. He had won. He had died for a purpose and had risen to secure the greatest victory ever won. We left our food, never even told the inn-keeper we were going, and we ran all the way back to Jerusalem. . . .

We found the disciples where we had left them, but they were hardly even the same men. We had left eleven broken men who had no place to go, men who were filled with terror and afraid to go outside of the room, afraid of themselves, of the authorities, of death, of life. . . . When we walked into that room again, we found that the eleven had been joined by other men and women and all of them were singing and crying with joy. Again and again they chanted: "The Lord is risen indeed! Simon has seen him!" It was like a litany. Everyone glowed with joy and confidence. They were like slaves just freed, like condemned prisoners given pardon. They had not been wrong in their hopes. They were vindicated and, even more important, the universe was vindicated. Evil didn't always win. Love is stronger. There is something to live for, and death no longer need be feared. All of this rang through their words and actions.

They asked what had happened to bring us back, and we told them about meeting a stranger who wondered why we were so sad. We told them how He explained our sorrow and how He made the scriptures clear, making our hearts burn. We described stopping at the inn and how He took bread and broke it and gave it to us, so that we saw who it was. We had finally seen that it was

Jesus, and He had been with us all that way and we had not known Him.

As we were still talking a light filled the place and there He was in our midst, right among us. Peter and Cleopas and I knew it was the Lord, but the others were frightened. The chilling touch of the holy sent shivers down their spines, and they shook with fear. They feared that a ghost, or something destructive, had come to haunt them, and they fell back in dread and terror. Humans are so used to meeting the destructive that they react to anything overwhelming in the same way, even when they should be able to see that it is Love. We cannot believe that love can conquer and that kindness could be triumphant.

Jesus spoke to us. He was human. He understood our fear and wanted to relieve it. "Why are you so troubled?" He said. "Why are these doubts coming up, and filling your minds? Look at my hands and my feet and see that it is I, myself. Feel me, and you will see, for a ghost doesn't have flesh and bones, and you can see that I have."

His words broke the spell. We crowded round Him. Gingerly at first we reached out, and then each of us embraced Him and knew His strength and life and victory. As we touched Him this strength and life and victory was ours.

And still some of our group could not believe. It was too good to be true. They were so filled with wonder that they didn't know what to believe. Then He asked us, "Do you have anything to eat here?" We gave Him a piece of broiled fish and he took it and ate it right before our eyes.

Then He spoke to us about the scripture, revealing the deepest meaning of all things just as He had done with the two of us on the road to Emmaus. After that He told us: "You are my witnesses, witnesses to others that love has conquered over death. It was right for the Messiah to suffer and die and rise again. All people must have a chance to learn that there is forgiveness for all who know the need for it. This message is for everyone. I know that you do not have the power to spread it by yourselves, but I will send you power and wisdom. Stay together and wait until it comes." Then He blessed us and disappeared from our sight.

We were a joyous band. There was no thought of sadness. No one wanted to write an elegy, because He is still with us. I find that I can turn within and He is there, and I can talk with Him even now. What a day that Sunday was! I will never forget it, and I doubt if it will ever be forgotten by the people of this world. It may have been the greatest day that ever was.

VII

The Man Who Fell among Thieves

Several years ago, on the road from Jerusalem to Jericho, I was attacked by a band of thieves. The experience nearly killed me, but it was the turning point of my life. It opened my eyes. I certainly would not choose an experience like that, but one can learn a lot if one survives.

I should have known better than to go from Jerusalem in any direction without an armed guard, but I was greedy. The caravans had come in from the south and I had new merchandise, choice oils and incense that had been in short supply. If I could only get to Jericho first, I could make a killing. I argued with myself that I hadn't heard of any recent raids on caravans or any people killed along the road. I thought it was worth the chance.

I had not gone far before I began to change my mind. It was a dark and foreboding day. I had had restless dreams the night before, but thinking about the pile of money I would make put them out of my mind. Now they began to come back, and I felt uneasy. I was quite watchful for a while. But then the sun came out, I saw Jericho ahead, and speeded up, forgetting my caution. Suddenly a rock struck my head. I staggered and fell. Then four bandits swooped down on me. I didn't have a chance. They tore off the pack I carried and then ripped off my clothes to see if I had any money hidden on my body. I was still conscious, although just barely, so they beat me some more. I must have gone limp enough to look dead, and with that they left me beside the road, bleeding, with only a few shreds of clothing left on my body.

When I came to I had plenty of time to think. . . . What a fool I have been! How stupid to risk everything for a little more money. Even if I am young, how stupid to build bigger barns when I may not live to see them filled . . . I swore that I would change my priorities if I survived, I'd spend more time with the children, and some time in silence and complain less at my wife. And since then I have. I am looking for meaning, some ultimate purpose that even death cannot rob me of.

I can almost thank those thieves for stopping me in my tracks. . . . Of course they wanted only to strip what I had and kill me, but even evil can be changed into good if one is not destroyed. Being the target of destructive violence reminded me that the same element is also in me. I am no saint. I could have been one of them, say, if I were poorer and driven from my home by the Romans. I might even have done the beating. I know that destructive part of me which pokes fun at hunchbacks and ridicules people who are weak. Perhaps this side was striking at me by starting me out on the road to Jericho. I have really been quite naïve and unconcious about myself. I wonder if all of us don't need to keep an eye on this part of ourselves. . . .

The pain began to get worse. Every time I moved another rock poked into my flesh. My shoulder was still bleeding, but the worst pain was thirst. In a few hours my mouth felt like leather and my tongue was swollen. What I would have given for just a sip of cold water . . . I thought of how little I have understood sickness. I have always been healthy, and sick people simply seemed weak to me because they complained about their sickness. I shall never treat sickness that way again. . . . As I drifted off and then came to again, I knew that I would never forget this pain. If only I lived, I would reach out a little more to the pain and sickness that surround me.

I had just about given up hope when I heard footsteps. . . . It was difficult to open my eyes, but I squinted down to see the robes of a priest and breathed a sigh of relief. Certainly this servant of the temple, this servant of God would stop and bring me some comfort and send for help. But he only stopped long enough to murmur something about: "Poor fellow, probably drunk . . . such brawls . . . I'd better get away before his friends show up. . . ." In his last sidelong glance he saw that I was still conscious. I was hurting too much to be angry. I must have drifted off again because the next thing I knew there were more footsteps, and I saw it was a Levite, a temple servant. I expected less of him. He knew it was good business to be above reproach and not get mixed up with bad characters. He pulled up his robes and hurried by, the very picture of rectitude, watching every rock for fear I had friends around.

I was aware enough to be disgusted. . . . These representatives of conventional religion, these impeccable, orthodox fellows couldn't even stop to find out if I needed help. But I couldn't really complain . . . my own religious attitude was just as indifferent to people's troubles. It kept me from reaching out, even to find out if someone needed healing . . . these men had shown me a lot about religious people, myself included.

I began to think the end had come, and I fought to stay conscious . . . was that an animal approaching? Yes, there was a donkey, and I closed my eyes in fear and hatred as I made out the rider. It was a vile, despised Samaritan, probably a lecher, as well as an underhanded fighter. The jig is up, I thought. He will kick my head in with that heavy boot. I wouldn't blame him, the way we Jews have treated them. We spit at Samaritans if they even walk on the same side of the street with us. They're the worst of men, ugly, cannibal-like . . . they desecrate the faith, even worse than Romans or Greeks or barbarians. . . . I cringed as I heard him dismount, heard his shoes crunch on the gravel as he approached. . . .

But instead of kicks or blows, I felt a gentle touch, actually a loving touch. He was feeling my pulse. Then he raked away the gravel, and went over and opened his pack. He laid out a piece of cloth and placed me on it. He brought some wine for me to sip. Nothing had ever tasted like that before. He poured some oil and wine into my wounds and gave me another sip of wine. Such healing kindness . . . and I let myself drift off. When I came to again, this man who might have kicked me was dressing my wounds. Then he picked me up, for he was very strong. He placed me on his beast and started off, walking along beside to hold me on. I can't remember much about that ride, but we finally reached a little inn. He let me down from the donkey and got the innkeeper to come and help carry me inside.

How grateful I was for that beast . . . I thought of how often I had beaten the animals I owned. Maybe worse, I have beaten my own animal nature, mistreated it . . . right then I resolved to do better. I was also thanking God that there are inns and people who keep them . . . why had I always complained about their prices? It's a blessing that someone provides these places where the sick can be cared for, or we can go and leave the world behind and care for our own bru·sed and battered souls. . . . When I retire, I thought, I'll keep an extra room just like this one as a retreat and try to help sick and tired people who need such a place. . . .

But that Samaritan . . . the one I had despised and feared . . . what a person he was. He knew my prejudice and so he did not try to make conversation. He asked for no thanks. He didn't even leave me his name, but he paid the innkeeper enough money to take care of me until I recovered. And if that wasn't enough, he said, he would make up the difference when he came this way again. . . . There were no strings attached . . . this man taught me more than all the instruction and angry insistence I've known most of my life.

How superficially I've regarded myself and other people . . . I've looked only at the outside, seeing with bigoted and prejudiced eyes. That Samaritan has made me look deeper . . . he was capable of kindness, this man that I had thought was the scum of the earth, with nothing good about him. He gave me kindness knowing that I might even resent having my life saved by a Samaritan. That is caring . . . thank heaven I got the message. I wish I could get it across to the fellows at the tavern. I guess it takes a real smashing from life to change our attitudes . . . I'm glad I don't have to judge people by appearances any more. And the same goes with myself. . . . Some of the things I used to despise the most in myself keep offering me the hope of healing now that I begin to accept them. . . .

But when I despise some person or some part of myself, I rob myself of the healing that person or that part is trying to bring. I have seen that even the darkest and worst part of me can go to work patching my hurts and putting me together. . . . That foreigner taught me the most that I know about wholeness . . . that I had better face what I am and not judge parts of me and try to eliminate them. . . . I have asked and tried to find him, but I've never been able to track him down. I would like to thank him for teaching me to treat myself and others the way he treated me. Often, these days, I stop to give someone a cup of cold water, or bind up a wound, or pick up a frightened child . . . and I feel like I am living more and more fully. All this I learned from a despised Samaritan who saved my life.

VIII

REFLECTIONS ON THE RAISING OF A MAN FROM DEATH

. . . And so Lazarus rose from the dead. So what? It showed that Jesus had unique power. He could heal the sick and raise the dead. I think that this happened, and that this was undoubtedly the event which turned the religious leaders against him once and for all. A thing like that could not be kept quiet and it gave Jesus a following which they couldn't tolerate. But does this event really speak to us today?

Jesus gave His message by actions as well as in teachings and parables. And one of the best ways to learn from these events is to let imagination play upon them as if we were listening to Jesus telling a story. Such an event or action of Jesus is myth as well as history. The things that He did express our relation to God and the nature of heaven which broke into the world with Him. They can often tell us as much about His significance to us as the things He expressed in words.

The story of Lazarus begins when Mary and Martha sent for Jesus because they knew that their brother was probably dying. They knew that He got the message, but He did not come right away. When Jesus finally came, He found the sisters grieving. Their brother had died. They did not try to pretend that everything was all right and that it was the will of God. They said reproachfully: "Lord, if you had come our brother would not have died." And Jesus felt their sorrow and His own loss of a friend, and He also wept.

Religion so often fails right here. We won't come out and say it . . . "Lord, we asked for something and you failed us." This kind of honesty is absolutely necessary if we are to find the power of Jesus. When we are phony there is not much that God or the Holy Spirit can do for us. When we are afraid or resentful or lost and bitter, we cannot get much help until we admit that this is the way we feel.

So often when we ask God to take over—in whatever kind of situation— He seems to tarry. He waits, needlessly, it seems, until what is sick in us has died . . . our hope, our courage, our capacity to love may be sick unto death. And when it dies we are bitter and angry, and we need to admit that we are bitter and angry, and that it looks to us as if the world doesn't care.

Then the only thing left for us to do is just to weep. . . . If you have ever lost someone you really loved, you know what grief is. The current idea that we should not give way to emotion, but that we should be heroic and not burden God or the world with our grief, is both bad psychology and bad religion. I am so glad for that shortest verse in the Bible . . "Jesus wept." It sanctifies human sorrow and agony. Jesus knew that He would raise Lazarus from death, but in that moment of pain and hurt and loss His own humanity joined the two sisters whom He loved, and He wept. . . .

The emotion of sorrow is never outgrown. We may know that the dead whom we love are not totally lost, but they are lost to our present ordinary conversation and touch, and it is right to weep. There is nothing worse psychologically than to bury the pains deep and let them lie unnoticed in hidden recesses of heart and mind so that they fester and poison the whole of us. Weeping is even physically therapeutic since tears carry a bacteria-destroying enzyme. How different Jesus's way is from the passionless way of some religions that tell us to get off the world, to become totally detached and merge with the cosmic mind so that nothing will ruffle us.

And when it is something within us which has died, it often seems that we are lost and can never, never measure up. We are dead. We have reason to be bitter, and the only thing to do is to weep. I wonder if it is possible to have an inner resurrection without such an honest confrontation and tears. Is this not the meaning of real contrition? Is it not what the Eastern Fathers meant when they spoke of healing weeping?

When Jesus asked the sisters where they had buried Lazarus, Mary told Him to come and see. Jesus and all the mourners then went with her out to the tomb. And Jesus told them to take away the stone. Immediately the crowd objected and Martha, the practical one, voiced their fear: "He has been buried four days and will be decomposed." The King James version of the Bible puts it more dramatically . . . "He has been buried four days and he stinketh." But Jesus insisted that this is the way to see the glory of God, and the stone was taken away.

This is another point at which much of our religion today fails us. It tries to avoid the dead parts of our lives. If we avoid them, we need not weep. If we avoid the stinking mess, we need not face our helplessness, and we need not come into real relationship with God by demanding to be helped by Him. If we avoid it, we can do without the courage it takes to face the stench of death. But then we also do without the transformation . . . no stench, no resurrection. . . .

With the tomb open, Jesus prayed a prayer of certainty and called out in a loud voice, "Lazarus, come forth!" And Lazarus came forth, still bound in his burial wrappings. Then Jesus spoke to the people again with His final command: "Unbind him."

To come alive we have to be sorry for the dead part of ourselves, sorry enough to say what needs to be done, and strong enough to face up to the evil which caused it to die. We have to act with firmness, to cry out with a loud voice. We have to be sorry enough, and to want life enough to pray for it with all of our being. Then, with faith and certainty, we can call out in a loud voice. And the dead within us comes forth, still in the cyst that was forming, and we are ready for the final action of setting it free. New life seldom comes forth without decisive action and a loud cry. Sometimes we remain dead simply because it is less effort and less painful than being alive. Yet the pain goes with the quickening, much like the pain of walking on a leg that has gone to sleep.

In their amazement at seeing Lazarus come out of the tomb, those people might have let the risen man smother in his grave clothes. But Jesus awakened them to action. The same thing is true when something has been raised within us. It must be set free or it can die again and negate the resurrection. We have to face the fact that it is dangerous to let the dead parts of us be raised. We probably let them die for good reason . . . usually for the reason that it is less dangerous just to be dead. . . .

Nothing is completely dead within us . . . so dead that it cannot be raised. And this story puts the question: What is the dead Lazarus within me? What part of me did I allow to die so that I am living as only a partial human being, busy getting more and more set in my one-sided, half existence? This event, this parable, written in the fabric of history, tells what is necessary for the dead parts of me to come to life again.

After this meaning had unfolded before my imagination, I then prepared two sermons on the miracle of Lazarus and gave them on two consecutive Sundays. Shortly after they were preached, a young man with whom I had been working for some time without much success came to me with a dream. In it one of his brothers had died, and he stood by the casket and raised the dead youth back to life. With only a little prompting he realized that it was a part of himself that had died, and he soon found that it was his capacity to reach out to another person with love and caring. He then went at the job of making the dream a reality, of bringing that capacity within himself back to life, and he was successful. The Biblical story unfolded in its deep meaning, and the parallel dream brought the young man to himself and was a turning point in his life. He learned to love, and his whole life changed. He came alive. The image was verified. Jesus still raises people from the dead.

IX

A Story

Many, many years ago there was a princess who lived in the fabled Empire of China. She was the emperor's only daughter, and she was as beautiful as she was intelligent. She was the center of the great court of the noblest of emperors.

The time came for her to marry and, after consulting with her father, she decided not to select just one of the court or some man she happened to know. She wanted to meet the finest and most handsome and interesting man in the whole kingdom. She believed that a person's appearance showed what one truly was and that the depth of a person's inner being showed forth in that person's face. The leaders of the court were sent out into every corner of the kingdom to announce that the handsomest young men were to appear at court on the appointed day. The best of those who came would then be taken before the princess herself in the royal palace.

In one far off province of the empire there lived a very crafty man. He was anything but good looking. Indeed one could tell from the hardness of his face that he was cruel and harsh. This man was a thief and a murderer, but he hit upon a plan. He went to the best mask-maker in China and ordered the most lifelike and handsome mask this craftsman could imagine. The thief paid well for his mask with the money he had gotten by violence.

In those days mask-making was one of the highest of the arts. Even so, when the thief saw the mask he had ordered, he was amazed, even startled. He looked in a mirror and gasped in astonishment. Instead of the cruel and hard look of the murderer, he saw before him a man of refinement and gentleness, a man of power and dignity, of strength and honesty, of kindness and generosity. He could hardly believe his eyes.

When he came to the court, there was no question about his passing the first test, and he was sent on with others to the royal palace itself. There he mixed with the greatest and finest people of the kingdom. And there the princess saw him. She was struck by his appearance at first sight. She was not easily swayed, but as she compared the masked thief with all the others, there was no comparison. The day came for the final selection, and he was the one she chose.

The princess was far too wise to order anyone to be her husband, and so, after the other guests had left, she asked this handsomest of all men to come into her private chambers, and there they talked. She asked him if he would marry her. Suddenly he saw the impossible alternatives. If he said no, he would certainly be discovered and brought to justice. And if he married her, she would soon learn the truth and have him executed. He regretted the day when he had started out on such a foolhardy venture. He was silent for a while. But then he hit on a plan that might work. He told the princess that he had never dreamed of being selected, and that he needed time to consider the obligations that were involved. He said that on this day, one year from then, he would return and give his answer.

The princess was most understanding. This seemed a wise decision, and so they parted. The thief now found his life quite altered. He could no longer disappear. He was now known as the most handsome man in the kingdom, and he had to act out the role that he had assumed. He had to guard every word so that it would not betray him. He had to learn to act with charm and grace and courage. He learned kindness and generosity, those qualities that were so manifest in his face. He began to show understanding and mercy, often consoling the sad and comforting the unhappy.

And all the time he was acutely conscious that he was quite different from his mask. Never for a moment could he forget what he truly was. You can imagine the agony he felt as a masked fraud. How careful he had to be. How much effort and energy he put into his acting. All the time his heart was on fire, hidden within. When people appreciated his actions or spoke well of him, he shuddered inside because he knew what he really was. He was horrified at how easily people could be deceived by one's actions. But the worst horror was the realization that the time was approaching for him to return to the princess.

The day came for the meeting. He finally decided to tell her the whole truth and take the consequences, whatever he might have to endure. Probably he would be beheaded for his treachery. They met once more in the great hall of the palace, and as they approached each other, the thief fell to the floor at the feet of the princess and sobbed out loud that he had deceived her. "I am only a thief and a scoundrel," he cried, "and I had this mask made so that I might get a chance to come inside and see the royal palace and meet the princess who is renowned above all other women. I am truly sorry, for I have delayed your plans for a whole year."

At first the princess was very angry. But then she decided that at least she should learn from the experience. She was still intrigued by the mask and wondered what the man was like underneath it. So she finally reached her hand out to raise him to his feet and said, "Yes, I have been deceived, but give me one pleasure and I will let you go free. Take off your mask and let me see what you really look like, and then you can go." In fear and trembling the thief removed his mask.

It was then that the princess cried out in real anger, "Why have you deceived me? Why did you have a mask made just like your real face?" The masquerader shook his head in confusion. The princess then handed him a mirror. Yes, it was true. His real face had become the same as the mask. For a whole year he had suffered and struggled to live up to the mask he wore, and finally he had become what he was trying to be.

Of course the story ended just as we would expect. The couple were married and the transformed thief became one of the greatest emperors that China ever had.

X

AFFIRMATION

This excellent introduction to a period of meditation is adapted from a form suggested by Roberto Assagioli[1] and used by the High Point Foundation in Pasadena, California.

Having stepped into the silence, comfortable, relaxed, breathing quietly, I remind myself . . .

My Body

I have a body, but I am not my body. My body may be in different conditions of health or sickness. It may be rested or tired. But it is not my real "I."

My body is my precious instrument of experience and action, but it is only an instrument. I treat it well; I seek to keep it in good health, but it is not my total self. I have a body, but I am not my body.

My Emotions

I have emotions, but I am not my emotions. They are countless, contradictory, changing, and yet I know that I always remain I, myself, in times of hope or despair, in joy or pain, in a state of irritation or calm. Since I can observe, understand and judge my emotions, and then increasingly direct and use them and bring them to a transforming center to be changed, it is evident that they are not myself. I have emotions, but I am not my emotions.

My Desires

I have desires, but I am not my desires. They, too, are changeable and contradictory, with alternations of attraction and repulsion. I have desires, but they are not myself. They give me energy and power, but they are not me.

My Intellect

I have an intellect, but I am not my intellect. It is more or less developed and active; it is undisciplined, but teachable; it is an organ of knowledge and judgment in regard to the outer world as well as to the inner world. But my intellect is not myself. I have an intellect, but I am not my intellect.

My Psyche

I am a psyche capable of growth, infinite growth. I have an ego and a will, but they cannot bring the growth. I need them in order to bring me to the transforming center, the divine Lover, the Christ, and He will give me growth. He will heal my body, quiet my emotions, empower the desires which lead to growth, enlighten my intellect and make me gradually into the likeness of Him upon whom I look. I am not this divine Lover, but I can be transformed into His likeness and image as I bring myself before Him. I can become an instrument of that kind of love toward myself and toward others. I am a psyche capable of infinite growth when I come and remain in His presence.

XI

TWO POETIC ENCOUNTERS WITH THE CHRIST

One of the most magnificent pieces of imaginative poetry ever written came from St. John of the Cross. His religious poetry is incomparable both as poetry and as religion. It expresses St. John's experience of fellowship with the Christ far more adequately than his longer prose manuals on the devotional life. Several of his devotional works are in fact expositions or commentaries on his poetry.

Another example of this quality of religious poetry is Francis Thompson's

The Hound of Heaven, which came out of a different life experience from that of St. John of the Cross. In one case the writer was a man striving for perfection and finding opposition and persecution from his religious community. The erotic tone in his work might be suspect in a lesser person. Francis Thompson, on the other hand, was a derelict, a drug addict, whose inner vision led him through the stench and agony within him until, through a powerful and religious friendship, he was saved and transformed.

There are hundreds of other examples I could have chosen. One can find them in any anthology of mystical or religious poetry, but these are two which happened to touch the core of my being. My suggestion is to read them as experiences, rather than with any idea of trying to write like either of these men. They were both consummate artists, and most of us have no such gift at all. On the other hand, we can know the experiences in our own lives. We can encounter as much as these poets, express it, and reap fully as great a harvest of our own if we do not sacrifice it by trying to imitate them. The point is to learn from them by identifying with their experience in imagination, letting it become one's own. The experience they describe is as real as that of a spectacular sunrise, for instance, seen through the eyes of a poet.

STANZAS OF THE SOUL[2]

1. On a dark night, Kindled in love with yearnings—oh, happy chance!—
   I went forth without being observed, My house being now at rest.
2. In darkness and secure, By the secret ladder, disguised—oh, happy chance!—
   In darkness and in concealment, My house being now at rest.
3. In the happy night, In secret, when none saw me,
   Nor I beheld aught, Without light or guide, save that which burned in my heart.
4. This light guided me More surely than the light of noonday,
   To the place where he (well I knew who!) was awaiting me—
      A place where none appeared.
5. Oh, night that guided me, Oh, night more lovely than the dawn,
   Oh, night that joined Beloved with lover, Lover transformed in the Beloved!
6. Upon my flowery breast, Kept wholly for himself alone,
   There he stayed sleeping, and I caressed him, And the fanning of the cedars made a breeze.
7. The breeze blew from the turret As I parted his locks;
   With his gentle hand he wounded my neck And caused all my senses to be suspended.
8. I remained, lost in oblivion; My face I reclined on the Beloved.
   All ceased and I abandoned myself, Leaving my cares forgotten among the lilies.

—St. John of the Cross

THE HOUND OF HEAVEN

I fled Him, down the nights and down the days;
I fled Him, down the arches of the years;
I fled Him, down the labyrinthine ways
   Of my own mind; and in the mist of tears
I hid from Him, and under running laughter.
      Up vistaed hopes I sped;
      And shot, precipitated,
Adown Titanic glooms of chasmèd fears,
  From those strong Feet that followed, followed after.
      But with unhurrying chase,
      And unperturbèd pace,
   Deliberate speed, majestic instancy,
      They beat—and a Voice beat
      More instant than the Feet—
'All things betray thee, who betrayest Me.'

     I pleaded, outlaw-wise,
By many a hearted casement, curtained red,
  Trellised with intertwining charities;
(For, though I knew His love Who followed,
      Yet was I sore adread
Lest, having Him, I must have naught beside).
But, if one little casement parted wide,
  The gust of His approach would clash it to.
  Fear wist not to evade, as Love wist to pursue.
Across the margent of the world I fled,
  And troubled the gold gateways of the stars,
  Smiting for shelter on their clangèd bars;
      Fretted to dulcet jars
And silvern chatter the pale ports o' the moon.
I said to Dawn: Be sudden—to Eve: Be soon;
  With thy young skiey blossoms heap me over
      From this tremendous Lover—
Float thy vague veil about me, lest He see!
  I tempted all His servitors, but to find
My own betrayal in their constancy,
In faith to Him their fickleness to me,
  Their traitorous trueness, and their loyal deceit.
To all swift things for swiftness did I sue;
  Clung to the whistling mane of every wind.

But whether they swept, smoothly fleet,
   The long savannahs of the blue;
      Or whether, Thunder-driven,
   They clanged His chariot 'thwart a heaven,
Plashy with flying lightnings round the spurn o' their feet:—
   Fear wist not to evade as Love wist to pursue.
      Still with unhurrying chase,
      And unperturbèd pace,
   Deliberate speed, majestic instancy,
      Came on the following Feet,
      And a Voice above their beat—
   'Naught shelters thee, who wilt not shelter Me.'

I sought no more that after which I strayed
      In face of man or maid;
But still within the little children's eyes
      Seems something, something that replies,
They at least are for me, surely for me!
I turned me to them very wistfully;
But just as their young eyes grew sudden fair
      With dawning answers there,
Their angel plucked them from me by the hair.
'Come then, ye other children, Nature's—share
With me' (said I) 'your delicate fellowship;
      Let me greet you lip to lip,
      Let me twine with you caresses,
         Wantoning
      With our Lady-Mother's vagrant tresses,
         Banqueting
      With her in her wind-walled palace,
      Underneath her azured daïs,
      Quaffing, as your taintless way is,
         From a chalice
Lucent-weeping out of the dayspring.'
      So it was done:
I in their delicate fellowship was one—
Drew the bolt of Nature's secrecies.
      I knew all the swift importings
      On the wilful face of skies;
      I knew how the clouds arise
      Spuméd of the wild sea-snortings;
         All that's born or dies

Rose and drooped with; made them shapers
Of mine own moods, or wailful or divine;
    With them joyed and was bereaven.
    I was heavy with the even,
    When she lit her glimmering tapers
    Round the day's dead sanctities.
    I laughed in the morning's eyes.
I triumphed and I saddened with all weather,
    Heaven and I wept together,
And its sweet tears were salt with mortal mine;
Against the red throb of its sunset-heart
    I laid my own to beat,
    And share commingling heat;
But not by that, by that, was eased my human smart.
In vain my tears were wet on Heaven's grey cheek.
For ah! we know not what each other says,
    These things and I; in sound *I* speak—
Their sound is but their stir, they speak by silences.
Nature, poor stepdame, cannot slake my drouth;
    Let her, if she would owe me,
Drop yon blue bosom-veil of sky, and show me
    The breasts o' her tenderness:
Never did any milk of hers once bless
      My thirsting mouth.
      Nigh and nigh draws the chase,
      With unperturbèd pace,
    Deliberate speed, majestic instancy;
      And past those noisèd Feet
      A Voice comes yet more fleet—
    'Lo! naught contents thee, who content'st
      not Me.'

Naked I wait Thy love's uplifted stroke!
My harness piece by piece Thou hast hewn from me,
    And smitten me to my knee;
    I am defenceless utterly.
    I slept, methinks, and woke,
And, slowly gazing, find me stripped in sleep.
In the rash lustihead of my young powers,
    I shook the pillaring hours
And pulled my life upon me; grimed with smears,
I stand amid the dust o' the moulded years—

My mangled youth lies dead beneath the heap.
My days have crackled and gone up in smoke,
Have puffed and burst as sun-starts on a stream.
  Yea, faileth now even dream
The dreamer, and the lute the lutanist;
Even the linked fantasies, in whose blossomy twist
I swung the earth a trinket at my wrist,
Are yielding; cords of all too weak account
For earth with heavy griefs so overplussed.
  Ah! is Thy love indeed
A weed, albeit an amaranthine weed,
Suffering no flowers except its own to mount?
  Ah! must—
  Designer infinite!—
Ah! must Thou char the wood ere Thou canst limn with it?
My freshness spent its wavering shower i' the dust;
And now my heart is as a broken fount,
Wherein tear-drippings stagnate, spilt down ever
  From the dank thoughts that shiver
Upon the sighful branches of my mind.
  Such is; what is to be?
The pulp so bitter, how shall taste the rind?
I dimly guess what Time in mists confounds;
Yet ever and anon a trumpet sounds
From the hid battlements of Eternity;
Those shaken mists a space unsettle, then
Round the half-glimpsèd turrets slowly wash again.
  But not ere him who summoneth
  I first have seen, enwound
With glooming robes purpureal, cypress-crowned;
His name I know, and what his trumpet saith.
Whether man's heart or life it be which yields
  Thee harvest, must Thy harvest-fields
  Be dunged with rotten death?

  Now of that long pursuit
  Comes on at hand the bruit;
That Voice is round me like a bursting sea:
  'And is thy earth so marred,
  Shattered in shard on shard?
Lo, all things fly thee, for thou fliest Me!
Strange, piteous, futile thing!

Wherefore should any set thee love apart?
Seeing none but I makes much of naught' (He said),
'And human love needs human meriting:
  How hast thou merited—
Of all man's clotted clay the dingiest clot?
  Alack, thou knowest not
How little worthy of any love thou art!
Whom wilt thou find to love ignoble thee,
  Save Me, save only Me?
All which I took from thee I did but take,
  Not for thy harms,
But just that thou might'st seek it in My arms.
  All which thy child's mistake
Fancies as lost, I have stored for thee at home:
  Rise, clasp My hand, and come!'
 Halts by me that footfall:
 Is my gloom, after all,
Shade of His hand, outstretched caressingly?
 'Ah, fondest, blindest, weakest,
 I am He Whom thou seekest!
Thou dravest love from thee, who dravest Me.'

FRANCIS THOMPSON

XII

TWO EUCHARISTIC MEDITATIONS

For several years I have used these two imaginative pieces of poetry as preparation for the experience of the Eucharist. They have touched me and many others as a setting for coming to this most central act of Christian worship.

THE EUCHARIST[4]

He was old,
  tired,
   and sweaty,
pushing his homemade cart
down the alley, stopping now and then
to poke around in somebody's garbage.

I wanted to tell him about EUCHARIST
But the look in his eyes,
    the despair on his face,
    the hopelessness of somebody else's life in his cart,
Told me to forget it.
So I smiled, said "Hi"—and gave him EUCHARIST.

She was cute,
    nice build, a little too much paint,
wobbly on her feet as she slid from her barstool, and on the make.
"No, thanks, not tonight,"—and I gave her EUCHARIST.

She lived alone,
    her husband dead,
        her family gone,
And she talked at you, not to you,
    words, endless words, spewed out,
So I listened—and gave her EUCHARIST.

Downtown is nice,
    Lights change from red to green, and back again,
Flashing blues, pinks and oranges.
    I gulped them in,
Said, "Thank you, Father,"—and made them EUCHARIST.

I laughed at myself,
    and told myself,
"You, with all your sin,
    and all your selfishness,
I forgive you,
    I accept you,
        I love you."
It's nice, and so necessary to give yourself EUCHARIST.

My Father, when will we learn—You cannot talk EUCHARIST—you cannot
    philosophize about it. YOU DO IT.
You don't dogmatize EUCHARIST.
Sometimes you laugh it, sometimes you cry it, often you sing it.
Sometimes it's wild peace, then crying hurt, often humiliating, never deserved.

You see Eucharist in another's eyes, give it in another's hand held tight,
    squeeze it in an embrace.

You pause EUCHARIST in the middle of a busy day, speak it in another's ear,
     listen to it from a person who wants to talk.

For EUCHARIST is as simple as being on time
and as profound as sympathy.
I give you my supper,
     I give you my sustenance,
          I give you my life,
               I give you me,
I give you EUCHARIST.

R. Voight

THE BALLAD OF JUDAS ISCARIOT[5]

This old ballad tells the story of when Judas committed suicide and his soul wandered through the universe bearing his body and seeking a place for it to rest. Hell would not take it in; the earth would not receive it; the sun refused to shine on it. Judas could find no resting place in all creation.

At last, in a nameless region of darkness and ice and snow the soul of Judas saw a lighted hall and the shadows of people moving about within. He laid his body in the snow and ran back and forth outside the windows. Although Judas did not know it, inside Jesus sat at a table with His guests, ready to receive the fleeing soul and relieve Judas of the burden of that body lying in the snow.

'Twas the Bridegroom sat at the table-head,
     And the lights burned bright and clear—
"Oh, who is that?" the Bridegroom said,
     "Whose weary feet I hear?"

'Twas one looked from the lighted hall,
     And answered soft and slow,
"It is a wolf runs up and down
     With a black track in the snow."

The Bridegroom in his robe of white
     Sat at the table-head—
"Oh, who is that who moans without?"
     The blessed Bridegroom said.

'Twas one looked from the lighted hall,
    And answered fierce and low,
"'Tis the soul of Judas Iscariot
    Gliding to and fro."

'Twas the soul of Judas Iscariot
    Did hush itself and stand,
And saw the Bridegroom at the door
    With a light in his hand.

        ....

'Twas the Bridegroom stood at the open door,
    And beckoned, smiling sweet;
'Twas the soul of Judas Iscariot
    Stole in, and fell at his feet.

"The Holy Supper is spread within,
    And the many candles shine,
And I have waited long for thee
    Before I poured the wine!"

Robert Buchanan

XIII

A True Story

Jesus told the story of the prodigal son . . . or perhaps it should be called the story of the father prodigal with love. It is a great story. It is the story of an impudent son . . . who went on to become profligate, immoral, and finally lost . . . being welcomed home again. It tells of his being given not only his father's affection, his warm and heartfelt forgiveness and embrace, but the best robe and even a ruby ring. What a symbol of profligate love that ring is, what a symbol of the senseless graciousness of God. Of all useless things, that ring. . . .

And then the feast, the banquet, the celebration with music and dancing. . . . At a conference in Germany several years ago one group was studying symbols and symbolism, and they acted out the story of the prodigal for the rest of us. It was in pantomime with a small orchestra giving an appropriate musical background. At the point where all were gathered together to portray the feast, tables were brought out and the whole group shared in a Eucharist. We also shared in recognizing how the father's embrace in that story symbolizes the healing touch of Jesus, and how the celebration foreshadows and suggests the Eucharist. . . .

This is a wonderful story. But there is an even more wonderful one, and that is one that tells the central story of Christianity, the story of Easter, the story of the actual love of God for us, then and now.

The story that Jesus lived was better than the one that He told. His life had to be lived to be believed. Few people would have taken it seriously otherwise. In the real story the prodigal does not come to himself until he knows that life and death story within. That prodigal is you, me and all of humankind. Remember that much of the world to which Jesus came was actually living like a scene from a pornographic movie.

In this other story, the prodigal leaves home in arrogance. He goes to a city of foreigners, built for pleasure, where the baths are places of immorality. There he spends every penny he has for wine, women and song. Finally the young man wakes up in prison, charged with killing a man in a drunken brawl. To his horror he finds that he is condemned to die. The time approaches for his execution. There is nothing he can do. He is rotting away in prison because of his own willfulness and unconsciousness.

The prodigal's father goes out each day to peer into the distance, hoping for some sign of his lost son. But there is none, and the father decides to go and search for him. When he reaches the city, he finds a disgusting trail of evidence which leads him to the prison where his son is held. The day of beheading is only a few days off. He goes to see his son, but the young man is too ashamed to face his father, too guilty even to talk with him. He pushes his father away in shame and guilt.

The father goes to the authorities. He asks if there is anything that he can do to save his son. There is only one hope. There is an ancient law in that land that a criminal may be freed and forgiven if someone else will offer his life in the place of the criminal. There is no other way. And who would offer to give up life for a person like this useless son? When he can find no other way, the father offers his own life. He turns himself over to the authorities in place of the son. On the appointed day he is taken to the executioner and slain, and the wayward son is free.

Bewildered and frightened, the son is released. He is given the money and belongings of his father, for it is an honest country . . . and then it breaks in upon the son, too late, the love his father had for him. Too late. . . . He is weeping and broken-hearted as he starts back from that far country toward home. Is there anything worse than to be loved this much and not to realize it? Why hadn't he met his father halfway and tried to show that *he* cared?

On the way home the son meets a stranger, a ragged beggar. Ordinarily he would have avoided someone as low as this, but now it is different. He knows that no one could be worse than he. He even shares his bread with the beggar, and they walk along the road together. The beggar listens as he tells his tale of failure and debauchery and sin.

Finally they come to the doorway of the father's house. The beggar turns and holds out his arms to the young man. He is revealed to the son. The stranger is his father risen from the dead. In that country which had claimed the father's life, an even older law has allowed it to be restored. According to the deep magic law from beyond the dawn of time, those who give of themselves expecting nothing in return cannot truly die. And so the father has risen from the dead.

Together they rejoice that each has been given another chance to show how much he cares. And they have a feast, a double feast, to give thanks for the son released and for the father risen from the dead. . . .

This is a representation of the central story of Christianity. Love is victorious and man is released. Death is overcome. This is what Christianity is all about—victorious, reconciling, transforming love. This is the love that Jesus of Nazareth brings. This is a story much like the story of His death and resurrection.

XIV

Two Meditations for a Hurt and Angry Friend

A.

Spew forth, oh noble Aetna, spew . . .
Break forth, oh molten belly of the hill,
Oh mountain, hot within and breaking forth.
Let all the primal rage and heat belch forth . . .
Let the fire burn and rip the mountain side
And vomit out the cinders and the melted rock,
The mud and muck, the steam, the red hot rock. . . .
Let go and turn the heavens black, the earth red and sorry
For her conception and her part in letting all the fire be.

Why now the heat? Why now the molten fury?
Why the burning in my belly, the belly of the earth . . .
The burning of the star and galaxies innumerable?
    Why is life burning, and burning life, and coolness death?
It is not fair or right or good or hope fulfilling.
And so we live upon a thin crust between the death
Of too much heat and too much cold,
Between conflagration and fury and freezing death. . . .

One thin crust which quavers, shakes between two deaths
Of heat and cold. And yet at the right moment, for a span of time
There conditions do exist and there Eros reigns
Between the deaths, between the furnace and the ice. . . .
　　And so spew forth to remind me where I am.

Perhaps the crust is the final meaning, and the time
Will come when inner meaning will grow and the crust
Will thicken, grow more solid, more secure . . .
Perhaps an inner crust toward which all things move,
Where we can taste the fire and chill and know some deeper reality
Than all three. . . . Perhaps, perhaps. . . .

B.

Comrade on the impossible way . . .
There is no hope, and yet there is hope. . . . I am not me, but another and
yet I am me also! You know love through me not because I am love,
but an instrument of an incredible love . . .
a love like Aslan . . . a strange self-giving thing . . .
The only power which turns back the demons,
restores the dismembered bodies . . .
I died this week, and so I am much more alive.
I saw my body lying there dead, and just because of this I am alive again . . .
and this aliveness I send on you, this gift of death, this resurrection,
renewal, hope, peace and rest. It strikes you in the liver and renews it . . .
It gives you yet another heart . . . new veins and sinews.
The valley of dry bones becomes an oasis of living men . . .
Life is more real than death . . .
something than nothing.
You have been dismembered and you shall come back into wholeness with
　　power . . .
a promise.
It has already begun.
It is real and coming.
Even trying you can't avoid the life and hope which comes to you. It is
as sure as the wind blowing from the ocean at Coronado . . . as sure as
heat in Phoenix in July . . .
You are destined to recovery and transformation. It is your lot.
You can't stay dead. The greater lover has ordained it.
He is there. . . . I am his harbinger, the first robin of spring, the first
　　tender, reddish shoot . . .

The long cold winter, the deadness of Persephone is coming to a close.

Christ has risen, Apollo is transformed.
Death is eaten up in victory . . .
and we can see the death of death in death.
Dracula is doomed. What is worse he'll be redeemed and forgiven . .
How unfair, unfair, unfair, unfair . . .
The last laborer receives as much as the first . . .
Damned unfair, but the way is beyond unfairness . . .

all things will be brought together in harmony,
within the love which moves the sun and all the other stars. . . .

It is ordained. It will be so.
Look up and watch it come. .   .

XV

Five Encounters in Silence

The Way

Alone, the climb was hard, my flesh was bruised,
Long hours, steep walls, sharp rocks, and now
The summit here at last, barren and cold,
The cold, cold wind against my face and hands, and eyes
Too tired to cry. Alone, alone with rock
And wind and heart quite full of emptiness—

I look around, see the mountain ranges
Which stretch in broken majesty forever.
The thunder rolls, the lightning strikes. The earth
In sympathy now heaves and quakes. The rain
Beats down. The mountain ranges disappear.

Oh Lord, a cave, a still small voice . . .
Where are you now? Where? Where? I am alone
And waiting here upon this crag, within.
The storm which nearly always rages. Alone
I wait and wait and wait. A message, Lord,
For me? Some word, some voice, some touch?
A little sign? It comes. A still small voice,

"You're not all bad. Keep on, keep on. The way
Ahead will soon become quite clear. Be kind
And do your best. One foot before the next.
See yonder crag the lightning strikes. That is
The way. Keep on. Be kind and love. Doors will
Open and the way will soon emerge. On. On."

My eyes are wet with rain and tears. I feel
A presence there, within and very close and warm.
"Thank you, my Lord, I'll try. I'll try. Keep close.
I don't do so well alone or have much courage,
Not very wise or bright or good. Stay close. Stay close."
I hear again. "Stop, stop and listen for the dawn,
The dayspring from on high. I'm here. I'm here."
Mid lightning strokes I see a cave, a narrow ledge
Of rock where I can lie. 'Tis time to rest
And sleep. Tomorrow is another day.
I'll do my best, but now I sleep refreshed,
And grateful for the words and place to rest.
        I rested quiet, grateful for the sight,
The vision of the way I had forgot. The onward struggling,
The warfare spiritual which does not end . . .
I see the path now, stretching into the bend
Of sight, the horizon lost in mist and grey,
And yet ahead another pinnacle to climb,
Another goal, another height, one battle more,
And then yet another, then on and on.
There is no end—So forward on the way . . .
It is the way, forever on and on.

Beside, within, He stands, ready down to stoop,
As battling on with courage I press on.
There is a way, hard, steep and real for me,
For all, and He there stands waiting to give
New hope and strength. There is a way. Keep clear
My heart's eyesight. On, on. Courage and love.
With mine and His together joined by Him I'll keep
Upon that way, my way, the way. I'll sleep
And tomorrow I'll venture forth again.
And morning's light will set me free again.
Life is the way, the way is life. On, on.
Eternally, now and forever on . . . on the way.

The path of heart is there,
The only one that brings us through.
I'll go on't, where'er it leads.

It is divine and human both, this track.
I see. I'll try. Let me forget not what
I dimly see, this vision of the way. . . .
Help me often to stop and listen
To the voice, and feel the presence,
And step out again upon the way.

Dying Daily

I die, but this time more easily.
So must I each day, each day.
It is the way, the way, the way.

> And then I sit upon a rock
> And gaze upon the deep.
> It was real, not mere fantasy.
> I think I know.
> The way is hard.
> The rock is real.
> A crystal lies
> Within my heart,
> Of sapphire blue.
> Death destroys not.
>   It gives the stone.
>   One does not die.

An open palm, not grasping anything.
Two warm arms embrace.
The king is there, the triune king.
He lives, and so do I.
Death and dying have pushed death away.
Willed dying, giving up is dawn.

> The rock, the vast deep, the soft wind,
> And dawn, the presence . . .
> I'll rest a while,
> And then go on. . . . . .

The Cloud

Sometimes when we try to be still it seems as if we are caught in a gray cloud, a fog . . . and we perceive and feel nothing . . . caught up in grayness. Sometimes it seems to be real blackness so that we are afraid to be still . . . afraid to enter into our little soul room, for there in the intensity of our inner being we are so alone . . . so alone . . . and yet, if we do not go into that aloneness nothing can precipitate the cloud and give us the clarity to see Thee. . . .

Our own willingness to face our inner cloud of loneliness is like cloud-seeding . . . like dropping little bits of chemical into the clouds so that drops of moisture begin to form . . . and then a rain comes, and perhaps the whole cloud system dissolves into rain showers so that the sun can begin to shine through. . . .

So it is with us . . . when we turn into our own loneliness and darkness. . . . Strange that sometimes it is only the pain of our being alone that can precipitate the fog around us and cause it to drop . . . how strange it is that running from the darkness only makes it darker, whereas entering into it causes it to dissolve, and then we can see . . . see that there in the corner of the room one has been standing all the time . . . the separation was only in us, our own cloud which we had not precipitated and let clear, because we would not deal with it. . . .

And then there is a ray of light . . . and the person standing quietly there at the edge of the room, waiting for us to speak . . . "Lord, have you been there all the time, and I didn't know?" "Yes, I have been here waiting for you to pass through yourself and find that I was here. I have been here all the time, but I force myself on no one."

Lord, it is almost as though we cannot find Thee as long as we have any other place outside to seek for Thee . . . as long as we seek for satisfactions in the outer world, we do not see Thee standing there . . . as long as we seek to be comforted by the outer world, filled by the outer world . . . person or thing . . . then we do not come into our aloneness and find Thee waiting there . . . Lord, I would not have thought of Thee as shy, Thou who art the maker of the universe.

And He says, "I must be shy with you human beings, or I would overpower you. That is why I came as a baby in a forgotten corner of the Roman Empire. If I were to reach out for you, I could not be sure that you sought me of yourself, that you would seek me. Then nothing would be truly real. Or if you sought me because I could bring you great power, or make bread from stones, or govern the world, you would not find me. Probably no one whose soul is filled ever wants me. But those who look deep within themselves and find the darkness and emptiness and loneliness, they are the ones who really need me and find me.

"Blessed are you . . . because it is you for whom I have been waiting."

A Mountaintop

The howling wind abated, and it was still.
The sky was clear, the dark and angry clouds
Vanished, and the sun was there in crimson glory—
or was it gold—more gold than red. As if the world
Had been bathed in golden pollen, rich Turner gold.

The storm had ceased, at least for now, peace, peace.
The gnarled and twisted trunk so long had stood against
Each storm, each fury, wind, torrent, falling stone,
Its tenuous deep-rooted grip so long been threatened
That peace was hard to understand . . . and even more
The stranger who wandered by, or even, it seems,
Had seen the strangeness of the pine
At timberline and, drawn by the inner struggle
Which held it there at crag's edge fierce and calm,
Made the tortuous ascent from rock to rock, around
Impossible walls of stone, up crevices until
He stood there and touched the ancient bark,
So twisted and so gnarled, caressed the roots,
Clinging deeply to the rock and penetrating far
Into the earth's heart, and there deriving nourishment.
His eye ran along the broken plumage of branch
And limb . . . some which gave life, and others eloquent
Of storms past and foreboding others yet to come.

As he stood there, the storm broke, the sky cleared,
The wind died, the calm came, the peace, and then
The gold, the golden bath suffusing everything
With life, meaning, deep understanding,
Deep like the earth. Release from storm and presentiments

Of a better day were in that gold, and more.

The hunchback was no hunchback, but like a man
Who won against insuperable odds, who had some grace
To give. Grace revealed grace. The storm
Would come again, but the memory of the golden calm
Would never fade, that moment when the sun broke forth
And everything was turned to gold . . . rock, snow-capped peak,
Root, branch, the traveler who struggled up to see
And know the tree which clung at timberline.
Even the tree was gold, dead branch, contorted root,
Trunk and all. The age of gold was not an idle fable.
It is real and will come again.

Sandcastles

I'm tired, but relatively happy . . .
It's fearful to see the world as good,
Or even partially so, for then the limb
May crash from out the oaks, crash
And break our feeble hopes and smash
Our fragile bodies, and leave us weeping
At the ocean's shore as the tide comes in
And washes away our castles built with so much effort
        and love and fear. . . .

And yet, is it not better to look for good,
For light, for green, for God who breaks
Through in whirlwind or in fire,
Than just to mope and fear as men
Who bury their one talent and growl
That life is a hard and bitter lord.

And so in spite of tide and limb half broke,
In spite of earthquake, flood and storm,
I'll give the best I can in love.
In hope, in reaching out, to those who will
Receive me. While it is light, I'll play,
And when comes the dark, or falls the branch,
I'll gird my loins and strive to
The infinite with all the hope that I can muster.

And I'll cry to my friends
To bear my woe as I have tried
To bear theirs. Between us we shall see
The dawn, another castle in the beach,
Another spring, and in the end,
My friend, an eternal day begins,
Where love is king and sovereign, now
And forever—always—and yet now.

XVI

Three Violent Meditations

These meditations are not for the person who cannot and should not look at the pain and agony found within the depths of the human soul. Some of us may need to meditate on gentleness in order to be healed, and if this is so we should not worry about the encounters in these pages. But these were real meditations done by one in agony, and they brought that person through despair to hope again.

I have found, when all masks are off, that this agony is in most human souls. We can avoid it by staying behind our masks, and so we try not to take them off. Then we usually make others carry the agony for us. And if there is a way of victory, we do not find out about it.

In each case the meditation starts with a mood, a threatening and destructive mood. The mood is faced, stepped into and allowed to transform itself into images, and also into voices that speak from within. At the darkest and deepest point a change takes place, as the Christ figure comes into the imagination and restores and renews. And each time a transformation of the images actually occurred, and the mood began to lift. This is the way of allowing Christ to do His atoning work by letting him into the deep and dark places within. This is theology in action.

The Desert

A feeling of separation and dryness is upon me. There is no destructive voice attacking. I only feel separate and alone, with no one who can take the whole of me. From the outside things go quite well. I function well enough. But inside all is dried out, dessicated. There seems to be no place to go, no meaning, no future, no horizon. I simply grind out what is required, sleep, get up and do it all over again. Life has lost its zest and sparkle . . . nothing to enjoy and nothing to look forward to. There is no particular fear; death does not seem to be on my tracks. Life is simply dull and dry.

I realize that I have had this gnawing feeling at the back of my heart for a long time. As I stop and look inward, I can feel it become more and more oppressive. I have a momentary desire to get back to busy-ness, to activity, and avoid the confrontation. But I know that this is no escape. I must deal with the mood, with what I feel, or it will keep at my heels. If I try to escape it, I may even flee so hard that I fall and break a bone or make myself sick. And then I will have both the mood of uselessness and dryness and the physical pain as well to deal with. It is better to deal with it now. . . .

I sit down at the typewriter and start writing what I feel, stepping into the depth of the mood . . . into its very heart so that the dryness swirls about me like a dry desert wind, burning my skin with the heat and sand. . . .

It is then that the image comes. I almost seem to open my eyes to find out what direction the wind is coming from . . . and I am sitting on a mound in a great deserted valley like the Arizona or Mojave deserts. I look around. It is perhaps fifty miles long, with jagged, tiger-tooth mountains on either side. In the distance I can see that each end is walled in. Here and there a little whirlwind plays with the dry sand. One of them has swept around me.

There is only one sign of habitation in the whole desolate expanse, and that is where I am sitting . . . beside a desert shack that has fallen in. It has been abandoned for a long time. . . . The windows are empty sockets. They look out on the debris of some former owner. A piece of tar paper flaps in the wind. A door, still hanging to its frame, whines as it swings back and forth . . . no other habitation in all that valley . . . just sagebrush and sand and rock. . . . I wonder if it goes on forever. Is there any other place? Is this all there is?

I have a view, because the mound is higher than most of the valley. Then I look down and find that I am sitting on the dumpheap . . . the accumulated residue of years of desert living, now abandoned. All the useless things have been thrown onto this spot . . . the broken china, the tin cans, the donkey dung, some warped two-by-fours, the crumpled door of a car, pieces of corrugated metal roofing. . . . The desert winds have poured sand around them and built a little mountain. . . . And there I sit like Job, examining the ashes and decay of former lives.

And the sun . . . always streaming down, now high overhead, burning, always bright, glaring day after day, drying out the skin, deadening the eyes, endlessly burning, relentless and incessant. . . . And when it drops, the night and cold come quickly. The shadows move and coyotes howl, and then I shudder and long for the sun, for day to come. . . .

This is what life seems like, what it feels like . . . absurd, burning, dry, meaningless and useless, alone, separate. I feel the full brunt of the vacancy, the vacuum, the searing vacuum, the dry and burning nothingness. And where does one look for help and where is there to go?

Is life meant to be like this, I wonder? There is a story that we were made for glory, for transformation, for God and joy. I laugh to myself. There is a story that once God came as a man to rescue humankind from their desert and give them life, to bring a promised land, a kingdom flowing with milk and honey, into their reach. . . . What harm to think about it? I have faced all that there is to face here. It may even be cowardice not to look for more than just this all-encompassing emptiness. . . . Could there be one who would seek me out and bring me back to myself and into touch with other human beings? I decide that it will not hurt to explore this possibility. . . .

I say: Lord, come to me; if you are real, come to me in my desolate isolation and make me human once again. . . . Of course, nothing happens. I expect a thunder clap, some lightning, and out of the explosion some triumphant figure with a chariot of fire to carry me away. But nothing. . . . All a fraud, I think. . . . No, let's hope. I keep scanning the valley for a sign. . . .

And then on the far side of the valley, miles away, I make out a moving spot, tinier than the tiniest leaf from where I sit. But before long I can see that it is moving as if alive. Are my eyes deceiving me? I watch as the sun, past its height, begins to drop into the West. The figure keeps moving, comes closer. Could it be coming my way, coming from the East? I keep staring dumbly as the figure comes still nearer. It really is a person, tall, a strong man in His very prime, erect, powerful, and yet He walks with grace. His clothes are very plain, but sturdy. And when He comes close enough so that I can see His face, I see one that makes me truly hope for the first time in years . . . kind, warm, compassionate, with a smile of humor as if this were some divine joke, this trip of His.

He comes right up to my dump heap. I have not moved or said a word. Nor has He spoken. He reaches out a hand to lift me down. Automatically I stretch out mine toward Him in return. As I step down He embraces me with a great hug . . . as if He were my mother, father, brother and sister, friend, beloved, all rolled into one, and I a small pouting child . . . as if I had tried to run away from home and had been found tired and frightened on the edge of a gloomy forest with night coming on. . . . He embraces me with all of my grime and sand and dried sweat and caked hair, just as I am. . . .

Then I lay my head upon His shoulder and murmur: "Thank you." After a moment I stand straight and ask Him: "Lord, why did you wait so long in coming?" And He replies: "Because you didn't ask. You thought you could do it by yourself. It is difficult to give you something when you don't know you want it. As long as people are satisfied with dryness or deserts or have no hope, they are so difficult to touch." I say: "Give me everything you have to give." "Come with me," He says.

Behind the dump heap where I had sat, a mass of granite rises from the earth, thrust up in some primeval age. He leads me there. He strikes the rock, and water gushes out. It falls into a basin below the rock. When the pool is filled, the water makes a stream down past the desert shack. He bids me bathe in the pool, and while I lie in the cool water, He takes my clothes and washes them and lays them on a rock to dry. Along the little stream vines spring up and grow, and soon they cover the broken shell of a cabin.

I come out of the water clean and so refreshed. I feel as if my skin was drinking in the moisture as the caked sand and mud melted. I put my clothes on again . . . I had forgotten that my coat had once been brightly colored. I dance with joy as I see myself reflected in the pool . . . clean, even dapper. He has a meal for me. There is milk and bread and honey, fish and berries. I look at Him and ask why He has come and why He is so kind. He tells me that it is because He loves us human beings and He wishes to fill them whenever their hands are opened to receive.

That night I sleep in peace. No more haunting dreams. And in the morning we leave the pool of water and the vine-covered house. We cross one ridge, and still there is desert . . . another and we see some junipers, and then piñon pine, and then the forest, green and rich. The land is rugged, but at last we come to the coast where people live. And there I have fellowship with others who have opened their hands to Him, and are beginning to open them to one another. And there I settle down to live and become stronger, and start to learn. . . . Someday I shall set out as He does. But for now it is the time to stay put and learn and grow. . . .

The Destroyer

Here I am Lord, broken and with the world tumbling down about me. Everything seems lost and broken. I don't know where to turn. I am in the midst of a great battlefield. . . . It stretches all around me. I am torn and bleeding, cut to pieces, fragmented. All around me is desolation and pain, ugliness and pain. Men are screaming and jabbing bayonets at each other . . . no meaning, no hope. . . . How can anything help us?

Dark Voice: So at last you listen. You stupid fool. You are the worst of fools . . . the most horrible of wretches. You have trusted in love, and it let you down. I have you here. You are in pain, and rightly so. You are lost. There is nothing but pain and guilt and tension and horror for you . . . I have come to finish you off and tear you apart. You have been tempted with hope, and there is none . . . only me here to laugh at you and drive you mad and finally destroy you . . . I will let you howl at the edge of eternity, in the black horror where traitors are placed and left to hurt forever, forever. If there is any meaning, it would have nothing to do with you . . . oh vomit of the earth, excrement, failure. No one loves you. No one could love you. There is nothing anywhere around but the awful battlefield, with men's guts streaming out of them, and you among them. You thought you had been raised to a place of consideration and honor . . . but it was just to let you be torn down and mocked and ridiculed. . . .

I can hear the creature, the man-woman monster of the dark depth laughing and laughing . . . I can feel chills of numinous horror, but I cannot see IT yet. . . .

I have been slashed at until almost dead, and then there on the battlefield I am seized by powerful arms. I'm drawn and quartered, but I cannot die. The evil one is all around me and yet I cannot see IT. . . .

The fragments of me are being carried to hell itself. The pit, the stench and smoke, and cries of other victims . . . there IT is clawing and tearing at me and every part of me feeling IT and its wrath. IT is around me and in me, tearing and destroying. I long only to die, to cease to exist, and I cannot. Then the voice cries out within me and around me:

Dark Voice: Oh fraud, deceiver and fraud, hopeless, miserable fool . . .

From the black cloud I see Attila the Hun emerge . . . There is Frankenstein's monster, the Baba Yaga, the Dracula . . . all bent on destroying forever and forever . . .

Dark Voice: And there is no one to turn to . . .

Me: Oh, but sometimes I have known a savior, a hope, The Christ . . . Come, come . . .

Dark Voice: Why would anyone come to you?

Me: I'm not all bad . . .

Dark Voice: But it makes no difference. I have you and no one will come. There is no one to come, for I am the only one. . . .

Then in the distance I see a light, the light of a lamp. It grows brighter . . . I can make Him out. It is the crucified One. The dark cloud of horror retreats. I am lying by the side of the road. He picks up the pieces of me and puts them together. . . .

Me: Lord, why have you not come before?

The Lord: Because you did not seek me. You even thought you were the only one who cared. I died that this dark one might not have power over you, or over anyone. I am real. . . .

Me: Why don't you destroy IT, or banish it forever and stop its depredations? It comes into the hearts of people, and through them it kills and hates and destroys.

The Lord: I would have to kill all people in order to destroy it, and I want to save you all, and even IT. I want to bring it to life along with you.

Me: But there is so much suffering and pain . . . so much, so much. . . .

He weeps over me and those around me. He is one and many. His tears are the healing elixir of life. In the midst of me He places a stone, and gradually

I mend and come together. He takes me in His hand, and I am like clay in an artist's hand. He breathes upon me. His tears are my life, and then He sweats blood, and it is my blood, and my heart begins to beat and I am alive. The pain begins to subside. He puts me on the ground and I can walk. Indeed I am more whole than before.

The Lord: Why, child, have you avoided me? Why did you wait so long?

Me: I thought that I had to get along by myself . . . and then I was taken in by the evil one, and I thought that you did not want me and would not have me.

The Lord: Child, child. I died for you. I love you. Here, come to me and let me hold you.

He holds me like a father holding his frightened child who has just awakened from a nightmare, like a child who has been hurt. . . .

Me: Even though you hold me, I still can't believe that you can love me . . . I know that you have saved me and brought me together, but help me to feel that you are with me and that love has power . . . your love. . . .

The Lord: Just let me hold you. You will die and rise again. You have already died and are alive.

Hours go by. He continues to hold me. The warmth of His body begins to touch my soul, and I begin to have a little peace.

Me: I am still afraid.

The Lord: It has tried to kill you, and I have saved you. Now you must die to everything . . . hang onto nothing. Hanging onto things is what gives the evil one control over you. What do you fear. . . ?

Me: I fear that all my evil will come out, and then all my attempts to love will be turned sour and become hate. I am afraid I cannot take the tension. I am afraid that I will be dropped into nothingness. I am afraid that IT will get me again . . . whenever I try to love, it seems to misfire.

The Lord: You have played God. You have looked for results. Just be, and I will be with you and with those whom you try to love. . . . Things will work out. . . . Continue, my son, my child.

Me: I fear for those I love. I am afraid I will bring destruction. I am still afraid. . . .

The Lord: You have reason to fear, but I am with you. I will not forsake you. The fear will die as you die. As you stop trying to play God, the fear will go away, and love and peace will take its place. I am with you, and I will use you silently and secretly if you will just take one step after another. I will protect you from IT . . . my power is just beginning. . . .

All this while He holds my trembling body. He kisses me, and His tears continue to flow. They are the balm of Gilead . . . I begin to relax.

The Lord: Part of this is physical. It is the power of evil in the body. . . .

Me: Yes, Lord, and I am not so afraid of IT . . . if everything is stripped from me, I can still go on as long as I have you. I can even bear the pain that I cause others unwittingly, because you can heal them . . . I begin to feel love again, love for those close to me. You become more real. Thank you, Lord, for coming, for your love and your healing.

The Lord: I am the one to thank you for calling and allowing me to heal. I created the world that it might be healed, and most people run from me. When the way is hard, they give up, and then the Dark Cloud seizes them and tortures them. Stay with me, and I will bring you through . . . nothing has to be done today. I will watch over the people and the things that really worry you. The way will not be easy, but they will come through . . . there is much pain . . . but my love keeps on when yours gives way. I can restore the wrongs you have done, those you may still do.

Me: I will try to keep going . . . thank you, thank you, and stay with me.

The Pit

Me: Down into the pit. The Christ cannot change what you do not face . . . down into the pit of slime and hate, of tornadoes and cruelty, of human agony and misery. . . . Men and women seeking only for themselves . . . and I as well . . . making a hopeless and meaningless world by trying to destroy and grasp. . . . The evil one having his way almost without anything to stop him. . . . We are chained here on a beach with waves of foulness rolling over us . . . depression, agony, hatred, slime and dung, and everywhere foul asps which slither over us and poison us . . . one bloats and suffers, but cannot die, for if one dies it is only more of the same . . . another life of hell and pain without meaning. . . . That laugh!

Dark Voice: And what is the use? All is hopeless. Nothing you do has any value, any meaning. The battle is done and the forces of light have lost. The crucifixion is complete. The best of men is strung upon a cross and dies and there is no resurrection, no new life. Nothing is victorious but death, and you cannot die to get out of it. You who are supposed to stand for some hope and victory . . . you are a sad, perverse, lying joke, a wicked liar. You don't believe any of it. It is all false. If there is any light or joy or hope, it is a mistake with no power. It merely comes from darkness, because a little light makes the ultimate victory of foulness and hate seem more horrible. If there were no light, then the darkness would not seem so black. . . . Lie down and let the slime and ugliness and pain crawl over you and through you, forever and ever . . . amen. . . .

Me: Go on, dear friend, dear sweet friend. You have tormented me so much that I don't have to like you. You can make it no worse. You have me in the pit, in the horror of the pit. You have had me there for some time, and I did not know it. But I can spit in your damnable face . . . and if there be no Christ, no victory, even then I'll continue to believe. Thinking of the war and hate, the pain, criticism, the lack of love, of understanding and sensitivity, you do seem to have the edge. . . . But light still tries to break through, and flowers still come up through the dung. . . . Even if it is not true, I will hang on to it . . . better than you.

Dark Voice: You work hard at nothing. You are busy, and what good does it do? You only get criticism from everyone. Why don't you just give up and admit that there is no hope, that everything runs on to greater darkness, greater pain, pulled by the pit into the devouring maw of death . . . everything about you is in vain. You are a laughingstock to any realistic man or woman. All you do is try to hold on to illusion. . . .

Me: Even though you stand forever jabbing that pitchfork into me and trying to make me recant, I will still hang on to hope. I should have turned and talked to you the other day.

Dark Voice: When in your self-righteous busy-ness would you have had time, you fool? You only love because you are misshapen and depraved . . . it is not love, but lust, which will turn to ashes in your mouth. You lie and tell meaningless stories, which help no one . . . you only make people's pain worse and try to satisfy your own vanity without success. You hypocrite . . . you are too proud to admit that you can never rise above the hate and retaliation, the dirty politics, the jagged pieces of broken lives, the slums, the unloving parents. . . . Give up your specks of light and join the company of those who know enough to hate and despair . . . you'll give in to the jaws of meaningless death in the end.

And the pitchfork goes in and out of me, each thrust accompanied by the laughter of my tormentors . . . how they enjoy seeing me writhe . . . I think of the bayoneted victims in Bangladesh, twisting and crying out as the crowd applauded the soldiers . . . of the crowd who gathered to mock and eat their lunches while they watched the crucifixion . . . the horror of Holy Week . . . Him abandoned, the perfect symbol of our human state. The better one is the more one suffers. And the voice goes on and on . . . No hope, no hope, no hope . . . no, no. . . .

Me: Against this I have no power. I cannot defeat it. I can hang on only because I cannot join it. . . . This I cannot join, and there are only two sides, only two. Before this I am defenseless. It has me, and the pitchfork keeps picking some new spot not yet insensitive to the pain. . . .

Dark Voice: And something in you says that you must keep this copy for another book. You do not even take seriously what you experience within . . . a fraud, a pickpocketing fraud . . . not even a first-class one . . . a miserable worm with no value. . . . You are hard to crush out, but in the end I will finish you. . . .

Me: Aha, weakness. You cannot kill me. You can pitchfork and dismember me, but as long as I hang on, you don't seem to be able to destroy completely.

With fury they come upon me and cut me apart, and into smaller pieces, and drench the parts in polluted, slimy death . . . but the parts don't die. . . .

Me: There is something else here, something else. Lord, where are you?

And a voice thunders out.

Voice: I am here, brooding over the darkness, trying to draw it to me that it may be shaped by me and renewed. But you only turn to me when you know your own helplessness. . . . You still have friends. You are not hanging on an outer cross.

At the sound of that Voice the great waves of horror tremble and recoil. . . . The ocean of hate and destruction draws away from the beach leaving wreckage and debris and the fragments of my torn body . . . there seems to be only a poor bum left, a dissolute and terrible looking character. He picks up the pieces of flesh and bone and puts them in a heap, mixed with all the filth and excrement from the ocean of ugliness. Then I notice . . . for somehow I am there . . . that he wears a crown of thorns. And this Samaritan places it on the dismembered parts, and then he weeps. And his tears are like living water, the elixir of life. He is simply so ugly that the ocean has left him alone and paid no attention to him. . . .

And gradually I come back to life and am a man again. . . . As I come back to life I find the crown on my head, and I take it off and give it to him, for I am certainly not worthy of it. Then I embrace him, who has saved me. . . . And there is a bolt of lightning . . . the ugly one is first a child, and then the strong youth, the magnificent young man, and the father . . . all separately and all in one. I cry out, "Why? Why?" He only shakes his head, and the father holds me close and speaks of love, and the youth holds me and tells me of his self-giving love, of the eternal beauty and wonder on the other side of dismemberment. . . .

Me: Why, again and again?

And the Creative Voice answers: You could not stand much light. Only God can. And so there is black night, and then dawn and again sunset and deep night and another day. Only so can you survive. Come, child, you are not alone. We go with you. We shall go with you this week. There is hope; there is light; there is love and joy. You shall feel them and give them . . . Lo, the dawn cometh. Love cometh and is more powerful than death and pain and cruelty and hate and selfishness and greed. Love is real, and in the end of time it will redeem all things . . . all things. . . .

We walk along the desolate shore covered with the wreckage of so many lives and hopes. And He stops and makes little piles of broken human fragments and weeps again. And He asks me to help in this task, for there are so many, so very many . . . the task seems endless. And the day wanes, and sunset comes, and at last I lie down to refreshing sleep . . . without fear. . . .

XVII

THE MEDITATIVE PROCESS AT WORK IN DREAMS

The following series of dreams was given to me by a student. They occurred during the summer, fall and winter of what would have been his second year in college. He calls them his "treasure; icons picturing the way of my conversion to Christianity." They are included because the reality that was encountered in sleep is clearly the same that is sought through meditation, and in either dreaming or meditation, it is found emerging through the same deep level of the psyche. These dreams tell their own story.

Dream One: occurred early in the summer. I had left home to live with a group of leftist leaning students in what was to be an experiment in communal living. My father, though consenting to my leaving, was very upset. To him people who lived in communes were communist.

Early in the morning, with the dawn, I arise. The stillness of the hour is full of anticipation. I am excited. The dawn holds for me the promise of an important day. The early morning hours come, bringing with them purpose and strength. They are also hours of confidence; I am confident. Still no one else in the house has awakened. My father still sleeps, my brothers and sisters still sleep. I leave the house to be refreshed by the morning air. Outside I expand into the space about me. The air and I are as one. There is joy.

It is necessary to return to the house. I realize that I must make the return, although in part it will be unpleasant, for I foresee what it is that I must do, and at first it will be difficult. At the door of the house my father waits, stern and stiff. He is himself as a door. The house has awakened; all is ready now. I approach, silently. Confidence is still with me. A few feet short of the door I stop and slowly begin to raise my head which had been lowered as I approached the door. I meet my father's eyes. For a second he braces himself. Then, with pain, he steps aside. His eyes are now those of a weeping boy. I pass through beside him. I realize that this must be. I realize that I can do nothing for my father. He must weep alone. His son could never be capable of drying his tears.

Inside the house the children have been waiting. They were quiet as they saw me pass through the door beside my father. Now they are waiting for me, watching me with expectant eyes. I motion. They arise. I smile. They laugh gently, cautiously. Then, turning, I walk to the door and they follow. As the last of them passes over the threshold, it is as if some evil spell which the house held over the children at last has been broken. At once they come alive with dance and song, and I too am filled with a boundless joy. I dance about them all, hugging them and lifting them high above my head. They laugh with glee and dance and jump and sing some more. The sound of their happiness only increases as I lead them from the yard to the road, and down the road to the house of the beautiful young lady.

Dream Two: occurred sometime in August. I only recall that disillusion with the "communal experiment" was already creeping in. It seemed that I was the only one interested in whether or not the dishes were done and the bathroom was kept clean.

I am alone in the desert. It is midday and the sun, high overhead, shines on the distant mountains and the cactus about me. The intense light of the sun fills the mountains and the cactus with an uncanny beauty. I could lose myself in contemplating them.

Suddenly before me, close to me, between myself and the mountains which only a second ago I was looking at, stands an old Indian chief. He looks toward the sun and his face shines like the sun. The lines on his face tell of hard years and deep wisdom gained through them. Just as suddenly I realize that he is listening, that I am not alone with him in the desert. There is with us a Spirit to whom the Indian is listening. I do not know how to listen as this old Indian does. I know only that there are three beings present and that the ground is sacred.

The old Indian does not speak. I dare not question.

Dream Three: actually did occur about one week into the fall semester of that year. About two weeks later I dropped out of school.

The first semester of the school year is a week old. Already I have lost interest in my courses. I want to travel; to hitchhike away, if only for a weekend. Giving way to the wanderlust that is in me, I pack my bag with cheese and bread, fasten my sleeping bag tight, and head for the toll road entrance. It is Friday morning.

The first car stops for me. I run up to it and see two friends from school in it. We exchange greetings and they ask me where I am going. I tell them that I am heading for New Mexico. Chicago is where they are going, and they tell me I'm welcome to ride that far with them. I decline, since it would take me too far out of my way, saying that it should be easy for me to catch another ride. Then the driver, as if he had just waked up to where I am going, asks in surprise how I expect to get there and back to South Bend for classes on Monday morning. I am a bit confused. It had apparently not occurred to me that hitchhiking to New Mexico and back would take longer than one weekend. I shrug my shoulders as if to answer, "Who knows?" They laugh and drive on.

Then my attitude changes. "So what," I say to myself, "I won't mind in the least if I do not make it back in time for classes on Monday morning. And I continue to look for a ride.

Dream Four: occurred about a month and a half later. I actually did build and live in the room described.

I have worked long and hard on building my room in the basement of the house on Hill street. For three weeks I had worked on it, sweeping, washing, painting the floors and walls, building desk, table, chair, bed, and doorway, putting in a window, and laying a carpet. I like the room hidden there in what had been a dusty, dirty storage space for all kinds of junk. My work had caused a real transformation. When I started, no one else in the house thought it possible to make the room livable. I surprised them. In fact, I amazed them. For three weeks, every day, all day I worked with my hands on the room and it was all my own doing. I liked the room very much, and now all these people whom I did not know were screaming at me, commanding me to give my room up.

I could not understand why. There did not seem to be any reason why I should be made to give up my room. But there they were, all of them screaming at me to give it up. They were screaming from above, as I stood bowed, dejected in the middle of my room. I tried to reason with them. I pleaded with them that I had transformed wasted space into a livable room. If anything, I said, they should be grateful to me for doing this.

They were not moved by my pleas. They screamed the louder, and finally, broken by the great force of their relentless opposition, I fell to the floor and gave up my room.

Dream Five: came several weeks after that. I had decided to leave the South Bend-Notre Dame area after Christmas. Because of a number of complications, the "commune experiment" would be terminating with the end of the school semester. I had thought of going to Europe after Christmas. After having the dream, I decided not to go.

The motorcycle had been running well all day, and I was having great fun zooming over the cobblestone streets of a small village in Germany—until I tried to take the steepest hill in the village. As I neared the top, the motorcycle conked out and began to slide backwards down the hill. I looked over my shoulder and became terrified by what I saw. Less than a half block below me the street abruptly broke off. And below the street, some 300 yards down, was a lake with rough, black waters. I could do nothing. I could not stop the motorcycle from sliding. Its speed increased, and I could not even manage to jump off. I was frightened for my life.

The motorcycle, with me helplessly caught on it, did not stop, but continued sliding downwards over the street's end, falling towards the rough, black waters of the lake.

Dream Six: occurred some time around the 20th of January the next year. I had left home the day after Christmas and hitchhiked to California to visit a friend who taught high school in Berkeley. After spending two weeks with him, I started out again. This time I was heading toward New Mexico. A good friend of mine had told me of a small Benedictine monastery in the mountains. He had suggested that the monks would very likely let me spend some time with them. I did not want to go back home so soon and so, although I had no idea of what went on in a monastery, I wandered in there on January 17. The good monks would have allowed me to stay through May. I left on Easter Monday after spending nearly three months with them.

While I am asleep on the hard straw bed in the monk's cell, my heart begins to beat wildly. I remain half-asleep—half awake. It is as if I am too frightened to allow myself to awaken completely for fear that I am dying and that, if awake, the pain would be too great to bear. My heart continues to beat wildly for a few more minutes. Then gradually it begins to slow down, and at last it stops altogether.

Then there is a wonderful stirring inside of me, and I feel my spent heart being replaced by one much larger and much stronger. And, as the new life from the heart begins to fill my blood vessels, I am told that this heart was my mother's.

Dream Seven: occurred about midway through my stay at the monastery.

The cliffs are high and I fall off, straight down, an unknown distance. I have been told often of their danger. All of the people who live in the country around the cliffs know how dangerous they are, and only a few of the most courageous or the most foolish souls have ever dared to climb them. Even the Indians of old, who once lived in the country around the cliffs, as legend goes, showed fear when they talked of them. But, it is said, they seldom mentioned them.

I had set out to climb the cliffs. I took no heed of the warnings of the people. When I reached the top with little trouble at all, I thought that all of the people and the Indians of old had been mistaken. I felt proud, and from the top of the cliffs I sneered at all who lived below and had not dared the climb, mocking them and calling them timid grandmothers.

I walked along the rim at the top, peering over into the abyss below. Suddenly the edge cracked, and I fell into the abyss. The unbearable speed and twisting of the fall caused my body to be changed into a weed. When, after hours of falling, I hit the bottom, I, the weed, began to burn with flames that shot up to the rim of the cliffs, to the very edge where my fall had begun. I burned and burned until I, the weed, had become ashes covering the bottom of the abyss.

From a deep, hidden place that was even below the bottom of the abyss, a great but gentle voice came forth pleading, "Jesus, Jesus, Jesus," and with the sound of the voice I was resurrected.

Dream Eight: came on the following night.

I meet face to face a tall, strong, black-clad cleric. He pokes his log-like finger at me and shouts that I was to give no ear to the voice which pleaded for Jesus the night before, and that my resurrection experience was purely and simply an illusion. His words hit my face like bullets.

I am overwhelmed and frightened by his awful message. I am silent for a few minutes while I collect myself and try to steady my shaking legs. Once calmed a bit, I say to the cleric, with the conviction of my whole self, "No, you are wrong." The cleric makes no reply. He turns and leaves me.

Dream Nine: occurred nearly a year later, after I had returned to school.

I received a letter from a monk, an old and holy monk. The calligraphy is exquisitely beautiful, written with the patience and concentration of a medieval scribe. I cannot read the script, however, for it is an ancient language which the monk has used. This does not upset me. It only heightens the sense of mystery which I have about the letter.

Suddenly I notice for the first time a fish drawn in the margin of the letter. It is even more beautiful than the calligraphy. It is a rare tropical fish whose scales form fascinating patterns of stunning color. Just as suddenly, the fish comes alive and swims all over the letter. The paper has become water, and the script gentle waves. I watch the fish, amazed and delighted, and then I realize that the fish was not created out of nothing, as I had been taught to believe about dreams, and had believed for much of my life. Instead, it was created out of a diagram that Morton Kelsey uses to describe the psyche or soul. This insight tickles me to death. I laugh and laugh and continue to watch the fish swim, noticing now that its skeleton, which could be seen through the beautiful colors without detracting from them, is essentially the same as Morton's diagram.

MORTON KELSEY'S   THE FISH (2)
DIAGRAM (1)

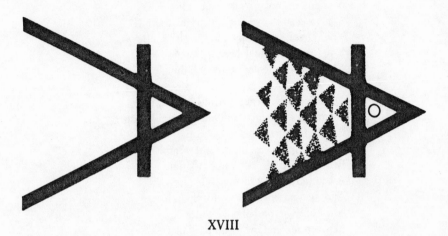

XVIII

I MET DEATH FACE TO FACE

I was in my fifties when my only brother died. He was several years older than I. I realized that I was now the oldest member of my immediate family. I was shaken by the bereavement and also by fear of death. The following words poured out of me into my journal. When I was finished the fear had far less hold on me and I was more at peace about my brother's death.

> There you stand glaring. No one could doubt
> Your identity, ancient foe of man and me.
> Face to face we stare at one another.
> "When does your boney index finger
> Reach out and touch me, chill me?
> You are not pretty, Death.
> I cannot stand against you; I have
> No power, no talisman to fight you off.
> I stand alone. So many times you've tried
> To finish me—sickness, rejection,
> Folly, guilt and fear. Have you some trick,
> Some new trick to undo me
> And so collect my rotting bones?
> When will you have your prey?
> Am I the next, the next in line?"
> I stand naked on the wild moor . . .
> The wind is howling and the sea

Screams against the crumbling cliffs——
"Why don't you take me, do your deed?
A silver filament is all that holds you back . . .
You do not move. You cannot move?
Oh, you can't cross over? It frightens you?
You, Death, are afraid and tremble?
You have died, have been defeated?"
My eyes become accustomed to the gloom.
The silver thread is more. It is a net,
Let down from heaven. And I look up—
There is a brightness and out of it flow images . . .
Comforting arms, tears like rain,
A dazzling perfect youth, father, mother,
Brother, lover, friend, ransom, guide.
A boundless jewel turning one face
And then another. From this there hangs
A net of silver and of gold which stands
Between me and the grinning skull,
Surrounds him as a silken pouch.
A voice like thunder shakes the net.
Shakes heaven, earth and even hell.
"He cannot have you long, this one.
His victory is for the moment only.
And he cannot even have his day
Until the time is ripe and full.
Death has died and so has lost his power.
He risked all and lost. His power's fear.
Only as you fear him can he control.
Only as you're drawn into the net,
Having given up in fear,
As rabbits move toward the snake's hypnotic eye.
Stare him down. Laugh in his face.
I am with you until the end,
With those you love whom death has touched.
They are not lost because they disappear.
Remember me, my child, my beloved.
I am here, always, and with love!"
The thunder rolls away. The rain falls.
I look Death in the face, straight on. I laugh.
He turns and slinks away.
Something deep within me speaks
And tells me that the day will come

When the voice of thunder will touch death's heart
And he will be one of us, the chosen, the redeemed, the loved.
Strange world, where death brings life,
If only, if only, I don't give up,
But struggle on in spite of dark and pain.
Oh death, where is your sting?
Oh grave, where is your victory?

XIX

A MEDITATION ON THE LORD'S PRAYER[6]

How does a person break through this physical world and come into contact with the light of God? How can we open ourselves to the creative principles in the universe in such a way that we are touched by the transforming, re-creating love of God? How can each of us find the inner renewal of the new light of Jesus Christ?

The disciples wanted to know the very same thing, and so they asked Jesus how to pray. He gave them instructions which have been misunderstood by many people. Often it is assumed that if we say the words of the Lord's Prayer, we are praying; but this is far from the truth. These words need to be *prayed*, not just said.

And so you ask: "How should I *pray* the Lord's Prayer?"

The first suggestion Jesus made was to address God directly and in a way that may seem strange: *Abba.* "Father." But *Abba* really means something closer to "Daddy."

We must know the one to whom we are turning, or we cannot address Him properly. If we treat a loving father as a vicious tyrant, or a distant oriental potentate, we do not make much contact. It is difficult for the father to relate with warmth when he is mistrusted or held at arm's length.

The image of our Father that comes to me is the father in Jesus's story of the prodigal son. Amazing man, this: he gave his son freedom to leave home and even gave him his share of the inheritance knowing full well what the results would be. Yet each day he would go and stand staring out into the desert, hoping against hope that he would see some trace of his son on a distant horizon, some sign or omen. And one day he spied a weary, broken figure and recognized him long before the son ever realized that his father was hurrying out to greet him.

The father ran up to his son and embraced him, while the son pleaded only to be granted a servant's status. Instead, the father gave him the best robe, sandals for his feet, rings for his fingers. Then he ordered a feast of the fatted calf so that all might rejoice with him that his son had returned home.

This is the kind of father to whom we pray when we say, "Our Father." He is so much better than anything we could have dreamed of or hoped for. Frankly, he is not "wish-fulfillment," because no one whom I know could imagine in the deepest part of being that such an overflowing love is the source and center of the world of which we are a part. It takes real faith to believe that the world can be like that when humans are what they are.

I find it helpful, as I say "Our Father," to see myself as the prodigal returning home after having loused up my life in nearly every conceivable way. I see the father there with open arms and gifts I dared not even dream of. This is the one to whom I turn in prayer. How important to imagine my standing there before the father. When I visualize this, then I realize that there is nothing I need hide, nothing I cannot share—no anger, no resentment, no guilt or fear.

Sometimes in my quiet time I repeat over and over the word "Father, Father, Father," until I know myself in His presence. A strange click occurs when suddenly you know, all by yourself, that you are not alone.

And then I hallow God's name. I simply tell him how grateful I am that there is one like Him in the center and core of the universe to whom I can turn now. I rejoice that at the heart of the world there is love like this. I praise Him that He cared so much for us and for me that he not only waited for me like the prodigal father—the father who was prodigal with that love—but even sent His beloved son into the world to submit to the cross for my sins, to rise again in order to rescue me from the powers of darkness—and this long before I thought of turning to Him.

Thank you, Father, for being like that.

Next I pray that this kingdom of His may come in my life, in my family, in my church, and in my community—this kingdom of love, concern, sacrificial caring. His kingdom is one in which there is understanding and fellowship, mutual awareness, mutual sensitivity, listening, generosity and kindness. I ask that I may be used as an instrument to bring that kind of kingdom into being, that my life may create the kind of conditions that result in such a kingdom.

Then I pray that God's will be done in me. I ask that I may know what He wants of me, how best I can do my part so that the kingdom of God may have more of a chance of being realized in this broken and unhappy world. I ask Him to give me the knowledge and power and love so that I may do His loving will toward myself and toward those around me.

Moreover I pray that I may put no limits on the possibilities of this kingdom or this love and that the power to change this world may flow through me. I pray that this kingdom of God and this will of God may come through me now and be realized here on earth just as it is and will be in heaven. What audacity! Had Jesus not taught me to do so, I would never have dared to pray that the kingdom might come on earth as it is in heaven.

And then I get around at last to asking for myself. I ask for daily bread—which is simply asking for all of my daily needs in a poetic image. I ask for health and freedom from pain; I ask for housing and warmth, for food and clothes, for psychological strength and companionship, as well as for physical sustenance and protection. It is like asking for everything that I need so that I can go out and do His will and prepare as best I can for His kingdom. I am to do this daily—not once a week, but *daily*.

But there is one condition. I ask that I may be forgiven. In doing this I acknowledge that there is so much that I need to have forgiven, so many follies and stupidities and some downright cruel and vicious acts.

There is no limit on the forgiveness. I think Judas Iscariot, the betrayer, could have found forgiveness, had he but turned and received it. And there is a betrayer in each of us, that part of us which sells short its best ideals and hopes, sells out for the meaner thing.

And we can be forgiven anything, if only we will forgive those who have hurt and misused and forgotten and slandered us. If we forgive, nothing is impossible. So I like to pray this way: "Lord, forgive me and help me to forgive; for I need your Spirit to be able to forgive and open myself to your forgiveness." Then can I be clean and free of my guilt and inner anguish and pain.

Next I ask that He may guide and direct me. Not only that He will not lead me into more than I can bear—no loving father would do that—but that He will guide me into the right road, the best path, the most creative way ahead. This is what I am praying when I ask that He lead me not into temptation.

Finally I ask Him to protect me from all the forces of evil in the world. Jesus believed in the reality of an evil one, a personal and very intelligent force for corruption and woe in the world, a force bent on perverting people and dragging them down and destroying them.

One Russian theologian observed, as he looked back over the Russian revolution and World Wars I and II, that one might think the evil powers were more intelligent than the powers of light. At least men have been more open to them. I ask that I may be protected from evil striking against me in the outer world, or striking within me in anxiety or depression, or striking through me at others with hatred or with a loose or vicious tongue or cruel act. How much I need this protection. I cannot stand alone on my own human ability against the evil one, but only as I have God's help. No one can. We become monsters the moment we do not have God. And so I ask for the protection which He wishes to give.

I then end with a paean of praise. I thank my Father for His being there and His being the kingdom and the power and the glory.

It takes less than a minute to recite or say the Lord's Prayer, but it may take fifteen or fifty minutes to pray it and to open oneself to the reality of the Father so that the love and power and strength and protection of God begins to enter my life and transform it.

After all, the Father sent Jesus Christ primarily that we might have that power, and He gave us this prayer so that we might know how to pray to become instruments of this incredible creativity and love.

Notes

Chapter 1

1. In his recent work, *Unsecular Man: The Persistence of Religion* (New York: Schocken Books, Inc., 1972), Andrew Greeley has reached much the same conclusions about humanity's continuing need for religion and its myths and symbols.

Chapter 2

1. This story told by Jesus is found in Matthew 20:1-16.

2. Louis Evely, *That Man Is You* (Paramus, N.J.: The Newman Press, 1965), pp. 16 and 26.

3. The types test is described by Isabel Briggs Myers in her excellent introductory work, *Introduction to Types*, privately printed (321 Dickinson Avenue, Swarthmore, Pa. 19081), 1970, and also in the *Manual: The Myers-Briggs Type Indicator* (Princeton, N.J., Educational Testing Service, 1963).

4. See Marie-Louise von Franz and James Hillman, *Lectures on Jung's Typology* (New York: Spring Publications, 1971).

Chapter 4

1. In five books and one shorter work I have described several very real ways in which the spiritual world affects people and their physical existence. Besides *Encounter with God* (Minneapolis: Bethany Fellowship, Inc., 1972), these are *Myth, History and Faith* (New York: Paulist Press, 1974), *God, Dreams, and Revelation* (Minneapolis: Augsburg Publishing House, 1974), *Healing and Christianity* (New York: Harper & Row, 1973), *Tongue Speaking* (Garden City, N.Y.: Doubleday & Company, Inc., 1964), and *The Reality of the Spiritual World* (Pecos, N.M.: Dove Publications, 1974).

2. See my article "Is the World View of Jesus Outmoded?" in *The Christian Century*, January 22, 1969, for further evidence about Jesus's understanding of the world.

3. The historical base of the gospel is convincingly shown by Günther Bornkamm in *Jesus of Nazareth* (New York: Harper & Row, 1960), and by Norman Perrin in *Rediscovering the Teaching of Jesus* (New York: Harper & Row, 1967). Also see Andrew M. Greeley, *The Jesus Myth* (Garden City, N.Y.: Doubleday & Company, Inc., 1971).

4. See Matthew 6:22-23 and Luke 11:34-35.

5. This is the point of view of the New Testament and the early church. See Gustav Aulén, *Christus Victor: An Historical Study of the Three Main Types of the Idea of the Atonement* (New York: The Macmillan Company, 1951).

6. An excellent review of the studies of religion and psychological health is found in *Research on Religious Development*, ed. Merton P. Strommen (New York: Hawthorn Books, Inc., 1971), pp. 391ff. The article is written by Russell J. Becker.

Chapter 5

1. This was Dietrich Bonhoeffer, a heroic man who committed his life to the strug-

gle against Nazism from within Germany. He really believed that the world was ready to follow the Christian message just because it is right for human beings, and without any metaphysical basis for faith or attention to the individual's inner spiritual life. Bonhoeffer was 39 when he was hanged in a Nazi concentration camp.

2. See my book *Healing and Christianity*, pp. 250ff., and the understanding I have tried to present there.

3. I have discussed these classes, which were part of my regular teaching schedule for several years, in an article entitled "Facing Death and Suffering: A Group Experiment in Affective Learning," *Lumen Vitae* (Brussels), Vol. 28, No. 2, 1973, pp. 281-295.

4. There are sections in both *Encounter with God*, pp. 116f., 149f., and 156ff., and *Healing and Christianity*, pp. 63ff. and 328ff., regarding this neglected aspect of reality. In addition I have discussed it in the pamphlet already mentioned, *The Reality of the Spiritual World*, and in two articles, "The Mythology of Evil," *Journal of Religion and Health*, Vol. 13, No. 1, 1974, pp. 7-18, and "Aggression and Religion: The Psychology and Theology of the Punitive Element in Man," *Religious Education*, Vol. 68, May-June 1973, pp. 366-386.

Chapter 7

1. The life of this remarkable woman is told by Baron Friedrich von Hügel in *The Mystical Element of Religion as Studied in Saint Catherine of Genoa and her Friends*, 2 vols. (London: J. M. Dent & Sons Ltd., 1927).

2. I have written about this in greater length in *The Art of Christian Love*, published in pamphlet form by Dove Publications, Pecos, N.M., 1974.

Chapter 8

1. C. G. Jung, *Memories, Dreams, Reflections*, recorded and edited by Aniela Jaffé (New York: Pantheon Books, 1963), pp. 176f.

2. *Ibid.*, p. 189.

Chapter 9

1. The opening shot in C. Northcote Parkinson's delightfully humorous study of administration, *Parkinson's Law* (Boston: Houghton Mifflin Company, 1957), p. 2.

2. St. Ignatius calls this form of praying "rhythmical recitation." See *The Spiritual Exercises of St. Ignatius*, translated by Anthony Mottola (Garden City, N.Y.: Doubleday & Company, Inc., 1964), pp. 108f.

Chapter 10

1. Søren Kierkegaard, *Fear and Trembling* and *The Sickness unto Death*, translated by Walter Lowrie (Garden City, N.Y.: Doubleday & Company, Inc., n.d.), pp. 197f.

2. Thomas Carlyle, *Sartor Resartus*, Book III, Chapter III.

3. From my book *Encounter with God, op. cit.*, p. 181.

4. C. G. Jung, *Memories, Dreams, Reflections, op. cit.*, p. 177. There is a psychological connection between images and emotions which we shall consider further in a later chapter. The relation between them is carefully discussed by James Hillman in *Emotion: A Comprehensive Phenomenology of Theories and Their Meanings for Therapy* (Evanston, Ill.: Northwestern University Press, 1964). I have discussed some of the same material in relation to Christian education in "The Place of Affect in Religious Education: Psychodynamics of Affectivity and Emotion," *Lumen Vitae* (Brussels), Vol. 26, No. 1, 1971, pp. 68-80.

It is possible to suppress emotions and images almost completely. Through the practice of yoga, for instance, so much control is sometimes possible that an individual can even face a striking cobra without flinching or showing any physiological manifestation of fear.

5. The reality of taboo deaths is discussed by Jerome D. Frank in *Persuasion and Healing* (New York: Schocken Books, 1969), pp. 39ff. Dr. Frank teaches medicine at Johns Hopkins University.

Chapter 11

1. See William Johnston, *Christian Zen* (New York: Harper & Row, 1971), pp. 77ff.

2. *The Spiritual Exercises of St. Ignatius, op. cit.*, pp. 108f.

3. *Writings from the Philokalia on Prayer of the Heart*, trans. E. Kadloubovsky and G. E. H. Palmer (London: Faber & Faber Ltd., 1954), p. 33.

4. *Ibid.*, pp. 192f. The use of the Jesus prayer is also described by Erhart Kaestner in *Mount Athos: The Call from Sleep* (London: Faber and Faber, 1961).

5. An interesting discussion of this way of prayer is found in *The Prayer of Jesus*, by "A Monk of the Eastern Church" (New York: Desclée Company, 1967). For a less sanguine appraisal of this movement by a Western writer, see Elmer O'Brien, S.J., *Varieties of Mystic Experience* (New York: The New American Library, 1965), pp. 83ff.

6. Dechanet's book is published in an illustrated edition; see Jean M. Dechanet, *Yoga in Ten Lessons* (New York: Harper & Row, 1966). *Be Here Now* by Baba Ram Dass is also illustrated; a new edition published in 1971 by Lama Foundation (Box 444, San Cristobal, N.M.) is distributed by Crown Publishers, Inc., New York. Swami Satchidananda's talks are available through Creative Sights and Sounds, Inc. (34 N. Jefferson Street, Dayton, Ohio 45402).

7. The Russian experiments are described by Sheila Ostrander and Lynn Schroeder in *Psychic Discoveries Behind the Iron Curtain* (Englewood Cliffs, N.J.: Prentice-Hall, Inc., 1970), pp. 20ff.

8. Aldous Huxley, *The Doors of Perception* (New York: Harper & Row, 1954), pp. 22f.

9. Further understanding of these devotional ways is found in three volumes of the *Papers from the Eranos Yearbooks*, ed. Joseph Campbell (Bollingen Series XXX, Princeton, N.J.: Princeton University Press); Vol. 4, *Spiritual Disciplines* (1960); Vol. 5, *Man and Transformation* (1964); Vol. 6, *The Mystic Vision* (1969). On a more popular level there are three books by Carlos Castaneda which describe how a Western graduate student found shamanistic experience. These books, whose popularity among college students attests to their appeal, are *The Teachings of Don Juan, A Separate Reality*, and *Journey to Ixtlan*.

Chapter 12

1. St. Gregory of Nyssa, *Commentary on the Song of Songs*, Sermon 10; quoted by Elmer O'Brien, S.J., *Varieties of Mystic Experience, op. cit.*, pp. 48f.

2. I have outlined these twelve different usages in Chapter 4 of my book *God, Dreams, and Revelation*, pp. 8off.

3. See Baron Friedrich von Hügel, *The Mystical Element of Religion, op. cit.*, Vol. II.

4. Russell J. Becker, "Religion and Psychological Health," in *Research on Religious Development, op. cit.*, pp. 391ff.

5. This outline of the kinds of religious experience is parallel in a way to von Hügel's description of the three elements of religion—the institutional-historical, the rational, and the mystical. When religious experience is understood in terms of the psycho-

logy of the unconscious, a great deal is revealed about each kind of experience. The vivid nature of the institutional-historical experience is revealed, while it is shown that there are two quite different strands of mystical experience. In the same way rational religion is shown to have two sides, one of them leading the highly developed rational person directly to contact with the divine so that all parts of that person's life and experience suddenly fall into order and harmony. Sir Isaac Newton's religion was probably of this kind.

It appears that these differences in religious experience are related to individual differences in personality type, which I have outlined briefly on pp. 21ff. The sensation and feeling types generally seem to lean toward institutional religious experiences, while the intuitive person usually seeks one form or the other of mysticism, and the thinking type naturally values experiences of rational harmony as the highest good.

Claudio Naranjo also suggests a threefold division of the kinds of meditation in a somewhat different way. He calls them the way of forms (the Apollonian), the expressive way (the Dionysian), and the negative way of negation and elimination. Claudio Naranjo and Robert E. Ornstein, *On the Psychology of Meditation* (New York: The Viking Press, 1971), p. 16 and the chapters that follow.

6. An excellent summary of Jung's thought on this subject is found in Hans Schaer's *Religion and the Cure of Souls in Jung's Psychology* (London: Routledge & Kegan Paul Ltd., 1951).

7. In several of his books Alan Watts has described this meditative goal, and Baba Ram Dass, in *Be Here Now, op. cit.*, shows a similar understanding of it.

8. See von Hügel, *The Mystical Element of Religion, op.cit.*, Vol. II, p. 131.

9. Roberto Assagioli, M.D., *Psychosynthesis: A Manual of Principles and Techniques* (New York: The Viking Press, 1971).

10. C. G. Jung, *Collected Works*, Vol. 11, *Psychology and Religion: West and East* (New York: Pantheon Books, 1958), p. 520.

11. *Ibid.*, p. 344.

12. William Johnston, *The Still Point: Reflections on Zen and Christian Mysticism* (New York: Harper & Row, 1971), p. 69.

13. St. John of the Cross, *Dark Night of the Soul*, trans. E. Allison Peers (Garden City, N.Y.: Doubleday & Company, Inc., 1959), pp. 67f.

14. For a careful, critical appraisal, both warm and understanding but aware of St. John's deficiencies, see David B. Burrell, C.S.C., "Understanding St. John of the Cross," *Cross and Crown*, Vol. 19 (1967), pp. 399-414.

15. John Calvin, *Institutes of the Christian Religion*, I.IX.6.

16. Andrew M. Greeley and William C. McCready, "Are We a Nation of Mystics?", *The New York Times Magazine*, January 26, 1975.

17. Charles Panati's *Supersenses: Our Potential for Parasensory Experience* (New York: Quadrangle/The New York Times Book Co., 1974), presents the recent scientific evidence developed in laboratories all over the world demonstrating the reality of this kind of experience.

18. Von Hügel, *The Mystical Element of Religion, op. cit.*, Vol. II, p. 127.

19. *Ibid.*, pp. 387f.

20. Von Hügel describes the Quietist controversy in detail. *Ibid.*, pp. 129ff.

21. C. G. Jung, *Collected Works*, Vol. 11, *op. cit.*, p. 337.

22. T. S. Eliot, *The Complete Poems and Plays: 1909-1950* (New York: Harcourt, Brace & World, Inc., 1952), p. 119.

Chapter 13

1. Helen Luke's interest in Dante began at Oxford where she studied Italian litera-

ture and continued through her psychological studies at the C. G. Jung Institute. *Dark Wood to White Rose* (Pecos, N.M.: Dove Publications), is a penetrating and valuable study which gives *The Divine Comedy* interest for each of us as an adventure story inward.

2. This work was done by Henry Reed and is described in a paper on "Modern Dream Incubation" which has not been published.

3. See R. Kalish and D. Reynolds, "On Post-Death Contact," *Journal for the Scientific Study of Religion,* Vol. 12, No. 2, pp. 209ff.

Chapter 14

1. C. G. Jung, *Analytical Psychology: Its Theory and Practice* (The Tavistock Lectures) (New York: Random House, 1970), p. 192.

2. *Ibid.,* p. 193.

3. *Ibid.,* pp. 190ff.

4. Rix Weaver, *The Wise Old Woman* (New York: Jung Foundation, 1973); Roberto Assagioli, *Psychosynthesis, op. cit.* See also Dr. Assagioli's more recent book, *The Act of Will* (Baltimore: Penguin Books, Inc., 1974).

5. In her excellent historical novel, *The Mask of Apollo,* Mary Renault gives a clear picture of the place of drama in Greek life.

6. See Chapter 10 of my book *Healing and Christianity* for a survey of the effects of emotions on one's body.

7. Roberto Assagioli, *Psychosynthesis, op. cit.,* pp. 57f.

8. In *Denial of Death* (New York: Free Press, 1973), Ernest Becker presents a superb analysis of the need for meaning in sociology and psychology and the failures that occur when thinkers fail to integrate such meaning into their ideas.

9. As already mentioned, I have discussed this relationship in an article published in *Lumen Vitae* on "The Place of Affect in Religious Education: Psychodynamics of Affectivity and Emotion," and James Hillman bears out the same understanding in his thorough study, *Emotion, op. cit.*

Chapter 15

1. This statement is quoted by Jim Elliott from an interview with Dr. Ira Progoff on "The Intensive Journal," released in duplicated form in 1971 for Dialogue House Associates by Explorations Institute, Berkeley, Calif.

2. Edward Fischer, "The Journal as Worship," *Worship,* Vol. 47, No. 8, pp. 473-481.

3. *Ibid.,* p. 477.

4. C. G. Jung, *Modern Man in Search of a Soul* (New York: Harcourt, Brace and Company, 1933), pp. 234f.

5. I have referred to this article on p. 148.

6. The entire section dealing with the investigation of dreams from a work by Pererius is found in the original edition of my book on dreams, *Dreams: The Dark Speech of the Spirit* (Garden City, N.Y.: Doubleday & Company, Inc., 1968), pp. 279-307.

Chapter 16

1. Walter Wink, *The Bible in Human Transformation* (Philadelphia: Fortress Press, 1973), pp. 49ff.

2. Franc Johnson Newcomb, *Hosteen Klah: Navaho Medicine Man and Sand Painter* (Norman, Okla.: University of Oklahoma Press, 1964), pp. 198ff.

3. George Maloney, *The Breath of the Mystic* (Denville, N.J.: Dimension Books, Inc., 1974), p. 183.

4. Quoted by Jaroslav Pelikan in *The Christian Tradition: A History of the Development of Doctrine*, Vol. 2, *The Spirit of Eastern Christendom (600-1700)* (Chicago: University of Chicago Press, 1974), p. 145. Professor Pelikan gives an excellent and sympathetic survey of the iconoclastic controversy.

5. See Martin Lings, *Shakespeare in the Light of Sacred Art* (New York: Humanities Press, Inc., 1966); also James Kirsch, *Shakespeare's Royal Self* (New York: G. P. Putnam's Sons for the C. G. Jung Foundation for Analytical Psychology, 1966).

6. Charles Panati in *Supersenses, op. cit.*, pp. 104ff., 110f., and 147, discusses recent experiments which show that the images of others can influence us even when we are not conscious of the influence.

7. Arthur Miller, *After the Fall* (New York: The Viking Press, 1964), pp. 21f.

8. *Ibid.*, pp. 113f.

Chapter 17

1. Roberto Assagioli, *Psychosynthesis, op. cit.*, pp. 118f.

2. St. John of the Cross, *Dark Night of the Soul, op. cit.*, pp. 33f.

3. *The Standard Book of British and American Verse* (Garden City, N.Y.: Garden City Publishing Co., Inc., 1932), pp. 661ff.

4. I was given this poem by a friend who did not know the source, and I have not been able to find where it comes from. I would appreciate hearing from any reader who knows where "The Eucharist" has been published, or can identify the author, R. Voight.

5. *The Standard Book of British and American Verse, op. cit.*, pp. 611ff.

6. This section is also published separately as a leaflet by Dove Publications, Pecos, N.M.